POWERSCORE
TEST PREPARATION

LSAT
READING
COMPREHENSION
BIBLE

**A Comprehensive Approach for Attacking the
Reading Comprehension Section of the LSAT**

Published by
PowerScore Publishing
57 Hasell Street
Charleston, SC 29401

Authors: David M. Killoran and Steven G. Stein

Manufactured in Canada
June 2012

ISBN: 978-0-9801782-9-6

LSAT Preparation Guides

PowerScore LSAT Logic Games Bible

- Ultimate guide for attacking the Logic Games section of the test
- Multiple drills with in-depth explanations and detailed methodology
- 30 real LSAT Logic Games, diagrammed with detailed analyses

PowerScore LSAT Logical Reasoning Bible

- Definitive guide to the Logical Reasoning section of the test
- Detailed discussions of the ideal approach to each Logical Reasoning question type
- Over 100 real LSAT questions analyzed and explained

LSAT Question Collections

PowerScore LSAT Game Type Training

- Includes every Logic Game and question from LSAT PrepTests 1 through 20
- 80 Logic Games games sorted according to the games classification system used in the *PowerScore LSAT Logic Games Bible*.

PowerScore LSAT Logical Reasoning Question Type Training

- Includes every Logical Reasoning question from LSAT PrepTests 1 through 20
- Nearly 1000 questions sorted by PowerScore question category

PowerScore LSAT Reading Comprehension Passage Type Training

- Includes every reading passage and question from LSAT PrepTests 1 through 20
- Passage types divided by category; answer keys provide line references

Ultimate LSAT Preparation

We Offer LSAT Courses Worldwide!

FULL-LENGTH LSAT COURSE $1295

- Over 125 course hours including 16 hours of proctored practice test time
- All of our instructors have scored in the 99th percentile on an official LSAT
- Free LSAT Homework Hotline and Online Student Center
- Thousands of pages of material, including many take-home LSATs

VIRTUAL LSAT COURSE $995

- Over 81 course hours including 36 hours of live online instruction
- Lessons taught by two of our senior LSAT experts, each of whom has scored in the 99th percentile on an official LSAT
- Thousands of pages of material, including many take-home LSATs
- Instant access to a recorded archive of each lesson from the course for review

WEEKEND LSAT COURSE $395

- 35 course hours including 16 live lecture hours and 19 online teaching hours
- All of our instructors have scored in the 99th percentile on an official LSAT
- Free Email Assistance and Online Student Center
- Hundreds of pages of course material
- Repeat the course for free within a year

"...the class showed me how to attack the LSAT in a way studying on my own never did. I would recommend this class to anyone!" –M. Smith • West Texas, A&M University

CONTENTS

CHAPTER ONE: INTRODUCTION

CHAPTER TWO: THE BASICS OF READING COMPREHENSION

CHAPTER THREE: PASSAGE ELEMENTS AND FORMATIONS

CHAPTER FOUR: DIAGRAMMING THE PASSAGES

Chapter Five: The Questions and Answer Choices

Chapter Six: Putting It All Together

Chapter Seven: Comparative Reading Passages

Chapter Eight: Common Passage Structures

CHAPTER NINE: COMMON PASSAGE THEMES

CHAPTER TEN: SECTION STRATEGY AND MANAGEMENT

CHAPTER ELEVEN: THE JUNE 2008 LSAT READING COMPREHENSION SECTION

CHAPTER TWELVE: TEST READINESS

APPENDIX

ENDNOTES

About PowerScore

PowerScore is one of the nation's fastest growing test preparation companies. Founded in 1997, PowerScore offers LSAT, GMAT, GRE, and SAT preparation classes in over 150 locations in the U.S. and abroad. Preparation options include Full-length courses, Weekend courses, Virtual courses, private tutoring, and admissions counseling services. For more information, please visit our website at www.powerscore.com or call us at (800) 545-1750.

For supplemental information about this book, please visit the *Reading Comprehension Bible* website at www.powerscore.com/lsatbibles.

THE POWERSCORE LSAT READING COMPREHENSION BIBLE

CHAPTER ONE: INTRODUCTION

Introduction

Welcome to the *PowerScore LSAT Reading Comprehension Bible*. The purpose of this book is to provide you with a powerful and comprehensive system for attacking the Reading Comprehension section of the Law School Admission Test (LSAT). By carefully studying and correctly applying the techniques we employ, we are certain that you can increase your Reading Comprehension score.

In an effort to clearly explain the fundamental principles of the Reading Comprehension section, this book contains substantial discussions of how to deconstruct the passages as you read, how to identify and attack the questions, and how to successfully avoid the traps set by the test makers. In doing so, we recommend techniques and approaches that have been tested in our live LSAT preparation classes, through individual tutoring, and on the LSAT itself. We feel the use of real Reading Comprehension passages is essential to your success on the LSAT, and no LSAT passage in this book has been modified from its original form.

This book has been carefully designed to reinforce your understanding of the concepts behind the Reading Comprehension section. In order to effectively and efficiently apply our methods, we strongly recommend that you thoroughly read and then reread each of the discussions regarding passage elements. We also suggest that as you finish each question you look not only at the correct answer choice, but also at the incorrect answer choices. Look again at the problem and determine which elements led to the correct answer. Study the analyses and explanations provided in the book and check them against your own work. By doing so, you will greatly increase your chances of scoring high on the Reading Comprehension section.

This book also contains a variety of drills and exercises that supplement the discussion of techniques and question analysis. The drills help strengthen specific skills that are critical for LSAT excellence; for this reason they are as important as the LSAT questions. In the answer keys to these drills we will often introduce and discuss important LSAT points, so we strongly advise you to read through all of the explanations.

Beginning on page 351 there is a complete quick-reference answer key to all of the problems in this book. This reference contains chapter-by-chapter answer keys, and on page 354 you will find a unique reverse lookup feature that lists all of the passages used in this book sorted by the LSAT administration date and PrepTest number.

If you are looking to further improve your LSAT score, we also recommend that you pick up a copy of the renowned PowerScore LSAT Logical Reasoning Bible and LSAT Logic Games Bible. The Logical Reasoning Bible contains our system for attacking the Logical Reasoning section of the LSAT, and the Logic Games Bible explains our methodology for attacking the Analytical Reasoning section. Both books are available through our website at www.powerscore.com.

Because new LSATs appear every several months, and access to accurate and up-to-date information is critical, we have devoted a section of our website to *Reading Comprehension Bible* students. This free online resource area offers supplements to the book material, answers questions posed by students, and provides updates as needed. There is also an official book evaluation form that we strongly encourage you to use. The exclusive *LSAT Reading Comprehension Bible* online resource area can be accessed at:

www.powerscore.com/lsatbibles

If we can assist you in your LSAT preparation in any way, or if you have any questions or comments, please do not hesitate to email us at lsatbibles@powerscore.com. Additional contact information is provided at the end of this book. We look forward to hearing from you!

A Brief Overview of the LSAT

The Law School Admission Test is administered four times a year: in February, June, September/October, and December. This standardized test is required for admission to any American Bar Association-approved law school. According to Law Services, the producers of the test, the LSAT is designed "to measure skills that are considered essential for success in law school: the reading and comprehension of complex texts with accuracy and insight; the organization and management of information and the ability to draw reasonable inferences from it; the ability to think critically; and the analysis and evaluation of the reasoning and arguments of others." The LSAT consists of the following five sections:

- 2 Sections of Logical Reasoning (short arguments, 24-26 questions per section)
- 1 Section of Reading Comprehension (3 long reading passages, 2 short comparative reading passages, 26-28 total questions)
- 1 Section of Analytical Reasoning (4 logic games, 22-24 total questions)
- 1 Experimental Section of one of the above three section types.

You are given 35 minutes to complete each section. The experimental section is unscored and is not returned to the test taker. A break of 10 to 15 minutes is given between the 3rd and 4th sections.

The five-section test is followed by a 35-minute writing sample.

The Logical Reasoning Section

Each Logical Reasoning Section is composed of approximately 24 to 26 short arguments. Every short argument is followed by a question such as: "Which one of the following weakens the argument?" "Which one of the following parallels the argument?" or "Which one of the following must be true according to the argument?" The key to this section is time management and an understanding of the reasoning types and question types that frequently appear.

Since there are two scored Logical Reasoning sections on every LSAT, this section accounts for approximately 50% of your score.

The Analytical Reasoning Section

This section, also known as Logic Games, is probably the most difficult for students taking the LSAT for the first time. The section consists of four games or puzzles, each followed by a series of five to eight questions. The questions are designed to test your ability to evaluate a set of relationships and to make inferences about those relationships. To perform well on this section you must understand the types of games that frequently appear and develop the ability to properly diagram the rules and make inferences.

At the conclusion of the LSAT and for five business days after the LSAT, you have the option to cancel your score. Unfortunately, there is no way to determine exactly what your score would be before cancelling.

The Reading Comprehension Section

This section is composed of three long reading passages, each approximately 450 words in length, and two shorter comparative reading passages. The passage topics are drawn from a variety of subjects, and each passage is followed by a series of five to eight questions that ask you to determine viewpoints in the passage, analyze organizational traits, evaluate specific sections of the passage, or compare facets of two different passages.

The Experimental Section

Each LSAT contains one undesignated experimental section which does not count towards your score. The experimental can be any of the three section types previously described, and the purpose of the section is to test and evaluate questions that will be used on *future* LSATs. By pretesting questions before their use in a scored section, the experimental helps the makers of the test determine the test scale.

The Writing Sample

For many years the Writing Sample was administered before the LSAT.

A 35-minute Writing Sample is given at the conclusion of the LSAT. The Writing Sample is not scored, but a copy is sent to each of the law schools to which you apply. In the Writing Sample you are asked to write a short essay that defends one of two possible courses of action.

You must attempt the Writing Sample! If you do not, Law Services reserves the right not to score your test.

Do not agonize over the Writing Sample; in law school admissions, the Writing Sample is not a major determining element for three reasons: the admissions committee is aware that the essay is given after a grueling three hour test and is about a subject you have no personal interest in; they already have a better sample of your writing ability in the personal statement; and the committee has a limited amount of time to evaluate applications.

The LSAT Scoring Scale

Each administered LSAT contains approximately 101 questions, and each LSAT score is based on the total number of questions a test taker correctly answers, a total known as the raw score. After the raw score is determined, a unique Score Conversion Chart is used for each LSAT to convert the raw score into a scaled LSAT score. Since June 1991, the LSAT has utilized a 120 to 180 scoring scale, with 120 being the lowest possible score and 180 being the highest possible score. Notably, this 120 to 180 scale is just a renumbered version of the 200 to 800 scale most test takers are familiar with from the SAT and GMAT. Just drop the "1" and add a "0" to the 120 and 180.

Although the number of questions per test has remained relatively constant over the last eight years, the overall logical difficulty of each test has varied.

This is not surprising since the test is made by humans and there is no precise way to completely predetermine logical difficulty. To account for these variances in test "toughness," the test makers adjust the Scoring Conversion Chart for each LSAT in order to make similar LSAT scores from different tests mean the same thing. For example, the LSAT given in June may be logically more difficult than the LSAT given in December, but by making the June LSAT scale "looser" than the December scale, a 160 on each test would represent the same level of performance. This scale adjustment, known as equating, is extremely important to law school admissions offices around the country. Imagine the difficulties that would be posed by unequated tests: admissions officers would have to not only examine individual LSAT scores, but also take into account which LSAT each score came from. This would present an information nightmare.

The LSAT Percentile Table

It is important not to lose sight of what LSAT scaled scores actually represent. The 120 to 180 test scale contains 61 different possible scores. Each score places a student in a certain relative position compared to other test takers. These relative positions are represented through a percentile that correlates to each score. The percentile indicates where the test taker ranks in the overall pool of test takers. For example, a score of 165 represents the 93rd percentile, meaning a student with a score of 165 scored better than 93 percent of the people who have taken the test in the last three years. The percentile is critical since it is a true indicator of your positioning relative to other test takers, and thus law school applicants.

Charting out the entire percentage table yields a rough "bell curve." The number of test takers in the 120s and 170s is very low (only 1.6% of all test takers receive a score in the 170s), and most test takers are bunched in the middle, comprising the "top" of the bell. In fact, approximately 40% of all test takers score between 145 and 155 inclusive, and about 70% of all test takers score between 140 and 160 inclusive.

The median score on the LSAT scale is approximately 151. The median, or middle, score is the score at which approximately 50% of test takers have a lower score and 50% of test takers have a higher score. Typically, to achieve a score of 151, you must answer between 56 and 61 questions correctly from a total of 101 questions. In other words, to achieve a score that is perfectly average, you can miss between 40 and 45 questions. Thus, it is important to remember that you don't have to answer every question correctly in order to receive an excellent LSAT score. There is room for error, and accordingly you should never let any single question occupy an inordinate amount of your time.

Since the LSAT has 61 possible scores, why didn't the test makers change the scale to 0 to 60? Probably for merciful reasons. How would you tell your friends that you scored a 3 on the LSAT? 123 sounds so much better.

There is no penalty for answering incorrectly on the LSAT. Therefore, you should guess on any questions you cannot complete.

The use of the LSAT in law school admissions is not without controversy. It is largely taken for granted that your LSAT score is one of the most important determinants of the type of school you can attend. At many law schools a multiplier made up of your LSAT score and your undergraduate grade point average is used to help determine the relative standing of applicants, and at some schools a sufficiently high multiplier guarantees your admission.

For all the importance of the LSAT, it is not without flaws. As a standardized test currently given in the paper-and-pencil format, there are a number of skills that the LSAT cannot measure, such as listening skills, note-taking ability, perseverance, etc. Law Services is aware of these limitations and as a matter of course they warn all law schools about overemphasizing LSAT results. Still, since the test ultimately returns a number for each student, it is hard to escape the tendency to rank applicants accordingly. Fortunately, once you get to law school the LSAT is forgotten. For the time being consider the test a temporary hurdle you must leap in order to reach the ultimate goal.

For more information on the LSAT, or to register for the test, contact Law Services at (215) 968-1001 or at their website at www.lsat.com.

The Law School Admission Council uses a variety of names that all refer to one or more portions of the entire operation that administers the LSAT and attendant services. These names include Law Services, LSAC, and LSAS, and you will see various references to those names throughout this book. There is no need for you to know the meaning of each specific name.

CHAPTER TWO: THE BASICS OF READING COMPREHENSION

The Reading Comprehension Section

The focus of this book is on the Reading Comprehension section of the LSAT, and each Reading Comprehension section contains four passage sets with a total of 26 to 28 questions. Since you have thirty-five minutes to complete the section, you have an average of approximately eight minutes and forty-five seconds to complete each passage set. Of course, the amount of time you spend on each passage set will vary with the reading difficulty of the passage(s), the difficulty of the questions, and the total number of questions per passage set. For virtually all students the time constraint is a major obstacle, and as we progress through this book we will discuss time management as well as time-saving techniques that you can employ within this section.

On average, you have 8 minutes and 45 seconds to complete each passage set.

Why Reading Comprehension?

Each section of the LSAT is designed to test abilities required in the study and/or practice of law. The Logical Reasoning sections measure your skills in argumentation and logic. The Logic Games section tests your ability to understand the interaction of different variables and the laws which govern their actions. Reading Comprehension, a section included in many standardized tests, provides a test of skills particularly important to both law students and attorneys. Law students are required to read significant portions of dense text throughout their legal studies, and lawyers must often be ready to do the same in their normal course of business; given that the misreading of a contract or legal judgment could lead to disastrous results for a lawyer's clients (not to mention the lawyer), it should not be surprising that Reading Comprehension is an integral part of the Law School Admission Test.

The Section Directions

Each Reading Comprehension section is prefaced by the following directions:

> "Each set of questions in this section is based on a single passage or a pair of passages. The questions are to be answered on the basis of what is <u>stated</u> or <u>implied</u> in the passage or pair of passages. For some questions, more than one of the choices could conceivably answer the question. However, you are to choose the <u>best</u> answer; that is, the response that most accurately and completely answers the question, and blacken the corresponding space on your answer sheet."

Because these directions precede every Reading Comprehension section, you should familiarize yourself with them now. Once the LSAT begins, *never* waste time reading the directions for any section.

Let us examine these directions more closely. Consider the following sentence: "The questions are to be answered on the basis of what is <u>stated</u> or <u>implied</u> in the passage or pair of passages." Thus, the test makers indicate that you are to use the statements of the author of the passage to prove and disprove answer choices. You do not need to bring in additional information aside from the typical ideas that the average American or Canadian would be expected to believe on the basis of generally known and accepted facts. For example, you would be expected to understand the *basics* of how the weather works, or how supply and demand works, but not the specifics of either. Please note that this does not mean that the LSAT cannot set up scenarios where they discuss ideas that are extreme or outside the bounds of common knowledge, such as a passage about a difficult scientific or legal concept. The test makers can and do discuss complex or extreme ideas; in these cases, they give you context for the situation by providing additional information.

Remember, the LSAT is used for admission to US and Canadian law schools, hence the test is geared towards those cultures.

The other part of the directions that is interesting is the sentence that states, "For some questions, more than one of the choices could conceivably answer the question. However, you are to choose the <u>best</u> answer; that is, the response that most accurately and completely answers the question." By stating up front that more than one answer choice could suffice to answer the question, the makers of the test compel you to read every single answer choice before making a selection. If you read only one or two answer choices and then decide you have the correct one, you could end up choosing an answer that has some merit but is not as good as a later answer. One of the test makers' favorite tricks is to place a highly attractive wrong answer choice immediately before the correct answer choice in the hopes that you will pick the wrong answer choice and then move to the next question without reading any of the other answers.

You should read all five answer choices in each question.

The Two Passage Types

The section directions also state that "Each set of questions in this section is based on a single passage or a pair of passages." Prior to June 2007, all LSAT Reading Comprehension sections consisted of four total passages, each accompanied by a series of five to eight questions. Each passage and its accompanying questions are known as a "passage set."

Starting with the June 2007 LSAT, the test makers introduced a new element to the test known as a Comparative Reading passage set, wherein two passages addressing the same topic are presented, and a set of questions follows. Comparative Reading passage sets and the special considerations that follow from their unique structure will be addressed in detail in Chapter Seven.

Passage Topics

Reading Comprehension passages are drawn from a wide variety of disciplines, including science, law, and humanities. Thus, you will typically encounter four passage sets with widely varying topical matter. However, even though passage subject matter differs, most sections are constructed from the same consistent set of topics, as follows:

4 Passage Sets

1   Law-related passage
1   Science-based passage
1   Humanities passage featuring diversity
1   Random passage, often Humanities

So, even though the exact subject matter of each passage changes from test to test, the typical LSAT contains one science passage, one law passage, and one humanities passage featuring diversity. The remaining passage is usually drawn from a humanities field such as history or economics, but occasionally the passage comes from science or law.

For a typical example, consider the topics from the December 2007 LSAT:

Topic	Subject Matter
Humanities/Diversity	Asian-American Poetry of Wing Tek Lum
Law	British Common Law
Humanities	University Research Commercialization
Science	Natural Predation and Cyclamen Mites

Please note that the topic of the passage is not necessarily indicative of the level of difficulty. That is, some Science passages are easy, some are difficult. The same goes for Law passages, Humanities passages, etc. In the next chapter we will discuss how to attack any type of passage, and we will discuss how the underlying structure of passages can be analyzed regardless of the passage topic. Topic is examined here so that you understand the nature of what you will be reading. In some cases, knowing the topic can help you make informed decisions about the viewpoints that will be presented therein, and in many cases, students perform better on passages that contain a subject matter that is familiar to them. And, although our primary analysis will focus on viewpoints and structure, later in this chapter we will examine passages from the most commonly occurring topics as a way to calibrate your test radar to the types of mechanisms and viewpoints put forth by the makers of the test.

To locate passages written in the desired style, test makers draw from various sources, which they adapt for use in the Reading Comprehension section. Academic, scientific, and scholarly journals tend to be written in a fairly sophisticated manner, and thus routinely provide materials for the LSAT; recent passage sources have included The University of California, Scientific American Library, and Johns Hopkins University. Articles are also drawn from publications devoted to the arts, including recent offerings from the American Academy of Arts and Sciences, and Poetry in Review Foundation. While the passages are drawn from a wide variety of sources, including newspapers, magazines, books, and journals, they tend to be written in a recognizable, academic style that generally evades simple analysis.

Approaching the Passages

Every Reading Comprehension passage set contains two separate parts: the passage(s) and the questions. When examining the two parts for the first time, students sometimes wonder about the best strategy for attacking the passages: Should I read the questions first? Should I skim the passage? Should I read just the first and last sentence of each paragraph of the passage? The answer is *Read the passage in its entirety and then attack the questions*.

That is, first read the entire passage with an eye towards capturing the main ideas, viewpoints, tone, and structure of the passage, and then proceed to the questions, answering them in order unless you encounter a question too difficult to answer. Although this may seem like a reasonable, even obvious, approach, we mention it here because some LSAT texts advocate reading the questions first or skimming the passage. Let us take a moment to discuss some of the various reading approaches that you *might* consider using, but should avoid:

We will discuss how to systematically break down each passage shortly.

1. **DO NOT** skim the passage, then do each question, returning to the passage as needed.

   In theory, it might seem that skimming could add some degree of efficiency, but in practice this is not the case. In fact, this approach actually reflects a fundamental misunderstanding of the nature of the Reading Comprehension section.

   Skimming might be sufficient to absorb lighter materials, such as newspapers or magazines, but that is because those types of materials are written with simplicity in mind. A newspaper editor wants readers to know half the story by the time they have read the headline, and magazines put the most attention-grabbing pictures on their covers; these publications are trying to draw you in, to entice you to make a purchase. The makers of the LSAT, on the other hand, are well aware that they are dealing with a captive audience; they do not feel any pressure to entertain (as you may have noticed), and passages are chosen based on completely different criteria.

   For many, skimming is a natural reaction to a time-constrained test, but unfortunately the test-makers are well aware of this tendency— the passages they use are chosen in part because they evade quick and simple analysis. In practice, the time "saved" on the front end skimming a passage is more than lost on the back end. In the question section, the skimmer invariably finds the need to go back and re-read, and is often not sufficiently familiar with the passage structure to locate relevant reference points quickly.

   Note: In Chapter Ten we will discuss the very limited contexts in which skimming is advisable.

2. **DO NOT** read just the first and last sentence of each paragraph of the passage, and then do each question, returning to the passage as needed.

This type of "super-skimming" may also sound good in theory; the idea of breezing through the passages, trying to pick up the big picture ideas, may sound appealing, but again, these passages unfortunately do not work that way. This shorthand and ineffective approach is based in part on the common misconception that the main idea of every paragraph appears in the first or last sentence. While this may often hold true, we will see that this is not always the case. After all, the makers of the LSAT are extremely sharp, and they are familiar with these common approaches as well. That may be why many passages will not follow this general rule—the test makers do not like for passages to follow such a simple prescribed formula.

This approach is basically an even more simplistic and ineffective variation of skimming that provides neither substantive knowledge of the information in the passage nor familiarity with the structure sufficient to locate important reference points.

3. **DO NOT** scan the questions first, then go to the passage and read it, answering questions as you come upon relevant information.

Like the two methods discussed previously, this approach may have some initial appeal. Proponents claim that a preview of the questions gives readers more direction when approaching the passage—if they know what will be asked, perhaps students can get a sense of what to look for when reading the passage. Then, proponents argue, students can save time and effort by skimming through the material that is not pertinent to any of the questions.

There are several problems with this approach: Because there are between five and eight questions per passage, students are forced to try to juggle a large amount of disparate information before even starting the passage. Not only does this make retaining the details of the questions challenging, but it also detracts from one's attention when reading the passage. Second, reading the questions first often wastes valuable time, since the typical student who applies this flawed approach will read and consider the questions, read the passage, and then go back and read each question again. This re-reading takes time without yielding any real benefit.

The bottom line is that your reading approach must be maximally effective for all passages. The flawed strategies above, although perhaps effective in some limited contexts, do not consistently produce solid results.

Having discussed some common practices to avoid, let us now consider the proper way to attack an LSAT passage:

In our experience, virtually all high-scoring LSAT takers read the passage before looking at the questions.

1. Always read the passage first. Read for an understanding of structure and detail, for viewpoints and themes, and for the author's tone. Make notations as needed.

2. After reading the passage, consider the questions in the order given. Return to the passage when necessary to confirm your answers.

3. If you encounter a question too difficult to answer, skip it and return to the question after completing the other questions in the passage set.

These are the basic steps to a proper approach to the Reading Comprehension section; each step will be discussed in greater detail.

Your Focus While Reading

LSAT reading is unlike the reading most people engage in on a day-to-day basis. For example, newspapers and magazines, and even most novels, are written with an eye towards presenting the material in the clearest and most interesting fashion possible. LSAT Reading Comprehension passages, on the other hand, are not written in this manner. They are often written in an academic style that is, at times, dense and complex.

Have you ever reached the second, or even third, paragraph of an article or reading passage and suddenly realized that you had no idea what you had just been reading? Many students have had this uncomfortable experience at some point. How are we able to read with our eyes while our minds are elsewhere? Ironically, it is our familiarity with the act of reading that has allowed many to develop the "skill" to do so without 100% focus. This approach might be fine for the morning newspaper or a favorite magazine, but these publications tend to be more simply written and they are unaccompanied by difficult questions. LSAT passages, on the other hand, are chosen for their tendency to elude this type of unfocused approach. Faced with this type of reading, many people "zone out" and lose concentration. Thus, your state of mind when approaching these passages is extremely important.

Giving yourself the simple instruction, "read the passage," allows your mind too much free reign to wander as your eyes gloss over the words. Instead, you should take a more active approach, breaking down the passage as you go, creating something of a running translation, and effectively outlining and notating, as we will discuss further. Yes, it can be difficult to focus for long stretches of time, but you must train yourself through practice to keep your concentration at as high a level as possible.

When starting a section, keep the following mindset tips in mind:

• Channel any nervous energy into intensity.

• Enjoy reading the passages—make them into a game or learning exercise.

- If you lose focus, take a deep breath, refocus, and then return to the task at hand.

- Read aggressively, not passively. Actively engage the material and think about the consequences of what you are reading.

Note: Strong readers have many advantages on this test, but becoming an effective reader obviously has significant value in many contexts. As you practice applying the approaches discussed in this book, keep in mind that they are applicable to reading in general, and not meant solely to help you achieve a high LSAT score (although this is obviously one of the benefits of having an effective approach to reading).

Your Attitude While Reading

Many students approach the Reading Comprehension section with anxiety, concerned about the prospect of reading dense passages with difficult structures and unfamiliar terminology. As is the case with every section of the LSAT, maintaining the proper mindset is vital; in this section, expectations of boredom or anxiety can become self-fulfilling prophecies. If you wish to perform well, you must approach the passages with a positive, energetic, and enthusiastic attitude.

It is vital that you avoid a negative attitude as you practice and improve your approach to reading. Some passages might cover topics that you do not find inherently interesting, but you should not resent the authors for it! These passages are presented not to delight and amuse, but rather to test your reading comprehension skills. Some students approach the passages as puzzles to solve, while others read the passages and try to learn new things from them. Either way, the truth of the matter is that if you do not try to enjoy reading the passages or get some value from them, you will be hard-pressed to perform well.

Some students get annoyed by the academic style of writing of the exam, but this is just part of the test. The passages in this section are not meant to be easy, and the test makers know that the way the passages are written and constructed can be off-putting to many students. You must simply ignore this situation, and take on the passages as a challenge.

> Many passages in the Reading Comprehension section discuss conflicts between different viewpoints, and this makes the reading inherently more interesting. Getting involved in the argument will make the passage more enjoyable for you and will also allow you to focus more clearly on the material.

> A positive attitude is perhaps the most underrated factor in LSAT success. Virtually all high-scoring students expect to do well on the LSAT, and this mind set helps them avoid distractions during the exam, and it helps them overcome any adversity they might face.

Understand the *Type* of Difficulty in the Reading Comprehension Section

There is a widespread misconception among test takers that because one's reading level is difficult to improve (having been developed over many years), one's performance on the Reading Comprehension section is also unlikely to change. This belief reflects a common misunderstanding about the specific type of difficulty associated with reading LSAT passages. Keeping in mind that the test makers only have about half of a page to get their points across, LSAT authors are limited as to the degree of depth that can be reached. This is not to say that these passages are simple, but that the challenge often comes from sources other than conceptual difficulty.

The LSAT is designed not only as a test of conceptual abilities—it is also a test of intimidation. So, how do the test makers ensure that the passages are challenging? Often by choosing subjects that seem daunting; many passages are based on esoteric topics, filled with sophisticated-sounding scientific or technical terms. It is vital that you avoid intimidation as a response to words or phrases which you have never seen. Since the makers of the LSAT do not expect or require outside knowledge with regard to Reading Comprehension passage topics, unfamiliar terms or phrases will almost always be surrounded by context clues. These issues will be covered further in our discussion of reading and notating strategy; for now it is important to understand that unfamiliar words or phrases do not necessarily make a passage any more conceptually difficult, as long as you do not react with discomfort at the prospect of seeing novel terms or phrases.

Reading Speed and Returning to the Passage

Given that you have an average of 8 minutes and 45 seconds to read each passage and complete the questions, the amount of time that you spend reading the passage has a direct effect on your ability to comfortably complete all of the questions. At the same time, the makers of the LSAT have extraordinarily high expectations about the level of knowledge you should retain when you read a passage. Many questions will test your knowledge of small, seemingly nitpicky variations in phrasing, and reading carelessly is LSAT suicide. Thus, every test taker is placed at the nexus of two competing elements: the need for speed (caused by the timed element) and the need for patience (caused by the detailed reading requirement). How well you manage these two elements strongly determines how well you perform.

Although it may sound rather ordinary, the best approach is to read each passage at the high end of your normal reading speed. If possible, you should try to step it up a notch or two, but reading too quickly will cause you to miss much of the detailed information presented in the passage and will force you to reread most of the passage. On the other hand, reading too slowly will prevent you from having adequate time to answer all of the questions.

In seeking to increase reading speed, some students ask us about speed reading courses. In our extensive experience, speed reading techniques do not work on LSAT passages because of the way they are written and constructed. LSAT passages are written in a detailed style filled with built-in traps and formations, and speed reading techniques are not designed to detect these elements.

One thing to be aware of as you read is that you do not need to remember every single detail of the passage. Instead, you simply need to remember the basic structure of the passage so you will know where to return when answering the questions. We will discuss this in more detail when we discuss passage structure.

Everyone's reading speed is different, but the fastest readers tend to complete each passage in somewhere around two to two and a half minutes. Readers moving at a more deliberate pace should finish the passage in around three to three and a half minutes. Once your reading time per passage exceeds the three and a half minute mark, the likelihood of being able to complete all of the questions drops considerably. At the end of this book we will discuss section management and how to handle situations where time is running out, and over the next several chapters we will focus on improving your LSAT reading ability. Improving your reading ability will, in part, consist of teaching you what to look for when reading the passages. Once your ability improves, you will be able to move through the passages and questions more quickly.

Please note that the primary aim of this book is not to just make you a *faster* reader (your natural reading speed has been developed over many years and is hard to increase by itself in a short period of time). Instead, as you become more adept with effective approaches to the passages, you will likely be able to attack the passage sets far more proficiently. The goal here is to make you a *better* reader with a greater knowledge of what to look for, and this will result in your becoming a faster reader.

Active Reading and Anticipation

The best readers read actively. That is, they engage the material and consider the implications of each statement as they read. They also use their involvement in the material to constantly anticipate what will occur next in the passage. This type of reading takes focus and a positive attitude, as discussed earlier, but it also takes practice.

The first part of this book is devoted to examining the theory of approaching the passages and questions, whereas the second part of the book is focused on applying those ideas and discussing passage elements.

Let us take a moment to examine several short sections of text, and use those sections to highlight the idea of how active reading leads to anticipating what comes next:

> Governmental reforms, loosening of regulations,
> and the opening of markets each played a role in fueling
> China's economic growth over the last quarter-century.

After reading this section, one could deduce that there are a number of directions this passage could go. For example, a detailed analysis of each of the three listed factors in the economic growth could be presented, or further implications of the growth could be discussed. Let's add the next two sentences—which complete this paragraph— and see where the author goes:

> Governmental reforms, loosening of regulations,
> and the opening of markets each played a role in fueling
> China's economic growth over the last quarter-century.
> Within the economy, the two most important segments
> (5)   are industry and agriculture. However, industry has
> grown at a significantly faster pace than agriculture.

If you were reading this passage, when you reached this juncture, you should have a fairly good idea of the possible directions the author can take with the *next* paragraph. Consider for a moment the information that has been presented thus far:

- Three factors were named as playing a role in China's economic growth over the last quarter-century.

- The economy is stated to have two key segments.

- One of those two segments is said to have grown at a much faster rate than the other segment.

Clearly, the logical direction to take at this point would be to either explain why industry has grown at a faster rate or why agriculture has grown at a slower rate, or both. There does seem to be a slightly higher likelihood that the author will focus on industry because the exact phrase used was, "industry has grown at a significantly faster pace than agriculture," and this phrasing puts the emphasis on "industry."

Let's see which direction the author chose:

> Governmental reforms, loosening of regulations, and the opening of markets each played a role in fueling China's economic growth over the last quarter-century. Within the economy, the two most important segments
> (5) are industry and agriculture. However, industry has grown at a significantly faster pace than agriculture.
> The growth in industry has occurred largely in the urban areas of China, and has been primarily spurred by a focus on technology and heavy manufacturing. This
> (10) emphasis, however, has not come without costs.

Not surprisingly, the author chose to address the industrial side of the economic growth, in this case by focusing on the segments within industry that have been the most important. Of course, as you continue to read, being correct in your anticipation should not cause you to stop reading actively. As the passage moves forward you should continue to "look ahead" mentally. For example, the last sentence in the text above suggests that the next topic of discussion will be the costs associated with the industrial economic growth.

As a reader, anticipating what will come next in the passage is a habit you should seek to cultivate. By constantly thinking about the possible directions the author can take, you will gain a richer perspective on the story being told by the author. Of course, at times, you might be incorrect in your prediction of what will come next. This is not a problem—you will still be able to absorb what is presented and there is no associated time loss. Simply put, there are tremendous benefits gained from actively reading.

Active Reading Drill

The following drill is presented to reinforce the valuable habit of reacting to important verbal cues. Most students are likely to be familiar with the meanings of important transitional words such as "furthermore" and "however," but again, the most effective readers react when they see these sorts of transitions, which can often allow the reader to predict the next turn of the passage. After each of the following examples, take a moment to consider what is likely to come next in the passage, and write down your predictions. *Answers on the next page*

1. After developing her initial hypothesis, early studies yielded consistently positive results; in fact,...

_____

_____

_____

2. As a result of his childhood accomplishments, Rhee found many opportunities that would have been inaccessible to lesser known talents. Notwithstanding his early successes,...

_____

_____

_____

3. Martindale was generally scorned by his contemporaries, who characterized him as an artist who lacked the imagination to create anything truly original, as well as the self-awareness to perceive his own shortcomings. Modern critics, however...

_____

_____

_____

4. Many American constitutional scholars argue that in making legal determinations, the Supreme Court should comply whenever possible with the original intent of drafters of the Constitution. At the same time,...

_____

_____

_____

5. Most experts in the field who were first told of Dr. Jane's hypothesis were initially skeptical, but...

_____

_____

_____

1. In this case, the words "in fact" tell us that the next information provided will likely continue to support the positive results yielded by early studies.

2. "Notwithstanding," which basically means "in spite of," tells us that the passage is about to take a turn; although Rhee did apparently enjoy early success, we are soon likely to be told of some challenge(s) that appeared in spite of Rhee's early achievements and opportunities.

3. The word "however" in this example is a clear indication that there is contrast between contemporaries' characterizations and those of modern critics, so it is likely that modern critics are going to have nicer things to say about Martindale.

4. If taken out of context, "at the same time" might appear to continue a thought, but the phrase is often more akin to "on the other hand." Here, the author begins by telling us that, according to many, Supreme Court decisions should be based on the Constitution's original intent. "At the same time" is likely in this case to be followed by some limitation on the advisability of this notion (e.g., "At the same time, many facets of modern life were not envisioned by the founders.")

5. "But" is a fairly obvious clue that the passage is about to take a new turn. If we are told of skepticism at first, followed by "but," then it is likely that the author is about to discuss how the hypothesis was confirmed, or possibly how Dr. Jane was able to overcome the initial skepticism of the experts.

Remember, after you have ascertained the topic, as you progress into the passage you must carefully track the following five key elements:

This is the order that we will discuss the five elements in, not the order they appear in the acronym. This is the most logical order for discussion purposes.

1. The various groups and viewpoints discussed within the passage.
2. The tone or attitude of each group or individual.
3. The argument made by each group or individual.
4. The main point of the passage.
5. The structure of the passage and the organization of ideas.

To remember these five critical elements, we use the acronym VIEWSTAMP:

VIEW	= the different **VIEW**points in the passage
S	= the **S**tructure of the passage
T	= the **T**one of the passage
A	= the **A**rguments in the passage
MP	= the **M**ain **P**oint

Let us examine each of these five elements in detail.

1. Viewpoint Identification and Analysis ▮▮▮▮▮▮

A viewpoint is the position or approach taken by a person or group. On the LSAT, Reading Comprehension passages typically contain anywhere from one to six different viewpoints. These viewpoints can be the author's or those of groups discussed by the author.

This section discusses the "VIEW" in VIEWSTAMP. The "VIEW" stands for Viewpoints.

As you read, you must identify each viewpoint that is presented in the passage. This is a fairly easy process—whenever a new group or individual viewpoint is discussed, simply note the presence of that group. Consider the following opening paragraph:

>   File sharing, the practice of allowing the electronic exchange of files over a network such as the Internet, has in recent years led to the emergence of a new and complex set of legal issues for intellectual property
> (5) owners. The rapid and often undetectable movement of digital copies of copyrighted material has made identifying offenders particularly difficult, and has made prosecuting such offenses time-consuming and expensive. The owners of certain types of intellectual
> (10) property, such as music, have claimed that enforcement of these violations is necessary in order to send a signal to other possible offenders. File sharers, on the other hand, typically claim that they did not know they were sharing copyrighted material, and that regardless, the
> (15) widespread use of file sharing networks renders the protection of copyrights impossible.

Let us take a moment to analyze this paragraph, section by section.

Lines 1-9

Many Reading Comprehension passages begin with a Viewpoint Neutral discussion that provides context for the passage.

Not all of the text on the LSAT is presented with a definable viewpoint. Many Reading Comprehension passages begin with a statement of facts or a description of the situation. In these sections, no viewpoint is presented. Throughout this book, we will refer to these sections as "viewpoint neutral." The first eight and a half lines of this passage are viewpoint neutral, simply providing a description of file sharing and the fact that this system raises legal issues. Yes, "intellectual property owners" are mentioned, but since no viewpoint is ascribed to them (as yet), there is no need to note them as a group.

Lines 9-12

The ninth line of the paragraph presents the first identifiable viewpoint of the passage, held by "The owners of certain types of intellectual property." These owners have an identifiable viewpoint, namely that "enforcement of these violations is necessary in order to send a signal to other possible offenders." You can note the presence of this viewpoint element in a variety of ways, from underlining or circling the name of the group to placing a visual marker off to the side (we will discuss passage notation in more detail in a later course segment).

Lines 12-16

Not unusually, a second viewpoint is also presented in the first paragraph. This viewpoint, of "File sharers," is somewhat contrary to the previous viewpoint presented.

Test takers might ask, "What is the value of tracking all of the viewpoints in a given Reading Comprehension passage?" There are several important reasons:

1. Tracking the viewpoints will help you disentangle the mass of information contained in every Reading Comprehension passage.

2. Within the questions, you will be asked to identify the viewpoints presented in the passages and to differentiate between those viewpoints. Answer choices will often present different viewpoints in order to test your ability to distinguish between groups.

In the paragraph under examination, the two viewpoints are presented "back-to-back." This is done intentionally so that the test makers can test your ability to compare and contrast different views. Of course, some test takers fail to distinguish these views, and they are much more prone to fall prey to questions that test the difference between these viewpoints.

In the above paragraph, the views are presented very clearly, and each group is easy to identify. Unfortunately, viewpoints will not always be presented with such clarity. Consider the following opening paragraph from a different passage:

> Literary critics have praised author Toni Morrison for her deft handling of female character development in novels that typically feature powerful and troubling themes. While some have called the author a feminist,
> (5) Morrison has never referred to herself as such, asserting that she seeks to craft viewpoints which embrace equality for all. But one of the strengths of her writing is the uniquely female point of view her characters bring to situations of intolerance and oppression. By their very
> (10) nature, Morrison's dynamic portrayals assert that women deserve equal rights in any forum.

The first sentence introduces the view of "Literary critics" and how they view the work of Toni Morrison. The second sentence (line 4) begins with "some have called," a reference to the views of some commentators, and then the second half of that sentence (line 5) refers to Morrison and how she views herself. So, the first two sentences contain three different groups and viewpoints. The third and fourth sentences may at first appear to be viewpoint neutral, but in fact this section is an opinion, and as this opinion is not ascribed to any particular group, it must be the opinion and viewpoint of the author. Thus, this paragraph contains four separate viewpoints:

An opinion presented without reference to any group is typically the author's opinion.

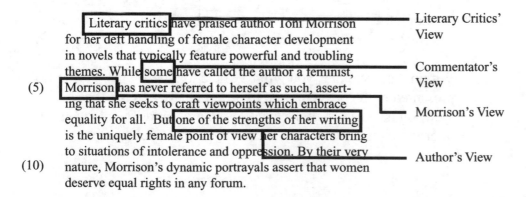

Of course, not all viewpoints are presented in separate sentences. In an effort to confuse test takers, the test makers sometimes introduce two viewpoints in a single sentence, as in the following example:

> While the proponents of the Futurism art movement
> believed that the past was an era to be ignored, some
> critics assert that, ironically, for the Futurists to break
> from the past would have required a more thorough
> (5)   understanding of history on their part.

In the sentence above, two views are introduced: those of the proponents of Futurism and of the critics of Futurism. However, although the sentence contains two opposing views, tracking those elements is no more difficult than when the views are presented in separate sentences. Again, we will discuss notating the views in a later section.

When we begin our discussion of the questions that typically accompany LSAT passages, we will revisit the importance of a viewpoint-based analysis. In the meantime, always remember to identify the various viewpoints that you encounter in a Reading Comprehension passage.

2. Tone/Attitude

Identifying the group or individual behind each viewpoint is usually easy. Identifying the tone or attitude of each group can sometimes be more challenging. Attitude is the state of mind or feeling that each group takes to the subject matter at hand, and for our purposes, "attitude" and "tone" will be used interchangeably.

This section discusses the "T" in the VIEWSTAMP acronym. The "T" stands for Tone.

The author's attitude is revealed through the author's choice of words. For example, is the author indifferent? Critical? Convinced? Skeptical? Hopeful? To make a determination of attitude, you must carefully examine the words used by the author. Is the opinion of the author positive or negative? By how much?

In most passages, LSAT authors tend not to be extreme in their opinions (there are exceptions to this rule, which will be discussed later). As mentioned earlier in this chapter, most passages are drawn from academic or professional publications, and the authors in these publications attempt to offer reasoned arguments in support of their position, arguments that will sway the average reader. In doing so, they often present counterarguments and acknowledge the position of the other side. This fact does not mean that they cannot have strong opinions; it just means that they will not use extremely passionate or fiery language. Thus, one does not often see an author whose tone would be described as "jubilant," "tempestuous," or "depressed."

Most LSAT authors do not display an extreme attitude or tone.

Note also that tone is representative of the passage as a whole, and not just of a single section. An author who exhibited strong support for a position throughout a passage but then at the very end of the passage acknowledged that critics existed would not be said to be "concerned" or "negative." In other words, the tone exhibited in the last few lines would not override or outweigh the positive support that the author displayed earlier. Instead, such a section would simply modify the overall tone of the author, to something along the lines of "reasoned optimism" or "positive but realistic."

Of course, the author is not the only one with a distinct tone. Each viewpoint group can have a tone as well, but determining that tone can sometimes be far more difficult because their position is filtered through the author's words. That is, the author chooses all of the words in the passage, so the viewpoint of each group is harder to discern at times because their views are given to you secondhand. This typically results in a limited range of tones. So, although an author's tone can be quite complex, usually the tone of other viewpoint groups is less so, and can often be reduced to a simple agree/disagree position. Thus, although you must know the viewpoint of each group in the passage, as far as attitude, you are primarily concerned with the attitude of the author.

Let us analyze a few excerpts and examine the idea of tone further. Consider the following section of text:

> There are signs that the animosity between the two
> companies is diminishing.

In the section above, the author's attitude towards the occurrence appears to be neutral. The information is presented factually, and no valuation of the diminishing animosity is provided. Consider, however, how this passage would read if one additional word was inserted:

> Fortunately, there are signs that the animosity between
> the two companies is diminishing.

With the addition of "fortunately," the author's attitude towards the occurrence is now clear—the diminishment of the animosity is a positive occurrence. Other word choices would obviously have a different effect. For example, choosing "unfortunately" instead of "fortunately" would reverse the author's position on the diminishing animosity.

Of course, LSAT passages are comprised of more than a single sentence, and sometimes no indicator words are present. The following text segment from the prior section typifies how a passage can begin:

> File sharing, the practice of allowing the electronic
> exchange of files over a network such as the Internet,
> has in recent years led to the emergence of a new and
> complex set of legal issues for intellectual property
> (5) owners. The rapid and often undetectable movement
> of digital copies of copyrighted material has made
> identifying offenders particularly difficult, and has
> made prosecuting such offenses time-consuming and
> expensive. The owners of certain types of intellectual
> (10) property, such as music, have claimed that enforcement
> is necessary in order to send a signal to other possible
> offenders. File sharers, on the other hand, typically
> claim to have been unaware that they were sharing
> copyrighted material, and that regardless, the widespread
> (15) use of file sharing networks renders the protection of
> copyrights impossible.

Lines 1-9 are viewpoint neutral, and thus the tone is neutral as well. The author simply presents the topic at hand, and he or she does so in a matter-of-fact manner. One would not say that the author is "happy," or "serious," or "sad."

Lines 9-12 present the first definable group in the passage, "Intellectual property owners." We know from prior analysis that their viewpoint is

---

that enforcement is a necessity, but their tone is harder to discern. Are they furious? Belligerent? Reasonable? There is really no way to know because no indication of their attitude is made other than the obvious fact that they believe enforcement is important and thus they disagree with other groups who believe it to be impossible. How they approach that disagreement, however, is not stated in the passage.

Lines 12-16 present a new viewpoint, that of "File sharers." However, other than understanding that this group's viewpoint is somewhat contrary to the owners of intellectual property, we cannot make a determination of the tone of their argument. There is no indication that they are focused, or intense, or happy. Like the previous group, there is simply not enough information to determine their exact attitude toward the subject matter.

Now, let's take a moment to examine another section of text:

> Altering the legal protections available to intellectual property owners would thus be misguided because it creates an environment where the consequences of copyright violation are greater than warranted, and the mere threat of legal action is enough to create a "chilling effect" on the creative environment.

Consider the author's position in this section of text. The choice of the words "misguided" reveals the author's attitude to be strongly negative toward changing the legal protections available to the owners. The "negative" part is easy to spot, but how do you know it is "strongly negative?" Think for a moment of some of the other words the author could have chosen instead of "misguided" that would also convey negativity. Here are just a few examples, each of which conveys negativity, but not to the degree conveyed by "misguided" :

> "Altering the legal protections available to intellectual property owners would thus be *concerning* because it...

> "Altering the legal protections available to intellectual property owners would thus be *troubling* because it..."

> "Altering the legal protections available to intellectual property owners would thus be an *issue* because it..."

In each example, the word chosen to convey negativity is not as strong or as harsh as "misguided." In the annals of LSAT passages, "misguided" is a relatively strong negative term. Of course, the author could have chosen to be even more negative, but that would begin to sound unreasonable:

"Altering the legal protections available to intellectual property owners would thus be *ridiculous* because..."

"Altering the legal protections available to intellectual property owners would thus be *preposterous* because..."

"Altering the legal protections available to intellectual property owners would thus be *disastrous* because..."

These word choices, while possible, tend not to occur on the LSAT because they convey such extreme emotion. Regardless, the point is that in examining attitude, you must carefully consider the word choices used by the author of the passage. The rule is that small changes in word choice can have a large effect on the overall tone of the passage.

Because tracking viewpoints and tone is such a critical ability, the next several pages contain a drill that will help test and strengthen your ability to identify various viewpoints and their accompanying tones.

Viewpoint and Attitude Identification Drill

Read each of the following paragraphs. Then, in the spaces that follow each paragraph, fill in the proper line references, respective viewpoints, and any associated tone or attitude. *Answers on Page 31*

Passage 1:

Federal rules of evidence have long prohibited the presentation in court of many types of "hearsay" (evidence recounted second-hand, rather than reported directly by a witness), based on the notion
(5) that only the most readily verifiable evidence should be allowed consideration by any court in making its determinations. Dr. Kinsley has argued, however, that the rules of evidence as currently written are unacceptably overreaching, defining
(10) as hearsay too many types of evidence whose value would far outweigh any associated detriment if allowed court admissibility. But modern hearsay rules have been written with good reason.

Lines: _____
Viewpoint: _____

Lines: _____
Viewpoint: _____

Lines: _____
Viewpoint: _____

Passage 2:

In the years which preceded Roger Bannister's record breaking performance, it was widely believed that the human body was not equipped to complete a mile-long run in under four minutes;
(5) human lungs, many leading experts asserted, could never deliver sufficient oxygen, and the heart could not undergo such physical stress. Bannister, undeterred, believed that he could reach the goal that he had set in 1952.

Lines: _____
Viewpoint: _____

Lines: _____
Viewpoint: _____

Passage 3:

Many of Joyce's phrasings are less than readily
decipherable, and as a result his works provide
seemingly endless opportunity for speculation about
construction and meaning. Consensus
(5) among literary scholars is often elusive, which is
why outlier academics sometimes gain notoriety in
the short term with questionable but well-publicized
claims concerning proper interpretation. For
example, one Joyce scholar in Ireland recently
(10) announced plans to publish "Finn's Hotel," a
collection of early notes which he asserts to be "a
previously unknown Joyce work," notwithstanding
the fact that the stories have all been published
before.

Lines: _____
Viewpoint: _____

Lines: _____
Viewpoint: _____

Lines: _____
Viewpoint: _____

Passage 4:

The first cardiac pacemaker was the brainchild of
John Hopps, a Canadian electrical engineer who, in
1941, while researching hypothermia and the use
of heat from radio frequencies to restore
(5) body temperature, found that mechanical or
electrical stimulation can restart a heart that has
stopped under conditions of extreme cold. The
earliest versions of the pacemaker were heavy
pieces of equipment which were far too large for
(10) implantation, and instead had to be rolled on
wheels and kept attached to the patient at all times.
Modern science has seen a striking decrease in the
size of these devices, which are now small enough
to be surgically placed under the skin, allowing
(15) them to remain virtually undetectable externally.

Lines: _____
Viewpoint: _____

Viewpoint and Attitude Identification Drill

On the other side of the interpretation debate
are those who believe that the Constitution was
meant to be a "living document," whose proper
construction would readily adapt to an evolving
(5) nation. Judges who subscribe to this perspective
are often referred to by strict constructionists as
judicial activists who are trying to take law-making
power away from the legislative branch of
the government. These judges, however, consider
(10) themselves interpreters, not activists. The framers
specifically allowed for constitutional amendment,
and afforded significant power to the judicial
branch; they felt that the Constitution was to
provide a framework but would have to adapt to a
(15) changing nation.

Lines: _____
Viewpoint: _____

Lines: _____
Viewpoint: _____

Lines: _____
Viewpoint: _____

Lines: _____
Viewpoint: _____

Viewpoint and Attitude Identification Drill Answers

1. <u>Lines 1-7</u>: This section is not attributed to any particular party, so it must come from the author. As this portion is purely informational, there is no tone at this point.

    <u>Lines 7-12</u>: This is the perspective of Dr. Kinsley. By using the term "unacceptably," Kinsley appears to have a fairly strong negative opinion about the breadth of hearsay prohibitions as currently written.

    <u>Lines 12-13</u>: This excerpt is also not attributed to anyone, so it is the author at this point who takes issue with Kinsley's argument, asserting that the hearsay rules have a reasonable foundation.

2. <u>Lines 1-7</u>: In the beginning of this paragraph, the author apprises us of a widely held belief about the body's limitations, followed by a more specific attribution of related assertions to many leading experts.

    <u>Lines 7-9</u>: Here the author makes the switch to the perspective of Bannister. There is not too much attitude reflected here, although Bannister is characterized as fairly confident.

3. <u>Lines 1-4</u>: This portion contains no clear opinion; it is thus <u>viewpoint-neutral</u>.

    <u>Lines 5-7</u>: Here is the <u>author</u>'s view: "outlier academics" (a seemingly derogatory reference) sometimes publicize questionable claims for the sake of short term fame.

    <u>Lines 9-10</u>: The viewpoint presented here is that of the Irish <u>Joyce scholar</u>.

4. <u>Lines 1-15</u>: This excerpt does not provide multiple viewpoints; it is simply the author's presentation of information about the history of the cardiac pacemaker and its inventor. As is sometimes the case with science passages, this selection reflects a relatively neutral tone.

5. <u>Lines 1-5</u>: This is the viewpoint of the "living document" proponents, and the tone is fairly matter-of-fact.

    <u>Lines 5-9</u>: Here the author presents the perspective of the strict constructionists, who take a negative tone with regard to the "living document" judges.

    <u>Lines 9-10</u>: At this point we are presented with the perspective of the so-called "judicial activists," who believe that they are simply offering interpretations rather than newly made laws.

    <u>Lines 10-12</u>: Here we are provided with information about the beliefs of the framers, with an attitude that lends more support to the idea of the Constitution as a living document.

3. Passage Argumentation

This section discusses the "A" in VIEWSTAMP. The "A" stands for Arguments.

Identifying viewpoints and tone is critical to getting a generalized feel for how a passage unfolds. Understanding the arguments will help you understand the details of the passage. So, let us first focus on the specifics of argumentation.

LSAT Reading Comprehension passages consist of premises and conclusions just as in the Logical Reasoning section. In the *PowerScore LSAT Logical Reasoning Bible* we detail how to identify premises and conclusions. Herein, we present a summary of the main points from that section, with additional notes and sections to account for the fact that Reading Comprehension passages are broader and more complex than Logical Reasoning questions.

Law Services says you are expected to possess, in their words, "a college-level understanding of widely used concepts such as argument, premise, assumption, and conclusion."

Identifying Premises and Conclusions

For LSAT purposes, a premise can be defined as:

"A fact, proposition, or statement from which a conclusion is made."

A premise gives a reason why something should be believed.

Premises support and explain the conclusion. Literally, the premises give the reasons why the conclusion should be accepted. To identify premises, ask yourself, "*What reasons has the author used to persuade me? Why should I believe this argument? What evidence exists?*"

A conclusion can be defined as:

"A statement or judgment that follows from one or more reasons."

A conclusion is the point the author tries to prove by using another statement.

Conclusions, as summary statements, are supposed to be drawn from and rest on the premises. To identify conclusions, ask yourself, "*What is the author driving at? What does the author want me to believe? What point follows from the others?*"

Because language is the test makers' weapon of choice, you must learn to recognize the words that indicate when a premise or conclusion is present. In expressing arguments, authors often use the following words or phrases to introduce premises and conclusions:

Premise Indicators	Conclusion Indicators
because	thus
since	therefore
for	hence
for example	consequently
for the reason that	as a result
in that	so
given that	accordingly
as indicated by	clearly
due to	must be that
owing to	shows that
this can be seen from	conclude that
we know this by	follows that

Make sure to memorize these word lists. Recognizing argument elements is critical!

Because there are so many variations in the English language, these lists cannot be comprehensive, but they do capture many of the premise and conclusion indicators used by LSAT authors. As for frequency of appearance, the top two words in each list are used more than any of the other words in the list.

When you are reading, always be aware of the presence of the words listed above. These words are like road signs; they tell you what is coming next. Consider the following example:

> Humans cannot live on Venus because the surface temperature is too high.

Identifying conclusions often helps in identifying the main point of a passage.

As you read the first portion of the sentence, "Humans cannot live on Venus," you cannot be sure if you are reading a premise or conclusion. But, as soon as you see the word "because"—a premise indicator—you know that a premise will follow, and at that point you know that the first portion of the sentence is a conclusion. In the argument above, the author wants you to believe that humans cannot live on Venus, and the reason is that the surface temperature is too high.

In our daily lives, we make and hear many arguments. However, unlike on the LSAT, the majority of these arguments occur in the form of conversations (and when we say "argument," we do not mean a fight!). Any LSAT argument can be seen as an artificial conversation, even the basic example above:

Author:	"Humans cannot live on Venus."
Respondent:	"Really? Why is that?"
Author:	"The surface temperature of Venus is too high."

If at first you struggle to identify the pieces of an argument, you can always resort to thinking about the argument as an artificial conversation and that may assist you in locating the conclusion.

Here are more examples of premise and conclusion indicators in use:

1. "The economy is in tatters. Therefore, we must end this war."

   "Therefore" introduces a conclusion; the first sentence is a premise.

2. "We must reduce our budget due to the significant cost overruns we experienced during production."

   "due to" introduces a premise; "We must reduce our budget" is the conclusion.

3. "Fraud has cost the insurance industry millions of dollars in lost revenue. Thus, Congress will pass a stricter fraud control bill since the insurance industry has one of the most powerful lobbies."

   This argument contains two premises: the first premise is the first sentence and the second premise follows the word "since" in the second sentence; the conclusion is "Congress will pass a stricter fraud control bill."

Notice that premises and conclusions can be presented in any order—the conclusion can be first or last, and the relationship between the premises and the conclusion remains the same regardless of the order of presentation. For example, if the order of the premise(s) and conclusion were switched in any of the examples above, the logical structure of the argument would not change.

Also notable is that the premise(s) and the conclusion can appear in the same sentence, or can be separated out into multiple sentences. Whether the ideas are together or separated has no effect on the logical structure of the argument. This is especially important to recognize in Reading Comprehension passages, because sections of an argument can be separated by many lines or spread out over an entire passage.

One Confusing Sentence Form

Because the job of the test makers is to determine how well you can interpret information, they will sometimes arrange premise and conclusion indicators in a way that is designed to be confusing. One of their favorite forms places a conclusion indicator and premise indicator back-to-back, separated by a comma, as in the following examples:

"Therefore, since..."
"Thus, because..."
"Hence, due to..."

A quick glance would seemingly indicate that what will follow is both a premise and a conclusion. In this instance, however, the presence of the comma creates a clause that, due to the premise indicator, contains a premise. The end of that premise clause will be closed with a second comma, and then what follows will be the conclusion, as in the following:

"Therefore, since higher debt has forced consumers to lower their savings, banks now have less money to loan."

"Higher debt has forced consumers to lower their savings" is the premise; "banks now have less money to loan" is the conclusion. So, in this instance "therefore" still introduces a conclusion, but the appearance of the conclusion is interrupted by a clause that contains a premise.

Additional Premise Indicators

Aside from previously listed premise and conclusion indicators, there are other argument indicator words you should learn to recognize. In the Reading Comprehension section, the author will often make an argument and then for good measure add other premises that lend support to the argument but are non-essential to the conclusion. These are known as additional premises:

Additional Premise Indicators (Continuing the same idea)

furthermore
moreover
besides
in addition
what's more
after all

Following are two examples of additional premise indicators in use:

1. "Every professor at Fillmore University teaches exactly one class per semester. Fillmore's Professor Jackson, therefore, is teaching exactly one class this semester. Moreover, I heard Professor Jackson say she was teaching only a single class."

   The first sentence is a premise. The second sentence contains the conclusion indicator "therefore" and is the conclusion of the argument. The first sentence is the main proof offered by the author for the conclusion. The third sentence begins with the additional premise indicator "moreover." The premise in this sentence is non-essential to the argument, but provides additional proof for the conclusion and could be, if needed, used to help prove the conclusion separately (this would occur if an objection was raised to the first premise).

2. "The city council ought to ease restrictions on outdoor advertising because the city's economy is currently in a slump. Furthermore, the city should not place restrictions on forms of speech such as advertising."

   The first sentence contains both the conclusion of the argument and the main premise of the argument (introduced by the premise indicator "because"). The last sentence contains the additional premise indicator "furthermore." As with the previous example, the additional premise in this sentence is non-essential to the argument but provides additional proof for the conclusion.

Counter-argument Indicators

In a passage, an author will sometimes bring up a counter-argument—an argument that contains an idea that is counter to the prior argument discussed by the author. In Reading Comprehension passages, counter-argument indicators usually introduce an entirely new viewpoint, and thus tracking these indicators is critical.

Counter-argument indicators can also introduce ideas that compare and contrast with the argument, or work against a previously raised point. In this sense, the counter-argument will generally present an idea that is in some way different from another part of the argument.

> Counter-argument indicators, also called adversatives, bring up points of opposition or comparison.

Counter-argument Indicators (Introducing a new idea)

but
yet
however
on the other hand
admittedly
in contrast
although
even though
still
whereas
in spite of
despite
after all

> Note that some terms, such as "After all," can appear on multiple indicator lists because the phrase can be used in a variety of ways. As a savvy LSAT taker, it is up to you to identify the exact role that the phrase is playing in the argument.

The following is an example of a counter-argument indicator in use:

1. "The United States prison population is the world's largest and consequently we must take steps to reduce crime in this country. Although other countries have higher rates of incarceration, their statistics have no bearing on the dilemma we currently face."

   The first sentence contains a premise and the conclusion (which is introduced by the conclusion indicator "consequently"). The third sentence offers up a counter-argument as indicated by the word "although."

Recognizing Conclusions Without Indicators

Many of the arguments we have encountered up until this point have had conclusion indicators to help you recognize the conclusion. And, many of the arguments you will see on the LSAT will also have conclusion indicators. But you will encounter arguments that do not contain conclusion indicators. The following is an example:

> "The best way to eliminate traffic congestion will not be easily found. There are so many competing possibilities that it will take millions of dollars to study every option, and implementation of most options carries an exorbitant price tag."

An argument like the one above can be difficult to analyze because no indicator words are present. How then, would you go about determining if a conclusion is present, and if so, how would you identify that conclusion? Fortunately, there is a fairly simple trick that can be used to handle this situation, and any situation where you are uncertain of the conclusion (even those with multiple conclusions, as will be discussed next).

Aside from the questions you can use to identify premises and conclusions (described earlier in this chapter), the easiest way to determine the conclusion in an argument is to use the Conclusion Identification Method™:

> Take the statements under consideration for the conclusion and place them in an arrangement that forces one to be the conclusion and the other(s) to be the premise(s). Use premise and conclusion indicators to achieve this end. Once the pieces are arranged, determine if the arrangement makes logical sense. If so, you have made the correct identification. If not, reverse the arrangement and examine the relationship again. Continue until you find an arrangement that is logical.

Let us apply this method to the argument at the top of this page. For our first arrangement we will make the first sentence the premise and the second sentence the conclusion, and supply indicators (in italics):

> *Because* the best way to eliminate traffic congestion will not be easily found, *we can conclude that* there are so many competing possibilities that it will take millions of dollars to study every option, and implementation of most options carries an exorbitant price tag.

Does that sound right? No. Let us try again, this time making the first sentence the conclusion and the second sentence the premise:

> *Because* there are so many competing possibilities that it will take millions of dollars to study every option, and implementation of most

options carries an exorbitant price tag, *we can conclude that* the best way of eliminating traffic congestion will not be easily found.

Clearly, the second arrangement is far superior because it makes sense. In most cases when you have the conclusion and premise backward, the arrangement will be confusing. The correct arrangement always sounds more logical.

Complex Argumentation

Up until this point, we have only discussed simple arguments. Simple arguments contain a single conclusion. While many of the arguments that appear on the LSAT are simple arguments, Reading Comprehension passages are typically made up of more complex arguments. Complex arguments contain more than one conclusion. In these instances, one of the conclusions is the main conclusion, and the other conclusions are subsidiary conclusions (also known as sub-conclusions).

While complex argumentation may sound daunting at first, you make and encounter complex argumentation every day in your life. In basic terms, a complex argument makes an initial conclusion based on a premise. The author then uses that conclusion as the foundation (or premise) for another conclusion, thus building a chain, or a ladder with several levels. Let us take a look at the two types of arguments in diagram form:

The makers of the LSAT love to use complex argumentation because the presence of multiple conclusions tends to confuse test takers, making attractive wrong answer choices easier to create.

In abstract terms, a simple argument appears as follows:

Conclusion

↑

Premise

As discussed previously, the premise supports the conclusion, hence the arrow from the premise to the conclusion. By comparison, a complex argument takes an initial conclusion and then uses it as a premise for another conclusion:

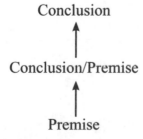

Conclusion

↑

Conclusion/Premise

↑

Premise

Thus, a statement can be both a conclusion for one argument and a premise for another. In this sense, a complex argument can appear somewhat like a ladder, where each level or "rung" represents the next level. Given enough time you could build an argument with hundreds of levels. In LSAT Reading Comprehension passages, however, there are typically four or five levels at most. Let us look at an example of a complex argument:

> "Because the Colts have the best quarterback in football, they therefore have the best offense in football. Because they have the best offense in football, they will win the Super Bowl next year."

In this argument, the first sentence contains a premise followed by a conclusion. This initial conclusion is then used in the second sentence as a premise to make a larger conclusion:

> Premise: "Because the Colts have the best quarterback in football,"

> Sub-Conclusion (conclusion of the previous premise/premise for the following conclusion): "they therefore have the best offense in football."

> Main Conclusion: "they will win the Super Bowl next year."

In this argument, the two premises lead directly to the conclusion. Unlike the previous argument, the author's conclusion seems reasonable based on the two premises. Note that the strength of this argument is based solely on the degree to which the premises prove the conclusion. The truth of the premises themselves is not an issue in determining whether the argument is valid or invalid.

Relationship Indicators

One of the purposes of the LSAT is to test how closely you read. One of the ways the LSAT tests whether you have this skill is to probe your knowledge of exactly what the author said. Because of this, you must at times read parts of a passage incredibly closely, and you must pay special attention to words that describe the relationships under discussion. For example, if an author concludes, "Therefore, the refinery can achieve a greater operating efficiency," do not make the mistake of thinking the author implied that greater operating efficiency *will* or *must* be achieved.

When it comes to relationships, the makers of the LSAT have a wide variety of modifiers in their arsenal. The following are two lists of words that should be noted when they appear, regardless of where they appear in the passage.

Quantity Indicators	Probability Indicators
all	must
every	will
most	always
many	not always
some	probably
several	likely
few	would
sole	not necessarily
only	could
not all	rarely
none	never

Quantity Indicators refer to the amount or quantity in the relationship, such as "some people" or "many of the laws." Probability indicators refer to the likelihood of occurrence, or the obligation present, as in "The Mayor should resign" or "The law will never pass." Many of the terms fit with negatives to form an opposing idea, for example, "some are not" or "would not."

Words such as the Quantity and Probability Indicators are critical because they are a ripe area for the LSAT makers to exploit. There are numerous examples of incorrect answer choices that have attempted to capitalize on the meaning of a single word in the passage, and thus you must commit yourself to carefully examining every word on the test.

A Word About Indicator Words

Over the past several pages, we presented lists of indicator words. These indicator lists are important for several reasons:

1. They help you identify the main elements of the author's argument.

2. They help you identify supplementary argument points made by the author.

3. They show you when the author introduces viewpoints other than his or her own.

4. They alert you to changes in the direction of the argument.

5. They alert you to the strength of the various points made by the author.

Your ability to track the flow and direction of the argumentation is critical, and thus we strongly recommend that you become extremely familiar with the words presented in each indicator list. These words will serve as road signs as you navigate your way through each passage.

Because of their importance, we will also discuss indicator words again in the chapter on diagramming passages.

4. The Main Point

In the previous Passage Argumentation section, our discussion of passage argumentation was at the detail level, discussing the words that authors use to introduce certain types of argumentative elements. Identifying ideas at the elemental level is an important ability, and one that will serve you well throughout the LSAT, as well as in law school. However, a large number of Reading Comprehension questions will ask you broad questions such as the Main Point of the author's argument. Consequently, you must also see the "big picture" as you read, and develop an ability to track the author's major themes and intents.

The main point of a passage is the central idea, or ultimate conclusion, that the author is attempting to prove. Although in the majority of passages the main point is stated in the first paragraph, it is not always the case that the main point appears in the first or second sentence. The main point of many passages has appeared in the final sentence of the first paragraph or in the first sentence of the second paragraph, or, at times, in the last paragraph. So, although the main point is often in the first paragraph, the test makers have the ability to place the main point anywhere in the passage.

As you read, you must identify the author's conclusions and track how they link together. What is the ultimate aim of the author's statements? What is he or she attempting to prove? Are some conclusions used to support others? If so, which is the primary conclusion? The key to identifying a main point is to remember that, although the main point may be stated succinctly in a sentence or two, all paragraphs of the passage must support the main point. Thus, the main point will not just reflect the argument contained in a single paragraph.

When we discuss Main Point questions in Chapter Five, we will discuss this part of passage identification in more detail, and then, as we break down passages we will also examine main points in detail.

This section discusses the "MP" in the VIEWSTAMP acronym. The "MP" stands for Main Point.

The main point of a passage is the central idea that the author is attempting to prove or relay.

5. Passage Structure

This section discusses the "S" in the VIEWSTAMP acronym. The "S" stands for Structure.

Many students, when they first begin working with Reading Comprehension passages, attempt to remember every single detail of the passage. Given the limits of human short-term memory, this is an impossible task. Fortunately, it is also an unnecessary one. Built into your test taking strategy should be the expectation that you will frequently return to the passage during the questions to confirm and disconfirm answer choices.

In order to successfully return to the passage, however, you must attempt to identify the underlying logical structure of the passage as you read. This will help you quickly find information once you begin to answer the questions. For example, some passages open by stating the background of a thesis that will be challenged later in the passage. In the following paragraphs the author will present an alternative viewpoint to the thesis and perhaps specific counterexamples which provide support for the alternative view. Awareness of this general structure will allow you to reduce the time you spend searching for information when you need to refer back to the passage.

The structure description to the right is taken from one of our explanations of a real LSAT passage.

Fortunately, identifying the logical structure of a passage does not require any training in logic or in logical terminology. You simply need to be able to describe in general terms the order in which things are presented in the passage. This is most often connected to specific paragraphs of a passage, as in, "The first paragraph introduces the jury unanimity requirement, and then presents the viewpoints of the critics of unanimity. At the start of the second paragraph, the author takes a strong position that jury unanimity is essential. The second and third paragraphs support that position—paragraph two states that the costs of hung juries are minimal, and paragraph three states that unanimous verdicts lead to fairer verdicts." With a brief synopsis such as this one, you could confidently return to the passage as needed. Question about the critic's position? Most likely the answer will be found in the first paragraph. Question about verdict fairness? Most likely the answer will be found in the last paragraph.

Do not worry that you will not be able to remember every detail. Remember, the answers to every problem are already on the page, and thus your task is simply to be able to identify the correct answer, not to remember every single thing about the passage.

Note that your structural analysis is *not* written down during the exam; instead, you simply hold the idea mentally. Thus, in a nutshell, your structural analysis must be compact enough to be mentally retained, and it must also provide enough basic detail to serve as a guide when you return to the passage. Also keep in mind that if you need to refresh your memory, you can glance at your markings on the passage itself for clues (we will discuss passage diagramming in Chapter Four).

Of course, the Viewpoint Analysis approach we discussed briefly before will also help you identify and control the structure of the passage. Understanding the views of the various players in the passage will greatly assist in your ability to understand the passage as a whole. Identifying the main point and author's tone will also make this task easier.

Let us try an example using the opening paragraph from an LSAT passage:

> The Canadian Auto Workers' (CAW) Legal
> Services Plan, designed to give active and retired
> autoworkers and their families access to totally
> prepaid or partially reimbursed legal services, has
> (5) been in operation since late 1985. Plan members have
> the option of using either the plan's staff lawyers,
> whose services are fully covered by the cost of
> membership in the plan, or an outside lawyer. Outside
> lawyers, in turn, can either sign up with the plan as a
> (10) "cooperating lawyer" and accept the CAW's fee
> schedule as payment in full, or they can charge a
> higher fee and collect the balance from the client.
> Autoworkers appear to have embraced the notion of
> prepaid legal services: 45 percent of eligible union
> (15) members were enrolled in the plan by 1988.
> Moreover, the idea of prepaid legal services has been
> spreading in Canada. A department store is even
> offering a plan to holders of its credit card.

A written analysis of the paragraph would appear as follows:

> The paragraph opens by introducing the concept of a pre-paid legal
> service plan, and specifically the one used by Canadian Auto Workers
> (CAW). There are several important elements that define the plan:
>
> 1. Members receive prepaid or partially reimbursed legal services.
> 2. Plan staff lawyers are fully covered by the plan.
> 3. Members can use outside lawyers, who may or may not charge
>   an additional fee.
>
> The plan has operated since 1985, and as of 1988 included 45 percent
> of eligible CAW members, so it seems there has been a good response
> to the plan in the short term. The idea is also spreading—other
> organizations are starting to offer similar plans.

The analysis above is too much to keep in your head while reading, so you
must distill the essence of the paragraph into a brief description that is easy
to remember (and of course, you may choose to make some markings on the
passage that will help reinforce certain points you deem notable). Such an
analysis would probably consist of:

> The prepaid legal service plan for Canadian Auto Workers covers legal
> costs for members and has been successful.

Does this description capture every detail of the first paragraph? No, but it
does not need to. You simply need to get the gist of what is occurring in this
paragraph so you can quickly return if needed to answer a question.

Let us examine the second paragraph of the same passage:

(20)   While many plan members seem to be happy to get reduced-cost legal help, many lawyers are concerned about the plan's effect on their profession, especially its impact on prices for legal services. Some point out that even though most lawyers have not joined the plan as cooperating lawyers, legal fees

(25)   in the cities in which the CAW plan operates have been depressed, in some cases to an unprofitable level. The directors of the plan, however, claim that both clients and lawyers benefit from their arrangement. For while the clients get ready access to

(30)   reduced-price services, lawyers get professional contact with people who would not otherwise be using legal services, which helps generate even more business for their firms. Experience shows, the directors say, that if people are referred to a firm and

(35)   receive excellent service, the firm will get three to four other referrals who are not plan subscribers and who would therefore pay the firm's standard rate.

Bypassing a complete written analysis for the moment, our distilled, structural analysis of this paragraph would be along the lines of:

> Lawyers are concerned about the plan's effect on prices; directors of the plan claim that everyone benefits.

Again, this description misses certain details, but it does indicate that there are two viewpoints presented in this paragraph, and that those two viewpoints are opposing. Should a question ask about the views of lawyers, you would know to return to the first half of this paragraph. On the other hand, should a question ask about the directors, the second half of this paragraph would be the proper starting point. Consider, for example, the following question which accompanied this passage:

5. The passage most strongly suggests that, according to proponents of prepaid legal plans, cooperating lawyers benefit from taking clients at lower fees in which one of the following ways?

    (A)   Lawyers can expect to gain expertise in a wide variety of legal services by availing themselves of the access to diverse clientele that plan participation affords.

    (B)   Experienced cooperating lawyers are likely to enjoy the higher profits of long-term, complex cases, for which new lawyers are not suited.

    (C)   Lower rates of profit will be offset by a higher volume of clients and new business through word-of-mouth recommendations.

    (D)   Lower fees tend to attract clients away from established, nonparticipating law firms.

    (E)   With all legal fees moving downward to match the plans' schedules, the profession will respond to market forces.

With regard to this question, it is valuable to be familiar with the passage organization, since the proponents' arguments can all be found in the second paragraph. Further, since the author presents conflicting viewpoints in that paragraph, we should focus on the second half, in which the author presents proponents' arguments in favor of the plan (The correct answer to the question above is answer choice (C), which summarizes the argument presented in lines 33-37 of the passage).

Let's complete our analysis by reviewing the final paragraph of the passage:

> But it is unlikely that increased use of such plans will result in long-term client satisfaction or in a
> (40) substantial increase in profits for law firms. Since lawyers with established reputations and client bases can benefit little, if at all, from participation, the plans function largely as marketing devices for lawyers who have yet to establish themselves. While
> (45) many of these lawyers are no doubt very able and conscientious, they will tend to have less expertise and to provide less satisfaction to clients. At the same time, the downward pressure on fees will mean that the full-fee referrals that proponents say will come
> (50) through plan participation may not make up for a firm's investment in providing services at low plan rates. And since lowered fees provide little incentive for lawyers to devote more than minimal effort to cases, a "volume discount" approach toward the
> (55) practice of law will mean less time devoted to complex cases and a general lowering of quality for clients.

Again, we can bypass a complete written analysis, and instead look at the distilled, structural analysis of this paragraph:

> The author concludes that the plan is unlikely to benefit clients or lawyers, and then offers reasons why.

Again, this synopsis misses some details, but that is immaterial. The point is to understand the general idea of what happened in the passage. You should also note that the first several lines of this paragraph contain the author's main point.

Putting all three analyses together, the entire structure appears as:

> The prepaid legal service plan for Canadian Auto Workers covers legal costs for members and has been successful.

> Lawyers are concerned about the plans effect on prices; directors of the plan claim that everyone benefits.

The author concludes that the plan is unlikely to benefit clients or lawyers, and then offers reasons why.

Note that this analysis not only describes the structural elements—viewpoints, for example—but also provides basic details of each. Compare this to a more logic-based analysis that eliminates the details of each viewpoint:

Paragraph 1: Introduce one example of a prepaid legal service plan

Paragraph 2: Present arguments for and against this type of plan

Paragraph 3: Assess these plans as unlikely to be beneficial, listing several specific reasons for this assertion.

This analysis is factually correct, but for our purposes it would not provide a very helpful guide when answering the questions. For example, the above characterization of the second paragraph is perfectly accurate, but as a mental tool for use in returning to the passage, it would be inadequate. Again remember the rule of structural analysis stated earlier:

Your structural analysis must be compact enough to be mentally retained, and it must also provide enough basic detail to serve as a guide when you return to the passage.

Passage Analysis and Structure Identification Drill

Using the principles described in this section, please provide a distilled and basic structural analysis of the following passage excerpts. *Answers on Page 52*

Example:

> Chinchillas, which are native to the Andes Mountains in South America, are rare in the wild due to overhunting. The trade in chinchilla fur extends as far back as the 1500s, but by the early 1900s demand for chinchilla pelts was so great that chinchillas became almost extinct. A series of trade prohibitions that outlawed the trade of chinchilla fur slowed the decline. Today, Chinchillas are still endangered but no longer on the brink of extinction.

Basic Summary: Chinchillas, native to the South American Andes, are rare because of the demand for their pelts, which began in the 1500s and put them near extinction in the 1900s. Trade prohibitions have slowed the decline.

Structural Analysis: Introduce the Chinchilla, its overhunting, and the trade prohibitions which saved the animal from the verge of extinction.

Passage 1:

> Many early scientists operated under the mistaken assumption that the continents were fixed in place, static and incapable of independent movement. As a result most ignored the fact that the east coast of South America and the west coast of Africa appeared to line up, mocking assertions that they two continents had at one time been part of a larger mass. Later, scientists began to consider the possibility of continental drift, and the likelihood that the two continents had indeed been linked at some point in the past.

Basic Summary:_____
_____
_____
_____

Structural Analysis:_____
_____
_____

Passage 2:

Political commentators have long advocated
direct monetary aid as an effective way to help
resolve the political and economic struggles
of many African nations. In her recent book,
however, Dambisa Moyo makes the startling
argument that western nations should discontinue
direct governmental aid on the grounds that such
aid actually worsens conditions for the general
population. Although she grants that some direct
investment in the economies of Africa—in the
form of business loans and credit—is desirable, her
belief is that debt levels have become intolerably
high and that foreign aid has facilitated the creation
of corrupt regimes. Critics have labeled her views
cruel and callous, attacking her for providing a
rationale for western neglect of Africa.

Basic Summary:_____
_____
_____
_____

Structural Analysis:_____
_____
_____

Passage 3:

The success of a small local business can
often depend on issues different from those which
determine the success of a large or national business.
Although many factors can contribute to the failure
of a local business, experts point to three significant
areas that commonly cause problems. First, poor
management of business operations can doom even
the best small business to failure. Management
covers a gamut of items, from accounting to
customer service to employee management, and
a weakness or lack of oversight in any of these
areas can quickly lead to serious problems. Second,
local businesses tend to rely heavily on location.
A poor location fails to attract customers, which
translates directly into low sales. Finally, because
these companies are by definition small, they must
rely heavily on advertising for success, so a weak
(or nonexistent) marketing strategy can have an
exaggerated impact on health of the business.

Basic Summary:_____
_____
_____
_____

Structural Analysis:_____
_____
_____

Passage 4:

The integral role played by the law in promoting public health is irrefutable. Eliminating lead in paints, banning smoking in public buildings, and requiring the posting of nutritional content on food labels are just a few types of public protection that have resulted from public health legislation. Within the nutritional law community, experts agree that these legal efforts have produced demonstrable benefits nationally. One burgeoning area of nutritional law is obesity law; proposed legislation in this area focuses largely on food warnings and additional labeling to apprise the public of risks associated with the overconsumption of certain foods. Participants in this debate must weigh the needs of all stakeholders, considering the rights of food producers while also considering the health of the general population.

Basic Summary: _____
_____
_____
_____

Structural Analysis: _____
_____
_____

Passage 5:

The fall of the Berlin Wall in 1989 is interpreted differently by different groups, depending in many cases on their ideology and their location. Observers in the United States often credit Ronald Reagan with the fall, due to his aggressive anti-communist agenda and large military budget. Europeans tend to perceive the event differently, believing that a policy of accommodation and productive engagement towards East Germany ultimately lead to the political upheaval that resulted in the fall of the Wall. Russians often view the event in a negative light, with a concomitant loss of geopolitical influence and control. Many Russians argue that post-fall events left Russia on the periphery of European politics, while Europe enjoyed an atmosphere that was more inclusive and cooperative.

Basic Summary: _____
_____
_____
_____

Structural Analysis: _____
_____
_____

Passage Analysis and Structure Identification Drill Answer Key

Note: It is unlikely that your answers will exactly match the answers below; these are merely suggested analyses of the passage excerpts. However, you should focus on whether your analysis of each excerpt provides similar sufficient basic detail and can be easily understood and retained.

Passage 1:

Basic Summary: Early scientists believed that continents couldn't move on their own, and thus failed to see the relationship between the coasts of South America and Africa. Later scientists considered the possibility that the continents had been linked in the past.

Structural Analysis: Introduce the misconceived perspective among "many early scientists" regarding static continents, these scientists' failure to note the evidence, and later scientists' considerations of a possible continental link.

Passage 2:

Basic Summary: Basic Summary: While many have advocated direct financial aid as a way to help Africa, Moyo disagrees, asserting that debt levels have grown too great, and foreign aid had led to corruption among the powerful. Moyo's critics attack her views, saying that these views justify western neglect.

Structural analysis: Introduce traditional beliefs regarding economic aid to Africa, followed by contrary perspective of Moyo, who sees this traditional approach as detrimental. Finally, introduce viewpoint of Mayo's critics, who consider her perspective to have damaging consequences.

Passage 3:

Basic Summary: Small, local businesses' success can depend on different factors than those of large, national businesses. Factors that commonly lead to problems are as follows: poor management of business operations, poor location, and weak or non-existent marketing strategy.

Structural Analysis: Assert that the small local businesses and large businesses can often rely on different factors for success. Introduce and briefly discuss three factors that can cause problems for small local businesses.

Passage 4:

Basic Summary: The law plays an important part in protecting the public health, with regard to such examples as lead paint and second hand smoke. Recently some have proposed expanding legislation regarding food labeling and warnings. The decision will require consideration of the producers' perspective as well as that of the general public.

Structural Analysis: Discuss importance of public health law; provide specific examples. Introduce new area of consideration—that of obesity law, the question of expanded labeling legislation, and the sides of the issue to be considered.

Passage 5:

Basic Summary: Different groups interpret the fall of the Berlin Wall in different ways, often depending on their ideology and location. Americans tend to credit Reagan, who had a large military budget to back a strongly anti-communist sentiment. In Europe they tend to credit "productive engagement" and eventual political upheaval, while Russians often perceive the event negatively, believing that it put Russia out on the political fringe.

<u>Structural Analysis</u>: Introduce general topic of differing viewpoints on the fall of the Berlin Wall, and reasons for differences in perspective. Briefly expand on the general viewpoints on the matter in the US, Europe, and Russia.

Take several minutes to read the following LSAT passage (time is not critical for this exercise). Look for the five crucial elements of VIEWSTAMP that we discussed within this chapter:

1. The various groups and viewpoints discussed within the passage. (VIEW)
2. The tone or attitude of each group or individual. (T)
3. The argument made by each group or individual. (A)
4. The main point of the passage. (MP)
5. The structure of the passage and the organization of ideas. (S)

Please note that we will not examine any of the questions just yet.

Economists have long defined prosperity in terms of monetary value, gauging a given nation's prosperity solely on the basis of the total monetary value of the goods and services produced annually.
(5) However, critics point out that defining prosperity solely as a function of monetary value is questionable since it fails to recognize other kinds of values, such as quality of life or environmental health, that contribute directly to prosperity in a broader sense.
(10) For example, as the earth's ozone layer weakens and loses its ability to protect people from ultraviolet radiation, sales of hats, sunglasses, and sunscreens are likely to skyrocket, all adding to the nation's total expenditures. In this way, troubling reductions in
(15) environmental health and quality of life may in fact initiate economic activity that, by the economists' measure, bolsters prosperity.

It can also happen that communities seeking to increase their prosperity as measured strictly in
(20) monetary terms may damage their quality of life and their environment. The situation of one rural community illustrates this point: residents of the community value the local timber industry as a primary source of income, and they vocally protested
(25) proposed limitations on timber harvests as a threat to their prosperity. Implicitly adopting the economists' point of view, the residents argued that the harvest limitations would lower their wages or even cause the loss of jobs.
(30) But critics of the economists' view argue that this view of the situation overlooks a crucial consideration. Without the harvest limitations, they say, the land on which the community depends would be seriously damaged. Moreover, they point out that the residents

(35) themselves cite the abundance of natural beauty as one of the features that make their community a highly desirable place to live. But it is also extremely poor, and the critics point out that the residents could double their incomes by moving only 150 kilometers
(40) away. From their decision not to do so, the critics conclude that their location has substantial monetary value to them. The community will thus lose much more—even understood in monetary terms—if the proposed harvest limits are not implemented.
(45) Economists respond by arguing that to be a useful concept, prosperity must be defined in easily quantifiable terms, and that prosperity thus should not include difficult-to-measure values such as happiness or environmental health. But this position dodges the
(50) issue—emphasizing ease of calculation causes one to disregard substantive issues that directly influence real prosperity. The economists' stance is rather like that of a literary critic who takes total sales to be the best measure of a book's value—true, the number of
(55) copies sold is a convenient and quantifiable measure, but it is a poor substitute for an accurate appraisal of literary merit.

This passage begins with the introduction of the viewpoint of the economists, who have long defined a nation's prosperity solely in terms of exact monetary value. In line 5, the opposing viewpoint of the critics is introduced, namely that defining prosperity in just economic terms is a poor measure because it fails to include important non-economic measures of prosperity, such as quality of life. The remainder of the first paragraph provides an example that supports the position of the critics.

In the first paragraph, the author does not make a strong statement of position, but there is a suggestion that the author supports the critics: in line 14, the author uses the term "troubling" in reference to reductions in environmental health and quality. This modifier suggests that the author agrees with the critics that non-economic measures of prosperity have value.

From a tone standpoint, thus far we simply have the economists and critics disagreeing over the measure of prosperity, with the author possibly on the side of the critics. No main point has been presented yet (that is, no conclusion has been drawn by the author). Structurally, we have two opposing views and an example supporting the critics' view.

The second paragraph suggests more strongly that the author agrees with the critics. The paragraph opens by indicating that communities who measure prosperity in strictly monetary terms can jeopardize their quality of life and their environment. The author's use of the words "It can also happen" and "may damage" suggest that the author believes these communities are harming themselves (and thus that the critics are correct in measuring prosperity in other terms besides just economic ones). The remainder of the paragraph is devoted to an example where a community uses an economic justification to oppose limits on timber harvests.

From a viewpoint, tone, and main idea standpoint, this paragraph adds very little. Structurally, the paragraph is comprised of a sentence that supports the critics, and an example that shows a community using an economic justification for a decision.

The third paragraph opens with the critics' response to the example in the second paragraph, namely that residents of the community have failed to consider that scenic beauty is a critical factor in their choice of residence. The community thus stands to lose a considerable amount if timber harvest limits are not imposed.

Similar to the second paragraph, this paragraph adds very little new information in the way of viewpoint, tone, or main point. The third paragraph is simply a continuation of the critics' view.

The final paragraph returns to the view of the economists, indicating that they believe that prosperity must be defined in easily quantifiable terms, and that therefore prosperity should not be defined to include quality of life values. At this point, the author finally enters and presents a defined viewpoint, that the economists' position is weak. The phrasing used in line 49—"But this position..."—attributes the view to no particular group, and thus the view must be that of the author. The passage then ends with further criticism of the economists. This final criticism reveals the main point of the passage, which is that the economists have defined prosperity too narrowly. Structurally, the last paragraph opens with the economists' position on how to define prosperity, and ends with the author's rebuttal of that position.

Let us take a moment to review each of the five critical VIEWSTAMP elements in the passage:

1. The various groups and viewpoints discussed within the passage.

   There are three main viewpoints presented in the passage: the economists', the critics', and the author's. The critics and the author are in agreement, and both oppose the economists.

2. The tone or attitude of each group or individual.

   The economists and the critics are at odds, but the tone of the disagreement does not appear to be acrimonious. For example, critics "point out" and "argue." Those are fairly mild words that simply indicate general disagreement, not animosity or particularly strong opposition.

   The author appears to disagree with the economists to a greater degree. In lines 49-57, the author uses terms like "dodges the issue" and "poor substitute" to indicate that he or she has a fairly negative view of the economists' position.

3. The argument made by each group or individual.

   The economists argue that prosperity should be defined in solely economic terms. Any measure of prosperity must be easily quantifiable, and thus any difficult-to-measure value should be rejected.

   The critics and the author disagree with the economists, and argue that a solely economic stance fails to account for other values that contribute to prosperity (such as quality of life), which are difficult to quantify but nonetheless important.

4. The main point of the passage.

Noting the main point of the passage will always be valuable, in part because recognition of the main point is vital to a complete understanding of the passage, and in part because a very significant percentage of Reading Comprehension passages are accompanied by a Main Point question—including this one. In this case, the main point is presented at the end of the passage, where the author indicates that the economists' definition of prosperity is too narrowly drawn.

1. Which one of the following most accurately states the main point of the passage?

    (A) According to critics, communities that seek to increase their prosperity recognize the need to gauge the value and ensure the long-term health of their local environment.
    (B) Economists' definition of prosperity strictly in terms of monetary value is too narrow to truly capture our ordinary conception of this notion.
    (C) If economists were to alter and expand their definition of prosperity, it is likely that the economic and environmental health of most communities would appear worse under the new definition than under the old definition.
    (D) In contrast with the views of economists, some critics believe that prosperity can be neither scientifically measured nor accurately defined, and as a concept is therefore of little use for economists.
    (E) While they are generally an accurate and practical measure of current economic prosperity, figures for the total expenditures of a nation do not aid in providing an indication of that nation's future economic prospects.

As prephrased above, the main point of the passage is that a monetary definition is too narrow to cover our notion of prosperity, so the correct answer choice is (B).

5. The structure of the passage and the organization of ideas.

The structure of the passage is as follows: The first paragraph presents the economists' view of prosperity, the critics' opposing view, and a supporting example of the critics' viewpoint. The second paragraph is a sentence that supports the critics, and an example that shows a community using an economic justification for a decision. The third paragraph is a further criticism of the economists, framed against the example from the second paragraph. The last paragraph opens with a further discussion of the economists' position on how to define prosperity, and ends with the author's main point—a rebuttal of the economists' position.

Overall, this is a solid passage—several viewpoints exist, clear authorial position and attitude are presented, and reasonably clear structure and argumentation exist. Granted, the topic may not be the most exciting, but the examples given are not uninteresting and you can engage yourself by focusing on the disagreement between the parties.

One final note: If you can consistently apply the five VIEWSTAMP ideas we have discussed throughout this chapter, you will be in an excellent position to attack the questions. And, our discussions of passage formations and passage diagramming in the next two chapters will only serve to make you an even stronger test taker. By the time we begin examining the questions in a few chapters, you will have a powerful arsenal of tools to dissect each problem, and, in many cases, you will discover that you know what the correct answer will say before you even begin reading the five answer choices.

Chapter Three: Passage Elements and Formations

Chapter Preview

This chapter will cover sources of passage difficulty and examine the elements and formations that appear in passages which tend to generate questions. That is, we will look at why passages are hard and what passage elements the test makers tend to ask about. In this sense, this chapter continues the discussion begun in Chapter Two. Chapter Two introduced the "big picture" elements that you must always track, whereas this chapter will discuss the more detailed elements that you should note. In the following two chapters we will then talk about how to physically notate these elements and then examine individual question types.

Sources of Difficulty: The Test Makers' Arsenal

There are several general ways the makers of the test can increase the level of difficulty of any given passage. Before examining the specific elements that the test makers like to test, reviewing the general methods that can be used to increase difficulty is helpful.

The following five methods are the primary ways used by the test makers to alter the perception of difficulty that students have about individual passages:

Challenging Topic or Terminology

In some passages, the choice of topic makes the passage seem more difficult to some students. For example, many students fear the appearance of a science-related passage on the LSAT. As we will discuss later, you should not be afraid or unduly worried by science passages (or any passage, for that matter). That said, an unfamiliar or complex topic can make a passage harder, but only incrementally so because the test makers are forced to explain the main concepts of the passage, regardless of the topic. Thus, there may be a few moments of anxiety while you are forced to adjust to an unknown topic, but the test makers will always give you the information needed to answer the questions. As outlined below, other methods are far more effective at making a passage difficult.

The use of complicated terminology usually concerns students as well. Reading a passage that contains words or ideas that you do not recognize is intimidating and usually confusing. As mentioned in Chapter Two, you should not be intimidated by unknown concepts, mainly because the test makers must *always* define any term or concept not in common public usage.

When you encounter unknown words, they will fall into one of two categories: new terms related to the concept under discussion or unknown vocabulary words. In the case of terms related to the concept under discussion (such as *Scar Art* or *LHB*), the test makers will define the term or concept for you in the text, sometimes briefly using synonyms, sometimes in greater detail. Unknown vocabulary words can be more challenging, but you can use context clues from the surrounding text to help determine the meaning of words you do not recognize. We will briefly discuss this point again later in this chapter.

Challenging Writing Style

The test makers carefully choose whether a passage will have a clear, easy-to-read writing style or a dense, convoluted writing style. Obviously, writing style has a tremendous effect on passage difficulty because even the easiest of concepts can become difficult to understand if the writing style is intentionally complex.

In the first few lines of a passage, it is difficult to tell whether the writing style will be challenging. If you do encounter a passage that has a very difficult-to-read style, use some of the tips in the next section to focus on the elements most likely to be tested.

There is no easy way to combat a passage written in an intentionally convoluted style other than carefully reading and clearly marking the passage.

Multiple Viewpoints

In Chapter Two we discussed the importance of tracking viewpoints while reading. We will discuss this again in a few pages, but be aware that one easy way for the test makers to increase difficulty is to add more viewpoints. Tracking viewpoints in a passage with only two viewpoints is easy; tracking viewpoints in a passage with six viewpoints is considerably more challenging. The more viewpoints present, the easier it is to confuse them, or forget who said what. This is especially true because when more viewpoints are present, the test makers typically insert extensive compare-and-contrast sections, which makes separating and mastering each view more difficult.

Later in this section we will address "compare and contrast" sections, and in Chapter Four we will discuss methods for tracking viewpoints in a concrete and easy-to-identify fashion.

Difficult Questions/Answers

The difficulty of a passage can also be altered by the nature of the questions. For example, if there are a large number of questions, or if the questions are unusual in nature, or, most frequently, if the answer choices are difficult to separate, then the passage set itself will be difficult or time-consuming. Thus, even an easily understandable passage can turn challenging once you start attacking the questions. In Chapter Five we will discuss question type in detail, and provide you with an effective approach for attacking any question you face.

Order of Presentation

Another very important factor is one which you should be thinking about from the outset. There is a common misconception among test takers that Reading Comprehension passages are presented in order of difficulty. The LSAC is not necessarily interested in making things easy on the reader (indeed, even if this were the intent, many topics are easy for some readers and difficult for others). Thus, sometimes the hardest passage on the test appears first, second, or third. To combat this situation, you should take advantage of the fact that this is a paper-based test—if, for example, you can already tell after reading the first few lines of a passage that it looks particularly challenging, you might consider moving on to another passage. This can be a bit disconcerting at first, because by the time you decide that a passage is difficult, you may feel that you have already invested significant time and effort into that passage. This is natural, but most students tend to overestimate the amount of time they have taken to read the first portion of a passage. In reality, within 10 to 15 seconds of *reading* a passage (not skimming), it is often possible to assess two very important factors:

1. Whether or not the topic is one of inherent interest to you.
2. Whether the passage is written in a style that you find relatively easy to understand.

Although you will be reading all of the passages of the section at some point, it can be far more efficient to start with those that you find most enjoyable and accessible; starting with your favorites will allow you to move more adeptly through the passages.

This test makers' weapon (the order of presentation) is one of the easiest to overcome: If you know that the passages might not be presented in ideal order, simply choose your favorites first. Some students prefer the comparative reading passages, which tend to be shorter, so those are the first they consider when beginning the Reading Comprehension section.

Passage Elements That Generate Questions

As you read, there are certain specific passage elements that should jump out at you, primarily because history has reflected the test makers' tendency to use these elements as the basis of questions.

For purposes of clarity, we will divide these elements into two groups: viewpoint-specific elements and text-based elements.

Viewpoint-Specific Elements

Analysis of viewpoints is one of the major approaches we use in attacking the passages, and in Chapter Two we discussed this approach in depth. Because separating viewpoints allows you to divide the passage into logical, trackable units, the process helps you to more easily understand the passage and to disentangle the many disparate ideas in each passage. Viewpoints also play a large role in the main themes of the passage, so they also are the source of many of the questions asked by the test makers. For example, questions about the main point, authorities cited by the author, or the perspective of any of the players in the passage are all related to viewpoints, and thus tracking viewpoints not only makes understanding the passage itself easier, it automatically assists you in answering a *significant* portion of the questions. Thus, while reading you must always focus on identifying each viewpoint in the passage.

Competing perspectives offer differing opinions on the same subject.

When considering viewpoints, be aware that one of the favorite tricks of the test makers is to use competing perspectives, a trick that involves presenting two or more viewpoints on the same subject, with each viewpoint containing slightly different elements (but often sharing some similar elements). Here is an example:

Topic: Nuclear power

Viewpoint 1: Nuclear power plants are efficient generators of energy, but they present serious long-term environmental concerns because of the problems associated with storing radioactive waste in the form of spent fuel.

Viewpoint 2: Nuclear power is the most efficient way to produce energy, and the waste problems associated with them, while significant, are lesser than those associated with more traditional energy production methods, such as those involving coal.

In the form above, the difference and similarity in viewpoints is easy to identify, but subtleties exist ("efficient generators" vs "most efficient way," and "serious long-term environmental concerns" vs "significant, are lesser," to name two). But imagine for a moment that the two views are woven together in a passage, and some extraneous information is also interspersed. When you finally attack the questions a few minutes later, it would be very easy to have forgotten the exact similarities and differences, especially if other viewpoints were present.

Thus, competing perspectives can be quite tricky because it is easy to confuse different views, and, of course, questions about these elements make certain to closely test whether you understand the exact differences between the different viewpoints.

Because viewpoint analysis was a main feature in Chapter Two, we will move on for the moment, but in all of the passages we analyze in later chapters we will prominently feature this element (and all the elements in VIEWSTAMP) in our analysis.

Text-based Questions

In one sense, all questions are based on the text. In using the name "text-based," we refer to elements that appear directly in the text as an identifiable part—definitions, lists, compare/contrast sections, or dates, for example—and not the broader and somewhat more abstract elements such as main points, author's purposes, or passage structure. Under this definition, text-based questions will often be smaller pieces, sometimes just a single word, but sometimes short sections of the text. In this sense, these are the "nuts and bolts" elements that you should be aware of when reading.

These are the elements we will discuss (not in order of importance):

1. Initial Information/Closing Information
2. Dates and Numbers
3. Definitions
4. Examples
5. Difficult words or phrases
6. Enumerations/Lists
7. Text Questions

Note these elements as you encounter them in the passages; you are likely to see them again in the questions.

1. Initial Information/Closing Information

The information presented in the first five lines of a passage—especially the details—is often forgotten by students. This occurs because at the very beginning of a passage you are focused on figuring out the topic and the author's general position, and thus seemingly minor details are hard to retain.

Similarly, the information presented in the last five lines is often forgotten because the average student is eager to jump to the questions and thus skims over the material at the very end of the passage. Thus, the test makers occasionally question you on your knowledge of information contained at the very beginning or end of the passage, so you must always make sure to check these areas if you are having difficulty answering a question, especially when you seem to have no idea where the answer might be (again, this would most likely occur with detail or fact-based questions).

2. Dates and Numbers

When an LSAT author references more than one date or era, creating a simple timeline can be an effective way to maintain relative perspective, whether the comparisons span days or centuries.

Dates often provide useful markers within a passage, allowing you "before" and "after" points to return to when searching for answers. While in some passages the use of dates is incidental, in other passages, a chronology is created, and then some of the questions will test your ability to understand the timeline. The general rule is that the more dates you see in a passage, the more important it is that you make note of them.

Numbers are usually less important than dates, but when numbers are used in a comparative sense, or as part of an explanation, the test makers will sometimes check your comprehension of their meaning.

3. Definitions

Identifying definitions serves two purposes: in those cases where you do not understand the term or concept it helps you to clarify the idea, and even when you do understand the concept the test makers will sometimes test you on your understanding of the definition.

The typical definition is presented in the immediate vicinity of the word or concept, like so:

> This landmark case established that in order to prevail against a publisher for defamation and libel, a public figure must be able to prove "actual malice," which means that the publisher either knowingly printed false statements about the public figure in question, or showed reckless disregard with respect to the truth or falsity of such statements when publishing them.

In the section above, the clause after the comma provides the definition for the legal term *actual malice*. Of course, some definitions are much shorter, such as this sentence which includes the one word definition of *mitigate*:

> While the plaintiff does have legal rights in such cases, there also exists
> a duty when possible to mitigate, or reduce, damages sustained as a
> result of negligence on the part of the defendant.

Regardless of the length of a definition, you should make sure that you are comfortable with the term being defined. If you encounter an idea or term that you think should be defined but do not see a definition in the immediate vicinity, then the definition will probably be presented relatively soon (explicitly or through context clues), and the test makers are simply trying to trick you with a "trap of separation," which we will discuss later in this chapter.

4. Examples

LSAT authors often use examples to explain or underscore the points they are making. Logically, these examples serve as broad premises that support the conclusion of the author. Functionally, they help you to understand the typically more abstract point that the author is making, and so they can be quite helpful especially when you are having difficulty understanding the argument.

Examples can be short and specific to a single point, or they can be substantial and involved and appear throughout the passage. Always remember, though, that the example is not the main conclusion or point of the author; generally, examples are provided to support or explain the main conclusion.

The words "for example" are the most common way that examples are introduced, but the following terms all have been used:

> For example
> For instance
> A case in point is
> As shown by
> As demonstrated by

Whenever you see these terms, immediately note what point is being shown. Here is an example:

> In science, serendipity often plays a crucial role in discoveries. For
> instance, Teflon was discovered by a scientist attempting to find a new
> gas for use in refrigeration.

Above, the author introduces a concept (that good luck often plays a part in new discoveries), and immediately exemplifies the concept with the introductory phrase "for instance."

5. Difficult words or phrases

The circumpolar vortex is the high-altitude westerly winds that circle the Northern hemisphere at the middle latitudes.

"Vituperate" means to berate or address harshly.

As mentioned earlier, challenging words or phrases are items that you should note while reading, but you should not become overly distressed if you do not immediately know what the terms mean. Terms outside the common public domain of knowledge (such as *circumpolar vortex*) are always explained, and unknown vocabulary words (such as *vituperate*) can often be defined by the context of usage. Acronyms are always explained.

The key thing to remember is that even if you do not understand a word, you will still understand virtually all other words in the passage, and so the possible downside of not knowing one word is very small. Simply bypass the word and then see if it is explained in some way later in the text or by context.

6. Lists and Enumerations

A number of passages feature sections where the author explains an idea by providing a list of points that support or explain the position. When these lists occur, you are almost always tested on your understanding of some or all of the items on the list.

The listed items do not appear as bullet points. Rather, they usually appear using constructions similar to one of the following:

> "First...Second...Third..."
> "First...Second...In addition..."
> "First...Second...Third...Last..."
> "(1)...(2)..."
> "Initially...And...Further..."
> "One possibility is...another possibility is...A final possibility..."

The lists usually contain one of two types of items: a list of reasons (premises) that explain why an action was taken or why a circumstance came into being, or a list of examples that relate to the point at hand.

A list of premises may appear as follows:

> The move towards political systems less dependent on monarchical structures came about for several reasons. First, the monetary and military abuses of the royalty placed several governments in severe financial hardship and created a strong undercurrent of discontent and resentment among the populace. Second, the uncertainty over personal human and property rights caused select elements within the upper class to become convinced that a more concrete and accountable political system was necessary, one insulated from the vagaries of royalty. And finally, problems with succession created a political environment fraught with uncertainty and turmoil.

A list of examples might appear as follows:

> Developing nations have used a number of ingenious methods to increase energy production—and therefore gross economic capacity—while at the same time maintaining a commitment to sustaining the environment. Microfinanced solar projects in India, Brazil, and Vietnam have all yielded power systems able to sustain towns and villages in remote areas, all without a material impact on local resources. A wind farm in Morocco is a successful collaboration between three commercial firms and the government, and now outputs 50 megawatts. In Tibet, where there are no significant or obtainable fossil fuel resources, the Nagqu geothermal energy field provides 300 kilowatts of power in a more cost-effective fashion than could any fossil fuel generators.

In the example above, the listed items are not numbered or introduced as list items, but a list of examples connected to specific countries is presented nonetheless. When reading, you must be prepared to encounter lists of items that are not clearly marked in the text. Any time an author presents a series of examples, you should recognize it and expect to capitalize on that list when you begin answering the questions.

7. Text Questions

When an author poses a question in the passage, in most instances the author goes on to immediately answer that question. Thus, tracking the presence of text questions is critical because it provides you with an outline for where the passage will go next. And, because these questions are often central to the theme of the passage, there is usually a question that revolves around the answer to the question.

Most often, text questions are posed in the traditional manner, with a question mark, as follows:

> So, what was the ultimate impact of the court's ruling on property rights for the Aleutian Islanders?

However, questions can be posed without the traditional question mark, as in this example:

> And thus, researchers concluded that some other explanation was needed to account for the difference in temperatures.

Text questions can be explicitly or implicitly presented in the passage.

In the example, the sentence implies that there is a question regarding the temperature difference, and this implicit question is likely to then be answered in the text.

Causal reasoning and conditional reasoning appear frequently in the Logical Reasoning sections of the LSAT, but less so in the Reading Comprehension section. Still, recognizing each reasoning type when it appears is extremely helpful because this can provide a framework that helps you understand the arguments being made.

Let's briefly review causal and conditional reasoning:

Causal Reasoning

The PowerScore LSAT Logical Reasoning Bible contains chapters on causality and conditionality that are considerably more extensive than the short section in this book. This is because those reasoning forms appear far more frequently in the Logical Reasoning sections than in the Reading Comprehension section.

Cause and effect reasoning asserts or denies that one thing causes another, or that one thing is caused by another. The cause is the event that makes the other occur; the effect is the event that follows from the cause. By definition, the cause must occur before the effect, and the cause is the "activator" or "ignitor" in the relationship. The effect always happens at some point in time after the cause.

Causality in Reading Comprehension usually is discussed in the context of why certain events occurred. The terms that typically introduce causality—such as *caused by*, *reason for*, or *product of*—are still used, but then the author often goes on to discuss the reasons behind the occurrence in depth.

Causality, when it appears in Reading Comprehension, is not normally viewed as flawed reasoning, and LSAT authors usually make an effort to explain the reasoning behind their causal assertions.

Conditional Reasoning

Conditional reasoning is the broad name given to logical relationships composed of sufficient and necessary conditions. Any conditional relationship consists of at least one sufficient condition and at least one necessary condition. A sufficient condition is an event or circumstance whose occurrence indicates that a necessary condition must also occur. A necessary condition is an event or circumstance whose occurrence is required in order for a sufficient condition to occur. In other words, if a sufficient condition occurs, you automatically know that the necessary condition also occurs. If a necessary condition occurs, then it is possible but not certain that the sufficient condition will occur.

Conditional relationships in Reading Comprehension passages tend to be unobtrusive, usually occurring as a sideline point to a larger argument. For example, a passage might discuss monetary policy, and in the course of doing so make a conditional assertion such as, "The only way to decrease monetary volatility is to tightly control the supply of money." In this sense, conditionality is usually not the focus or Main Point of a passage, but instead it is a type of reasoning that occurs while discussing or supporting other points.

Of the two types of reasoning, causal reasoning appears more frequently than conditional reasoning in the Reading Comprehension section. This difference is due to the fact that many passages attempt to address why certain events occurred, and in doing so they naturally fall into causal explanations.

When either of the two reasoning types appear, they are usually discussed in more expansive terms, and the casual or conditional argument is broad and seldom based on single words or sentences. For example, consider the following paragraph:

> While prescriptions for medications are at an all-time high, hyperactivity in children appears to be attributable in many cases to diet. Excessive ingestion of processed sugars, for example, has been linked to various disorders. In a recent study of children diagnosed with hyperactivity, many subjects displayed a more positive response to sugar restriction than to traditionally prescribed medication.

In the first sentence, a cause-and-effect relationship is asserted, and then the remainder of the paragraph builds the case for the assertion. Of course, causal or conditional reasoning assertions need not be limited to a single paragraph; entire passages can be built around a single causal or conditional idea.

While there are many concrete elements to track when reading a passage, there are also a number of text formations and configurations you should recognize. These formations are often used to generate questions, and in this sense they function as possible "traps" for the unwary test taker. The following section reviews the most frequently appearing traps, and examines each in detail.

Traps of Similarities and Distinctions™

These sections of text discuss in detail items that have both similarities and differences. By comparing and contrasting the items in a continuous section of text, the test makers create the possibility of confusion (by comparison, if the discussion of the concepts were separated into discrete sections, the information would be easier to control). Here is an example of a compare-and-contrast section of text:

> Geologically, rocks generally fall into one of three categories: igneous, sedimentary, or metamorphic. Igneous rocks are the result of cooled lava or magma, sedimentary rocks are the result of pressures and accumulations that often result in layers, and metamorphic rocks are igneous or sedimentary rocks that undergo a change caused by conditions underground.
>
> The role of heat in the formation of rocks is varied, and somewhat dependent on location. Igneous rocks are often formed within the earth, and the release of high levels of heat through cooling leads to the formation of the rock. Sedimentary rocks are formed at the earth's surface (often underwater) by the addition of low levels heat, and metamorphic rocks are formed in virtually any location by the addition of low or high levels of heat.
>
> Within each classification, texture, "or "microstructure," is an important determinant of type. Texture occurs throughout a rock, and is an important means of identifying the origin of a rock. While sedimentary rock microstructures tend to reveal condition of the sediment or layer the rock originated from, metamorphic rock microstructures tend to reveal the nature and timing of the change that lead to the creation of the rock. Igneous rock textures depend on several factors, including the cooling rate and mineral composition of the magma or lava. They are often characterized by grains or crystals.

If a list of comparisons and contrasts starts to get complicated, a bracket to the side with a simple note ("textures compared") allows you to keep that section in perspective and move on to the rest of the passage.

You should not become bogged down in trying to get every detail straight in a section like the one above. Instead, make a simple notation next to the section (we will discuss this in the next chapter) so that if you are asked about the details you can quickly return to the passage and sort out the specifics.

Compare-and-contrast sections appear very frequently in Reading Comprehension passages, and you should expect to see one or more on your exam.

Trap of Separation™

One favorite trick of the test makers is to take a long discussion of a given topic, inserting a discussion about a distinct but related topic into separate pieces of the longer discussion. Then in the questions, the test makers require you to understand the bigger-picture discussion, testing your ability to track related concepts even when separated by many lines (or entire paragraphs) in the passage. Consider the following example:

> Market control is the ability to affect and influence trends in pricing, quantities available, and other aspects of a given market. Market control factors can lead to four distinct major market structures. In a case of perfect competition, there are many sellers producing similar goods, none of the participants have market control, and there are limited barriers to entry into the market. While such scenario is considered optimal, it is nearly impossible to achieve or maintain. In a monopoly, a single seller of a particular product or service exists, and that seller has complete control over supply and pricing. Monopolies typically arise in industries that have significant barriers to entry, such as high capital costs or centralized resource control. In both an oligopoly and a duopoly, only a small number of sellers exist, and each maintains a degree of market control.
>
> Within monopolistic and oligopolistic market structures, the potential for market abuse is significant. Monopolists face no competition and can thus restrict supply in order to maintain artificially high prices. Each member of an oligopoly is typically aware of the decisions and actions of other members, increasing the prospects for collusion and other such restrictive trade practices. Because both monopolies and oligopolies can work against the general public interest, industrialized societies often put in place legal restrictions to control the behavior of such firms, in some cases preventing the formation of monopolies or oligopolies altogether.
>
> A fourth market structure tends to require less governmental oversight. Monopolistic competition, also known as a competitive market, exists when there are many producers and many consumers, with products and services that might be similar but are sufficiently distinctive to allow for continued competition in the marketplace. Such a system is preferable to the monopoly and the oligopoly, each of which is conducive to unfair degrees of market manipulation.

In the above section of text, the author introduces the idea of four major market structures, and goes on to expand upon three of the four structures (perfect competition, monopoly, duopoly) in the first paragraph. Following this partial expansion, the entire second paragraph is used to discuss potential market abuses and restrictions to protect the public interest. In the final paragraph, the author returns to the topic of the first paragraph's list, finally presenting monopolistic competition as the fourth and final portion of the discussion of major market structures.

In some especially insidious instances, the question stems will specifically refer you to just one of the places where the concept is discussed (for example,

"In lines 12-14, the author..."), but this will not be the place in the passage that contains the information needed to answer the question. This trap, known as the Trap of Question Misdirection, can be very difficult to handle because most questions that specifically refer you to a place in the passage are indeed referring you to the area where the information needed to answer the question resides. In Chapter Five we will discuss specific reference questions in more detail.

One reason this trick works is that there is a natural tendency on the part of readers to assume that pieces of information that are related should be in close proximity. The logical and linear writing style used in newspapers and textbooks tends to support this belief, and many students bring those beliefs to the LSAT. However, as we have already discussed, the test makers want to present passages that test your ability to comprehend difficult material, and so they use certain methods to create greater complexity in the passages.

Of course, just as information that is separated can be related, information that is in close proximity does not have to be connected, as discussed next.

Trap of Proximity™

Just because two ideas are presented in close physical proximity to one another within a passage does not mean that they are related. In the Market Structures passage on the previous page, we noted that the second paragraph provided a discussion that was not particularly relevant to the classification list. Regardless, this sidebar is cleverly placed between the first three classifications in the opening paragraph, and the fourth classification in the last paragraph.

As mentioned in the prior section, the expectation of most readers is that information that is physically close together will be related. This does not have to be the case, and the makers of the LSAT will set up situations to test your ability to make that distinction.

Trap of Inserted Alternate Viewpoint ™

Another trick of the test makers is to present several different viewpoints, forcing the reader to track both the topical information and the various perspectives. For example:

> Some critics have complained that Faulkner's storytelling in *The Sound and the Fury* was "disorganized and incoherent" to such a degree that understanding the novel seems "deliberately incomprehensible." What such critics fail to see is that Faulkner's use of different narrators was meant to provide a broader perspective, through alternative views of the story. Falkner himself admitted, however, that he had failed in his attempt to tell the story in a way he found satisfactory, and some critics agree.

In the above excerpt, the author quickly jumps from the perspective of "some critics" to that of the passage author, to Falkner's own view (a perspective with which some critics agree!). This technique is meant to test your ability to track different perspectives and to understand who said or believed what.

Traps of Chronology™

Traps of chronology relate to the placement and order of items within the passage, and the tendency of many readers to believe that when one item is presented before another, then the first item occurred first or caused the second item. These two traps are called the Trap of Order and the Trap of Cause:

<u>Trap of Order</u>

Some students make the mistake of believing that because an item is discussed before another item, the first item likely predated the second item. Unless explicitly stated or inherently obvious, this does not have to be the case.

<u>Trap of Cause</u>

Some students make the mistake of assuming that when one item is discussed before another item, then the first item must have caused the second item. This assumption is unwarranted. The easiest way to discern the author's intentions is to carefully examine the language used by the writer because causal relationships almost always feature one or more of the words that indicate causality (such as *caused by*, *produced by*, *determined*, etc).

The simple truth is that the order of presentation of the items in the passage does not necessarily indicate any temporal or causal relationship between those items.

Passage Topic Traps™

Previously we discussed how passages on any topic could be easy or difficult. Difficulty is more a function of writing style, the number of viewpoints, and the exact concepts under discussion than of the general topic of the passage. That said, the test makers will occasionally use the topic to catch test takers off-guard. This can occur because when the typical student begins reading a passage, the topic often frames their expectation. For example, science passages are thought to be challenging whereas passages about humanities are less feared. The test makers are well aware of these ingrained expectations, and they at times play a sort of "bait and switch" game with students, especially by making a passage initially look hard or easy and then radically changing the level of difficulty after the first few lines or first paragraph.

As you develop the ability to see through the topic and focus on the writing style, you will notice that many passages are not as complex as their topics might suggest.

An example occurred on the June 2006 LSAT. The last passage opened with a discussion of the cultivation of maize, and most students immediately relaxed. After all, this was a passage about corn, and we are all familiar with good ol' corn, so how hard could it be? After the first paragraph, however, the passage turned brutally difficult. On the other hand, on the September 2006 LSAT the second passage began with a discussion of modern bankruptcy law that looked rather ominous. However, as the passage unfolded, the argument was easy to follow and the passage as a whole was fairly simple to understand. There are, of course, other examples from LSAT history.

The point to draw from this discussion is that you should not assume that a topic or passage will be easy or hard just from the first line or paragraph. The test makers love to play with the expectations of students, and one of their favorite tricks is to turn those expectations on their head.

Final Chapter Note

In review, the approach we advocate is a multi-level one. While reading, you should constantly track the five major VIEWSTAMP elements discussed in Chapter Two: the various groups and viewpoints discussed within the passage, the tone or attitude of each group or individual, the argument made by each group or individual, the main point of the passage, and the structure of the passage and the organization of ideas. At the same time, you must also keep an eye on the smaller elements that appear throughout the text; items such as examples and definitions, or forms of reasoning, to name a few. While this approach may sound complicated, with practice it becomes second nature, and soon you will find that you are able to answer many questions very quickly and with more confidence. In Chapter Six we will present a review of all of the ideas from the first few chapters in order to give you a concise guide to approaching any passage.

In addition, to help you juggle all of this information, in the next chapter we will discuss how you can make physical notations on the passage to help you effectively track all of these elements. Prior to that, however, on the following pages is a drill that will test your ability to recognize the elements discussed in this chapter.

Passage Elements and Formations Recognition Drill

Analyze the following passage excerpts, noting the components discussed in this chapter. In the space provided, list any of the notable passage formations, elements, or reasoning structures, and then provide a brief summary of the material in each excerpt. *Answers on Page 78*

Passage 1:

The quagga, an extinct subspecies of the zebra, was initially classified as an entirely separate species (*Equus quagga*) in 1778, based in part on its distinctive coat, which included stripes on only the front half of the animal's body. Recent DNA studies conducted at the Smithsonian Institution, however, indicate that the animal was actually a subspecies of the plains zebra (*Equus burcelli*). Based on the discovery of the close relationship between quaggas and extant zebra species, those conducting the "Quagga Project" in South Africa began selectively breeding existing plains zebras and have successfully produced animals whose outward appearance is very similar to that of preserved quagga specimens.

Analysis: _____
_____
_____
_____
_____
_____
_____

Passage 2:

What is the "right" that the Second Amendment to the US Constitution was intended to protect? This amendment, which states that "A well regulated militia, being necessary to the security of a free state, the right of the people to keep and bear arms, shall not be infringed," has largely been subject to two very different interpretations. Some argue that the amendment guarantees every citizen the right to own a gun. Others believe that the founders intended to assure the right to those who were members of the necessary "well regulated militia," but that this right does not necessarily extend to every individual citizen.

Analysis: _____
_____
_____
_____
_____
_____

Passage 3:

The Great Depression was an era of nationwide financial devastation which led to a significant increase in the number of married women working outside the home; the percentage of wives in the workplace increased from 12% in the early 1930's, to 15% by the start of World War II. After the war, the expansion of business and public sectors led to an increase in the number of jobs available, and by 1960 almost one third of married women were working outside the home.

Analysis: _____
_____
_____
_____
_____
_____
_____

Passage 4:

Radioactivity causes many nuclei to be unstable, leading to a chain of *decay* (emission of atomic particles), which occurs until a stable nucleus is achieved. Radioactive decay generally takes one of three forms: The first type is known as Alpha decay, which describes the emission of an alpha particle from the nucleus. The second type is called Beta decay, which takes place when the ratio of neutrons to protons is too great, which can lead to the emission of an electron or a positron. Gamma decay is the third class of radioactive decay, which takes place when excessive energy is present in the nucleus and involves the emission of a gamma particle.

Analysis: _____
_____
_____
_____
_____
_____
_____

Passage 5:

One alternative to antibiotics is the use of localized bioactive phytochemicals. Certain plant species have an almost limitless ability to synthesize aromatic substances (phytochemicals), which in many cases serve as plant defense mechanisms against predation by insects, herbivores, and, most significantly, micro-organisms. Scientists investigating this antimicrobial activity have found that these phytochemicals can also inhibit the growth of pathogenic bacteria in humans, and, since these agents appear to have structures and operational effects that are distinct from currently utilized antibiotics, the effects of pre-existing antibiotic resistance on phytochemicals should be minimal.

Analysis: _____

_____

_____

_____

_____

_____

Passage Elements and Formations Recognition Drill Answer Key

Passage 1: In this passage we are presented with a scientific topic and many unfamiliar and <u>difficult words</u> (most of which are Latin!). As long as we don't get intimidated by the scientific terminology, the concepts presented here are not overly complex:

> The quagga is a subspecies of the zebra. At first thought a totally different species, it was called equus quagga. Recent DNA studies show it to be a relative of plains zebras—equus burcelli—still in existence today. Thus, members of the "Quagga Project" have selectively bred plains zebras and developed an animal which looks outwardly like the extinct quagga.

Passage 2: The author opens this passage with a <u>text question</u>. When we see such a question in an LSAT passage, we should always take note; it often presents an inquiry central to the discussion (as is the case here). This passage also provides an example of <u>multiple viewpoints</u>—one of the test-makers' methods of adding complexity. The passage can be distilled as follows:

> What is protected by the Second Amendment?
> Some say it protects the right of every individual to own a gun.
> Others say it protects the rights of the "well regulated militia" but not of every individual citizen.

Passage 3: Here the author provides us with the percentage of working married women at three different points in time. Since there are several different <u>dates and numbers</u> to consider, the creation of a simple <u>timeline</u> can be helpful in tracking information and developing a clear perspective:

Early 1930's	Beginning of WWII	1960
12%	15%	almost 33%

Passage 4: The author of this passage discusses a <u>challenging topic</u>—radioactive decay—and provides a <u>definition</u>, which we should note: in this context, decay means particle emission. The author then presents a <u>list</u> of the three different types of such decay. Whenever an LSAT author provides a list, we should take note, because we are likely to see related questions. The three types are as follows:

> A. Alpha decay: emission of an alpha particle
>
> B. Beta decay: emission of electron or positron
>
> C. Gamma decay: emission of a gamma particle

Passage 5: If there is a common element reflected here it is the author's <u>challenging writing style</u>; this selection is not written in a particularly accessible way, and begins with some unfamiliar and <u>difficult terminology</u>. The passage can be distilled as follows:

Bioactive phytochemicals (<u>defined</u> as aromatic substances) can be used in place of antibiotics. Certain plants can create such substances, which can defend against plant predators, including micro-organisms. Scientists have found that these substances can also help defend against pathogens in humans. Further, phytochemicals are different enough from antibiotics that antibiotic resistance should have no effect on such substances.

CHAPTER FOUR: DIAGRAMMING THE PASSAGES

Passage Diagramming

Because of the amount of information contained in each Reading Comprehension passage, most students naturally make some markings and notations on the passage as they read. These notations, when made in an organized fashion, create a "visual summary" of the information in the passage. This "summary" can then be used to help mentally organize the information in the passage, and that helps save time when returning to the passage because the location of information is more obvious. Both of these benefits help answer the questions more quickly.

Within this section, we discuss two types of diagram elements: markings and notations. Passage markings are the marks—brackets, circles, boxes, etc.— you make on the text of the passage, whereas passage notations are the written notes or symbolizations that you make to the left or right of the passage (or above and below). The combined product of your marks and notations creates what we term the "passage diagram."

> "Markings" refer to marks made directly on the text of the passage. "Notations" refer to written notes or symbolizations made next to the text. "Passage diagrams" include the marks and notations on the passage.

Note: **The proper approach to diagramming varies from person to person, and there is no correct or incorrect way to notate a passage**. The methods we discuss provide an idea of the types of diagramming that can be done—this is not to suggest that every element must be diagrammed. We suggest becoming familiar with these tools, and using your practice time to establish the type and amount of diagramming that works best for you.

What to Use to Diagram

You have two choices for highlighting implements: your pencil or the highlighter pen allowed by LSAT rules. Some students, used to using highlighters while in school, prefer to use the highlighter for the majority of passage markings. We prefer the pencil because it allows you to not only mark the passage, but also make side notes when necessary. The choice is yours, but be aware that if you choose the highlighter, you will likely still find yourself reaching for your pencil frequently.

Marking the Passage Text

When marking the passage, you have a number of choices regarding the actual marks you make. Underlining, circling, boxing, and bracketing are among the main tools you have to choose from. Although most students have their own personal preferences when it comes to marking, let us first consider the available identifiers, and then in the next section we will expand on which markings are best for certain situations.

Basic Underlining

This is the simplest and most common technique of all: pick out words or phrases that give decisive information or indicate a turning point in the passage, and then underline those portions. Underlining can help crystallize the information, allowing you to more easily handle the material. Here is a brief example:

> While the proponents of the Futurism art movement
> believed that <u>the past was an era to be ignored</u>, some
> critics assert that, ironically, for the Futurists to break
> from the past would have required a more thorough
> (5) understanding of history on their part.

The key point to remember is that while *some* underlining is very helpful, a large amount of underlining actually makes things more confusing. Be judicious when choosing what to underline. For example, consider the following:

> While the <u>proponents of the Futurism art movement</u>
> believed that <u>the past was an era to be ignored</u>, some
> <u>critics assert that, ironically, for the Futurists to break</u>
> <u>from the past would have required a more thorough</u>
> (5) <u>understanding of history on their part</u>.

In this case, the underlining has no value because almost all of the text has been marked as important or notable. The key is to mark those few sections that you feel have high value. We will discuss this in more detail when we look at further examples of passage diagramming.

Circling

At times, some students prefer to circle (or, more accurately, oval) key words or phrases instead of underlining. This provides a visual change from underlining, and can make certain elements of the passage stand out more clearly.

> While the proponents of the Futurism art movement
> believed that the past was an era to be ignored, some
> critics assert that, ⬭ironically,⬭ for the Futurists to break
> from the past would have required a more thorough
> (5) understanding of history on their part.

Boxing

Boxing is a variation on circling. However, in our marking system we reserve boxing for identifying viewpoints and viewpoint changes, as in the following:

While the ⬚proponents of the Futurism art movement⬚ believed that the past was an era to be ignored, some ⬚critics⬚ assert that, ironically, for the Futurists to break from the past would have required a more thorough
(5)   understanding of history on their part.

Viewpoints are marked with boxes.

This marking is usually accompanied by a "V" side notation as well. More on this notation in the Passage Notations section.

Bracketing Text

This technique is best for marking a section of text too unwieldy or large to underline. Here is an example using a bracket to identify the Main Point of a passage:

But it is unlikely that increased use of such plans will result in long-term client satisfaction or in a
(40)   substantial increase in profits for law firms. Since lawyers with established reputations and client bases can benefit little, if at all, from participation, the plans function largely as marketing devices for lawyers who have yet to establish themselves. While
(45)   many of these lawyers are no doubt very able and conscientious, they will tend to have less expertise and to provide less satisfaction to clients. At the same time, the downward pressure on fees will mean that the full-fee referrals that proponents say will come
(50)   through plan participation may not make up for a firm's investment in providing services at low plan rates. And since lowered fees provide little incentive for lawyers to devote more than minimal effort to cases, a "volume discount" approach toward the
(55)   practice of law will mean less time devoted to complex cases and a general lowering of quality for clients.

MP

If you encounter a lengthy portion of text you think is notable, or a dense section of text you think will generate a question, use a bracket to identify the section.

The "MP" stands for "Main Point."

Passage notations are notations that you make to the right or left side of the passage, and usually they are letters that stand for certain elements within the passage, such as "V" for viewpoint or "MP" for Main Point.

Some students ask if they should write out notes next to each paragraph or important element. In general, the answer is No. Writing out more than a word or two usually takes too long. The better choice is to mark that element in such a way that it stands out as significant to you. The exception to this rule is when you are having extreme difficulty with retaining the structure or main ideas of a passage (this is a problem that non-native English speakers sometimes have, for example). In these cases, the best strategy is to write out a short description of each paragraph or of the passage as a whole.

These are the passage notations we frequently use:

"V" for Viewpoint

Typically this is accompanied with a subscript to identify the owner of the viewpoint, such as in V_A for the viewpoint of the author, or V_C for the viewpoint of a critic. Here is an example, using our boxing section markings:

> While the | proponents of the Futurism art movement | V_P
> believed that the past was an era to be ignored, some
> | critics | assert that, ironically, for the Futurists to break V_C
> from the past would have required a more thorough
> (5) understanding of history on their part.

The V notation is typically used when the viewpoint is first introduced, and then again if the viewpoint reappears later in the passage. This makes tracking viewpoints extremely easy, and also helps identify the structure of the passage.

"MP" for Main Point

As shown in the discussion of bracketing in the marking section, the MP notation is placed whenever you identify the Main Point of the passage. Often, the MP notation appears in conjunction with a bracket, but that is a personal and contextual choice.

"CC" for Compare and Contrast sections

As discussed in the last chapter, the makers of the LSAT frequently include dense sections of text where ideas or positions are compared and contrasted. Because identifying connected positions using markings is challenging in these sections, often the best approach is to simply place a "CC" notation next to the section of compare and contrast material. This notation then provides a quick reference point to return to if a question comes up about one or more of the groups involved. At that point you can sort out which viewpoint is which.

"Def" for Definitions

As discussed in the last chapter, definitions are often tested in the questions, either directly or indirectly. Consequently, notating definitions when they appear is beneficial. The best approach is to simply place a "Def" notation next to the definition in the text. This notation then provides a quick reference point to return to if a question comes up about the definition.

"Ex" for Examples

As previously discussed, examples are used to support the arguments in the passage, and they help readers gain a greater understanding of the concept under discussion. Thus, examples are often tested in the questions. Because some examples stretch over many lines, the best approach is to simply place an "Ex" next to the section containing the example.

Circled numbers for Enumerations

As discussed in the last chapter, LSAT authors often list out the reasons behind a specific action or occurrence. When this occurs, you should underline the word that indicates each item and place a circled number next to the section, as in the following example:

(10)   Historians have indicated that support for the legislation
       was broad-based. <u>First,</u> active members of the armed   ①
       forces benefited directly from the educational incentives
       provided by the law. <u>Second,</u> colleges and universities   ②
       were ardent supporters of the legislation due to the
(15)   financial advantages afforded by thousands of new
       students. And <u>finally,</u> employers ultimately benefited   ③
       from the presence of a better educated workforce (albeit
       not immediately).

"Q" for Questions posed by the author

Questions raised by the author are almost always followed immediately by further information that answers the question. Tracking these questions—when they appear—helps you to track the flow of information within the passage. Simply place a "Q" next to the question posed in the text.

With practice, many test takers find that marking and notating becomes second nature. When this occurs, the amount of time used for diagramming the passage is minimal. The key, though, is to be extremely familiar with the kinds of marks and notations you prefer to make.

What to Diagram—Reviewed by Diagram Element

The first rule of passage diagramming is this: do not over-diagram! The key to successfully diagramming a passage is to mark and notate the elements that routinely appear in the questions and to do so consistently. With this in mind, let us take a moment to briefly review the passage diagrams, along with notes on what each diagram element should designate.

Markings:

Underlining

- Use to mark words, phrases or sentences that are important, such as tone indicators.

- Use with indicator words for numbered lists.

Circling

- Use to mark words that change the direction of the passage, such as "but" or "although."

Boxing

- Use solely to mark viewpoints and viewpoint changes.

Bracketing

- Use to identify sections of text too unwieldy or large to underline.

- Use with the MP, CC, or Def notation where appropriate.

<u>Notations</u>:

V Use with a box for Viewpoints, with a subscript identifying the group or person.

MP Use to identify the Main Point of the passage.

CC Use to denote Compare and Contrast sections, sometimes with a bracket.

Def Definitions of words, phrases, or ideas, sometimes with a bracket.

Ex Place next to Examples used in the passage.

1, 2, etc. Place these numbers, with a circle around each, next to the items in numbered lists. Underline each item indicator.

Q Use to note Questions posed by the author in the text.

Let us reformulate the table on the prior page, and now list some of the passage formations that typically create questions (as discussed in the last chapter) along with suggested marks and notations for each.

Words, phrases or sentences that are important — underline

Words that change the direction of the passage — underline

Viewpoints and Viewpoint changes — box and side "V" notation

Unwieldy or large sections of text — bracket

Main Point — side "MP" notation

Compare and Contrast sections — side "CC" notation

Definitions — side "Def" notation

Examples — side "Ex" notation

Numbered lists — circled side "1, 2, 3, etc" notation and underlined indicator words

Questions in the text — side "Q" notation

With the MP, CC, or Def notation — bracket

Final Chapter Note

The marks and notes above are not the only possible ones; they are simply the ones we will use in this book. If you have a different mark or note that you find helpful, by all means use it. Developing a system that works for you is one of the goals of this book.

Remember, diagramming systems are simply a helpful tool to keep track of the information in each passage. Although they will help you organize and quickly locate information, you are still responsible for identifying the conclusion and overall structure of the passage. Most importantly, be consistent in your notations! By always noting the same elements in the same way, you can move through the test as fast as possible with maximum accuracy.

Passage Diagramming Drill

Diagram each of the following passages, using the marks and notations discussed in this chapter. Then summarize the basic structure of each paragraph. *Answers on Page 92*

Passage 1:

The Law and Economics movement seeks to apply economic theories to the law. Within the movement there are two approaches: the positive and the normative. Positive economic analysis of law attempts to predict the economic outcomes of different legal rules. For example, a product liability case would require examination of the various economic outcomes produced under negligence claims, as compared with those produced under statutory claims. Normative economic analysis incorporates the positive economic analysis and adds to it by making policy recommendations based on the various outcomes. The defining guideline under a normative analysis is to advocate for the most efficient outcome in economic terms.

Critics of the Law and Economics movement compellingly argue that academic economic models are unsuitable for the analysis of real-world legal scenarios. Because the most complicated economic models, they argue, are still unable to reflect the complexities of actual human behavior and motivations, an economic analysis can never produce fully accurate results. In addition, because a number of desirable social values—such as free speech—cannot be easily quantified, the economic values assigned are somewhat arbitrary and most likely egregiously inaccurate.

Defenders of the Law and Economics movement argue that the general value of an economic analysis is enough to justify adopting the approach, and that precise outcomes are hard to predict regardless of the model used. Further, advocates argue that the field is developing, and recent developments attempt to account for some of the criticisms. These arguments provide some defenses against the critics, but in the main fall short of validating the movement.

Summary: _____

_____

_____

_____

_____

_____

_____

_____

_____

_____

Passage 2:

Although there has been progress in attempting to attain equality for women in the workplace, there is still much to be done before equality is achieved. In particular, certain workplace initiatives would likely attract more women, including those with families. Accordingly, experts have identified several areas where employers should improve job options and benefits. The two most notable recommendations in regards to working mothers are increased flex-time options and expansion of the virtual workplace.

Flex-time, which allows for a variable work schedule, addresses the needs of working mothers by helping to foster a balance between work and family obligations. Schedules can accommodate four-day work weeks, irregular hours (including nights and weekends), and rotating schedules subject to routine changes. The flex-time option, which should be mandatory where possible, benefits employers as well: happy, satisfied workers have been proven to be more productive, and offering this option makes the employer more attractive in the labor market.

Another worthy initiative is the expansion of the virtual workplace. The advent of the internet, more easily available high-speed digital data transfer, and new telecommunications technology has made working from home a viable option for many. Working mothers benefit from time saved (less travel time between work and home, less time needed to get ready for work) and from the convenience of working in an environment where family emergencies can be countered or even avoided. The virtual workplace, in combination with flex-time, offers the flexibility required of many working mothers, and employers should be legally compelled to offer these options.

Summary: _____

_____

_____

_____

_____

_____

_____

_____

_____

_____

Passage 3:

    The World Anti-Doping Agency defines "Gene Doping" as "the non-therapeutic use of cells, genes, genetic elements, or of the modulation of gene expression, having the capacity to improve athletic performance." Some argue that the best way to gain any degree control over the problem of gene doping, which can be both costly and difficult to detect, is to legalize it. After all, they assert, if a professional golfer can have eye surgery to improve his game, then perhaps other types of athletes should be allowed certain limited genetic modifications. Moreover, the argument goes, legalization and regulation would bring the imposition of safety standards.

    But isn't gene doping different? Does it violate the basic spirit of fair competition? The overwhelming consensus is that it does. The Olympic committee believes that gene doping is wrong, and this perspective is shared by several professional and college sports leagues, all of which have added gene doping to their lists of official prohibitions. It is quite doubtful, however, that all of these groups will be able to match strong objection with practical enforcement.

Summary: _____

_____

_____

_____

_____

_____

_____

_____

_____

_____

Passage 4:

Monetarism, an economic theory formulated and espoused primarily by Milton Friedman, contends that controlling the supply of money will lead to a stable, growing national economy. A central tenet of monetarism is that inflation—the rising of prices—has a deleterious effect on economic growth, and that judiciously controlling the supply of money within an economy will help curb inflation and eventually lead to a greater quantity of goods and services.

Friedman's theory, which was ironically born from the Keynesian demand side economics theories of the early 1930's, did not simply propose that the monetary supply should be fixed or arbitrarily regulated. Instead, Friedman argued that the money supply should not be allowed to grow any faster than the desired rate of economic growth within an economy. If the money supply were allowed to expand beyond desired rates of growth, Friedman argued, inflation would result because people would not simply hold the extra money idly; they would instead spend that money, and the resulting buying surge would result in increased demand and, eventually, increased prices. On the other hand, if the money supply was reduced, people would instead save money and the resulting drop in demand would eventually decrease prices.

In sum, Friedman suggested monetary manipulation to bring the supply a demand for money to an artificial equilibrium, but, as Margaret Thatcher and many others have since learned, the application of these principles in the real world often brings about results contrary to those predicted from the ivory towers of abstract economic theory.

Summary: _____

_____

_____

_____

_____

_____

_____

_____

_____

_____

<u>**Passage 5:**</u>

Those who describe themselves as "strict constructionists" argue that the Constitution should be interpreted to accurately reflect the original intent of its framers. Judges of this ilk believe that the words of the document should be considered "black letter law," to be construed strictly and literally. A sincere belief that the Constitution should be interpreted as a static list of directives, however, seems rather archaic in the modern era.

On the other side of the interpretation debate are those who belief that the Constitution was meant to be a "living document," whose proper construction would readily adapt to an evolving nation. Judges who subscribe to this perspective are often referred to by strict constructionists as judicial activists who are trying to take law-making power away from the legislative branch of the government. These judges, however, consider themselves interpreters, not activists. The framers specifically allowed for constitutional amendment, and afforded significant power to the judicial branch; they felt that the Constitution was to provide a framework but would have to adapt to a changing nation.

Summary: _____

_____

_____

_____

_____

_____

_____

_____

_____

Passage Diagramming Drill Answer Key

Do not be concerned if your diagram and summary do not match ours exactly. The point of this drill is to get you thinking about how to diagram, and about the types of notations that can be made. Again, the proper approach to notating passages varies from person to person. **There is no correct or incorrect way to diagram.**

Passage 1:

The Law and Economics movement seeks to apply economic theories to the law. Within the movement there are two approaches: the positive and the normative. ① Positive economic analysis of law attempts to predict the economic outcomes of different legal rules. For example, a product liability case would require examination of the various economic outcomes produced under negligence claims, as compared with those produced under statutory ② claims. Normative economic analysis incorporates the positive economic analysis and adds to it by making policy recommendations based on the various outcomes. The defining guideline under a normative analysis is to advocate for the most efficient outcome in economic terms.

V₁ Critics of the Law and Economics movement compellingly   Critiques:
argue that academic economic models are unsuitable for   ①
the analysis of real-world legal scenarios. Because the most
complicated economic models, they argue, are still unable
to reflect the complexities of actual human behavior and
motivations, an economic analysis can never produce fully
accurate results. In addition, because a number of desirable   ②
social values—such as free speech—cannot be easily
quantified, the economic values assigned are somewhat
arbitrary and most likely egregiously inaccurate.

V₂ Defenders of the Law and Economics movement argue that   Defenses:
the general value of an economic analysis is enough to justify ①
adopting the approach, and that precise outcomes are hard to
predict regardless of the model used. Further, advocates argue ②
that the field is developing, and recent developments attempt
to account for some of the criticisms. These arguments provide

Vₐ some defenses against the critics, but in the main fall short of
validating the movement.

Summary:

Here we have a very nicely structured passage which can be distilled simply as follows:
Law and Economics movement (def.): application of economic theory to law. Two approaches:
1) Positive, which tries to predict economic results of different laws; and
2) Normative, which makes recommends policy based on positive approach.

Critics Viewpoint (and arguments list): 1) Economic models don't work like the real world; and 2) Social values are difficult to quantify, and attempts to do so will be inaccurate.

Defenders's Viewpoint (and arguments list): 1) General value justifies the approach; and 2) Recent developments in this new field may respond to some critiques.

Author's Viewpoint: There are defenses of the movement, but they don't validate it.

Passage 2:

Although there has been progress in attempting to attain equality for women in the workplace, there is still <u>much to be done before equality is achieved</u>. In particular, certain workplace initiatives would likely attract more women, including those with families. Accordingly, experts have identified several areas where <u>employers should improve</u> job <u>options and benefits</u>. The two most notable recommendations in regards to working mothers are increased <u>flex-time</u> options and expansion of the <u>virtual workplace</u>.

V_A

Recommendations:
① ②

<u>Flex-time</u>, which allows for a <u>variable work schedule</u>, addresses the needs of working mothers by helping to foster a <u>balance between work and family</u> obligations. Schedules can accommodate four-day work weeks, irregular hours (including nights and weekends), and rotating schedules subject to routine changes. The flex-time option, which (should) be mandatory where possible, benefits employers as well: happy, satisfied <u>workers</u> have been proven to be <u>more productive</u>, and offering this option makes the <u>employer more attractive</u> in the labor market.

helps mothers

helps employers

V_A

① ②

Another worthy initiative is the expansion of the <u>virtual workplace</u>. The advent of the internet, more easily available high-speed digital data transfer, and new telecommunications technology has made working from home a viable option for many. <u>Working mothers benefit from time saved</u> (less travel time between work and home, less time needed to get ready for work) and from the <u>convenience</u> of working in an environment where family emergencies can be countered or even avoided. The virtual workplace, in combination with flex-time, offers the flexibility required of many working mothers, V_A and employers (should be) legally compelled to offer these options.

helps mothers

① ②

⎤ MP

Summary:

This passage is written entirely from the perspective of the author, whose view is first presented in the opening sentence: there is much to do before the workplace is equitable to both genders. The author then presents the short list of the two "most notable" recommendations (again, the author's opinion): 1) flex time; and 2) the virtual workplace.

Flex time (def): variable work scheduling.
Beneficial for working mothers: offers work/family balance.
Benefits for employers: 1) satisfied workers are more productive, and 2) employers that offers flex time are more attractive to workers

Virtual office (def): working from home via internet and other new tech.
Benefits for working mothers: 1) preparation and travel time saved, and 2) convenience of working from home

We might note the author's use of the word "should" several times. Since these value-judgements are not attributed to anyone else, they must represent the perspective of the author, whose main point is stated at the close of the passage: these are improvement and should be required.

Passage Diagramming Drill Answer Key

Passage 3:

Def.

V₁

     The World Anti-Doping Agency defines "Gene Doping" as "the non-therapeutic use of cells, genes, genetic elements, or of the modulation of gene expression, having the capacity to improve athletic performance." Some argue that the best way to gain any degree control over the problem of gene doping, which can be both costly and difficult to detect, is to legalize it. After all, they assert, if a professional golfer can have eye surgery to improve his game, then perhaps other types of athletes should be allowed certain limited genetic modifications. Moreover, the argument goes, legalization and regulation would bring the imposition of safety standards.

Q:

V₂

V_A

     But isn't gene doping different? Does it violate the basic spirit of fair competition? The overwhelming consensus is that it does. The Olympic committee believes that gene doping is wrong, and this perspective is shared by several professional and college sports leagues, all of which have added gene doping to their lists of official prohibitions. It is quite doubtful, however, that all of these groups will be able to match strong objection with practical enforcement.

Summary:

The first paragraph opens with a definition of gene doping, followed by the viewpoint of "some" who suggest legalization of gene doping, comparing it to eye surgery. While this is a rather unconvincing argument, safety standards are offered as another possible justification.

The second paragraph opens with two text questions, immediately followed by an answer, with a shift to the viewpoint of the Olympic committee and many other athletic organizations who oppose the practice of gene doping. The closing sentence shifts to the viewpoint of the author, who is clearly skeptical about the prospects for enforcement.

Passage 4:

> Monetarism, an economic theory formulated and espoused primarily by Milton Friedman, contends that controlling the supply of money will lead to a stable, growing national economy. A central tenet of monetarism is that inflation—the rising of prices—has a deleterious effect on economic growth, and that judiciously controlling the supply of money within an economy will help curb inflation and eventually lead to a greater quantity of goods and services.

Def.

V_M

> Friedman's theory, which was ironically born from the Keynesian demand side economics theories of the early 1930's, did not simply propose that the monetary supply should be fixed or arbitrarily regulated. Instead, Friedman argued that the money supply should not be allowed to grow any faster than the desired rate of economic growth within an economy. If the money supply were allowed to expand beyond desired rates of growth, Friedman argued, inflation would result because people would not simply hold the extra money idly; they would instead spend that money, and the resulting buying surge would result in increased demand and, eventually, increased prices. On the other hand, if the money supply was reduced people would instead save money and the resulting drop in demand would eventually decrease prices.

V_M

> In sum, Friedman suggested monetary manipulation to bring the supply a demand for money to an artificial equilibrium, but, as Margaret Thatcher and many others have since learned, the application of these principles in the real world often brings about results contrary to those predicted from the ivory towers of abstract economic theory.

V_M

V_A

Summary:

This passage begins with an introduction to (and limited definition of) Monetarism: the theory which asserts that control of the money supply will curb inflation, leading to stable growth. This paragraph functions to introduce the theory and relay the perspective of Friedman and the Monetarists.

In the second paragraph we are told that Monetarism was "ironically" born from Keynesian economics (Keynes, we should infer, must have developed different theories). We are then presented with a two theoretical outcomes to monetary manipulation, from the viewpoint of the Monetarists:
Expansion beyond desired growth: increases inflation, spending, demand, and eventually prices.
Reduction of money supply: increases savings, decreases demand, and eventually drops prices.

In the final paragraph the author sums up Monetarist theory, and finally provides some insight into the author's viewpoint. Friedman sought, in theory, an artificial equilibrium. Apparently, however, Margaret Thatcher attempted to apply these principles in the real world and, we can infer from the last words of the passage, the outcome was contrary to what was predicted by Monetarist theory.

Passage 5:

Those who describe themselves as "strict constructionists"   V₁
argue that the Constitution should be interpreted to accurately
reflect the original intent of its framers. Judges of this ilk
believe that the words of the document should be considered
"black letter law," to be construed strictly and literally. A
sincere belief that the Constitution should be interpreted as a
static list of directives, however, seems rather archaic in the   Vₐ
modern era.

On the other side of the interpretation debate are those
who believe that the Constitution was meant to be a "living   V₂
document," whose proper construction would readily adapt to
an evolving nation. Judges who subscribe to this perspective
are often referred to by strict constructionists as judicial   V₁
activists who are trying to take law-making power away
from the legislative branch of the government. These judges,
however, consider themselves interpreters, not activists. The   V₂
framers specifically allowed for constitutional amendment, and   V_F
afforded significant power to the judicial branch; they felt that
the Constitution was to provide a framework but would have to
adapt to a changing nation.

Summary:

The author begins the first paragraph with the perspective of the strict constructionists: The
Constitution should be interpreted as originally intended. In the *author*'s opinion, the strict
constructionists' perspective is outdated ("archaic").

The second paragraph provides an opposing perspective, of those who see the Constitution as
adaptive to change. These people perceive themselves as interpreters, and the author supports
their perspective by pointing out that the *framers*—those who wrote the Constitution—foresaw
the need for change. In this passage, the author clearly shares and supports the viewpoint of the
second group (the "interpreters").

CHAPTER FIVE: THE QUESTIONS AND ANSWER CHOICES

The Questions

In this chapter, we will focus solely on the questions that accompany single passage sets. In the Comparative Reading chapter, we will discuss in detail the question types that accompany dual passage sets.

In single passage sets, a group of five to eight questions follows each passage, and each of the questions is directed at the passage. The question stems cover a wide range of tasks, and will variously ask you to:

- describe the main point or primary purpose of the passage

- describe the structure and organization of the passage

- identify the viewpoint of the author or the viewpoint of subjects discussed within the passage

- identify details of the passage or statements proven by the passage

- describe the meaning, function, or purpose of words or phrases in the passage

- strengthen, weaken, or parallel elements of the passage

- augment or expand the passage

On average, you typically have less than 1 minute to complete each question.

Analyzing the Question Stem

At first glance, Reading Comprehension sections appear to have a multitude of different types of question stems. The test makers create this impression by varying the words used in each question stem. As we will see shortly, even though they use different words, many of these question stems are identical in terms of what you are asked to do.

In order to easily handle the different questions, we categorize the question stems that appear on the LSAT. Fortunately, every question stem can be defined as a certain type, and the more familiar you are with the question types, the faster you can respond when faced with individual questions. Thus, one of your tasks is to learn each question type and become familiar with the characteristics that define each type. We will help you accomplish this goal by including a variety of question type identification drills and by examining each type of question in detail.

Make sure to read each question stem very carefully. Some stems direct you to focus on certain areas of the passage and if you miss these clues, the problem becomes much more difficult.

All Reading Comprehension question stems provide some insight into where in the passage you should begin your search for the correct answer. This element is called "location," and you should always establish location as you read each question stem.

Location can be divided into three categories—Specific Reference, Concept Reference, and Global Reference:

Specific Reference (SR). These question stems refer you to a specific numbered line, paragraph, or sentence. For example:

> "The author of the passage uses the phrase 'rational expectations' (line 39) primarily in order to"

> "Which one of the following best defines the word 'pragmatic' as it is used in the second paragraph of the passage?"

> "Which one of the following would best exemplify the kind of theory referred to in the final paragraph of the passage?"

In some Specific Reference questions, the answer choices refer you to specific lines within the passage:

> Which one of the following, in its context in the passage, most clearly reveals the attitude of the author toward the 'academics' described in the passage?
>
> (A)   "new process" (line 8)
> (B)   "progressed" (line 55)
> (C)   "challenged" (line 12)
> (D)   "questionable intentions" (line 21)
> (E)   "contrarian" (line 60)

Although the correct information in a Specific Reference question is not always found in the exact lines referenced, those line references are always an excellent starting point for your analysis.

To attack Specific Reference questions, return to the passage and start reading three to five lines above the reference, or from the most logical nearby starting point such as the start of a paragraph.

To attack Specific Reference questions that refer to an exact line number or sentence, always return to the passage and start reading three to five lines above the reference, or from the most logical nearby starting point such as the start of a paragraph. To attack Specific Reference questions that refer to a paragraph, return to the passage and consider the paragraph in question. We will discuss this approach in more detail when we begin dissecting individual passages.

Concept Reference (CR). Some questions refer you to ideas or themes within the passage that are not identified by a specific line or paragraph reference, but that are identifiable because the ideas are clearly enunciated or expressed within one or two areas of the passage. When reading questions that contain concept references, you should typically know where to search in the passage for the relevant information even though no line reference is given. Examples include:

> "The passage suggests which one of the following about the behavior of elk in conflict situations?"

> "The author's discussion of telephone answering machines serves primarily to"

> "The passage indicates that prior to the use of carbon dating, at least some historians believed which one of the following?"

In each of the above instances, although no specific location reference is given, an engaged student would know where in the passage to begin searching for the correct answer, and he or she would then return to the passage and take a moment to review the relevant information.

A thorough understanding of the organization of the passage allows for quick access to the information necessary to attack Concept Reference questions.

Global Reference (GR). Global Reference questions ask about the passage as a whole, or they fail to identify a defined area or isolated concept within the question stem. For example:

> "Which one of the following most accurately expresses the main point of the passage?"

> "The primary purpose of the passage is to"

> "Information in the passage most strongly supports which one of the following statements?"

Although they might at first seem intimidating, many Global questions can be answered from your initial reading of the passage. For example, you know that you are always seeking to identify the main point of the passage as you read, so the presence of a Main Point question should not alarm you or cause you any undue work. On the other hand, Global questions that ask you to prove statements drawn from the passage can be time-consuming because they typically require you to return to the passage and cross-check each answer choice.

Understanding the "big picture" is vital, since at least half of the questions on any given passage are likely to be Global Reference questions.

Note that not every question stem that refers to a concept is a Concept Reference question. For example, if an entire passage is about the poet Rita Dove, and the question stem asks about the views of Rita Dove, that question would be classified as Global. We will discuss this classification in more detail when we examine individual questions.

Throughout this book, all questions are first classified as one of these three types. There are also additional indicators designating question type, etc.

As we classify Reading Comprehension questions, location will always appear as the first element of the classification. Thus, every question classification in this book will begin with the shorthand reference of SR, CR, or GR.

The concept of location should not be an unexpected one. Reading Comprehension passages are roughly 50-60 lines in length, and with a passage of that size, you should expect that the test makers will want to ask about different parts of the passage.

Throughout this section we will indicate how frequently each type of question appears. Assessing just the Location element, this is the frequency of appearance per section (the typical section is 26-28 questions in length):

> Frequency of SR Questions: 20 - 30% overall
> Frequency of CR Questions: 15 - 25% overall
> Frequency of GR Questions: 50 - 60% overall

Location Designation Drill

Each of the following items contains a sample Reading Comprehension question stem. In the space provided, categorize each stem into one of the three Location designations: Specific Reference (SR), Concept Reference (CR), and Global Reference (GR). While we realize that you have not yet worked directly with each question type, by considering the designations you will now have an advantage as you attack future questions. Later in this chapter we will present more comprehensive Identify the Question Stem drills to further strengthen your abilities. *Answers on Page 102*

1. Question Stem: "Which one of the following most accurately describes the organization of the material presented in the passage?"

   Location Designation: _____

2. Question Stem: "The third paragraph of the passage provides the most support for which one of the following inferences?"

   Location Designation: _____

3. Question Stem: "The discussion of Muniz' first theory is intended to perform which of the following functions in the passage?"

   Location Designation: _____

4. Question Stem: "The author mentions the number of species (lines 20-23) primarily in order to support which of the following claims?"

   Location Designation: _____

5. Question Stem: "Which of the following is mentioned in the passage as an important characteristic of each of the three theories discussed in the passage? "

   Location Designation: _____

6. Question Stem: "Which one of the following titles most completely and accurately describes the contents of the passage?"

   Location Designation: _____

Location Designation Drill Answer Key

The typical student misses a few questions in this drill. Do not worry about how many you miss; the point of this drill is to acquaint you with the idea of Location as it is presented in different question stems. As you see more examples of each type of question, your ability to correctly identify the Location element will improve.

1. Location Type: Global Reference

Because this stem asks about the "organization of the material presented in the passage," it references the passage as a whole and is thus best described as a Global Reference question.

2. Location Type: Specific Reference

This stem specifically references the "third paragraph of the passage," and so this is a Specific Reference question.

3. Location Type: Concept Reference

This question stem does not refer to a specific line or paragraph, so it cannot be a Specific Reference question. The reference to a particular theory is enough to suggest that this is more specific than a Global Reference question, so this example can be classified a Concept Reference question.

4. Location Type: Specific Reference

This stem specifically references the "lines 20-23," and therefore this is a Specific Reference question.

5. Location Type: Concept Reference

This question stem does not refer to a specific line or paragraph, so it cannot be a Specific Reference question. However, the question also does not refer to the passage in general, and the idea mentioned in the stem is specific enough to suggest that this is a Concept Reference question.

6. Location Type: Global Reference

This stem discusses the "contents of the passage," and is thus best described as a Global Reference question.

Reading Comprehension Question Types

After establishing Location, the next element you must identify when reading question stems is the type of question that you face. The questions in the Reading Comprehension section are similar to the questions asked in the Logical Reasoning section, and virtually all question stems that appear in the Reading Comprehension section of the LSAT can be classified into one of six different types:

1. Must Be True/Most Supported
2. Main Point
3. Strengthen
4. Weaken
5. Parallel Reasoning
6. Cannot Be True

Many of the question types discussed in the LSAT Logical Reasoning Bible are also covered here.

Note that some of the other question types that appear in the Logical Reasoning section, such as Justify the Conclusion or Resolve the Paradox, *could* appear in the Reading Comprehension section, but they appear so infrequently that a discussion of those types is not useful.

You must correctly analyze and classify every question stem because the question stem ultimately determines the nature of the correct answer choice. A mistake in analyzing the question stem almost invariably leads to a missed question. Properly identifying the question stem type will allow you to proceed quickly and with confidence, and in some cases it will help you determine the correct answer before you read any of the five answer choices.

Occasionally, students ask if we refer to the question types by number or by name. We always refer to the questions by name, as that is an easier and more efficient approach. Numerical question type classification systems force you to add two unnecessary levels of abstraction to your thinking process. For example, consider a question that asks you to "weaken" the argument. In a numerical question classification system, you must first recognize that the question asks you to weaken the argument, then you must classify that question into a numerical category (say, Type 4), and then you must translate Type 4 to mean "Weaken." Literally, numerical classification systems force you to perform an abstract, circular translation of the meaning of the question, and the translation process is both time-consuming and valueless.

In the following pages we will briefly discuss each of the primary Reading Comprehension question types.

1. Must Be True/Most Supported

    This category is simply known as "Must Be True." Must Be True
    questions ask you to identify the answer choice that is best proven by
    the information in the passage. Question stem examples:

    > "If the statements above are true, which one of the following must also be true?"

    > "Which one of the following can be properly inferred from the passage?"

    Must Be True questions are the dominant category in the Reading
    Comprehension section; over 75% of the questions you face in
    each section can be categorized as Must Be True. Although at first
    glance this might seem like an unusually high percentage, keep in
    mind that Reading Comprehension is about trying to understand a
    lengthy passage of text. The best way to test your comprehension of
    this information is to ask a series of questions aimed at determining
    whether you understood the facts of what you read. Keep in mind that
    when selecting an answer choice, you must find one supported by the
    information in the passage. We call this the Fact Test™: The correct
    answer to a Must Be True question can always be proven by referring
    to the facts stated in the passage.

    Many of the Must Be True questions in the Reading Comprehension
    section ask you to perform a more specific action, such as to identify
    the author's viewpoint or the function of a word or phrase. In the next
    section we will examine these attributes in more detail and discuss
    each type of Must Be True question.

2. Main Point

    Main Point questions are a variant of Must Be True questions. As you
    might expect, a Main Point question asks you to find the primary focus
    of the passage. Question stem example:

    > "The main point of the argument is that"

    Main Point questions most often appear as the very first question in
    each passage set. This placement is beneficial because as you conclude
    your reading of the passage, you should already know the main point
    of what you have read.

*Over 85% of
LSAT Reading
Comprehension
passages are
accompanied
by a Main Point
question.*

    As a total in the section, Main Point questions appear approximately
    13% of the time, but they appear in over 85% of all passages. When
    considered in combination with Must Be True questions, therefore,
    the operation of finding facts and proving conclusions represents
    approximately 88% of the questions in a Reading Comprehension
    section.

3. Strengthen

    These questions ask you to select the answer choice that provides
    support for the author's argument or strengthens it in some way.
    Question stem examples:

    > "Which one of the following, if true, most strengthens the argument?"

    > "Which one of the following, if true, most strongly supports the statement
    > above?"

4. Weaken

    Weaken questions ask you to attack or undermine the author's
    argument. Question stem example:

    > "Which one of the following, if true, most seriously weakens the argument?"

    Considered together, Strengthen and Weaken questions only appear
    about 4% of the time.

5. Parallel Reasoning

    Parallel Reasoning questions ask you to identify the answer choice that
    contains reasoning most similar in structure to the reasoning presented
    in the stimulus. Question stem example:

    > "Which one of the following arguments is most similar in its pattern of
    > reasoning to the argument above?"

    Over the past several years Parallel Reasoning questions have appeared
    more frequently. Even so, these questions appear infrequently, perhaps
    only once or twice per section.

6. Cannot Be True

    Cannot Be True questions ask you to identify the answer choice that
    cannot be true or is most weakened based on the information in the
    stimulus. Question stem example:

    > "If the statements above are true, which one of the following CANNOT be
    > true?"

    These questions often appear with the modifier "Least," which will be
    discussed in more detail in a later section of this chapter.

Other question elements will also be discussed, most notably question variants
(such as Author's Perspective questions) and overlays (such as Principle
questions). Those will be discussed later in this chapter.

Question Classification (Up to this point)

From a classification standpoint, at this point we have established that every question in the Reading Comprehension section has two elements: Location and Question Type. When questions are classified in this book, those two elements are always listed in order, as follows:

Location, Question Type

Here are several sample question classifications featuring both elements:

SR, Must
(Location: Specific Reference, Type: Must Be True)

CR, Strengthen
(Location: Concept Reference, Type: Strengthen)

GR, MP
(Location: Global Reference, Type: Main Point)

SR, Parallel
(Location: Specific Reference, Type: Parallel Reasoning)

The next page contains a drill designed to strengthen your ability to correctly classify questions.

Identify the Question Type Drill

Each of the following items contains a sample Reading Comprehension question stem. In the space provided, categorize each stem into one of the three Location designations: Specific Reference (SR), Concept Reference (CR), and Global Reference (GR), and then categorize each stem into one of the six main Reading Comprehension Question Types: Must Be True, Main Point, Strengthen, Weaken, Parallel Reasoning, or Cannot Be True. While we realize that you have not yet worked directly with each question type, by considering the designations now you will have an advantage as you attack future questions. *Answers on Page 109*

1. Question Stem: "Which of the following, if true, would lend most support to the view attributed to Norton's critics?"

   Classification: _____

2. Question Stem: "The author would most likely disagree with which one of the following statements?"

   Classification: _____

3. Question Stem: "Which one of the following most accurately describes the author's purpose in referring to Johnson as being "unfairly criticized by his contemporaries" in the first sentence of the passage?"

   Classification: _____

4. Question Stem: "Which one of the following most accurately expresses the main point of the passage?"

   Classification: _____

5. Question Stem: "Which one of the following, if true, would most call into question the author's assertion in the last sentence of the passage?"

   Classification: _____

6. Question Stem: "The author's description of the relationship between the conductor and the orchestra (line 39) is most closely analogous to which of the following?"

   Classification: _____

7. Question Stem: "Which one of the following most accurately describes the organization of the passage?"

    Classification: _____

8. Question Stem: "Which one of the following, if true, most weakens the author's argument against international aid as a first line of defense?"

    Classification: _____

9. Question Stem: "The author of the passage would be most likely to agree with which one of the following statements?"

    Classification: _____

10. Question Stem: "Which one of the following would, if true, most strengthen the claim made by the author in the last sentence of the passage (lines 54-58)?"

    Classification: _____

11. Question Stem: "Which one of the following, if true, offers, the most support for Harper's hypothesis?"

    Classification: _____

12. Question Stem: "According to the passage, which one of the following is an obstacle to the creation of an effective treatment plan for patients in third world nations?"

    Classification: _____

13. Question Stem: "Which one of the following is most similar to the relationship described in the passage between the new methods of the building industry and pre-twentieth-century construction?"

    Classification: _____

14. Question Stem: "The third paragraph of the passage most strongly supports which one of the following inferences?"

    Classification: _____

Identify the Question Stem Drill Answer Key

The typical student misses about half of the questions in this drill. Do not worry about how many you miss; the point of this drill is to acquaint you with the different question stems. As you see more examples of each type of question, your ability to correctly identify each stem will improve.

1. CR, Strengthen
Location: Here we are asked to find the answer choice that would support a particular view referenced from the passage, so this is a <u>Concept Reference</u> question.
Type: The presence of the phrase "Which of the following, if true," generally introduces either a Strengthen or a Weaken question. In this case, since the correct answer will support the referenced view, this is clearly a <u>Strengthen</u> question.

2. GR, Cannot
Location: This example provides no direction, conceptual or otherwise, as to location in the passage. It is therefore a <u>Global Reference</u> question.
Type: This question requires you to find the answer choice with which the author would disagree. Because the correct answer choice will be inconsistent with the author's attitude, this question stem can be classified as a <u>Cannot Be True</u> question (that is, "according to the author, which of the following cannot be true?").

3. SR, Must
Location: This example provides the exact location of the referenced quote, so this is a <u>Specific Reference</u> question.
Type: The correct answer must pass the Fact Test; in this case it must provide an accurate description of the referenced quote's purpose in the passage. Therefore this question stem falls under the <u>Must Be True</u> category.

4. GR, MP
Location: This common question stem refers to the passage as a whole and is therefore a <u>Global Reference</u> question.
Type: Since this question stem asks for the main point of the passage, this is a clear example of a <u>Main Point</u> question. The correct answer choice will be the one which most accurately and completely reflects the central focus of the passage.

5. SR, Weaken
Location: Although no line reference is provided in this example, the reader is directed specifically to the last sentence of the passage, so this is a <u>Specific Reference</u> question.
Type: A question stem that begins with "Which of the following, if true" is nearly certain to be a Strengthen or Weaken question. In this case, the information in the correct answer will call the referenced assertion into question, so this should be classified as a <u>Weaken</u> question.

6. SR, Parallel
Location: Since an exact line reference is provided, this is a <u>Specific Reference</u> question.
Type: Here the reader is asked to find the answer choice which is most closely analogous to the referenced discussion, which makes this a <u>Parallel</u> question. The correct answer choice will reflect a relationship or other element similar to that discussed in the passage.

7. GR, Must

Location: Since this question stem deals with the entire passage, this is a <u>Global Reference</u> question.
Type: This question requires that the reader understand the overall structure of the given passage, and the correct answer choice must reflect that structure. This is a <u>Must Be True</u> question.

8. CR, Weaken

Location: Although this question does not provide a line reference, it refers to a very specific argument advanced by the author. It is thus a <u>Concept Reference</u> question.
Type: This is one of the more readily recognizable question types, since the word "weaken" is in the question stem; this is a standard <u>Weaken</u> question which in this case requires that the correct answer choice reduce the credibility of the author's referenced criticism.

9. GR, Must

Location: This question deals with the passage as a whole, so this is a <u>Global Reference</u> question.
Type: This common question requires that the reader understand the author's perspective. The correct answer choice must reflect the author's attitude, and pass the Fact Test, so this is a <u>Must Be True</u> question.

10. SR, Strengthen

Location: The line reference at the end of this question stem identifies this example as a <u>Specific Reference</u> question.
Type: The fact that we are asked to strengthen a claim means that this is a <u>Strengthen</u> question, and the correct answer choice must assist the author's argument in some way.

11. GR, Strengthen

Location: Without reading the passage, it might be difficult to assess the scope of this question's reference (although you should immediately recognize that this is <u>not</u> a Specific Reference question). If the passage is largely focused on the referenced hypothesis, this is a <u>Global Reference</u> question.
Type: Since the correct answer choice will somehow support the referenced hypothesis, this is a <u>Strengthen</u> question.

12. CR, Must

Location: This question stem requires the reader to identify a particular obstacle but does not provide its specific location in the passage, so this is a <u>Concept Reference</u> question.
Type: In this case, the correct answer choice will come directly from information provided in the passage, so this is a <u>Must Be True</u> question.

13. CR, Parallel

Location: This question refers to a specific relationship but offers no line references, thus it is a <u>Concept Reference</u> question.
Type: The question stem asks you to find an answer that is "most similar to the relationship" in the passage, and thus this is a <u>Parallel</u> question.

14. SR, Must

Location: Specification of "the third paragraph" makes this a <u>Specific Reference</u> question.
Type: Although this question stem uses the word "supports," the correct answer choice will be the one which, based on the passage, <u>Must Be True</u>.

Reading Comprehension Question Types Examined in Detail ▬▬

Must Be True/Most Supported Questions ▬▬▬▬▬▬▬▬

Percentage of passages containing Must Be True Questions: 100%

Must Be True questions are, by far, the most important Reading Comprehension question type. From a percentage standpoint, Must Be True questions make up approximately 88% of all of the questions in each Reading Comprehension section. Thus, to achieve a high score in the Reading Comprehension section, you must dominate Must Be True questions. In this section we will examine Must Be True questions, and then examine a variety of specific Must Be True subtypes. In each instance we will provide helpful tips and strategies to attack each type and subtype.

Must Be True questions require you to select an answer choice that is proven by the information presented in the passage. The correct answer choice can be a paraphrase of part of the passage or it can be a logical consequence of one or more parts of the passage. However, when selecting an answer choice, you must find the proof that supports your answer in the passage. Again, this is called the Fact Test.

> The correct answer to a Must Be True question can always be proven by referring to the facts stated in the passage.

The test makers will try to entice you by creating incorrect answer choices that could possibly occur or are likely to occur, but are not *certain* to occur. You must avoid those answers and select the answer choice that is most clearly supported by what you read. Do not bring in information from outside the passage (aside from commonsense assumptions); all of the information necessary to answer the question resides in the passage.

Must Be True questions are considered the foundation of the LSAT because the skill required to answer a Must Be True question is also required for every other LSAT question. Must Be True questions require you to read text and understand the facts and details that logically follow. To Weaken or Strengthen an argument, for example, you first need to be able to ascertain the facts and details. The same goes for every other type of question. Because every question type relies on the fact-finding skill used to answer Must Be True questions, your performance on Must Be True questions controls your overall Reading Comprehension score. For this reason, you must lock down the understanding required for this question category: what did you read in the passage and what do you know on the basis of that reading?

The statistics presented at the start of each section reference the percentage of all passages that contain the listed question type. In this instance, for example, every single LSAT passage is accompanied by at least one Must Be True question.

The vast majority of the questions in the Reading Comprehension section are Must Be True questions.

In the Reading Comprehension section from the June '05 LSAT, 100% of the questions fell under the category of Must Be True and its sub-types.

Attacking Must Be True Questions

Your approach to Must Be True questions will, in part, be dictated by the Location element specified in each question stem. That is, your approach to an SR, Must question will necessarily be different than your approach to a GR, Must question. Following, we examine how the difference in Location affects how you attack Must Be True questions.

Specific Reference

As mentioned in the Location section:

> To attack Specific Reference Must Be True questions—those which refer to an exact line number, sentence, or paragraph—always return to the passage and start reading three to five lines above the reference, or from the most logical nearby starting point such as the start of a paragraph.

The prevalence of Must Be True questions is incredibly beneficial to you as a test taker because the answer to all Must questions resides directly in the text of each passage.

As we will see when discussing specific passages and questions, the "three to five line" recommendation is open-ended because what you are seeking is the most logical starting point for your reading, and that starting point is typically the prior complete sentence or two.

For Specific Reference questions that refer to a paragraph, refer to the following rule:

> To attack Specific Reference questions that refer to a paragraph, return to the passage and consider the paragraph in question.

Concept Reference

With Concept Reference Must Be True questions, you must return to the areas in the passage mentioned in the question stem and quickly review the information. These questions are by nature more vague than Specific Reference questions and so you must rely on your passage diagramming or memory to return to the correct area.

Global Reference

Global Must Be True questions are usually Main Point, Purpose, or Organization questions (this subtype will be discussed on page 116), and you will typically not need to refer back to the passage prior to attacking the answer choices because you will already know the answer from your reading. Remember, if you seek to identify the five critical elements of each passage as identified in Chapter Two, you will automatically know the answer to every Global Must Be True question. Thus, you would only need to refer back to the passage to eliminate or confirm individual answer choices.

Percentage of passages containing Must Be True Question Subtypes: 100%

Although many of the questions in the Reading Comprehension section are straightforward Must Be True questions (this category comprises roughly 30% of all questions), about 60% of all questions are subtypes of the Must Be True category. Fundamentally, these subtypes are approached in exactly the same manner as regular Must Be True questions. That is, the Fact Test applies and you must still be able to justify your answer with evidence from the passage. However, some of these subtypes ask for very specific information, and thus an awareness of the existence of these question types is essential.

Main Point Questions (MP)

Percentage of passages containing a Main Point Question: 89%

Main Point questions may be the question type most familiar to test takers. Many of the standardized tests you have already encountered, such as the SAT, contain questions that ask you to ascertain the Main Point. Even in daily conversation you will hear, "What's your point?" Main Point questions, as you might suspect from the name, ask you to summarize the author's point of view in the passage.

The answer you select must follow from the information in the stimulus. But be careful: even if an answer choice must be true according to the stimulus, if it fails to capture the main point it cannot be correct. This is the central truth of Main Point questions: Like all Must Be True question variants, the correct answer must pass the Fact Test, but with the additional criterion that the correct answer choice must capture the author's point.

The key to identifying a main point is to remember that, although the main point may be stated succinctly in a sentence or two, all paragraphs of the passage must support the main point. Thus, the main point will not just reflect the argument contained in a single paragraph. To assess the situation, apply the viewpoint identification approach and argument identification methods discussed in Chapter Two. These two VIEWSTAMP items will direct you toward the Main Point during your reading of the passage. Thereafter, you will be in an excellent position to answer any Main Point question.

The Main Point question stem format is remarkably consistent, with the primary feature being a request for you to identify the conclusion or point of the argument, as in the following examples:

> "Which one of the following most accurately expresses the main point of the passage?"

> "Which one of the following statements best expresses the main idea of the passage?"

A complete understanding of any passage requires that you identify the main point, even in the rare case that a passage does not include a Main Point question.

Two types of *incorrect* answers frequently appear with Main Point questions:

1. Answers that are true but do not encapsulate the author's point.

2. Answers that repeat portions of the passage but not the Main Point.

Each answer type is attractive because they are true based on what you have read. However, neither summarizes the author's main point and therefore both are incorrect.

Purpose/Function Questions (P)

Historically, Purpose/Function questions have comprised approximately 1/5 of all Reading Comprehension questions.

Percentage of passages containing a Purpose Question: 87%

At the Specific Reference and Concept Reference level, Purpose questions ask why the author referred to a particular word, phrase, or idea. To determine the reasons behind the author's use of words or ideas, refer to the context around the reference, using context clues and your knowledge of the viewpoints and structure of the passage. Here are several example question stems:

"The author of the passage uses the phrase "clearly insufficient" (line 39) primarily in order to"

"The author's discussion of feline maternal instinct (lines 23-34) functions primarily to"

"The author's discussion of increased erosion over the last decade serves primarily to"

"Which one of the following best states the function of the third paragraph of the passage?"

Global Purpose questions are almost always phrased using the words "primary purpose" and ask for the author's main purpose in writing the passage. These questions ask you to describe why the author wrote the passage, and the correct answer is often an abstract version of the main point (and if not, at the very least the answer to a Global Purpose question will agree with the Main Point).

"The primary purpose of the passage is to"

"In the passage, the author seeks primarily to"

Perspective Questions

Percentage of passages containing a Perspective Question: 95%

This category contains questions about two of the five VIEWSTAMP elements identified in Chapter Two: viewpoints and tone. These two elements are very closely related, and we combine these two elements in our question classification, using the term "perspective" to capture the idea behind both elements.

Perspective questions can be divided into two categories: questions that ask about the author's views and tone, and questions that ask about the views and tone of one of the other groups discussed in the passage. These two types are discussed below.

Author's Perspective Questions (AP)

Percentage of passages containing an Author's Perspective Question: 84%

Author's Perspective questions ask you to select the answer choice that best reflects the author's views on a subject or the author's attitude toward a subject. Because identifying the position of the author is a critical part of your strategy when reading, normally these questions should be relatively painless.

> "The author of the passage would most likely agree with which one of the following statements?"

> "It can be inferred that the author of the passage believes which one of the following about the history of modern art?"

> "It can be reasonably inferred from the passage that the author's attitude is most favorable toward which one of the following?"

Understanding the author's viewpoint is an integral part of mastering any passage. About 20% of Reading Comprehension questions concern the Author's Perspective.

Subject Perspective Questions (SP)

Percentage of passages containing a Subject Perspective Question: 29%

In this question type, we use the term "subject" to refer to a person or group who is discussed in the passage. Subject Perspective questions ask you to select the answer choice that best reflects the views or attitude of one of the other groups in the passage. Because identifying all views is a critical part of your strategy when reading, you should be well-prepared for these questions.

> "Given the information in the passage, which one of the following is Kantor most likely to believe?"

Subject Perspective questions make up about 5% of Reading Comprehension questions overall.

"It can be inferred that Peter Goodrich would be most likely to agree with which one of the following statements concerning common law?"

These questions are considered Must Be True questions because the correct answer follows directly from the statements in the passage.

Organization Questions (O)

Percentage of passages containing an Organization Question: 25%

These questions usually appear in reference to either a specific paragraph or to the passage as a whole, and refer less frequently to specific lines.

At the line level, you are normally asked to identify the way in which pairs of lines relate to each other:

> "The logical relationship of lines 8-13 of the passage to lines 23-25 and 49-53 of the passage is most accurately described as"

At a specific paragraph level, you will either be asked to identify the structure of the paragraph, or to identify how one paragraph relates to another paragraph. Question examples include:

> "Which one of the following most accurately describes the relationship between the second paragraph and the final paragraph?"

> "Which one of the following most accurately describes the organization of the material presented in the second and third paragraphs of the passage?"

At the Global level, these questions ask you to describe the overall structure of the passage. For example:

> "Which one of the following best describes the organization of the passage?"

> "Which one of the following most accurately describes the organization of the material presented in the passage?"

> "Which one of the following sequences most accurately and completely corresponds to the presentation of the material in the passage?"

In both the Specific and Global versions, these questions are similar to the Method of Reasoning questions in the Logical Reasoning section, but they are generally broader. Given that you must track structure as you read, these questions should be fairly straightforward exercises in matching answer choices to what you already know occurred in the passage.

Although questions which specifically reference Passage Organization make up only about 4% of questions in this section, a strong grasp of the structure of a passage will allow you to attack Concept Reference and Specific Reference questions far more efficiently.

Expansion Questions (E)

Percentage of passages containing an Expansion Question: 10%

Expansion questions require you to extrapolate ideas from the passage to determine one of three elements: where the passage was drawn from or how it could be titled, what sentence or idea could come before the passage, and what sentence or idea could follow the passage. The following examples show the range of phrasing in these questions:

"Which one of the following would be most suitable as a title for this passage if it were to appear as an editorial piece?"

"Which one of the following titles most completely summarizes the contents of the passage?"

"If this passage had been excerpted from a longer text, which one of the following predictions regarding the future of aeronautics would be most likely to appear in that text?"

"Which one of the following sentences would most logically begin a paragraph immediately following the end of the passage?"

"Which one of the following is the most logical continuation of the last paragraph of the passage?"

"Which one of the following sentences could most logically be appended to the end of the last paragraph of the passage?"

Questions about the title or source of the passage typically reflect the Main Point of the passage. Questions asking you to identify pre- or post-passage sentences, however, are usually immediately dependent upon the two or three sentences at the beginning or end of the passage, and then more generally dependent upon the passage as a whole. These questions can be difficult because they ask you to infer the flow and direction of the passage from a somewhat limited set of clues.

Correct Answers in Must Be True Questions

Let us take a moment to discuss two types of answers that will always be correct in a Must Be True question and any Must Be True subtype (except for Main Point questions, as discussed previously).

1. Paraphrased Answers

   Paraphrased Answers are answers that restate a portion of the passage in different terms. Because the language is not exactly the same as in the passage, Paraphrased Answers can be easy to miss. Paraphrased Answers are designed to test your ability to discern the author's exact meaning. Sometimes the answer can appear to be almost too obvious since it is drawn directly from the passage.

2. Combination Answers

   Answers that are the sum of two or more passage statements

   Any answer choice that would result from combining two or more statements in the passage will be correct.

Should you encounter either of the above as an answer choice in a non-Main Point, Must Be True question, select the answer with confidence.

Incorrect Answers in Must Be True Questions

There are several types of answers that appear in Must Be True questions that are incorrect. These answers appear frequently enough that we have provided a review of the major types below. Each answer category below is designed to attract you to an incorrect answer choice. As we begin to look at actual passages and questions in the next chapter, we will examine instances of these types of answers.

1. Could Be True or Likely to Be True Answers

   Because the criteria in the question stem require you to find an answer choice that Must Be True, answers that merely could be true or are even likely to be true are incorrect. These answers are attractive because there is nothing demonstrably wrong with them (for example, they do not contain statements that are counter to the passage). Regardless, like all incorrect answers, these answers fail the Fact Test. Remember, you must select an answer choice that must occur based on what you have read.

   This category of "incorrect answers" is very broad, and some of the types mentioned on the next page will fall under this general idea but place an emphasis on a specific aspect of the answer.

2. Exaggerated Answers

Exaggerated Answers take information from the passage and then stretch that information to make a broader statement that is not supported by the passage. In that sense, this form of answer is a variation of a Could Be True answer since the exaggeration is possible, but not proven based on the information. Here is an example:

> If the passage states, "*Some* software vendors recently implemented more rigorous licensing procedures."

> An incorrect answer would exaggerate one or more of the elements: "*Most* software vendors recently implemented more rigorous licensing procedures." In this example, *some* is exaggerated to *most*. While it could be true that most software vendors made the change, the passage does not prove that it must be true. This type of answer is often paraphrased, creating a deadly combination where the language is similar enough to be attractive but different enough to be incorrect.

Here is another example:

> If the passage states, "Recent advances in the field of molecular biology make it *likely* that many school textbooks will be rewritten."

> The exaggerated and paraphrased version would be: "Many school textbooks about molecular biology will be re-written." In this example, *likely* has been dropped, and this omission exaggerates the certainty of the change. The paraphrase is also problematic because the passage referenced school textbooks whereas the paraphrased answer refers to school textbooks *about molecular biology*.

3. "New" Information Answers

Because correct Must Be True answers must be based on information in the passage or the direct result of combining statements in the passage, be wary of answers that present so-called new information—that is, information not mentioned explicitly in the passage or information that would not fall under the umbrella of a statement made in the passage. For example, if a passage discusses the economic policies of Japan, be careful with an answer that mentions U.S. economic policy. Look closely at the passage—does the information about Japanese economic policy apply to the U.S., or are the test makers trying to get you to fall for an answer that sounds logical but is not directly supported?

4. The Shell Game

The LSAT makers have a variety of psychological tricks they use to entice test takers to select an answer choice. One of their favorites is one we call the Shell Game: an idea or concept is raised in the passage, and then a very similar idea appears in an answer choice, but the idea is changed just enough to be incorrect but still attractive. This trick

Shell Game answers occur in all LSAT question types, not just Must Be True.

is called the Shell Game because it abstractly resembles those street corner gambling games where a person hides a small object underneath one of three shells, and then scrambles them on a flat surface while a bettor tries to guess which shell the object is under (similar to Three-card Monte). The object of a Shell Game is to trick the bettor into guessing incorrectly by mixing up the shells so quickly and deceptively that the bettor mistakenly selects the wrong shell. The intent of the LSAT makers is the same.

5. The Opposite Answer

As the name suggests, the Opposite Answer provides an answer that is completely opposite of the stated facts of the passage. Opposite Answers are very attractive to students who are reading too quickly or carelessly.

6. The Reverse Answer

Here is a simplified example of how a Reverse Answer works, using italics to indicate the reversed parts:

> The passage might state, "*Many* people have *some* type of security system in their home."

> An incorrect answer then reverses the elements: "*Some* people have *many* types of security systems in their home."

The Reverse Answer is attractive because it contains familiar elements from the passage, but the reversed statement is incorrect because it rearranges those elements to create a new, unsupported statement.

7. The Wrong View

Wrong View answers frequently appear in Perspective questions. For example, the question will ask you to identify a statement that agrees with the author's view, but then places one or more answers that would agree with the view of another group in the passage. You can avoid these answers by carefully tracking viewpoints as discussed earlier.

8. Hidden References

In some Specific Reference questions, you will be sent to a certain location in the passage but the information needed to answer the question will reside elsewhere in the passage, in a section that also touches on the issue in the Specific Reference. This can be difficult to handle if the information is a large number of lines away.

Reverse Answers can occur in any type of question.

Non-Must Be True Question Types

In this section we examine all other Reading Comprehension question types. As mentioned earlier, these questions appear with far less frequency than Must Be True questions.

Strengthen Questions

Percentage of passages containing a Strengthen Question: 8%

Strengthen questions ask you to identify the answer choice that best supports a section of the passage or a particular view from the passage. The correct answer choice does not necessarily prove the argument beyond a shadow of a doubt, nor is the correct answer choice necessarily an assumption of the argument. The correct answer choice simply helps the argument in some way.

Following are several Strengthen question stem examples:

> "Which one of the following would, if true, most strengthen the author's position regarding the practical applicability of the theory presented in the passage?"

> "Which one of the following would, if true, most strengthen the claim made by the author in the last sentence of the passage (lines 54-58)?"

> "Which one of the following, if true, would lend the most support to the claims of critics discussed in lines 9-17?"

50% of the LSAT is devoted exclusively to Logical Reasoning, so questions which test your critical reasoning ability, such as Strengthen or Weaken questions, are less common in the Reading Comprehension section.

How to Strengthen an Argument

Use the following points to effectively strengthen arguments:

1. Identify what you are trying to strengthen!

   Before you can examine the answer choices, you must know what it is that you must strengthen. When evaluating an answer, ask yourself, "Would this answer choice assist the position in question in some way?" If so, you have the correct answer.

2. Personalize the argument.

   Personalizing allows you to see the argument from a very involved perspective and can clarify your perspective as you assess the strength of each answer.

3. Look for weaknesses in the argument.

   This may seem like a strange recommendation since your task is to strengthen the argument, but a weak spot in an argument is tailor-made for an answer that eliminates that weakness. If you see a weakness or flaw in the argument, look for an answer that eliminates the weakness.

In other words, close any gap or hole in the argument.

Many Strengthen questions require students to find the missing link between a premise and the conclusion. These missing links are assumptions made by the author or by the party in question, and bringing an assumption to light strengthens the argument because it validates part of the author's thinking.

4. Remember that the correct answer can strengthen the argument just a little or a lot. This variation is what makes these questions difficult.

Three Incorrect Answer Traps

The following types of wrong answer traps frequently appear in Strengthen questions:

1. Opposite Answers. These answers do the exact opposite of what is needed—they weaken the position in question. Because of their direct relation to the argument they are tempting, despite the fact that they result in consequences opposite of those intended.

2. Shell Game Answers. Remember, a Shell Game occurs when an idea or concept is raised in the passage and then a very similar idea appears in the answer choice, but the idea is changed just enough to be incorrect but still attractive. In Strengthen questions, the Shell Game is usually used to support a conclusion or position that is similar to, but slightly different from, the one presented in the passage.

3. Out of Scope Answers. These answers simply miss the point of the argument and support issues that are either unrelated to the argument or tangential to the argument.

Some of the wrong answer types from the Must Be True section do not apply to Strengthen and Weaken questions. For example, the New Information answer is usually wrong in a Must Be True question, but not in a Strengthen or Weaken question because new information is acceptable in the answer choices.

These three incorrect answer traps are not the only forms that an attractive wrong answer may take, but they appear frequently enough that you should be familiar with each form.

Because the same types of wrong answer traps appear in Strengthen as in Weaken questions, the three items above apply to both this section and the following section on Weaken questions.

Percentage of passages containing a Weaken Question: 14%

Weaken questions require you to select the answer choice that undermines a position as decisively as possible. In this sense, Weaken questions are the polar opposite of Strengthen questions.

Note that the makers of the LSAT can use a variety of words to indicate that your task is to weaken the argument:

> weaken
> attack
> undermine
> refute
> argue against
> call into question
> cast doubt
> challenge
> damage
> counter

You do not need to find an answer that destroys the author's position. Instead, simply find an answer that hurts the argument.

Here are two Weaken question stem examples:

> "Which one of the following, if true, would most weaken Hart's argument regarding the recently excavated fossils?"

> "Which one of the following, if true, would most seriously challenge the position of the critics mentioned in line 34?"

When approaching Weaken questions, always remember to:

1. Isolate and assess the position you are attacking. Only by understanding the structure of the position can you gain the perspective necessary to attack that position.

2. Know the details of what was said in the passage.

3. Accept the answer choices as given, even if they include "new" information. Unlike Must Be True questions, Weaken answer choices can bring into consideration information outside of or tangential to the stimulus. Just because a fact or idea is not mentioned in the passage is not grounds for dismissing an answer choice. Your task is to determine which answer choice best attacks the position.

Weaken question stems tell you to accept the answer choices as true, so you cannot throw out an answer because it doesn't seem possible.

By focusing on the points above, you will maximize your chances of success on Weaken questions.

Parallel Reasoning Questions

Percentage of passages containing a Parallel Reasoning Question: 32%

Parallel Reasoning questions force you to evaluate five different arguments (six if you include the passage).

Parallel Reasoning questions ask you to identify the answer choice that contains reasoning most similar in structure to the reasoning in a section of the passage. Because each answer choice is a wholly new argument, these questions force you to evaluate five arguments in one question, and as such they can be quite time consuming (a fact known to and exploited by the test makers).

In the *LSAT Logical Reasoning Bible*, we detail a sophisticated and highly effective method for solving Logical Reasoning Parallel Reasoning questions. This method, while effective for Reading Comprehension questions, tends to be too advanced. The typical Reading Comprehension Parallel Reasoning question asks you to parallel the structure of a section or paragraph, and thus you usually need only understand the basic outline of what occurred in the section. Then, select the answer choice that contains the same structure. If you find yourself choosing between two or more answer choices, then simply compare some of the other elements in the passage—intent of the author or group, force and use of premises, the relationship of the premises to a conclusion, and the soundness of the argument.

Parallel Reasoning questions comprise about 5% of all Reading Comprehension questions.

Question stem examples:

> "Which one of the following is most analogous to the artistic achievements that the author attributes to Mangino?"

> "As described in the passage, the approach suggested by the Modernists is most similar to which one of the following?"

> "Based on the passage, the relationship between attorney and client is most analogous to the relationship between:"

Percentage of passages containing a Cannot Be True Question: 16%

As you can see, Cannot Be True questions occur infrequently in Reading Comprehension sections. Nonetheless, a familiarity with the principles behind these questions is helpful.

In Cannot Be True questions your task is to identify the answer choice that cannot be true or is most weakened by the information in the passage. Thus, instead of using the information in the passage to prove that one of the answer choices must be true, you must instead prove that one of the answer choices cannot occur, or that it disagrees with the information in the passage.

From an abstract standpoint, Cannot Be True questions can be viewed in two ways:

1. Polar Opposite Must Be True Questions

   Cannot Be True questions are the polar opposite of Must Be True questions: instead of proving an answer choice, you disprove an answer choice.

2. Reverse Weaken Questions

   Cannot Be True questions are like reverse Weaken questions: use the information in the stimulus to attack one of the answers.

Both question descriptions are similar, and neither sounds very difficult. In practice, however, Cannot Be True questions are tricky because the concept of an answer choice being possibly true and therefore wrong is counterintuitive. This type of question appears very infrequently, but the test makers are savvy and they know Cannot questions can catch test takers off-guard and consume more time than the average question. When you encounter a Cannot Be True question, you must mentally prepare yourself to eliminate answers that could be true or that are possible, and select the one answer choice that cannot be true or that is impossible.

Cannot Be True questions can be worded in a variety of ways, but the gist of the question type is to show that an answer cannot follow, as in the following examples:

> "Which one of the following, if true, is LEAST consistent with Alaimo's theory about aggressive behavior in wasps?"

> "Given the information in the passage, the author is LEAST likely to believe which one of the following?"

Question types that appear infrequently, such as Cannot Be True (which occur in about 3% of all questions), tend to consume more time because students are not used to seeing those types of questions.

When words such as "cannot," "least," and "except," are used in question stems, they are capitalized.

Certain words that sometimes appear in question stems have a powerful impact on the nature of the answer choice you are seeking. The most important of these words are discussed below.

"Most" and "Best" in Question Stems

Many question stems contain the qualifiers "most" or "best." For example, a typical question stem will state, "Which one of the following most accurately expresses the main point of the passage?" or "Which one of the following best expresses the main idea of the passage?" Astute test takers realize that the presence of "most" or "best" opens up a Pandora's box of sorts: by including "most" or "best," there is a possibility that other answer choices will also meet the criteria of the question stem (Main Point, Strengthen, Parallel, etc.), albeit to a lesser extent. In other words, if a question stem says "most weakens," the possibility is that every answer choice weakens the argument and you would be in the unenviable position of having to choose the best from a bunch of good answer choices. *Fortunately, this is not how it works*. Even though "most" or "best" will appear in a number of stems, you can rest assured that only one answer choice will meet the criteria. So, if you see a "most weakens" question stem, only one of the answers will weaken the argument. So, then, why does "most" or "best" appear in so many question stems? Because in order to maintain test integrity the test makers need to make sure their credited answer choice is as airtight and defensible as possible. Imagine what would occur if a question stem, let us say a Weaken question, did not include a "most" or "best" qualifier: any answer choice that weakened the argument, even if only very slightly, could then be argued to meet the criteria of the question stem. A situation like this would make constructing the test exceedingly difficult because any given problem might have multiple correct answer choices. To eliminate this predicament, the test makers insert "most" or "best" into the question stem, and then they can always claim there is one and only one correct answer choice.

"Except" and "Least" in Question Stems

"Except" is used more frequently in LSAT Reading Comprehension question stems than "least."

The word "except" has a dramatic impact when it appears in a question stem. Because "except" means "other than," when "except" is placed in a question it negates the logical quality of the answer choice you seek. Literally, it turns the intent of the question stem upside down. For example, if a question asks you what must be true, the one correct answer must be true and the other four answers are not necessarily true. If "except" is added to the question stem, as in "Each of the following must be true EXCEPT," the stem is turned around and instead of the correct answer having the characteristic of must be true, the four incorrect answers must be true and the one correct answer is not necessarily true.

Many students, upon encountering "except" in a question stem, make the mistake of assuming that the "except" charges you with seeking the polar opposite. For example, if a question stem asks you to weaken a statement, some students believe that a "Weaken EXCEPT" question stem actually asks you to strengthen the statement. This is incorrect. Although weaken and strengthen are polar opposites, because except means "other than," when a "Weaken EXCEPT" question stem appears, you are asked to find any answer choice other than Weaken. While this could include a strengthening answer choice, it could also include an answer choice that has no effect on the statement. Thus, in a "Weaken EXCEPT" question, the four incorrect answers Weaken the statement and the one correct answer does not weaken the statement (could strengthen or have no effect). Here is another example:

The true effect of "except" is to logically negate the question stem.

"Which one of the following, if true, strengthens the argument above?"

> One correct answer: Strengthen
> Four incorrect answers: Do not Strengthen

"Each of the following, if true, strengthens the argument above EXCEPT:"

> One correct answer: Does not Strengthen
> Four incorrect answers: Strengthen

As you can see from the example, the presence of except has a profound impact upon the meaning of the question stem. Because "except" has this powerful effect, it always appears in all capital letters whenever it is used in an LSAT question stem.

The word "least" has a similar effect to "except" when it appears in a question stem. Although "least" and "except" do not generally have the same meaning, when "least" appears in a question stem you should treat it *exactly the same* as "except." Note: this advice holds true only when this word appears in the question stem! If you see the word "least" elsewhere on the LSAT, consider it to have its usual meaning of "in the lowest or smallest degree."
Because "least," like "except," has such a strong impact on the meaning of a question stem, the test makers kindly place "least" in all capital letters when it appears in a question stem.

Of course, every once in a while two answer choices achieve the desired goal; in those cases you simply choose the better of the two answers. Normally, the difference between the two answers is significant enough for you to make a clear distinction as to which one is superior.

In the answer keys to this book, we will designate questions that contain "except" or "least" by placing an "X" at the end of the question stem classification. For example, a "Must Be True EXCEPT" question stem would be classified as "MustX." A "Parallel EXCEPT" question stem would be classified as "ParallelX" and so on. The only exception to this rule will be a question that states, "Each of the following could be true EXCEPT." Those questions will be designated "Cannot Be True."

Principle Questions

The word "proposition" or "precept" can be used in place of "principle."

Principle questions (PR) are not a separate question type but are instead an "overlay" that appears in a variety of question types. For example, there are Must Be True Principle questions (Must-PR), Strengthen Principle questions (Strengthen-PR), and Cannot Be True Principle questions (Cannot-PR), among others. In a question stem, the key indicator that the Principle concept is present is the word "principle." Here are two examples of Principle question stems:

> "Which one of the following principles can be most clearly said to underlie the author's arguments in the third paragraph?"

> "Given the information provided in the second paragraph, the author can most reasonably be said to use which one of the following principles to support the scientists' claims?

A principle is a broad rule that specifies what actions or judgments are correct in certain situations. For example, "Some companies are profitable" is not a principle because no rule is involved and no judgment can be drawn from the statement. "All companies should strive to be profitable" is a principle, and one that can be applied to any company.

The degree of generality of principles can vary considerably, and some are much narrower than others. For example, "Children at Smith Elementary School must wear uniforms" is a principle restricted to children attending Smith. The principle does not apply to a child attending a different school. On the other hand, the principle "Any person of voting age has an obligation to vote" applies to a large number of people regardless of background, education, wealth, etc.

Because a principle is by definition a broad rule (usually conditional in nature), the presence of the Principle indicator serves to broaden the scope of the question. The question becomes more abstract, and you must analyze the problem to identify the underlying relationships. Functionally, you must take a broad, global proposition and apply it in a specific manner, either to the answer choices (as in a Must or Parallel question) or to the passage (as in a Strengthen or Weaken question).

One of the aims of the test makers is to keep you off-balance. An unsettled, frustrated test taker is prone to make mistakes. By mixing up the types of questions you face as well as the location you must search in order to find the proper information, the makers of the test can keep you from getting into a rhythm. Imagine how much easier the Reading Comprehension section would be if you faced eight consecutive Local Must Be True questions with each passage. For this reason, you will always see a spread of questions within each section, and you will infrequently see the same exact question type twice in a row. Since this situation is a fact of the LSAT, before the test begins prepare yourself mentally for the quick shifting of mental gears that is required to move from question to question.

Location, Type, and Sub-type Drill

The following is another collection of sample Reading Comprehension questions. In the space provided, categorize each stem into one of the three Location designations: Specific Reference (SR), Concept Reference (CR), and Global Reference (GR), and then categorize each stem into one of the six main Reading Comprehension Question Types: Must Be True, Main Point, Strengthen, Weaken, Parallel Reasoning, or Cannot be True. In addition, include any relevant sub-type designations as discussed in this chapter: Purpose (P), Organization (O), Author's Perspective (AP), Subject Perspective (SP), Passage Expansion (E), Except (X), or Principle (PR). *Answers on Page 133*

1. Question Stem: "It can be reasonably inferred from the passage that the author's attitude is most favorable toward which one of the following?"

   Question Type: _____

2. Question Stem: "Which one of the following views can most reasonably be attributed to the experts cited in line 39?"

   Question Type: _____

3. Question Stem: "As described in the passage, the approach used by FEMA in collecting the data is most analogous to which of the following?"

   Question Type: _____

4. Question Stem: "Based on information in the passage, it can be inferred that which one of the following sentences could most logically be added to the passage as a concluding sentence?"

   Question Type: _____

5. Question Stem: "Which one of the following, if true, would most weaken the author's argument against contracts similar to those described in the passage?"

   Question Type: _____

6. Question Stem: "Which of the following, if true, lends the most credence to the author's argument in the last paragraph of the passage?"

   Question Type: _____

7. Question Stem: "Which one of the following best states the main idea of the passage?"

   Question Type: _____

8. Question Stem: "Which one of the following most accurately describes the organization of the passage?"

   Question Type: _____

9. Question Stem: "The passage provides information that answers each of the following questions EXCEPT:"

   Question Type: _____

10. Question Stem: "The author's primary purpose in the passage is"

    Question Type: _____

11. Question Stem: "The logical relationship of lines 7-9 of the passage to lines 23-25 of the passage is most accurately described as"

    Question Type: _____

12. Question Stem: "Which one of the following, if true, would most cast doubt on the author's interpretation of the study involving the family discussed in line 17?"

    Question Type: _____

13. Question Stem: "The passage contains information sufficient to justify inferring which one of the following?"

    Question Type: _____

14. Question Stem: "The author's attitude toward Zeno's development of a new hypothesis about atomic processes can most aptly be described as"

    Question Type: _____

15. Question Stem: "Which one of the following institutions would NOT be covered by the multi-tier classification system proposed by Jacobs?"

   Question Type: _____

16. Question Stem: "Which one of the following most closely expresses the author's intended meaning in using the term "unabashedly" (line 14)?"

   Question Type: _____

17. Question Stem: "The author's attitude toward the studies mentioned in lines 14-23 is most likely"

   Question Type: _____

18. Question Stem: "Based on the passage, the author would probably hold that which one of the following principles is fundamental to long-term reduction of recidivism rates?"

   Question Type: _____

19. Question Stem: "Which one of the following most accurately describes the organization of the material presented in the first and second paragraphs of the passage?"

   Question Type: _____

20. Question Stem: "In discussing the tangential details of events, the passage contrasts their original significance to witnesses with their possible significance in the courtroom (lines 52-59). That contrast is most closely analogous to which one of the following?"

   Question Type: _____

Location, Type, and Sub-type Drill Answer Key

The typical student misses at least half of the questions in this drill. Do not worry about how many you miss; the point of this drill is to acquaint you with the different question stems. As you see more examples of each type of question, your ability to correctly identify each stem will improve.

1. GR, Must, AP
Location: This question stem provides no reference points, so this is a Global Reference Question.
Type: The correct answer to this question must reflect the author's attitude as described in the passage, and it must pass the Fact Test. This is a Must Be True question.
Sub-Type: Since the question deals with the author's attitude, this is an Author's Perspective question.

2. SR, Must, SP
Location: This question stem provides a line reference, so this is a Specific Reference question.
Type: The correct answer must be consistent with the passage's description of the referenced experts, so this is a Must Be True question.
Sub-Type: Here we are asked about the views of experts cited in the passage, so we must understand their perspective to find the answer to this Subject Perspective question.

3. CR, Parallel
Location: This question stem refers to a particular approach discussed somewhere in the passage, so this is a Concept Reference question.
Type: Here we are asked to parallel the referenced approach, so this is a Parallel Reasoning question (as with most questions that contain the word "analogous").

4. SR, Must, E
Location: This question stem specifies the location by asking for a logical concluding sentence.
Type: The correct answer to this question must provide a logical conclusion, which can be determined based on information from the passage, so this is a Must Be True question.
Sub-Type: This question requires that a logical conclusion be added to the end of the passage, which makes this a Passage Expansion question.

5. CR, Weaken
Location: This question deals with a particular argument made by the author, so this is a Concept Reference question (if the entire passage were focused on this one argument, this would then be a Global Reference question).
Type: Since this question asks for the answer choice which will weaken the author's argument, this is of course a Weaken question.

6. SR, Strengthen
Location: The line reference makes this a Specific Reference question.
Type: In this case we are asked to "lend credence" to an argument (otherwise known as "strengthening"). This is a Strengthen question.

7. GR, MP
Location: This question stem regards the passage as a whole, so this is a Global Reference Question.
Type: Since this question asks for the central focus of the passage, this is a Main Point question.

---

8. GR, Must, O

Location: As this question provides no specific reference points, it is a Global Reference question.
Type: The answer to this question stem comes directly from information in the stimulus, so this is a Must Be True question.
Sub-Type: This is a clear example of an Organization question, which requires that you have an understanding of the overall structure of the passage.

9. GR, MustX

Location: This question references the passage in its entirety, so this is a Global Reference question.
Type: The information needed to answer this question comes directly from the passage, so this is a Must Be True question.
Sub-Type: This is an Except question, so the four incorrect answers in this case will be those choices that can be answered with information provided in the passage. The correct answer choice will be the one that cannot be answered by the passage.

10. GR, Must, P

Location: This common question stem refers to the passage as a whole, and is therefore a Global Reference question.
Type: The answer to this question will be based on information from the passage (and should be prephrased). This is a Must Be True question.
Sub-Type: Since this question asks for the author's main purpose, this is a Purpose question.

11. SR, Must, O

Location: This question refers us specifically to various locations in the passage, so this is a Specific Reference question.
Type: The answer comes from information from the passage, making this a Must Be True question.
Sub-Type: Because this question requires that you understand the structure of the passage, as well as the relationship between various sections of the passage, this is an Organization question.

12. SR, Weaken

Location: The reference to line 17 makes this a Specific Reference question.
Type: When we see a question begin with "Which of the following, if true," we can generally expect either a Strengthen or a Weaken question. In this case, because the correct answer will "cast doubt," this is a Weaken question.

13. GR, Must

Location: This stem gets no more specific than "The passage," so this is a Global Reference question.
Type: Although the wording in this case is somewhat convoluted, if an answer choice must be a "sufficiently justified inference," then it Must Be True.

14. CR, Must, AP

Location: This question stem refers to a particular hypothesis, which makes this a Concept Reference question.
Type: A proper description of the author's attitude will come directly from information in the passage (and therefore should certainly be prephrased), so this is a Must Be True question.
Sub-Type: This question requires an understanding of the author's attitude, so it is an Author's Perspective question.

15. CR, Cannot

Location: This question stem deals with a proposed classification system. If this system were the focus of the passage as a whole, this would be a Global Reference question. In the actual passage, however, that is not the case, making this a Concept Reference question.

Type: Since the correct answer choice cannot be covered by the proposed classification, this is a Cannot question.

16. SR, Must, P

Location: This question refers us to line 14, which makes this a Specific Reference question.

Type: The answer to this question should be prephrased, as it will come directly from information offered in the passage. It is a Must Be True question.

Sub-Type: Since this question stem requires that we consider the intended meaning of the given term, it is a Function/Purpose question.

17. SR, Must, AP

Location: This question stem specifies that the study is mentioned in lines 14-23, so this is a Specific Reference question.

Type: This question regards information about the author which comes directly from the stimulus, and the answer must pass the Fact Test. This is a Must Be True question.

Sub-Type: This example requires an understanding of the author's attitude, so it is an Author's Perspective question.

18. GR, Must, AP, PR

Location: If this question deals with a passage which focuses on recidivism rates, then this is a Global Reference question. If recidivism had only made up a part of the discussion, this would have been a Concept Reference question.

Type: The answer to this question will come from the information offered in the passage, so this is a Must Be True question.

Sub-Type: Since this question regards the author's attitude, it is an Author's Perspective question, and because the answer will involve fundamental principles, it is also a Principle question.

19. SR, Must, O

Location: This question refers to a specific portion of the passage, so it is a Specific Reference question.

Type: The answer to this Must Be True question will come from information provided in the passage, and should be prephrased.

Sub-Type: This question stem requires an understanding of the structure of the passage, as it is a Passage Organization question.

20. SR, Parallel

Location: Since this question refers to lines 52-59, it is a Specific Reference question.

Type: This question requires that we find an "analogous contrast," which basically means that we have to find a parallel scenario. This is a Parallel Reasoning question.

Prephrasing Answers

Most students tend to simply read the question stem and then move on to the answer choices without further thought. This is disadvantageous because these students run a greater risk of being tempted by the expertly constructed incorrect answer choices. One of the most effective techniques for quickly finding correct answer choices and avoiding incorrect answer choices is prephrasing. Prephrasing an answer involves quickly speculating on what you expect the correct answer will be based on the information in the passage.

Although every answer you prephrase may not be correct, there is great value in considering for a moment what elements could appear in the correct answer choice. Students who regularly prephrase find that they are more readily able to eliminate incorrect answer choices, and of course, many times their prephrased answer is correct. In part, prephrasing puts you in an attacking mindset: if you look ahead and consider a possible answer, you are forced to involve yourself in the problem. This process helps keep you alert and in touch with the elements of the problem.

Keep in mind that prephrasing is directly related to attacking the passage; typically, students who closely analyze the five critical elements of the passage can more easily prephrase an answer.

Keep in mind, however, that while the answers to *many* questions can be prephrased, not *all* answers can be prephrased. A question that asks, "Which one of the following most accurately states the main point of the passage?" should immediately bring an answer to mind. On the other hand, if a question asks, "To which one of the following questions does the passage most clearly provide an answer?" you cannot prephrase an answer, because you are not given sufficient information to pre-form an opinion. Yes, you will have some general knowledge based on your reading, but because the test makers can choose any angle from the passage, you will probably not come up with a strong prephrase to this question. This should not be a concern—prephrase when you can, and if you cannot, move ahead.

The Answer Choices

All LSAT questions have five lettered answer choices and each question has only one correct, or "credited," response. As with other sections, the correct answer in a Reading Comprehension question must meet the Uniqueness Rule of Answer Choices™, which states that "Every correct answer has a unique logical quality that meets the criteria in the question stem. Every incorrect answer has the opposite logical quality." The correctness of the answer choices themselves conforms to this rule: there is one correct answer choice; the other four answer choices are the opposite of correct, or incorrect. Consider the following specific examples:

1. Logical Quality of the Correct Answer: Must Be True
   Logical Quality of the Four Incorrect Answers:
   > The opposite of Must Be True = Not Necessarily True (could be not necessarily the case or never the case)

2. Logical Quality of the Correct Answer: Strengthen
   Logical Quality of the Four Incorrect Answers:
   > The opposite of Strengthen = Not Strengthen (could be neutral or weaken)

3. Logical Quality of the Correct Answer: Weaken
   Logical Quality of the Four Incorrect Answers:
   > The opposite of Weaken = Not Weaken (could be neutral or strengthen)

Even though there is only one correct answer choice and this answer choice is unique, you still are faced with a difficult task when attempting to determine the correct answer. The test makers have the advantage of time and language on their side. Because identifying the correct answer at first glance can be quite hard, you must always read all five of the answer choices. Students who fail to read all five answer choices open themselves up to missing questions without ever having read the correct answer. There are many classic examples of Law Services placing highly attractive wrong answer choices just before the correct answer. If you are going to make the time investment of analyzing the stimulus and the question stem, you should also make the wise investment of considering each answer choice.

As you read through each answer choice, sort them into Contenders and Losers. If an answer choice appears somewhat attractive, interesting, or even confusing, keep it as a contender and quickly move on to the next answer choice. You do not want to spend time debating the merits of an answer choice only to find that the next answer choice is superior. However, if an answer choice immediately strikes you as incorrect, classify it as a loser and move on. Once you have evaluated all five answer choices, return to the answer choices that strike you as most likely to be correct and decide which one is correct.

The Contender/Loser separation process is exceedingly important, primarily because it saves time. Consider two students—1 and 2—who each approach the same question, one of whom uses the Contender/Loser approach and the other who does not. Answer choice (D) is correct:

Student 1 (using Contender/Loser)

> Answer choice A: considers this answer for 10 seconds, keeps it as a Contender.
> Answer choice B: considers this answer for 5 seconds, eliminates it as a Loser.
> Answer choice C: considers this answer for 10 seconds, eliminates it as a Loser.
> Answer choice D: considers this answer for 15 seconds, keeps it as a Contender, and mentally notes that this answer is preferable to (A).
> Answer choice E: considers this answer for 10 seconds, would normally keep as a contender, but determines answer choice (D) is superior.

> After a quick review, Student 1 selects answer choice (D) and moves to the next question. Total time spent on the answer choices: 50 seconds (irrespective of the time spent on the passage).

Student 2 (considering each answer choice in its entirety)

> Answer choice A: considers this answer for 10 seconds, is not sure if the answer is correct or incorrect. Returns to stimulus and spends another 15 seconds proving the answer is wrong.
> Answer choice B: considers this answer for 5 seconds, eliminates it.
> Answer choice C: considers this answer for 10 seconds, eliminates it.
> Answer choice D: considers this answer for 15 seconds, notes this is the best answer.
> Answer choice E: considers this answer for 10 seconds, but determines answer choice (D) is superior.

> After a quick review, Student 2 selects answer choice (D) and moves to the next question. Total time spent on the answer choices: 65 seconds.

Comparison: both students answer the problem correctly, but Student 2 takes 15 more seconds to answer the question than Student 1.

Some students, on reading this comparison, note that both students answered the problem correctly and that the time difference was small, only 15 seconds more for Student 2 to complete the problem. Doesn't sound like that big a difference, does it? But, the extra 15 seconds was for just one problem. Imagine if that same thing occurred on every single Reading Comprehension problem in the section: that extra 15 seconds per question would translate to a loss of 6 minutes and 45 seconds when multiplied across 27 questions in a section! And that lost time would mean that student 2 would get to four or five fewer questions than Student 1, just in this one section. This example underscores an essential LSAT truth: little things make a big difference, and every single second counts. If you can save even five seconds by employing a certain method, then do so!

Occasionally, students will read and eliminate all five of the answer choices. If this occurs, return to the passage and re-evaluate what you have read. Remember—the information needed to answer the question always resides in the passage, cither implicitly or explicitly. If none of the answers are attractive, then you must have missed something key in the passage.

The individuals who construct standardized tests are called *psychometricians*. Although this job title sounds ominous, breaking this word into its two parts reveals a great deal about the nature of the LSAT. Although we could make a number of jokes about the *psycho* part, this portion of the word refers to psychology; the *metrician* portion relates to metrics or measurement. Thus, the purpose of these individuals is to create a test that measures you in a precise, psychological way. As part of this process, the makers of the LSAT carefully analyze reams of data from every test administration in order to assess the tendencies of test takers. As Arthur Conan Doyle observed through his character Sherlock Holmes, "You can, for example, never foretell what any one man will do, but you can say with precision what an average number will be up to." By studying the actions of all past test takers, the makers of the exam can reliably predict where you will be most likely to make errors. Throughout this book we will reference those pitfalls as they relate to specific questions and passage types. For the moment, we would like to highlight one mental trap you must avoid at all times in any LSAT section: the tendency to dwell on past problems. Many students fall prey to "answering" a problem, and then continuing to think about it as they start the next problem. Obviously, this is distracting and creates an environment where missing the next problem is more likely. When you finish a problem, you must immediately put it out of your mind and move to the next problem with 100% focus. If you are uncertain of your answer on the previous problem, simply make a note in the test booklet and then return to that problem later, if time allows. If you let your mind wander back to previous problems, you fall into a deadly trap.

Answer Transferring

Transferring your answers from the test booklet to your answer sheet is one of the most important tasks that you will perform on the LSAT. Our research indicates that approximately 10% of all test takers make some type of transcription error during a typical five section test. Since one question can mean a difference of several percentile points, we strongly advise you to follow one of the two approaches discussed below. The method you choose is entirely dependent upon your personal preferences.

1. <u>Logical Grouping</u>. This method involves transferring several answer choices at once, at logical break points throughout the test. For the Reading Comprehension and Logic Games sections, transfer answer choices after you complete the questions for each passage or game. For the Logical Reasoning section, transfer answer choices after you complete each two-page question group. This method generally allows for faster transferring of answers, but some students find they are more likely to make errors in their transcription.

2. <u>Question By Question</u>. As the name implies, this method involves filling in

the answer ovals on your answer sheet after you complete each individual question. This method generally consumes more time than the Logical Grouping method, but it usually produces a higher transfer accuracy rate. If you use the Logical Grouping method and find yourself making errors, use this method instead.

If you are concerned about making a transcription error (as are most test takers), use this simple trick when transferring answers: Once you have decided on an answer choice, say the question number and your chosen answer to yourself (silently, of course), and repeat it during the moments it takes to fill in the corresponding oval. If you say to yourself, for example, "23 B" as you move to the answer sheet, then you are very unlikely to go to the wrong question number or fill in the wrong answer oval.

Filling in the Ovals

Although Law Services prints dire warnings against making stray marks on the answer sheet or incompletely filling in the ovals, these errors are not fatal to your LSAT score. If you believe that Law Services has incorrectly scored your test due to an answer sheet problem, you can have your answer sheet hand scored for an additional fee. Although rarely an issue, machine scoring errors can occur from stray marks, incompletely or improperly filled-in ovals, partially erased answers, or creases in your answer sheet. Remember, answers in your test booklet will not be scored, and two fully blackened answer choices to the same question will be marked incorrect and will not be reviewed by hand scoring.

Be sure to blacken the entire oval for the answer choice you select. Do not use checks or Xs, and do not select two answers.

Practicing with Time

In the last chapter of this book we will discuss time management in detail. However, most students begin practicing with the ideas in this book before reaching that chapter, and we would like to take a moment to give you advice on how to properly practice for the timed element of the LSAT.

Students often ask if they should time themselves while practicing. While every student should take a timed practice LSAT at the very start of their preparation in order to gauge where they stand, not all preparation should be composed of timed exercises. When you learn a new concept or are practicing with a certain technique, you should begin by doing the first several problems untimed in order to get a feel for how the idea operates. Once you feel comfortable with the concept, begin tracking the time it takes you to complete each question. At first, do not worry about completing the passages within a specified time frame, but rather examine how long it takes you to do each passage when you are relaxed. How long does it take you to read the passage? How long to do each question? After doing several passages in this fashion, then begin attempting to read each passage and question set in the time frame allowed on the test (8 minutes and 45 seconds). Thus, you can "ramp up" to

Average completion times for the other two sections:

Logic Games: 8 minutes and 45 seconds per game.

Reading Comprehension: 8 minutes and 45 seconds per passage.

the appropriate time per passage.

A number of
LSAT PrepTests
can be purchased
through our
website, www.
powerscore.com.

We are also often asked if every LSAT PrepTest must be done as a timed exercise. The answer is No. Although we recommend doing as many PrepTests as possible, you can break up individual tests and do section challenges (completing just one or two sections in the required time) or simply work through a section as a challenge exercise where you focus on answering a variety of question types without worrying about the time component.

Final Chapter Note

This concludes our general discussion of the single passages that appear in the Reading Comprehension section. In the next chapter we will briefly review all of the ideas from Chapters One through Five, and then we will use those techniques to work through several complete single passages and question sets. If, in the future, you find yourself unclear about some of these ideas, please return to these initial chapters and re-read them.

If you feel as if you are still hazy on some of the ideas discussed so far, do not worry. When discussing the theory that underlies all questions and approaches, the points can sometimes be a bit abstract and dry. In the remaining chapters we will focus more on the application of these ideas to real questions, and working with actual questions often helps a heretofore confusing idea become clear.

CHAPTER SIX: PUTTING IT ALL TOGETHER

Chapter Preview

Up until this point we have focused on the methods needed to analyze the passages, and in doing so we have isolated individual sections of text that relate directly to each discussion. Now it is time to combine all of the information you have learned and analyze some complete passage sets. Accordingly, this chapter contains two sections:

1. A review of all of the elements of the approach we use for single passages.

2. Two actual LSAT passages, each with detailed analysis of the passage text and each question.

Reading Approach Review

The following section briefly reviews the reading approaches discussed in the second and third chapters of this book.

Chapter Two Review

After you have ascertained the topic, as you progress into the passage you must carefully track the following five key VIEWSTAMP elements:

1. The various groups and viewpoints discussed within the passage. (VIEW)
2. The structure of the passage and the organization of ideas. (S)
3. The tone or attitude of each group or individual. (T)
4. The argument made by each group or individual. (A)
5. The main point of the passage. (MP)

Chapter Three Review

Sources of Difficulty

There are four general ways the makers of the test can increase the difficulty of any given passage:

1. Challenging Topic or Terminology
2. Challenging Writing Style
3. Multiple Viewpoints
4. Difficult Questions/Answers

Passage Elements That Generate Questions

As you read, there are certain specific passage elements that should jump out at you, primarily because history has shown that the test makers use these elements as the basis of questions. For purposes of clarity, we will divide these elements into two groups:

Viewpoint-Specific Elements

1. Track all viewpoints
2. Be wary of competing perspectives

Text-based Elements

Text-based elements will often be smaller pieces, sometimes just a single word, but sometimes short sections of the text. In this sense, these are the "nuts and bolts" elements that you should be aware of when reading.

These are the seven elements (not in order of importance):
1. Initial Information/Closing Information
2. Dates and Numbers
3. Definitions
4. Examples
5. Difficult words or Phrases
6. Enumerations/Lists
7. Text Questions

Two Broad Reasoning Structures

Causal reasoning and conditional reasoning appear frequently in the Logical Reasoning sections of the LSAT, but less so in the Reading Comprehension section.

Causal Reasoning

Cause and effect reasoning asserts or denies that one thing causes another, or that one thing is caused by another. The cause is the event that makes the other occur; the effect is the event that follows from the cause. By definition, the cause must occur before the effect, and the cause is the "activator" or "ignitor" in the relationship. The effect always happens at some point in time after the cause.

Causality in Reading Comprehension usually is discussed in the context of why certain events occurred. The terms that typically introduce causality—such as *caused by*, *reason for*, or *product of*—are still used, but then the author often goes on to discuss the reasons behind the occurrence in depth.

Conditional Reasoning

Conditional reasoning is the broad name given to logical relationships composed of sufficient and necessary conditions. Any conditional relationship consists of at least one sufficient condition and at least one necessary condition.

Conditional relationships in Reading Comprehension passages tend to be unobtrusive, usually occurring as a sideline point to a larger argument.

Of the two types of reasoning, causal reasoning appears more frequently than conditional reasoning in the Reading Comprehension section.

Pitfalls to Avoid

There are a number of text formations and configurations you should recognize. These formations are often used to generate questions, and in this sense they function as possible "traps" for the unwary test taker.

Traps of Similarities and Distinctions

These sections of text discuss in detail items that have both similarities and differences. By comparing and contrasting the items in a continuous section of text, the test makers create the possibility of confusion.

Trap of Separation

One of the favorite tricks of the test makers is to take related pieces of information and then physically separate those pieces by a number of lines of text that discuss a different concept. Then, in the questions, the test makers ask you a question about the concept in order to examine your ability to track related concepts in the face of unrelated (and likely confusing) information.

The Trap of Question Misdirection

This trap occurs when the test makers use a specific line reference in the question stem to direct you to a place in the passage where the correct answer will not be found.

Trap of Proximity

Just because two ideas are placed in physical proximity in a passage does not mean that they are related.

Trap of Inserted Alternate Viewpoint

Another trick of the test makers is to discuss a particular viewpoint, and then in the middle of that discussion insert a new viewpoint.

Traps of Chronology

Traps of chronology relate to the placement and order of items within the passage, and the tendency of many readers to believe that when one item is presented before another, then the first item occurred first or caused the second item. These two traps are called the Trap of Order and the Trap of Cause:

Trap of Order

Some students make the mistake of believing that because an item is discussed before another item then the first item likely predated the second item. Unless explicitly stated or inherently obvious, this does not have to be the case.

Trap of Cause

Other students make the mistake of assuming that when one item is discussed before another item, then the first item must have caused the second item. This assumption is unwarranted. The easiest way to discern the author's intentions is to carefully examine the language used by the writer because causal relationships almost always feature one or more of the words that indicate causality (such as *caused by*, *produced by*, *determined*, etc).

The simple truth is that the order of presentation of the items in the passage does not indicate any temporal or causal relationship between those items.

Passage Topic Traps

The test makers will occasionally use the topic to catch test takers off-guard. Because most students have expectations of difficulty based on topic, the test makers at times play a sort of "bait and switch" game with students, especially by making a passage initially look hard or easy and then radically changing the difficulty after the first few lines or first paragraph.

On the following pages two actual LSAT passages are presented, along with a complete analysis of each passage and all of the corresponding questions.

To most effectively benefit from this section, time yourself on the first passage. Attempt to finish the passage in 8 minutes and 45 seconds, but if you cannot, continue working until you complete all of the questions and note your time. Then, read the entire explanation section. After reviewing the first passage, proceed to the second passage and try again.

If you experience trouble with time, do not worry. At the end of the book we will discuss timing and time management.

One last note: remember that maintaining a positive attitude is critical! Approach the passages with energy and enthusiasm and you will see your performance improve.

Attempt to finish each passage in 8 minutes and 45 seconds, but if you cannot, continue working until you complete all of the questions and note your time. Then, read the corresponding explanation section.

The use of computer-generated visual displays in courtrooms is growing as awareness of their ability to recreate crime scenes spreads. Displays currently in use range from still pictures in series that mimic
(5) simple movement to sophisticated simulations based on complex applications of rules of physics and mathematics. By making it possible to slow or stop action, to vary visual perspectives according to witnesses' vantage points, or to highlight or enlarge
(10) images, computer displays provide litigators with tremendous explanatory advantages. Soon, litigators may even have available graphic systems capable of simulating three dimensions, thus creating the illusion that viewers are at the scene of a crime or accident,
(15) directly experiencing its occurrence. The advantages of computer-generated displays derive from the greater psychological impact they have on juries as compared to purely verbal presentations; studies show that people generally retain about 85 percent of visual
(20) information but only 10 percent of aural information. This is especially valuable in complex or technical trials, where juror interest and comprehension are generally low. In addition, computers also allow litigators to integrate graphic aids seamlessly into
(25) their presentations.

Despite these benefits, however, some critics are urging caution in the use of these displays, pointing to a concomitant potential for abuse or unintentional misuse, such as the unfair manipulation of a juror's
(30) impression of an event. These critics argue further that the persuasive and richly communicative nature of the displays can mesmerize jurors and cause them to relax their normal critical faculties. This potential for distortion is compounded when one side in a trial
(35) does not use the technology—often because of the considerable expense involved—leaving the jury susceptible to prejudice in favor of the side employing computer displays. And aside from the risk of intentional manipulation of images or deceitful use
(40) of capacities such as stop-action and highlighting, there is also the possibility that computer displays can be inherently misleading. As an amalgamation of data collection, judgment, and speculation, the displays may in some instances constitute evidence unsuitable
(45) for use in a trial.

To avoid misuse of this technology in the courtroom, practical steps must be taken. First, counsel must be alert to the ever-present danger of its misuse: diligent analyses of the data that form the
(50) basis for computer displays should be routinely performed and disclosed. Judges, who have the discretion to disallow displays that might unfairly prejudice one side, must also be vigilant in assessing the displays they do allow. Similarly, judges should
(55) forewarn jurors of the potentially biased nature of computer-generated evidence. Finally, steps should be taken to ensure that if one side utilizes computer technology, the opposing side will also have access to it. Granting financial aid in these circumstances
(60) would help create a more equitable legal arena in this respect.

1. Which one of the following most accurately states the main point of the passage?

(A) Those involved in court trials that take advantage of computer-generated displays as evidence need to take steps to prevent the misuse of this evidence.

(B) The use of computer-generated displays has grown dramatically in recent years because computer aids allow litigators to convey complex information more clearly.

(C) The persuasive nature of computer-generated displays requires that the rules governing the use of these displays be based on the most sophisticated principles of jurisprudence.

(D) Litigators' prudent use of computer-generated displays will result in heightened jury comprehension of complex legal issues and thus fairer trials.

(E) Any disadvantages of computer-generated visual displays can be eliminated by enacting a number of practical procedures to avoid their intentional misuse.

2. Which one of the following most accurately describes the organization of the passage?

(A) The popularity of a new technology is lamented; criticisms of the technology are voiced; corrective actions to stem its use are recommended.

(B) A new technology is endorsed; specific examples of its advantages are offered; ways to take further advantage of the technology are presented.

(C) A new technology is presented as problematic; specific problems associated with its use are discussed; alternative uses of the technology are proposed.

(D) A new technology is introduced as useful; potential problems associated with its use are identified; recommendations for preventing these problems are offered.

(E) A new technology is described in detail; arguments for and against its use are voiced; recommendations for promoting the widespread use of the technology are advanced.

3. As described in the passage, re-creating an accident with a computer-generated display is most similar to which one of the following?

(A) using several of a crime suspect's statements together to suggest that the suspect had a motive

(B) using an author's original manuscript to correct printing errors in the current edition of her novel

(C) using information gathered from satellite images to predict the development of a thunderstorm

(D) using a video camera to gather opinions of passersby for use in a candidate's political campaign advertisements

(E) using detailed geological evidence to design a museum exhibit depicting a recent volcanic eruption

4. Based on the passage, with which one of the following statements regarding the use of computer displays in courtroom proceedings would the author be most likely to agree?

(A) The courts should suspend the use of stop-action and highlighting techniques until an adequate financial aid program has been established.

(B) Computer-generated evidence should be scrutinized to ensure that it does not rely on excessive speculation in depicting the details of an event.

(C) Actual static photographs of a crime scene are generally more effective as displays than are computer displays.

(D) Verbal accounts by eyewitnesses to crimes should play a more vital role in the presentation of evidence than should computer displays.

(E) Computer displays based on insufficient or inaccurate input of data would not seem realistic and would generally not persuade jurors effectively.

5. The author states which one of the following about computer displays used in trial proceedings?

(A) Despite appearances, computer displays offer few practical advantages over conventional forms of evidence.

(B) Most critics of computer-generated evidence argue for banning such evidence in legal proceedings.

(C) Judges should forewarn jurors of the potentially biased nature of computer-generated displays.

(D) Computer displays are used primarily in technical trials, in which jury interest is naturally low.

(E) Litigators who utilize computer-generated displays must ensure that the opposing side has equal access to such technology.

6. The author mentions each of the following as an advantage of using computer displays in courtroom proceedings EXCEPT:

(A) They enable litigators to slow or stop action.
(B) They can aid jurors in understanding complex or technical information.
(C) They make it possible to vary visual perspectives.
(D) They allow litigators to integrate visual materials smoothly into their presentations.
(E) They prevent litigators from engaging in certain kinds of unjustified speculation.

One of the intriguing questions considered by anthropologists concerns the purpose our early ancestors had in first creating images of the world around them. Among these images are 25,000-year-
(5) old cave paintings made by the Aurignacians, a people who supplanted the Neanderthals in Europe and who produced the earliest known examples of representational art. Some anthropologists see these paintings as evidence that the Aurignacians had a
(10) more secure life than the Neanderthals. No one under constant threat of starvation, the reasoning goes, could afford time for luxuries such as art; moreover, the art is, in its latter stages at least, so astonishingly well-executed by almost any standard of excellence
(15) that it is highly unlikely it was produced by people who had not spent a great deal of time perfecting their skills. In other words, the high level of quality suggests that Aurignacian art was created by a distinct group of artists, who would likely have spent
(20) most of their time practicing and passing on their skills while being supported by other members of their community.

Curiously, however, the paintings were usually placed in areas accessible only with extreme effort
(25) and completely unilluminated by natural light. This makes it unlikely that these representational cave paintings arose simply out of a love of beauty or pride in artistry—had aesthetic enjoyment been the sole purpose of the paintings, they would presumably
(30) have been located where they could have been easily seen and appreciated.

Given that the Aurignacians were hunter-gatherers and had to cope with the practical problems of extracting a living from a difficult environment, many
(35) anthropologists hypothesize that the paintings were also intended to provide a means of ensuring a steady supply of food. Since it was common among pretechnological societies to believe that one can gain power over an animal by making an image of it,
(40) these anthropologists maintain that the Aurignacian paintings were meant to grant magical power over the Aurignacians' prey—typically large, dangerous animals such as mammoths and bison. The images were probably intended to make these animals
(45) vulnerable to the weapons of the hunters, an explanation supported by the fact that many of the pictures show animals with their hearts outlined in red, or with bright, arrow-shaped lines tracing paths to vital organs. Other paintings clearly show some
(50) animals as pregnant, perhaps in an effort to assure

plentiful hunting grounds. There is also evidence that ceremonies of some sort were performed before these images. Well-worn footprints of dancers can still be discerned in the clay floors of some caves, and
(55) pictures of what appear to be shamans, or religious leaders, garbed in fantastic costumes, are found among the painted animals.

1. Which one of the following most accurately describes the author's position regarding the claims attributed to anthropologists in the third paragraph?

   (A) implicit acceptance
   (B) hesitant agreement
   (C) noncommittal curiosity
   (D) detached skepticism
   (E) broad disagreement

2. The passage provides information that answers which one of the following questions?

   (A) For how long a period did the Neanderthals occupy Europe?
   (B) How long did it take for the Aurignacians to supplant the Neanderthals?
   (C) Did the Aurignacians make their homes in caves?
   (D) What are some of the animals represented in Aurignacian cave paintings?
   (E) What other prehistoric groups aside from the Aurignacians produced representational art?

3. The author would be most likely to agree with which one of the following statements?

(A) The cave paintings indicate that the Aurignacians lived a relatively secure life compared to most other hunter-gatherer cultures.

(B) Skill in art was essential to becoming an Aurignacian shaman.

(C) Prehistoric hunter-gatherers did not create any art solely for aesthetic purposes.

(D) All art created by the Aurignacians was intended to grant magical power over other beings.

(E) The Aurignacians sought to gain magical power over their prey by means of ceremonial acts in addition to painted images.

4. The author mentions the relative inaccessibility of the Aurignacian cave paintings primarily to

(A) stress the importance of the cave paintings to the lives of the artists who painted them by indicating the difficulties they had to overcome to do so

(B) lay the groundwork for a fuller explanation of the paintings' function

(C) suggest that only a select portion of the Aurignacian community was permitted to view the paintings

(D) help explain why the paintings are still well preserved

(E) support the argument that Aurignacian artists were a distinct and highly skilled group

5. The passage suggests that the author would be most likely to agree with which one of the following claims about the Aurignacians?

(A) They were technologically no more advanced than the Neanderthals they supplanted.

(B) They were the first humans known to have worn costumes for ceremonial purposes.

(C) They had established some highly specialized social roles.

(D) They occupied a less hostile environment than the Neanderthals did.

(E) They carved images of their intended prey on their weapons to increase the weapons' efficacy.

Practice Passage I—June 2006 Passage #1 Answer Key

On the following pages you will find both practice passages, replicated and notated, each followed by an outline of the passage and complete explanations of the questions. Keep in mind that these notations are meant to provide examples—your markings will probably not look exactly like the ones below; your focus should be on the general effectiveness of your notation and outlining approach.

The use of computer-generated visual displays in courtrooms is growing as awareness of their ability to recreate crime scenes spreads. Displays currently in use range from still pictures in series that mimic
(5) simple movement to sophisticated simulations based on complex applications of rules of physics and mathematics. By making it possible to slow or stop action, to vary visual perspectives according to witnesses' vantage points, or to highlight or enlarge
(10) images, computer displays provide litigators with tremendous explanatory advantages. Soon, litigators may even have available graphic systems capable of simulating three dimensions, thus creating the illusion that viewers are at the scene of a crime or accident,
(15) directly experiencing its occurrence. The advantages of computer-generated displays derive from the greater psychological impact they have on juries as compared to purely verbal presentations; studies show that people generally retain about 85 percent of visual
(20) information but only 10 percent of aural information. This is especially valuable in complex or technical trials, where juror interest and comprehension are generally low. In addition, computers also allow litigators to integrate graphic aids seamlessly into
(25) their presentations.

Despite these benefits, however, some critics are urging caution in the use of these displays, pointing to a concomitant potential for abuse or unintentional misuse, such as the unfair manipulation of a juror's
(30) impression of an event. These critics argue further that the persuasive and richly communicative nature of the displays can mesmerize jurors and cause them to relax their normal critical faculties. This potential for distortion is compounded when one side in a trial
(35) does not use the technology—often because of the considerable expense involved—leaving the jury susceptible to prejudice in favor of the side employing computer displays. And aside from the risk of intentional manipulation of images or deceitful use
(40) of capacities such as stop-action and highlighting, there is also the possibility that computer displays can be inherently misleading. As an amalgamation of data collection, judgment, and speculation, the displays may in some instances constitute evidence unsuitable
(45) for use in a trial.

To avoid misuse of this technology in the courtroom, practical steps must be taken. First, counsel must be alert to the ever-present danger of its misuse: diligent analyses of the data that form the
(50) basis for computer displays should be routinely

performed and disclosed. Judges, who have the discretion to disallow displays that might unfairly prejudice one side, must also be vigilant in assessing the displays they do allow. Similarly judges should
(55) forewarn jurors of the potentially biased nature of computer-generated evidence. Finally steps should be taken to ensure that if one side utilizes computer technology, the opposing side will also have access to it. Granting financial aid in these circumstances
(60) would help create a more equitable legal arena in this respect.

Displays'
Explanatory
Advantages:
① to slow or stop
② to vary visual perspectives
③ to highlight or enlarge

CC

V_{SC}

*Potential
Problems*

V_{AUTH}
Steps to avoid misuse:
①

② (Similarly)
③ (Finally)

Paragraph One:

This passage begins with a presentation of facts from the author. Computer-generated visual displays are effective at recreating crime scenes, so they are becoming more widely used, in forms ranging from still pictures to complex simulations. These visual aids (soon available in 3-D) provide significant advantages, since people only retain 10% of what they hear, versus 85% of what they see, and trials are often complicated and uninteresting to jurors. Visual displays can be seamlessly integrated into a litigator's presentation.

Paragraph Two:

Having outlined the benefits of these displays, the author turns to the subject of potential for abuse, shifting to the viewpoint of "some critics," who warn that mesmerizing displays might throw off the jury's reasoning abilities, especially in a long, boring trial. The critics are also concerned that these displays are potentially unfair when only presented on one side of the argument, since juries might tend to be prejudiced in favor of the side with the visual displays. Displays that require too much speculation would be unsuitable for trial.

Paragraph Three:

In this paragraph the passage shifts to the author's viewpoint, that the following list of steps must be taken to avoid misuse:

1. Lawyers must avoid misuse of computer visual displays by analyzing and disclosing data used, and judges must prohibit prejudicial displays and analyze admissible ones.
2. Judges should forewarn jurors of the potential for bias.
3. Computer displays should be accessible to both sides; financial aid may ensure this.

VIEWSTAMP Analysis:

The **Viewpoints** presented in this passage are those of "some critics urging caution," (line 26) and the perspective of the author, who agrees with those critics about the need for prudence.

The **Structure** of this passage is as follows:

Paragraph One: Introduce the concept of computer-generated visual displays, and discuss several advantages associated with their seamless presentation and visual nature.

Paragraph Two: Discuss the disadvantages, including potential for abuse, potential to prejudice the jury, and potentially speculative basis for some such displays.

Paragraph Three: Provide three steps that must be taken to avoid misuse of the displays: analyze the data, prohibit prejudicial use, forewarn juries, and allow access to both sides.

The author's **Tone** is even-handed, discussing both pros and cons, but certainly cautionary with regard to court use of computer displays.

The main **Argument** in this passage is that these displays, though advantageous, should be used prudently in the court system to ensure equitability.

The **Main Point** of this passage is that these computer displays provide some advantage, but we must guard against their misuse.

Question #1: GR, Main Point. The Correct answer is (A)

We already know the Main Point, so this question should be relatively straightforward.

Answer choice (A): This is the correct answer choice. Those who make use of the advantages must guard against potential for abuse.

Answer choice (B): This statement does not reflect the main point of the passage, and we cannot even confirm its accuracy based on the passage; the author says that use of the displays is growing, but nothing about dramatic growth.

Answer choice (C): The author believes that the legal community should guard against abuse, but says nothing about basing rules on "the most sophisticated principles of jurisprudence."

Answer choice (D): While prudent use of the displays might increase jury comprehension, the author is concerned about the prospect for unfairness, so it would be inaccurate to claim that use of the displays would inherently result in fairer trials.

Answer choice (E): The author provides a list of steps that must be taken to guard against misuse of the visual displays, but avoidance of intentional misuse would not guarantee this outcome—the author specifies the prospect of unintentional misuse as well.

Question #2: GR, O. The correct answer choice is (D)

Again, we should seek to prephrase an answer. The organization of this passage is basically as follows: the author introduces the concept of computer visual displays, discusses advantages, possible problems, and steps to take to guard against misuse.

Answer choice (A): The popularity of the displays is not lamented; the author simply wishes to guard against their misuse. And the author does not necessarily want to stop their use, but rather to take steps to ensure proper use.

Answer choice (B): This answer choice overstates the author's perspective; the author does not endorse the displays, as much as present pros, cons, and protective measures. This answer choice does not even mention the disadvantages of the displays, which is an integral part of the passage.

Answer choice (C): The author does not discuss alternative uses of the computer visual displays, but rather suggests ways to ensure fairness in the way they are used.

Answer choice (D): This is the correct answer choice, as it restates our prephrase: new technology is introduced with pros, cons, and steps to avoid unfairness in its application.

Answer choice (E): In this passage, the author does describe a new technology, followed by a discussion of its benefits and potential problems, but this is not quite the same as arguing against its use in general. The author just believes that we need to take care in the use of visual displays. Further, the author is not necessarily interested in promoting its widespread use, but rather that the courts be prudent as the use of the displays grows in popularity.

Question #3: GR, Parallel. The correct answer choice is (E)

Here we are looking for something analogous to the use of computer generated displays, which translate information into a more visual re-creation.

Answer choice (A): Using a suspect's statements to suggest a motive does not even contain a visual component, so this is not analogous to the use of courtroom visual displays.

Answer choice (B): Using an original to correct printing errors is not parallel, because in such a case there would be no reason for concerns about accuracy or speculation. Also, there is no visual re-creation in this scenario, so this answer choice is incorrect.

Answer choice (C): This answer choice provides a scenario that involves prediction, as opposed to re-creation or representation, so this choice is not parallel.

Answer choice (D): While this answer choice does involve a visual component, this scenario does not involve a re-creation of any sort, so it is not analogous.

Answer choice (E): This is the correct answer choice. Here we have a situation where evidence is being gathered for the presentation of a visual re-creation, which is much like that created by computer-generated courtroom visual displays.

Question #4: GR, Must, AP. The correct answer choice is (B)

To answer this question, we must have a solid grasp on the author's tone, which is precautionary.

Answer choice (A): The author discusses the possible applicability of a financial aid program in the context of the newer technologies that are less accessible to those with less resources. Stop-action and highlighting would seem more broadly accessible, and the author does not discuss this matter specifically, so this answer choice is incorrect.

Answer choice (B): This is the correct answer choice. One of the reasons for caution specified by the author is the speculative content of computer-generated displays presented as evidence.

Answer choice (C): The author never makes this comparison, and in any case it seems unlikely that the author would agree with this assertion.

Answer choice (D): The author does not assert that computer displays should play a less vital role. Rather, the author is primarily concerned with the responsible use of this technology which can be used very effectively in court.

Answer choice (E): The author never discusses the persuasiveness of inaccurate data, but since the author is concerned that this evidence may be unfairly prejudicial, presumably this is based on the concern that inaccurate data could effectively persuade the jury, so this answer choice is incorrect.

Question #5: GR, Must: The correct answer choice is (C)

For a Must Be True question, we can apply the Fact Test to confirm the correct answer choice.

Answer choice (A): There is specific discussion of the possible advantages of the computer-generated visual displays, so the author would not agree with this assertion.

Answer choice (B): Critics of the technology don't necessarily want to see it banned; some just want to ensure that the courts are responsible in allowing and monitoring its use.

Answer choice (C): This is the correct answer choice. This is one of the steps the author provides in the list of steps which must be taken to avoid misuse in the courts.

Answer choice (D): The word that makes this answer choice incorrect is "primarily." We know that the computer-generated displays are used in technical trials, but the author provides no insight into how often the displays may be used in non-technical trials.

Answer choice (E): This answer choice provides a clever pitfall: the author believes in the principle of equal access to the modern displays, but does not place the burden on the litigators. The author asserts that the job of counsel (litigators) is to analyze the data and disclose findings, and it would appear to be the job of the court system to provide for financial aid and ensure equal access to the technology.

Question #6: GR, Must, X. The correct answer choice is (E)

In this Must Be True Except question, among the five answer choices, the four incorrect answer choices will be accurate based on the information in the passage, and the correct answer choice is the one that is not necessarily true.

Answer choice (A): The author mentions this advantage in line 7, so this answer choice is incorrect.

Answer choice (B): This advantage is discussed in line 21, so this accurate assertion is another incorrect answer.

Answer choice (C): This advantage is specifically mentioned in line 8 of the passage, so this answer choice is incorrect.

Answer choice (D): This is discussed at the end of the first paragraph, in lines 23-25. Since this answer choice is confirmed by the Fact Test, it must be incorrect in response to this Except question.

Answer choice (E): This is the correct answer choice. The author does not make this assertion—in fact the author is specifically concerned with the prospect of too much speculation going into the creation of the computer-generated displays. Since the assertion in this answer choice is definitely not true, this is the correct answer choice to this Must Be True Except question.

One of the intriguing questions considered by anthropologists concerns the purpose our early ancestors had in first creating images of the world around them. Among these images are 25,000-year-
(5) old cave paintings made by the Aurignacians, a people who supplanted the Neanderthals in Europe and who produced the earliest known examples of representational art. Some anthropologists see these V_{SA} paintings as evidence that the Aurignacians had a
(10) more secure life than the Neanderthals. No one under constant threat of starvation, the reasoning goes, could afford time for luxuries such as art; moreover, the art is, in its latter stages at least, so astonishingly well-executed by almost any standard of excellence
(15) that it is highly unlikely it was produced by people who had not spent a great deal of time perfecting their skills. In other words, the high level of quality suggests that Aurignacian art was created by a distinct group of artists, who would likely have spent
(20) most of their time practicing and passing on their skills while being supported by other members of their community.

Curiously however, the paintings were usually V_A placed in areas accessible only with extreme effort
(25) and completely unilluminated by natural light. This makes it unlikely that these representational cave paintings arose simply out of a love of beauty or pride in artistry—had aesthetic enjoyment been the sole purpose of the paintings, they would presumably
(30) have been located where they could have been easily seen and appreciated.

Aesthetics not the only reason

Given that the Aurignacians were hunter-gatherers and had to cope with the practical problems of extracting a living from a difficult environment, many V_{MA}
(35) anthropologists hypothesize that the paintings were also intended to provide a means of ensuring a steady supply of food. Since it was common among pretechnological societies to believe that one can gain power over an animal by making an image of it,
(40) these anthropologists maintain that the Aurignacian paintings were meant to grant magical power over the] MP Aurignacians' prey—typically large, dangerous animals such as mammoths and bison. The images ex. were probably intended to make these animals
(45) vulnerable to the weapons of the hunters, an explanation supported by the fact that many of the pictures show animals with their hearts outlined in red, or with bright, arrow-shaped lines tracing paths to vital organs. Other paintings clearly show some
(50) animals as pregnant, perhaps in an effort to assure plentiful hunting grounds. There is also evidence that ceremonies of some sort were performed before these images. Well-worn footprints of dancers can still be discerned in the clay floors of some caves, and
(55) pictures of what appear to be shamans, or religious leaders, garbed in fantastic costumes, are found among the painted animals.

Paragraph One:

The author begins this science passage with a factual, viewpoint-neutral tone, introducing the anthropological question of why our early ancestors created artistic images of their world. The Aurignacians, who emerged in Europe after the Neanderthals, created the first known representational art in cave paintings 25,000 years ago. At line 8, the author shifts to the viewpoint of "some anthropologists," who claim that the art speaks to the Aurignacians' secure environment, since they were able to focus on something beyond survival.

Paragraph Two:

In this paragraph the author presents evidence which weighs against artistic appreciation as the driving force of the cave paintings. Since the paintings were placed inaccessibly in unlit caves, it seems unlikely that aesthetic concern was the sole purpose for the creation of the cave paintings.

Paragraph Three:

In the final paragraph the author presents the viewpoint of "many anthropologists." The Aurignacians did have a difficult living environment, so they may have created the paintings to ensure a steady food supply; like other pretechnological societies, the Aurignacians may have believed that creation of an animal's image gives one power over that animal. This assertion is supported by images of animals being killed, images of pregnant animals, and evidence of ceremonial dances, which included costumed religious figures and took place near the cave paintings.

VIEWSTAMP Analysis:

These are the three **Viewpoints** presented in the passage: Those of "some anthropologists," discussed in the first paragraph, who believe that the cave paintings spoke to the Aurignacians' secure lifestyle; that of the author, who uses the second paragraph to question this belief; and the perspective of "many anthropologists," discussed in the third paragraph, who think the paintings were meant to gain power over the animals depicted.

The **Structure** of the passage is as follows:

> Paragraph One: Introduce question of why early peoples created images, and the first known representational art, the Aurignacians' cave paintings. Discuss hypothesis that such art reflects a secure lifestyle.

> Paragraph Two: Point out that the cave paintings were poorly lit and inaccessible, so aesthetics were probably not their primary purpose.

> Paragraph Three: Discuss the possibility that the paintings were intended to gain power over the animals depicted.

The author's **Tone** is somewhat academic, considering and then dismissing one hypothesis in favor of a different explanation for the cave paintings.

The **Arguments** in the passage are those of the first group of anthropologists mentioned, who assert that the cave paintings meant security, that of the author, who presents evidence to refute the notion that the paintings were purely aesthetic, and that of the second group of anthropologists, who believe they were meant to bring power.

The **Main Point** of the passage is to discuss what may have caused the Aurignacians to create the first known representational art; it was probably not aesthetics (they were low-lit and not readily accessible), but rather the Aurignacians' efforts to gain power over the animals depicted in the paintings.

Question #1: SR, Must, AP. The correct answer choice is (A)

To answer this question, it is helpful to have recognized the author's tone with regard to the various hypotheses. The author appears to agree with the reasoning of the anthropologists discussed in the third paragraph.

Answer choice (A): This is the correct answer choice. The author presents the hypothesis of "many anthropologists" at the beginning of the third paragraph, provides their evidence, takes a supportive tone, and never questions the validity of their argument. This is implicit acceptance.

Answer choice (B): The author does not appear hesitant to agree with the anthropologists, but rather supportive of their beliefs, so this answer choice is incorrect.

Answer choice (C): "Non-committal" does not describe the tone here; the author appears to agree with the reasoning of the anthropologists discussed in the third paragraph, so this answer choice is incorrect.

Answer choice (D): The author is skeptical about the theory in the first paragraph, but with regard to the anthropologists discussed in the third paragraph the author is neither detached nor skeptical.

Answer choice (E): Broad disagreement is certainly not reflected by the author in the third paragraph of this passage; the author appears to agree with the hypothesis and the supporting evidence, so this answer choice is incorrect.

Question #2: GR, Must. The correct answer choice is (D)

Answer choice (A): Although the author tells us that the Aurignacians supplanted the Neanderthals, the length of the Neanderthals' occupation of Europe is never discussed in the passage.

Answer choice (B): Again, the author mentions this supplanting, but does not specify how long it took, so this answer choice is incorrect.

Answer choice (C): The images discussed in the passage were created in caves, but the author never discusses whether or not the Aurignacians lived in caves.

Answer choice (D): This is the correct answer choice. In lines 42-43, the author tells us that some of the animals represented were large, dangerous animals such as mammoths and bison.

Answer choice (E): The only representational art discussed in the passage is that of the Aurignacians, the earliest known creators of such images. Since the author provides no information about other artistic prehistoric groups, this answer choice is incorrect.

Question #3: GR, AP. The correct answer choice is (E)

Answer choice (A): The first group of anthropologists, discussed in the opening paragraph, make this hypothesis, but the author appears to disagree, providing evidence to the contrary in the second paragraph.

Answer choice (B): The author maintains that the creators of the cave paintings were highly skilled, but these artists were not necessarily the same people as the shaman discussed in the last paragraph of the passage, so this answer choice is incorrect.

Answer choice (C): The word that makes this answer choice incorrect is "any." The author doesn't go so far as to say that *no* art was created for solely aesthetic reasons, only that the cave paintings' placement suggest that *they* weren't created just for artistic enjoyment.

Answer choice (D): Again, one word takes this question out of contention: "all." The discussion in the passage is limited to the cave paintings, and the author makes no such broad assertions regarding "all art" that the people created.

Answer choice (E): This is the correct answer choice. This answer choice is supported by the third paragraph of the passage, and discussed as a likely reason for the creation of the cave paintings.

Question #4: CR, Must. The correct answer choice is (B)

This is another question conducive to prephrasing, so we should try to get a good idea of the answer before considering the choices provided. In this case, the author discusses the relative inaccessibility of the cave paintings to show that they were probably not produced solely for artistic appreciation, leading to another explanation of what drove the Aurignacians to create the images.

Answer choice (A): The author does not delve into the personal lives of the artists, beyond mentioning the likelihood that these people apparently made up a distinct group in the Aurignacian society.

Answer choice (B): This is the correct answer choice, and is perfectly aligned with our prephrase. The author mentions the inaccessibility in order to set the stage for the alternative explanation that the images were created as part of the Aurignacians' ceremonial efforts to master their prey.

Answer choice (C): There is no suggestion that any segment of the Aurignacian society was prohibited from seeing the paintings—only that the images were placed in unlit, relatively inaccessible places.

Answer choice (D): While the placement of the paintings does provide a reasonable explanation for their preservation, this is not what led the author to discuss their placement, so this answer choice is incorrect.

Answer choice (E): The author does believe that the artists were a distinct group, but this is based on the quality of the work, and has nothing to do with the author's discussion of inaccessibility.

Question #5: GR, Must, AP. The correct answer choice is (C)

Answer choice (A): While both groups may have been nontechnological societies, the author makes no comparison of the technological advancement of the two groups. We know that the Aurignacians supplanted the Neanderthals, but that does not provide information about their respective technological advances, so this answer choice is incorrect.

Answer choice (B): The author does not assert that the Aurignacians were the first humans known to wear costumes for ceremonies, but rather that they were the first to create representational art. No information is provided concerning whether the Aurignacians' costumed ceremonies were preceded by such ceremonies in other cultures.

Answer choice (C): This is the correct answer choice. The author does support the belief that the artists played a distinct role, based on the level of excellence of the art, so this answer choice is supported by the information in the passage.

Answer choice (D): This is the assertion of the anthropologists discussed in the first paragraph of the passage. The author goes on to discuss the inaccessibility of the cave paintings to show that they were not necessarily reflective of a more secure lifestyle, but of a desire to gain power over their prey.

Answer choice (E): Weapon carving is not discussed in the passage, so this answer does not pass the Fact Test, and is incorrect.

CHAPTER SEVEN: COMPARATIVE READING PASSAGES

Dual Passages

In the first six chapters of this book we have focused on single passages. We now turn our attention to the dual passages—also known as Comparative Reading passages—that also occur on the LSAT.

Starting with the June 2007 LSAT, the makers of the test introduced the dual passage format to the exam, and every LSAT now features one dual passage set per section. The dual passage set can appear anywhere within the section (first, second, third, or last), and, as with single passages, the number of questions varies from five to eight.

Dual passages are very similar to the single passages, but rather than present just one selection from a single author, two passages are given on a similar or related subject (by two separate authors, generally with different points of view). Comparative reading sets are also distinguished from the other three single passages because the two passages in comparative reading are labeled, "**Passage A**" and "**Passage B**," respectively. Cumulatively, the two passages in comparative reading are also roughly the same length as a single standard reading comprehension passage (approximately 500 words) and line numbering occurs in the same way for all of the passages on the test, with line number references every five lines. The line numbering does not restart for the second passage, but continues on from the first passage.

The first thing that you should keep in mind when approaching comparative reading is that the strategies that you have learned thus far for the single passages still apply extremely well to the dual passages. That is, you must still read both comparative reading passages for ideas like viewpoints, tone, argumentation, main point, and general passage structure and function. Although the two passages in a dual set will differ somewhat from one another, the approach that you have taken towards the single passages— reading the passage first, making relevant notations within the passage, reading aggressively for viewpoints and main point ideas—will serve you quite well in comparative reading. In fact, many students find that they enjoy the dual passage format more than the single passage format, as the two passages provide a more complete and balanced perspective on the topic being discussed. This typically leads to a better understanding of the passages presented and, consequently, a better performance on the questions that follow. In addition, because each passage is shorter, the complexity of the arguments developed within each passage tends to be less than in single passages, and thus most students find that the reading itself is easier.

Comparative Reading passages were first introduced on the June 2007 LSAT.

All of the strategies we discussed in the single passage section apply to Comparative Reading.

As you read the passages, remember that they will relate to each other in various ways. As the test makers recently stated, "In some cases, the authors of the passages will be in general agreement with each other, while in others their views will be directly opposed. Passage pairs may also exhibit more complex types of relationships: for example, one passage might articulate a set of principles, while the other passage applies those or similar principles to a particular situation." Clearly the primary goal for comparative reading is to identify the main point and viewpoints of each passage and then to relate those ideas to each other, focusing on the passages' similarities and differences. Let's take a moment now to analyze those similarities and differences.

Similarities between Comparative Reading Passage Sets and Single Passages

- General reading strategy remains the same

- Difficulty of the subject matter is the same for single and dual passages, and the subject matter will be drawn from the same disciplines: humanities, social sciences, biological and physical sciences, and issues related to law

- Dual passage length and the number of questions that follow the passages are comparable to those of a single passage, so the total amount of reading is similar

- Difficulty of the questions is roughly the same for single and dual passages

- Question types are generally similar to those seen in the single passages, however the emphasis is more on global questions (main point, author's attitude, function) and passage relationship questions in comparative reading

- The same type of reading traps appear in both types of passages

- Questions should be answered exclusively on the basis of the information provided in the selection(s); no specific, subject-based knowledge is necessary

- Single and dual passages can all be diagrammed in the same ways

Differences between Comparative Reading Passage Sets and Single Passages

- There are two related passages in comparative reading as opposed to a single passage

- Two authors contribute to the reading selection in comparative reading, while single passage selections are drawn from only one author

- The majority of the comparative reading questions deal with the relationship between the two passages, while single passage questions tend to have a higher percentage of local questions

- The theme or main point of the comparative reading passages will often change from passage A to passage B, as opposed to the more consistent, singular purpose of an author in a single passage

- The ability to compare and contrast is paramount to success in comparative reading; success in singular passage reading comprehension is largely dependent upon a reader's ability to identify passage structure and organization

- The complexity of argumentation in each of the dual passages tends to be less than the complexity developed in a single passage. This is logical because there are fewer words in each of the individual dual passages

Passage Diagramming

You can use the same system of markings and notations for the dual passages as you used with the single passages. Simply recognize that there are two passages instead of one, and thus there will be two author's viewpoints, two main points, etc.

The diagramming system we discussed in the single passage section applies to Comparative Reading as well.

One additional strategy that some students have found helpful (especially those struggling with the Reading Comprehension section), particularly as they practice comparative reading before test day, is to make two columns in the small space available in the lower margin of their test booklet: the first column for Similarities, and the second column for Differences. If used, this diagram allows you to write out the various points on which the passages agree and disagree, and better delineate the sometimes subtle differences on which the questions tend to focus.

Comparative Reading Question Types

The questions in Comparative Reading passage sets tend to focus less on the detailed question indicators found in single passages—such as specific examples, new terms or phrases, lists, etc.—and more on broader, holistic ideas—main points, author's tone and opinion, and passage relationships.

Before examining the question types that appear specifically in the dual passage sets, it is important to note that all of the question types that appear in the single passage sets can and do appear in Comparative Reading. Thus, the list below should be considered to additionally include all of the question types discussed in Chapter Five.

Comparative Reading-Specific Questions

The hallmark of Comparative Reading-specific questions is that they ask about the relationship between the two passages. This makes sense because you have been presented the two passages for a reason, namely to test your ability to understand the connection between the two passages, including their similarities and differences. Hence, all of the questions in these sets can be classified based on whether they ask about both passages (passage commonality), just one passage (passage exclusivity), or the passages combined together (passage aggregate). Let us examine all three classifications in detail:

Passage Commonality™ Questions (PC)

Because there are two passages, the question types tend to focus on the relationship between the two passages.

Frequency of all Comparative Reading Questions: 72%

The most frequently appearing question type is known as Passage Commonality. These questions ask you to identify themes, viewpoints, and other elements that appear in *both* passages. Here are several question stem examples:

> "Both passages were written primarily in order to answer which one of the following questions?"

> "Each of the two passages mentions the relation of music to"

The Fact Test™ states:

The correct answer to a Must Be True question can always be proven by referring to the facts stated in the passage.

> "Which one of the following principles underlies the arguments in both passages?"

Although the exact nature of each of the above question examples is different (one is a Purpose question, one is a Principle question, etc.), the function of each question is to ask you to find an element that is common to both passages. To successfully solve these questions, you must use the statements of each passage to identify the answer that appears in both. That is, you must use the Fact Test. Passage Commonality questions are thus a variant of the Must Be True questions we are already very familiar with from earlier chapters.

While solving Passage Commonality questions should be a relatively straightforward and clear process, the test makers do have some answer choice traps in their arsenal. The following are three ways the test makers attempt to trap you in Passage Commonality questions:

1. The item appears in Passage A only

    This is the most dangerous of the three traps because some students, upon finding the information in Passage A, then only quickly glance at Passage B to see if it too contains the same information. With only a cursory review of Passage B, these students are far more likely to fall for an answer that is not fully supported by Passage B. Remember, the correct answer to a Passage Commonality question must appear in *both* passages.

2. The item appears in Passage B only

    This trap is the same as #1, but the information appears in Passage B only.

3. The item appears in neither passage

    Although this may seem like an easy answer choice to avoid, the test makers are savvy, and they present answers that relate to the topic at hand but are not actually discussed in either passage. Thus, at first glance, these answers look like possible candidates because they could seemingly follow from the discussion, but on second glance no supporting evidence is found in either passage for the answer choice.

If you focus on the fact that the correct answer to every Passage Commonality question must appear in *both* passages, you will find these questions very manageable. Simply find the evidence in each passage and then proceed.

While the majority of Passage Commonality questions can be proven by referring directly to the details of the passage, a small subset ask you to focus on the broad, abstract relationship between the two passages. These questions are known as Passage Relationship questions.

Passage Relationship Questions (PRel)

Frequency of all Comparative Reading Questions: 26%

Passage Relationship questions ask you to identify the abstract relationship between part or all of each passage. While these questions are a variant of the Passage Commonality questions just discussed, they are an abstract version.

To analogize these questions to Logical Reasoning questions, regular Passage Commonality questions are like Must Be True questions, whereas Passage Relationship questions are like Method of Reasoning questions. Both question types come from the same family, but one focuses on the details whereas the other is focused on broad, abstract concepts. Here are two examples:

"Which one of the following most accurately characterizes a relationship between the two passages?"

"Which one of the following most accurately describes a way in which the two passages are related to each other?"

To answer these questions, you must still use the Fact Test, but you must use it to identify the abstract elements described in each answer choice.

Additionally, two other Passage Commonality question types are based on the views of each author:

Author Agreement (AA)

Frequency of all Comparative Reading Questions: 8%

As you note the similarities and differences between the two passages, you should also be tracking the points of agreement and disagreement between the two authors. Author Agreement questions ask you to identify points of agreement between the authors, as in the following examples:

"The authors would be most likely to agree on the answer to which one of the following questions regarding musical capacity in humans?"

"It can be inferred from the passages that the authors believe that the increase constraint on access to scientific information and ideas arises from"

"It can be inferred from the passages that both authors hold which one of the following views?"

To ensure that you are prepared to attack such questions, remember to read the comparative reading passages actively: Pause and assess what you have read, including the similarities and differences between the two authors' perspectives, before moving on to the questions.

Author Disagreement (AD)

Frequency of all Comparative Reading Questions: 8%

When the authors of the two passages display divergent perspectives, draw different conclusions, or make contrary assertions, it is a good idea to track the points of contention. Author Disagreement questions ask you to identify differences in the attitudes, assertions, and conclusions of the two authors. Here are several examples of such question stems:

> "It can be inferred that the authors of the two passages would be most likely to disagree over whether"

> "The author of passage B would be most likely to make which one of the following criticisms about the predictions cited in passage A concerning a rise in sea level"

> "The authors of the two passages would be most likely to disagree over"

These questions are similar to Point at Issue questions, which are a variation of Must Be True/Author's Perspective questions. Thus, you can use the Agree/Disagree Test™ on those questions you feel you cannot solve in any other manner.

Remember, in order to successfully attack this question type, it is vital that you have a solid understanding of the respective tones used by the two authors.

Passage Exclusivity™ Questions (PE)

Frequency of all Comparative Reading Questions: 13%

Passage Exclusivity questions ask about information contained in only one of the two passages, such as:

> "Which one of the following most accurately expresses the main point of passage A?"

> "Which one of the following is discussed in passage B but not in passage A?"

Thus, these questions are the same exact questions as those that occur in the single passage sets. Occasionally, some of these questions will specifically ask you to exclude the other passage from consideration, but then, of course, you are still focused on the information contained in the cited passage.

The Agree/ Disagree Test is an advanced technique used for solving Point at Issue questions in the Logical Reasoning section. The technique can be used on applicable Reading Comprehension questions as well.

The test makers have two types of wrong answer choices that appear frequently in these questions:

1. The item appears in the other passage

   Under the pressure of the test, many students confuse the information in one passage for the information in the other passage. Passage Exclusivity questions are well-placed to expose this mistake, and the answer choices are designed to see if you will mix up the contents of each passage. While confusing the contents of the two passages is understandable, you can avoid this error by tightly tracking the five major VIEWSTAMP elements discussed in Chapter Two.

2. The item appears in neither passage

   Although this may seem like an easy answer choice to avoid, the test makers are savvy, and they present answers that relate to the topic in the specifically-referenced passage but that are not actually discussed in that passage. Thus, at first glance, these answers look like possible candidates because they could seemingly follow from the discussion, but on second glance no supporting evidence is found in the named passage for the answer choice.

By focusing on the passage specifically referenced in the question stem, you can avoid the two traps above.

Passage Aggregate™ Questions (PA)

Frequency of all Comparative Reading Questions: 13%

Passage Aggregate questions require you to treat the two passages as one.

Passage Aggregate questions ask you to consider the information from two passages in combination, or in the aggregate. In this sense, these questions ask you to treat the two passages as one whole passage. Here are several question stem examples:

> "Which one of the following can be most reasonably inferred from the two passages taken together, but not from either individually?"

> "Each of the following is supported by one or both of the passages EXCEPT:"

> "Together, the two passages disprove which one of the following assertions?"

Although these questions may initially appear intimidating, they are actually quite easy because the test makers are taking away the separating wall between the two authors. With this separating point removed, to attack these questions you can simply use the techniques discussed in the single passage sections.

One Special Consideration

In the final analysis, Comparative Reading questions are the same as single passage set questions, with the difference that the emphasis is on how well you can understand the similarities and differences between the two passages. All of the questions in these passages in some way test your ability to compare and contrast the two passages. With this in mind, we cannot overstress the importance of keeping track of the two passages, and knowing precisely where they are alike and where they differ. Within our passage explanations we will highlight the importance of making this comparison by setting aside the normal VIEWSTAMP analysis in favor of a similarities and differences analysis to help you better understand the crucial nature of this idea.

You must be aware of how the passages are similar and how they differ.

If you have any concern that you might become confused by the similarity between the two passages, then pause briefly after reading Passage A to organize your thoughts about what you have just read. Once you have taken a moment to ensure that you are comfortable with the information from the first passage, move on to Passage B and read with the intention of establishing the relationship between the approach and attitude of both authors.

A Comparative Reading Passage Analyzed ██████████████████

On the following page an actual LSAT Comparative Reading passage is presented, along with a complete analysis of the passage and all of the corresponding questions.

To most effectively benefit from this section, time yourself on the passages. Attempt to finish the passage in 8 minutes and 45 seconds, but if you cannot, continue working until you complete all of the questions and note your time. While reading, remember to look for the VIEWSTAMP elements within each passage, but concentrate equally on the similarities and differences between the two passages as those will be the focus of the questions. Then, read the entire explanation section and consider what elements you missed, and what you need to do to improve. Within the passage analysis we will directly discuss the passage similarities and differences.

If you experience trouble with time, do not worry. At the end of the book we will discuss timing and time management.

The passages discuss relationships between business interests and university research.

Passage A

As university researchers working in a "gift economy" dedicated to collegial sharing of ideas, we have long been insulated from market pressures. The
(5) recent tendency to treat research findings as commodities, tradable for cash, threatens this tradition and the role of research as a public good.

The nurseries for new ideas are traditionally universities, which provide an environment uniquely suited to the painstaking testing and revision of
(10) theories. Unfortunately, the market process and values governing commodity exchange are ill suited to the cultivation and management of new ideas. With their shareholders impatient for quick returns, businesses are averse to wide-ranging experimentation. And, what
(15) is even more important, few commercial enterprises contain the range of expertise needed to handle the replacement of shattered theoretical frameworks.

Further, since entrepreneurs usually have little affinity for adventure of the intellectual sort, they can
(20) buy research and bury its products, hiding knowledge useful to society or to their competitors. The growth of industrial biotechnology, for example, has been accompanied by a reduction in the free sharing of research methods and results-a high price to pay for
(25) the undoubted benefits of new drugs and therapies.

Important new experimental results once led university scientists to rush down the hall and share their excitement with colleagues. When instead the rush is to patent lawyers and venture capitalists, I
(30) worry about the long-term future of scientific discovery.

Passage B

The fruits of pure science were once considered primarily a public good, available for society as a whole. The argument for this view was that most of
(35) these benefits were produced through government support of universities, and thus no individual was entitled to restrict access to them.

Today, however, the critical role of science in the modern "information economy" means that what was
(40) previously seen as a public good is being transformed into a market commodity. For example, by exploiting the information that basic research has accumulated about the detailed structures of cells and genes, the biotechnology industry can derive profitable
(45) pharmaceuticals or medical screening technologies. In this context, assertion of legal claims to "intellectual property"-not just in commercial products but in the underlying scientific knowledge-becomes crucial.

Previously, the distinction between a scientific
(50) "discovery" (which could not be patented) and a technical "invention" (which could) defined the limits of industry's ability to patent something. Today, however, the speed with which scientific discoveries can be turned into products and the large profits
(55) resulting from this transformation have led to a blurring of both the legal distinction between discovery and invention and the moral distinction between what should and should not be patented.

Industry argues that if it has supported-either in
(60) its own laboratories or in a university-the makers of a scientific discovery, then it is entitled to seek a return on its investment, either by charging others for using the discovery or by keeping it for its own exclusive use.

15. Which one of the following is discussed in passage B but not in passage A?

(A) the blurring of the legal distinction between discovery and invention
(B) the general effects of the market on the exchange of scientific knowledge
(C) the role of scientific research in supplying public goods
(D) new pharmaceuticals that result from industrial research
(E) industry's practice of restricting access to research findings

16. Both passages place in opposition the members of which one of the following pairs?

(A) commercially successful research and commercially unsuccessful research
(B) research methods and research results
(C) a marketable commodity and a public good
(D) a discovery and an invention
(E) scientific research and other types of inquiry

17. Both passages refer to which one of the following?

   (A)   theoretical frameworks
   (B)   venture capitalists
   (C)   physics and chemistry
   (D)   industrial biotechnology
   (E)   shareholders

18. It can be inferred from the passages that the authors believe that the increased constraint on access to scientific information and ideas arises from

   (A)   the enormous increase in the volume of scientific knowledge that is being generated
   (B)   the desire of individual researchers to receive credit for their discoveries
   (C)   the striving of commercial enterprises to gain a competitive advantage in the market
   (D)   moral reservations about the social impact of some scientific research
   (E)   a drastic reduction in government funding for university research

19. Which one of the following statements is most strongly supported by both passages?

   (A)   Many scientific researchers who previously worked in universities have begun to work in the biotechnology industry.
   (B)   Private biotechnology companies have invalidly patented the basic research findings of university researchers.
   (C)   Because of the nature of current scientific research, patent authorities no longer consider the distinction between discoveries and inventions to be clear-cut.
   (D)   In the past, scientists working in industry had free access to the results of basic research conducted in universities.
   (E)   Government-funded research in universities has traditionally been motivated by the goals of private industry.

As with most Comparative Reading passages, we have two authors taking different tones in their discussions of the same general topic: the transformation that has taken place in the way research is developed and brought to market. The first author fears the ramifications of these changes, while the second is more accepting of the increasing role of industry in science's commoditization.

Your job as a reader is to first get a clear picture of Passage A. Let's take a moment to analyze the four paragraphs of **Passage A**:

Paragraph One: The author—who is apparently a university researcher, as indicated by the "we"—states that researchers have long been insulated from market pressures. The author now believes that this tradition has been threatened by the recent tendency to treat research findings like commodities that can be traded for cash. There is some clear tone in this initial paragraph: the author is a traditionalist who yearns for the old days, when universities worked toward the sharing of ideas, in service of the common good.

Paragraph Two: In this paragraph, the author continues the argument for universities as the ideal developers of new ideas: cultivation of new ideas, the author argues, is uniquely suited to universities. The latter half of this paragraph introduces two of the reasons the author believes businesses are ill-suited to the cultivation and management of new ideas, namely that the market is impatient with experimentation, desiring quick returns on investment and few businesses are expert enough to suggest new theories when old ones are disproved.

Paragraph Three: Here the author presents another problem—the entrepreneur's incentive to bury information that is potentially useful to the competition. We are also provided with the example of the biotech industry, which has developed new drugs and therapies, but at the cost of reduced sharing of research methods and results. Structurally, this paragraph explains the third of the three reasons businesses are unsuitable to managing new ideas.

Paragraph Four: In the final paragraph the author reasserts the nostalgic attitude from the first paragraph, along with a concern for the future if new discoveries will lead researchers not to their colleagues, but rather to their lawyers and corporate sponsors.

Overall, this author believes that universities provide a good system of idea development while allowing for freedom to experiment, share ideas, and develop new theories. The author argues that the old system is far preferable to the new system, which faces market pressures for quick returns and is emerging with the trend toward commoditization of research findings, and under which there are incentives to hoard information (as exemplified by the biotech industry). The author is concerned about the future if this trend continues. As a whole, the passage is reasonably interesting and the arguments made are not difficult to understand.

With a strong analysis of Passage A in hand, move to the second passage and perform a similar analysis on **Passage B**:

Paragraph One: This passage starts much like the first, with the author discussing the old days, when scientific discoveries were considered a public good. This perception was based on the fact that such discoveries were facilitated by government support of universities, and thus entitled to no one individual. However, the author separates himself from this view by using the phrase, "The argument for this view..."

Paragraph Two: With the transitional term "however," the author denotes a change in the direction of the discussion: In contrast to the old days, the author asserts, the "information economy" of today is transforming public goods into market commodities. The author provides the example of the biotech industry, which can take information about cell structures and turn it into profit through drugs or medical screening technologies. In such situations, the question of legal rights to such underlying intellectual property becomes critical.

Paragraph Three: In this paragraph, the author refers again to the old days, when the right to patent depended on the distinction between discoveries, which could not be patented, and inventions, which could. Today, the author asserts, the speed of the market in transforming discoveries to profitable products has led to a blurring of the previously existing legal and moral distinctions.

Paragraph Four: In this final paragraph the author presents the viewpoint of "Industry," which argues that if it has sponsored a discovery, on its own or through a university, then it should get a return on this investment, by charging others or maintaining exclusive use of the discovery.

Overall, this author believes that the new information economy is bringing inevitable change to our system of idea development. The old system was based on the government sponsorship of new scientific discovery; today, such discoveries can be so quickly converted to cash that the old legal and moral lines are becoming blurred. The author presents the argument of Industry: if a business sponsors a discovery, it is entitled to a return, through licensing or exclusive use.

This passage is a bit more difficult than Passage A, but you can still break down the passage fairly easily. The third paragraph is probably the one paragraph that causes students to slow down and possibly re-read.

With a clear understanding of the two passages, the next step is to make a basic analysis of the passage relationships:

> Passage Similarities: Both authors believe that the world is changing, and both discuss the changes that are taking place as scientific research is treated increasingly like a commodity. Interestingly, both authors use the example of the biotechnology field in their discussions of developing research results for the market. You should expect this shared biotech example to appear at least once in the questions or answer choices.

> Passage Differences: While the topics of the passages are similar, the authors' tones are quite different. They agree that the world is changing, but where the first author yearns for the past, the second author is clearly more resigned to, and more comfortable with, these changes. The first author discusses the example of biotech in the context of detriment that can come from the incentives of the new system. The second author brings up the example in order to reflect the increasing importance of determinations of intellectual property rights. The first author closes Passage A on a somber note, asserting concern for the future. The second author, in contrast, is more accepting of the changes, and closes Passage B with a presentation of Industry's argument.

The two passages are each easy to read, and the tone of each author is clear. After taking a moment to consider the similarities and differences between the two passages, you should feel quite confident about moving on to the questions.

Question #15: PE, Must. The correct answer choice is (A)

The first question in the passage is a Passage Exclusivity question, which is the less common of the two main question types.

Answer choice (A): This is the correct answer choice. The author of passage A does not refer to the blurring of legal lines, but the author of passage B discusses this issue in lines 50-59.

Answer choice (B): Both authors bring up the general issue of the effect of the market on the exchange of scientific knowledge, so this answer choice is incorrect.

Answer choice (C): Both passages begin with discussions of the old days, when scientific discoveries were generally considered public goods (line 6 in Passage A, and line 33 in Passage B), so this response is incorrect.

Answer choice (D): New pharmaceuticals are brought up in different contexts by both authors (in Passage A in line 25, and in Passage B in line 45), so this cannot be the correct response to this Passage Exclusivity question.

Answer choice (E): The restriction of access to research findings is discussed in lines 20-21 in Passage A, and on the last two lines in Passage B.

Passage Analysis—December 2007 Passage #3

Question #16: PC, Must. The correct answer choice is (C)

The remaining four questions are all Passage Commonality questions, which force you to evaluate the passages together. This particular question asks you to analyze pairs discussed in each passage.

Answer choice (A): Neither passage involves discussion of commercially successful versus unsuccessful research, so this answer choice is incorrect.

Answer choice (B): Both passages discuss research in terms of its status as a public good versus a commodity tradable for cash. Neither passage involves discussion of research methods versus research results.

Answer choice (C): This is the correct answer choice. Both authors discuss the old days in contrast with modern times, and the fact that research results are becoming less of a public good as they become more of a commodity. The author of Passage A tells us that "the recent tendency to treat research findings as commodities…threatens this tradition…of research as a public good." Passage B provides, "what was previously seen as a public good is being transformed into a market commodity."

Answer choice (D): Only the author of Passage B discusses the outdated distinction between an invention and a discovery. Passage A does not include this comparison, so this answer choice is incorrect.

Answer choice (E): The author of Passage A discusses the difference between university-run and non-university-run research, but neither author discusses any distinction between scientific research and other types of inquiry.

Question #17: PC, Must. The correct answer choice is (D)

This is a relatively easy question that tests your ability to seek a reference common to each passage.

Answer choice (A): Passage A refers to theoretical frameworks on line 17, but Passage B makes no reference to them, so this answer choice is incorrect.

Answer choice (B): Venture capitalists are referenced in Passage A, in line 29, with regard to the author's concern for the future, but they are not discussed in Passage B.

Answer choice (C): Neither author discusses physics and chemistry, so this answer choice is incorrect.

Answer choice (D): This is the correct answer choice. The biotech field is discussed in Passage A to exemplify the reduced sharing of information (lines 21-25), and in Passage B to reflect the importance of intellectual property given the speed of the market (lines 44-48).

Answer choice (E): Shareholders are discussed in Passage A as part of the problem (line 13), but they are not discussed by the author of Passage B, so this choice is incorrect.

Question #18: PC, Must. The correct answer choice is (C)

Attack this question by prephrasing the answer: both authors believe that this increased constraint comes from the pressures of the market.

Answer choice (A): Both authors credit (or blame) market processes, but neither discusses the increase of research volume, so this answer choice is incorrect.

Answer choice (B): Because neither passage discusses the desire of individual researchers for credit, this cannot be the correct response.

Answer choice (C): This is the correct answer choice; it is the market's desire for advantage that has led to constraints on access to research findings. Passage A provides, beginning in line 18, "…entrepreneurs…can buy research and bury its products, hiding knowledge useful to society or to their competitors." The author of Passage B presents Industry's argument, which is that if Industry has sponsored research, "…then it is entitled to seek a return…either by charging others…or by keeping it for its own exclusive use."

Answer choice (D): There is no discussion regarding moral reservations about research's social impact, so this answer choice is incorrect.

Answer choice (E): Neither author discusses a reduction in government funding for university research.

Question #19: PC, Must. The correct answer choice is (D)

This is the hardest question of the passage. The question stem itself is a simple PC-Must, but finding the correct answer choice is difficult.

Answer choice (A): Although both authors use the biotech industry to exemplify how research results are brought to today's market, neither makes any claim that researchers are leaving universities to work in biotech.

Answer choice (B): Neither author asserts any claims regarding invalid patents, so this answer choice is incorrect.

Answer choice (C): The blurring of the distinctions of legal lines is discussed only in Passage B, and not attributable to the nature of current scientific research—these lines are getting blurred by the speed of the market and the large profits that are now accessible.

Answer choice (D): This is the correct answer choice. Both authors discuss the fact that in the old days, the results of scientific research were generally considered public goods, which implies free access.

Answer choice (E): There are no claims made in either one of the passages regarding the motivations of government-funded research, so this answer choice is incorrect.

Two Comparative Reading Practice Passages

The next four pages contain two actual LSAT Comparative Reading passage sets. After the two passages, a complete analysis of each passage and all of the corresponding questions is presented.

To most effectively benefit from this section, time yourself on the first passage. Attempt to finish the passage in 8 minutes and 45 seconds, but if you cannot, continue working until you complete all of the questions and then note your time. Then, read the entire explanation section for the first passage. Afterwards, move to the second passage and repeat the process.

The following passages concern a plant called purple loosestrife. Passage A is excerpted from a report issued by a prairie research council; passage B from a journal of sociology.

Passage A

Purple loosestrife *(Lythrum salicaria),* an aggressive and invasive perennial of Eurasian origin, arrived with settlers in eastern North America in the early 1800s and has spread across the continent's
(5) midlatitude wetlands. The impact of purple loosestrife on native vegetation has been disastrous, with more than 50 percent of the biomass of some wetland communities displaced. Monospecific blocks of this weed have maintained themselves for at least 20 years.
(10) Impacts on wildlife have not been well studied, but serious reductions in waterfowl and aquatic furbearer productivity have been observed. In addition, several endangered species of vertebrates are threatened with further degradation of their
(15) breeding habitats. Although purple loosestrife can invade relatively undisturbed habitats, the spread and dominance of this weed have been greatly accelerated in disturbed habitats. While digging out the plants can temporarily halt their spread, there has been little
(20) research on long-term purple loosestrife control. Glyphosate has been used successfully, but no measure of the impact of this herbicide on native plant communities has been made.
    With the spread of purple loosestrife growing
(25) exponentially, some form of integrated control is needed. At present, coping with purple loosestrife hinges on early detection of the weed's arrival in areas, which allows local eradication to be carried out with minimum damage to the native plant community.

Passage B
(30)   The war on purple loosestrife is apparently conducted on behalf of nature, an attempt to liberate the biotic community from the tyrannical influence of a life-destroying invasive weed. Indeed, purple loosestrife control is portrayed by its practitioners as
(35) an environmental initiative intended to save nature rather than control it. Accordingly, the purple loosestrife literature, scientific and otherwise, dutifully discusses the impacts of the weed on endangered species-and on threatened biodiversity
(40) more generally. Purple loosestrife is a pollution, according to the scientific community, and all of nature suffers under its pervasive influence.
    Regardless of the perceived and actual ecological effects of the purple invader, it is apparent that
(45) popular pollution ideologies have been extended into the wetlands of North America. Consequently, the scientific effort to liberate nature from purple loosestrife has failed to decouple itself from its philosophical origin as an instrument to control nature
(50) to the satisfaction of human desires. Birds, particularly game birds and waterfowl, provide the bulk of the justification for loosestrife management. However, no bird species other than the canvasback has been identified in the literature as endangered by
(55) purple loosestrife. The impact of purple loosestrife on

furbearing mammals is discussed at great length, though none of the species highlighted (muskrat, mink) can be considered threatened in North America. What is threatened by purple loosestrife is the
(60) economics of exploiting such preferred species and the millions of dollars that will be lost to the economies of the United States and Canada from reduced hunting, trapping, and recreation revenues due to a decline in the production of the wetland
(65) resource.

7. Both passages explicitly mention which one of the following?

    (A) furbearing animals
    (B) glyphosate
    (C) the threat purple loosestrife poses to economies
    (D) popular pollution ideologies
    (E) literature on purple loosestrife control

8. Each of the passages contains information sufficient to answer which one of the following questions?

    (A) Approximately how long ago did purple loosestrife arrive in North America?
    (B) Is there much literature discussing the potential benefit that hunters might derive from purple loosestrife management?
    (C) What is an issue regarding purple loosestrife management on which both hunters and farmers agree?
    (D) Is the canvasback threatened with extinction due to the spread of purple loosestrife?
    (E) What is a type of terrain that is affected in at least some parts of North America by the presence of purple loosestrife?

9. It can be inferred that the authors would be most likely to disagree about which one of the following?

    (A) Purple loosestrife spreads more quickly in disturbed habitats than in undisturbed habitats.
    (B) The threat posed by purple loosestrife to local aquatic furbearer populations is serious.
    (C) Most people who advocate that eradication measures be taken to control purple loosestrife are not genuine in their concern for the environment.
    (D) The size of the biomass that has been displaced by purple loosestrife is larger than is generally thought.
    (E) Measures should be taken to prevent other non-native plant species from invading North America.

10. Which one of the following most accurately describes the attitude expressed by the author of passage B toward the overall argument represented by passage A?

(A) enthusiastic agreement
(B) cautious agreement
(C) pure neutrality
(D) general ambivalence
(E) pointed skepticism

11. It can be inferred that both authors would be most likely to agree with which one of the following statements regarding purple loosestrife?

(A) As it increases in North America, some wildlife populations tend to decrease.
(B) Its establishment in North America has had a disastrous effect on native North American wetland vegetation in certain regions.
(C) It is very difficult to control effectively with herbicides.
(D) Its introduction into North America was a great ecological blunder.
(E) When it is eliminated from a given area, it tends to return to that area fairly quickly.

12. Which one of the following is true about the relationship between the two passages?

(A) Passage A presents evidence that directly counters claims made in passage B.
(B) Passage B assumes what passage A explicitly argues for.
(C) Passage B displays an awareness of the arguments touched on in passage A, but not vice versa.
(D) Passage B advocates a policy that passage A rejects.
(E) Passage A downplays the seriousness of claims made in passage B.

13. Which one of the following, if true, would cast doubt on the argument in passage B but bolster the argument in passage A?

(A) Localized population reduction is often a precursor to widespread endangerment of a species.
(B) Purple loosestrife was barely noticed in North America before the advent of suburban sprawl in the 1950s.
(C) The amount by which overall hunting, trapping, and recreation revenues would be reduced as a result of the extinction of one or more species threatened by purple loosestrife represents a significant portion of those revenues.
(D) Some environmentalists who advocate taking measures to eradicate purple loosestrife view such measures as a means of controlling nature.
(E) Purple loosestrife has never become a problem in its native habitat, even though no effort has been made to eradicate it there.

Passage A

Readers, like writers, need to search for answers. Part of the joy of reading is in being surprised, but academic historians leave little to the imagination. The perniciousness of the historiographic approach became (5) fully evident to me when I started teaching. Historians require undergraduates to read scholarly monographs that sap the vitality of history; they visit on students what was visited on them in graduate school. They assign books with formulaic arguments that transform (10) history into an abstract debate that would have been unfathomable to those who lived in the past. Aimed so squarely at the head, such books cannot stimulate students who yearn to connect to history emotionally as well as intellectually.

(15) In an effort to address this problem, some historians have begun to rediscover stories. It has even become something of a fad within the profession. This year, the American Historical Association chose as the theme for its annual conference some putative connection to (20) storytelling: "Practices of Historical Narrative." Predictably, historians responded by adding the word "narrative" to their titles and presenting papers at sessions on "Oral History and the Narrative of Class Identity," and "Meaning and Time: The Problem of (25) Historical Narrative." But it was still historiography, intended only for other academics. At meetings of historians, we still encounter very few historians telling stories or moving audiences to smiles, chills, or tears.

Passage B

Writing is at the heart of the lawyer's craft, and so, (30) like it or not, we who teach the law inevitably teach aspiring lawyers how lawyers write. We do this in a few stand-alone courses and, to a greater extent, through the constraints that we impose on their writing throughout the curriculum. Legal writing, because of the purposes (35) it serves, is necessarily ruled by linear logic, creating a path without diversions, surprises, or reversals. Conformity is a virtue, creativity suspect, humor forbidden, and voice mute.

Lawyers write as they see other lawyers write, and, (40) influenced by education, profession, economic constraints, and perceived self-interest, they too often write badly. Perhaps the currently fashionable call for attention to narrative in legal education could have an effect on this. It is not yet exactly clear what role (45) narrative should play in the law, but it is nonetheless true that every case has at its heart a story-of real events and people, of concerns, misfortunes, conflicts, feelings. But because legal analysis strips the human narrative content from the abstract, canonical legal (50) form of the case, law students learn to act as if there is no such story.

It may well turn out that some of the terminology and public rhetoric of this potentially subversive movement toward attention to narrative will find its

(55) way into the law curriculum, but without producing corresponding changes in how legal writing is actually taught or in how our future colleagues will write. Still, even mere awareness of the value of narrative could perhaps serve as an important corrective.

7. Which one of the following does each of the passages display?

(A) a concern with the question of what teaching methods are most effective in developing writing skills

(B) a concern with how a particular discipline tends to represent points of view it does not typically deal with

(C) a conviction that writing in specialized professional disciplines cannot be creatively crafted

(D) a belief that the writing in a particular profession could benefit from more attention to storytelling

(E) a desire to see writing in a particular field purged of elements from other disciplines

8. The passages most strongly support which one of the following inferences regarding the authors' relationships to the professions they discuss?

(A) Neither author is an active member of the profession that he or she discusses.

(B) Each author is an active member of the profession he or she discusses.

(C) The author of passage A is a member of the profession discussed in that passage, but the author of passage B is not a member of either of the professions discussed in the passages.

(D) Both authors are active members of the profession discussed in passage B.

(E) The author of passage B, but not the author of passage A, is an active member of both of the professions discussed in the passages.

9. Which one of the following does each passage indicate is typical of writing in the respective professions discussed in the passages?

    (A) abstraction
    (B) hyperbole
    (C) subversion
    (D) narrative
    (E) imagination

10. In which one of the following ways are the passages NOT parallel?

    (A) Passage A presents and rejects arguments for an opposing position, whereas passage B does not.
    (B) Passage A makes evaluative claims, whereas passage B docs not.
    (C) Passage A describes specific examples of a phenomenon it criticizes, whereas passage B does not.
    (D) Passage B offers criticism, whereas passage A does not.
    (E) Passage B outlines a theory, whereas passage A does not.

11. The phrase "scholarly monographs that sap the vitality of history" in passage A (lines 6-7) plays a role in that passage's overall argument that is most analogous to the role played in passage B by which one of the following phrases?

    (A) "Writing is at the heart of the lawyer's craft" (line 29)
    (B) "Conformity is a virtue, creativity suspect, humor forbidden, and voice mute" (lines 37-38)
    (C) "Lawyers write as they see other lawyers write" (line 39)
    (D) "every case has at its heart a story" (line 46)
    (E) "Still, even mere awareness of the value of narrative could perhaps serve as an important corrective" (lines 57-59)

12. Suppose that a lawyer is writing a legal document describing the facts that are at issue in a case. The author of passage B would be most likely to expect which onc of the following to be true of the document?

    (A) It will be poorly written because the lawyer who is writing it was not given explicit advice by law professors on how lawyers should write.
    (B) It will be crafted to function like a piece of fiction in its description of the characters and motivations of the people involved in the case.
    (C) It will be a concise, well-crafted piece of writing that summarizes most, if not all, of the facts that are important in the case.
    (D) It will not genuinely convey the human dimension of the case, regardless of how accurate the document may be in its details.
    (E) It will neglect to make appropriate connections between the details of the case and relevant legal doctrines.

Passage A

Paragraph One:

This paragraph opens with a description of the passage's central focus: purple loosestrife, a Eurasian plant brought to eastern North America in the early 1800s. After a brief introduction, the author's attitude toward the spread of the perennial plant becomes clear, calling it "disastrous," discussing the plants demonstrated ability to sustain itself for as long as 20 years, and the resulting displacement (up to 50%) of some wetlands communities. Although no specific numbers are discussed in this context, "serious reductions in waterfowl and aquatic furbearer productivity have been observed," and some invertebrate endangered species are threatened by the effects on their habitat. The author closes the paragraph with the presentation (and qualification) of two approaches to the problem:

a. Digging out the plants can temporarily halt the spread, but little is known about long-term control.
b. Glyphosate has had success, but nothing is known about its impact on native plant communities.

Paragraph Two:

The author uses the brief final paragraph to conclude that the plant needs to be controlled. In the last sentence, the author asserts that the only way to cope with the weed is through early detection and local eradication with minimal damage to the native plant populations.

Passage Structure:

Paragraph 1: Introduce the purple loosestrife and characterize the plant as disastrous, discussing its ability to endure and displace local plant populations. Present two approaches to the problem, and the respective limitations of each.

Paragraph 2: Conclude that an integrative solution needs to be found, and present early eradication as the only way to cope with the problem.

Passage B

Paragraph One:

The introduction to this passage presents a rare instance of something approaching sarcasm from an LSAT author, who chooses very strong language from the outset ("tyrannical, life-destroying") to describe the purple loosestrife. While those who seek to control the weed say that they do so to save nature, the author tells us, perhaps they seek to control it. The author portrays the scientific community as "dutifully" focusing on possible threats to endangered species and biodiversity, closing the paragraph with another sarcastic exaggeration: "Purple loosestrife is a pollution…and all of nature suffers under its pervasive influence."

Paragraph Two:

The author opens the second paragraph implicitly questioning the seriousness of the effects of the "purple invader" (another shot at those who claim disaster). The "popular pollution ideologies" have spread to North American wetlands, and the author asserts the philosophical origin to be the desire to control nature. Concern for birds, particularly game and waterfowl, is characterized as "justification," and the author points out that only the canvasback is confirmed by literature to be endangered by the purple loosestrife. Although neither muskrat nor mink are endangered in North America, the effects on furbearing mammals are highlighted in literature, because of what the author believes to be the primary motivation behind the loosestrife concern to the U.S. and Canada: the millions of dollars in revenues that could be lost as a result of any decline in the furbearing population.

Passage Structure:

Paragraph 1: Present sarcastically exaggerated characterization of the purple loosestrife, suggest the concern about the plant as the intent to control nature.

Paragraph 2: Continue with the sarcastic characterizations of the "purple invader," and again suggest the intended desire to control nature. Assert the concern for birds to be merely a "justification," and economic considerations about furbearing mammals to be the true motivation behind efforts to control purple loosestrife.

Passage A Summary:

Purple loosestrife has spread across North America since it was brought to the continent in the early 1800s. The plant can sustain itself for twenty years or more, and can displace significant wetlands populations. Digging can work in the short term, but perhaps not for long-term control, and Glyphosate works but little is known about the herbicide's effects on other plants. While integrated control of the destructive year-round weed is needed, the only way to cope at present is through early detection and eradication to minimize collateral damage.

Passage B Summary:

The war on purple loosestrife is professed by its practitioners to be waged on behalf of nature, but this may be merely a justification, considering the fact that only one bird is documented to be at risk because of the purple weed. Although fur-bearing mammal populations are not currently threatened in North America, the concern may likely be based on prospective economic detriment to the U.S. and Canada.

Passage Similarities:

As is common among LSAT Comparative Reading passage sets, the two authors focus on the same topic, but from very different perspectives. Both passages focus the purple loosestrife and some of the ramifications of the weed's spread, and both authors discuss the plants ability to possibly reduce certain bird and furbearing mammal populations.

Passage Differences:

Both passages focus on the purple loosestrife and the effects of the weed's spread, but the author's attitudes are diametrically opposed. The first author is clearly quite concerned about the environmental ramifications of the weed's displacement of some wetlands, while the second author sees such concerns as alarmist, and questions the real motivations of those who claim to be fighting for the environment. While the first author discusses various approaches to loosestrife control, the second author asserts that such approaches are efforts to control nature, and suggests that those fighting for loosestrife control may really be more concerned with financial considerations of the potential detriments to certain very profitable species.

Question #7: PC. The correct answer choice is (A)

From the discussion of Passage Similarities above, we can prephrase some possible answers to this Passage Commonality question: both passages discuss the purple loosestrife and its spread, of course, and both authors point out detriment to some bird and furbearing mammal populations.

Answer choice (A): This is the correct answer choice. The author of passage A discusses aquatic furbearers (lines 11-12) and the author of passage B considers the threat to furbearing mammals as a likely cause for all of the concern about the weed. This discussion begins on line 55.

Answer choice (B): Only the author of passage A mentions this herbicide (line 21), or, for that matter, any particular approach to the control of the loosestrife.

Answer choice (C): The author of passage B presents this as a likely cause for the supposedly

environmental concerns, but the economic threat is not referenced at all in Passage A.
Answer choice (D): Only the author of passage B references these "pollution ideologies," on line 45.

Answer choice (E): While the author of passage A would likely be interested in such literature, it is only referenced in passage B (line 54).

Question #8: PC. The correct answer choice is (E)

The answer to this Passage Commonality question is difficult to prephrase, but must pass the Fact Test; both passages will provide sufficient information to answer only one of the questions presented in the answer choices.

Answer choice (A): The author of passage B does not discuss the history of the weed in North America, although the author of passage A answers this question on line 4.

Answer choice (B): Neither author discusses such literature or its abundance.

Answer choice (C): While we can infer that these two groups might agree on the need for control based on passage B, they are not mentioned by the author of passage A.

Answer choice (D): Although the author of passage A is clearly more concerned about the environmental impact of the spread of purple loosestrife, it is the author of Passage B who mentions the canvasback, intended to point out the existence of only one known threat associated with the weed (according to the referenced literature).

Answer choice (E): This is the correct answer choice. Both authors point to the wetlands as affected terrain (lines 5 and 46).

Question #9: PA, AD. The correct answer choice is (B)

Based on the discussion of passage Differences above, we can create a general prephrase to answer this Author Disagreement question: The main difference between the attitudes of the two authors is that while the first believes the weed to pose a serious environmental threat to North American wetlands, the author of passage B believes the threat to be overblown and the concern to be based on financial considerations.

Answer choice (A): While the author of passage A would agree with this statement (lines 15-18), the second author makes no reference to this comparison (additionally, there is no reason to infer that there would be any disagreement on this issue).

Answer choice (B): This is the correct answer choice, as prephrased above. The author of Passage A believes the threat to be serious, and the author of passage B questions the seriousness of the environmental impact, pointing out that the furbearing mammals in question are not threatened in North America.

Answer choice (C): The author of passage A would most likely disagree with this bold claim, but we cannot assess the attitude of the second author regarding this group's sincerity; it is possible that even those primarily concerned with financial impact might still have concern for the environment. Answer choice (D): This belief is not presented or alluded to in either passage.

Answer choice (E): Like incorrect answer choice (D) above, this is an issue that is not referenced by either author, so this can't be the right answer to this Author Disagreement question.

Question #10: PA, AD. The correct answer choice is (E)

Like question #9 above, we can confidently attack this question armed with an understanding of the different attitudes of the two authors. The author of passage B has a cynical attitude reflected through use of exaggeration of the problem, and a questioning of the motivations of those who fight to control the loosestrife—people like the author of passage A.

Answer choice (A): This answer choice is clearly incorrect, since there is no such agreement relayed by the author of passage B.

Answer choice (B): Like incorrect answer choice (A) above, this choice includes the word "agreement," ruling it out as a contender.

Answer choice (C): The author of passage B is certainly not neutral, but rather outspoken in questioning the motives behind the efforts to control the loosestrife.

Answer choice (D): The author of passage B is neither purposely neutral (as suggested by answer choice (C) above), nor ambivalent—the second author displays a strongly skeptical attitude.

Answer choice (E): This is the correct answer choice, as prephrased above: the author of passage B is clearly skeptical about the seriousness of the purple loosestrife spread as characterized in passage A.

Question #11: PA, AA. The correct answer choice is (A)

Since there is not much agreement apparent between the two authors, we can prephrase the answer to this Author Agreement question as well. They agree that the purple loosestrife can be detrimental to other populations, but they disagree as to the seriousness of ramifications and the basis of concern.

Answer choice (A): This is the correct answer choice. This is a major concern for the author of passage A, and even the author of passage B references some impact on certain species.

Answer choice (B): The author of passage A characterizes the weed's spread as disastrous, but the author of passage B would question this characterization.

Answer choice (C): Only the author of passage A even mentions herbicides, and merely points out that there is limited information regarding a certain herbicide's impact on other plants.

Answer choice (D): The first author believes the weed to be a major problem and would thus likely agree with this statement, but the second author would question whether bringing the plant to the continent was a "great ecological blunder."

Answer choice (E): Neither author references the weed's reaction to local elimination.

Question #12: PRel. The correct answer choice is (C)

Although a precise prephrased answer to this general Passage Relationship question would be difficult to produce, the discussions of the passage similarities and differences above should be sufficient to locate the correct answer choice.

Answer choice (A): There is no such direct counter, and the authors don't necessarily disagree about the evidence presented—they disagree about the ramifications of noted effects.

Answer choice (B): Since the two authors would broadly disagree about the seriousness of the discussed phenomenon, this incorrect answer choice should be quickly eliminated.

Answer choice (C): This is the correct answer choice. The author of passage B specifically references and questions the professed concerns of environmentalists like the first author, but the first author makes no reference to the claim that financial considerations drive the concern about the loosestrife.

Answer choice (D): The author of passage B simply questions the seriousness of the purple loosestrife spread, advocating no specific policy.

Answer choice (E): This incorrect answer choice provides an opposite answer: it is actually passage B which downplays the seriousness of claims made in passage A.

Question #13: PA, Weaken/Strengthen. The correct answer choice is (A)

This Passage Aggregate question presents a rare hybrid of a weaken and strengthen question. The correct answer choice will strengthen the conclusions in passage A (and the claim that the problem is serious) and weaken the dismissive assertions made in the second passage.

Answer choice (A): This is the correct answer choice. If this is true, then even those species that are not currently threatened might eventually be endangered.

Answer choice (B): This is an opposite answer, supporting the second author's suggestion that financial considerations and the human desire to control nature have led to concern about the purple loosestrife.

Answer choice (C): Like answer choice (B) above, this choice would strengthen the argument in passage B, making concerns about the loosestrife more likely attributable to such effects.

Answer choice (D): This strengthens assertions found in passage B, not passage A.

Answer choice (E): This is another opposite answer which would certainly not strengthen the arguments made in passage A, but would bolster passage B's general assertion that the weed should not be the cause of serious concern.

Paragraph One:

The author begins this passage by pointing out that readers need to search for and find answers, but that there is little surprise in traditional academic history. Interestingly, this passage is written in first person (denoted with the use of "I", "we," etc.), and the author is apparently a teacher (or has taught at some point). The author's viewpoint is critical of the traditional, "historiographic" approach to teaching history, which requires students to read lifeless, formulaic, scholarly works that are aimed solely at the intellect, facilitating little emotional connection with the reader. In the course of explaining his or her viewpoint, the author also indicates that historians are the ones requiring students to read such lifeless texts, visiting upon the students that which was visited upon them.

Paragraph Two:

Here the author discusses the views of "some historians" (line 15). These historians have begun to rediscover the storytelling as a method of teaching history. But the author criticizes these historians, giving the example of the American Historical Association conference, where the inclusion of a narrative component in the teaching of history gave evidence of a "fad" within the profession. Although the titles of several papers presented at the AHA conference did pay lip service to this idea, the author points out that they still exemplify historiography, intended solely for academics. The author's final conclusion is that historians still rarely elicit any real emotion in response to their accounts of history.

Passage A Summary:

The traditional, formulaic methods of teaching history fail to relay emotion, and academic required readings do not generally elicit any significant emotional connection with readers. One historical society included a narrative component in a recent convention, but the author believes that, with or without the word "narrative" in the title, much of this "historiography" is intended for academia, and still generally fails to bring any true emotional component to these accounts.

Passage Structure:

> Paragraph 1: Discuss problems with the traditional teaching approach (emotionless, scholarly history), identify author as a teacher through use of first person. Establish "historians" as a group with an different, inferior view of teaching history.

> Paragraph 2: Discuss the view of "some historians," who attempt to use a narrative component as one possible solution. Examine recent attempts to include this component, conclude that attaching the title "narrative"—without relaying to an audience any real emotion—does not solve the problems associated with the historiographic approach.

Passage B: Legal writing and a focus on the narrative

Paragraph One:

In this introductory paragraph, the author, who clearly teaches law ("we who teach the law" line 30), discusses the standard approach to legal writing instruction, through specific courses as well as general writing constraints imposed throughout law school. Legal writing, we are told, is traditionally done predictably, in linear fashion, avoiding surprise, humor, and too much creativity.

Paragraph Two:

Because traditional legal writing style is perpetuated by lawyers, the author asserts that attorneys often write poorly. One factor that might influence writing quality is the attention to narrative on the part of legal educators. Although unsure of what role this might play in the law, the author points out that with traditional legal analysis, students tend to disregard the narrative content when considering the facts of a given case.

Paragraph Three:

In the final paragraph the author asserts that there might be some positive outcome from an increased attention to narrative (the author refers to such a movement as "potentially subversive," in order to underscore the very traditional nature of legal writing and associated aversion to change). While terminology associated with a greater focus on the narrative may at some point be reflected in the law curriculum, though, the author believes that this will not necessarily bring changes to the way legal writing is produced or taught. The author concludes that even a simple awareness of the value of the narrative, however, might lead to improvement.

Passage B Summary:

Throughout the law school curriculum students are taught to write without creativity or surprise. Lawyers do the same, and according to the author this often means poor writing. Perhaps legal educators could improve on this situation through greater attention to narrative (as traditional legal analysis tends to downplay narrative content). While this will not necessarily improve legal writing or how it is taught, the author concludes that even an appreciation for the value of a narrative component could help the situation.

Passage Structure:

Paragraph 1: Identify author as a teacher of law through use of first person perspective. Specify problems with traditional methods of teaching legal writing.

Paragraph 2: Assert that the same problems are perpetuated by attorneys, many of whom are bad writers as a result. Introduce the notion of a greater focus on the narrative in legal education.

Paragraph 3: Conclude that more attention to the narrative component might be somewhat helpful, even if it does not change the manner in which legal writing is taught.

Passage Similarities:

Both passages are written in the first person, and both authors are teachers. Both authors believe that their respective fields might be improved with a greater attention to narrative content, and neither one appears completely satisfied with the current level of such focus.

Passage Differences:

The author of passage A has apparently taught history at some point, and the author of passage B appears to be a legal professor. While Author A seems completely unimpressed by the degree to which historians have actually applied the idea, Author B's tone is more optimistic, as manifest in the conclusion that simple awareness can be somewhat curative.

Question #7: PC, Must. The correct answer choice is (D)

Answer choice (A): The passages are not primarily discussions of what teaching methods would be most effective; rather, the authors discuss the possible value of introducing more narrative to their respective fields.

Answer choice (B): The authors do not show a concern about the representation of unfamiliar points of view—their concern is with the use of narrative (or lack thereof).

Answer choice (C): The word that makes this answer incorrect is cannot. The authors do not have a conviction that writing cannot be creatively crafted; they both believe that their respective discipline's writings might be improved with more attention to narrative.

Answer choice (D): This is the correct answer choice. Both authors manifest the belief that their field's writing might derive benefit from increased attention to storytelling.

Answer choice (E): Neither author asserts the need for purging of either discipline, so this answer choice is incorrect.

Practice Passage II—September 2007 Passage #2 Answer Key

Question #8: PC, PRel. The correct answer choice is (B)

We can certainly prephrase the answer to this question. The authors of both passages appear to belong to the professions that they discuss.

Answer choice (A): Since this is exactly opposite our prephrase, this answer choice is incorrect.

Answer choice (B): This is the correct answer choice, and restates our prephrase; the first author is a history teacher, and the second author is involved in legal education.

Answer choice (C): Both authors are members of the professions they discuss.

Answer choice (D): The profession discussed in Passage B is legal education, and since the author of Passage A only discusses history, this answer choice is incorrect.

Answer choice (E): Again, each author is a member of the field discussed.

Question #9: PC, Must. The correct answer choice is (A)

Answer choice (A): This is the correct answer choice. Both authors mention the degree of abstraction in their fields. The author of Passage A discusses the transformation of history into an abstract debate (line 10), and the author of Passage B asserts that "legal analysis strips the human narrative content from the abstract, canonical legal form of the case" (lines 48-50).

Answer choice (B): Neither author discusses hyperbole (also known as extreme exaggeration).

Answer choice (C): The author of Passage B refers to the narrative movement as "potentially subversive" (line 53) but does not assert that subversion is typical of legal writing. Additionally, subversion is not mentioned in Passage A at all.

Answer choice (D): Both authors believe that more attention to narrative might provide benefit, but neither asserts that narrative is typical of the writing in their respective fields.

Answer choice (E): Neither author asserts that imagination is typical of the writing in either field, so this answer choice is incorrect on both counts.

Question #10: PC, Must. The correct answer choice is (C)

This is an interesting question stem, because despite the presence of the words *NOT* and *parallel*, this is not a Parallel X question. Instead, this is actually a Must Be True question, since the correct answer choice must accurately describe how the passages *fail* to parallel one another.

Answer choice (A): Passage A does not present and reject an argument; rather, the author discusses recent focus on the narrative, but is somewhat unimpressed by the outcome.

Answer choice (B): Both passages provide evaluative claims, as both authors believe that their professions might benefit from the introduction of more narrative, so this answer choice is incorrect.

Answer choice (C): This is the correct answer choice. The author of Passage A discusses several history presentations with the word "narrative" in their titles, but criticizes the lack of emotion in historiography regardless. As this answer choice correctly reflects, the author of Passage B does not provide specific examples.

Answer choice (D): Both passages provide criticism, so this answer choice is incorrect.

Answer choice (E): Neither passage really outlines a theory—both just believe that more focus on narrative could bring benefits (if we consider this a theory, then this theory is offered in both passages—either way, this answer choice is incorrect.)

Question #11: PC, PRel. The correct answer choice is (B)

The referenced quote is the author's assertion that historiography is dry and unemotional. If we are looking for a quote that plays the same role in Passage B, we should seek the answer choice that presents legal writing in a similar light.

Answer choice (A): This quote does not present legal writing as dry or unemotional, so this answer choice is incorrect.

Answer choice (B): This is the correct answer choice. With this quote, it is clear that the author believes legal writing to be generally conformist and uninteresting, intended to lack humor, creativity, and individuality.

Answer choice (C): This quote deals with a facet of the self-perpetuating nature of legal writing style, but does not allude to the lack of creative or interesting presentation.

Answer choice (D): Unlike the referenced quote in the question stem, which criticized historiography as dry, the quote in this answer choice focuses on the other side—the emotional part of every legal case, so this answer choice is incorrect.

Answer choice (E): This quote is the hopeful closing note of the second passage; it does not play a role that is anything like that of the quote in question, so this answer choice is incorrect.

Question #12: PE, AP. The correct answer choice is (D)

Author B's perspective on most legal writing is quoted in the preceding question: "Conformity is a virtue, creativity suspect, humor forbidden, and voice mute."

Answer choice (A): The author of Passage B does not claim that legal writing lacks explicit advice, or that all legal writing is poorly written—only that it will tend to lack creativity or individuality.

Answer choice (B): The author does not believe that such legal documents are generally crafted like a piece of fiction; in fact, the author asserts that legal writing could use more of a narrative component, so this answer choice is incorrect.

Answer choice (C): The author does not make the claim that legal writing is always concise or well-crafted, so this answer choice is not accurate.

Answer choice (D): This is the correct answer choice. The author believes that legal writing as it stands is likely to lack depth and emotion, although it may present accurate details.

Answer choice (E): The author does not make the argument that all legal writing fails to tie relevant legal doctrine to case facts, so this answer choice is incorrect.

CHAPTER EIGHT: COMMON PASSAGE STRUCTURES

Chapter Preview

In this chapter we examine several general passage structures, each of which has appeared multiple times on the LSAT. As you develop your familiarity with these recurring structures you will find that the reading selections become more predictable, increasing both your understanding of the passages and your confidence as you move through the Reading Comprehension section.

Common Passage Structures and Layouts

All LSAT Reading Comprehension passages are expository in nature. That is, they are intended to explain or communicate ideas. Within this realm, the overall presentation of a passage depends on three elements: author's tone, author's writing style, and structure of the passage. For example, two authors using the same passage structure will produce very different passages if they use different writing styles, or different tones.

Most students recognize that there are many tones an author can choose. The author can be friendly or cold, neutral or passionate, conversational or aloof, etc. Normally, identifying tone is fairly easy, and most students have little difficulty in doing so. The test makers can also choose from a wide variety of writing styles, from dense and complicated to clear and simple. The writing style usually becomes evident once you begin reading, but other than recognizing what you are facing, there is little value in considering the range of possible styles before you begin reading. For our purposes, simply noting the tone and writing style as you read is sufficient.

Although many different tones and styles of writing exist, the number of ways to present an idea, structurally speaking, is considerably more limited. While it is impossible to catalogue every possible passage structure, there is a high degree of value in being familiar with some of the most frequently appearing forms. On the following pages we take a look at some of these structures.

> In structural terms, the number of ways to present an idea is limited.

One note: this section is not about the number of paragraphs contained in a passage. When we discuss passage structure, we do not mean five paragraph essays like the ones you may have written in high school. Passage structure in this context means the way in which the author presents the ideas.

A narrative is a story or account of events. Virtually all LSAT passages are narrative forms, whether they discuss a person's views, an occurrence, or the history behind an idea. Although narratives by definition can be either factual or fictitious, on the current LSAT the narratives are all true. That is, they contain accounts of actual events and views expressed by actual groups in the real world. Of course, as discussed in Chapter Two, you do not need any prior knowledge of these occurrences; everything you need to answer the questions will be presented in the passage or passages.

On the following pages we present some of the most commonly appearing Narrative Forms, along with a number of example passages. Please note that when presenting the passages, we only present a limited number of accompanying questions. This is because our focus in this section is on the types of reading passages you will encounter, and not as much on the questions that accompany those passages.

Narrative without Authorial Position

One of the key elements in any narrative is the position, if any, of the author. In a small set of passages, the focus is solely on the narrative and the author takes no position whatsoever.

Of course, when there is no authorial view, there can be no Author's Perspective questions. You are simply tested on the views of the subject under discussion, and various points concerning the details and structure of the passage.

The majority of passages have an authorial position, as discussed next.

Narrative with Authorial Position

While the absence of an authorial viewpoint is not uncommon, you are much more likely to encounter narratives in which the author does take a defined position. In narrative form passages, the author's viewpoint is most frequently presented at the end of the passage, but there are exceptions; the author's viewpoint is sometimes presented at the beginning of a passage, or, less often, somewhere in the middle. In reading the passage on the next page, you will notice that it does not take long to figure out the author's attitude about the artist under consideration (and when the author takes a position at the start of the passage, as in this case, the passage is normally devoted to justifying that position).

The paintings of Romare Bearden (1914-1988) represent a double triumph. At the same time that Bearden's work reflects a lifelong commitment to perfecting the innovative painting techniques he

(5) pioneered, it also reveals an artist engaged in a search for ways to explore the varieties of African-American experience.

By presenting scene, character, and atmosphere using a unique layered and fragmented style that

(10) combines elements of painting with elements of collage, Bearden suggested some of the ways in which commonplace subjects could be forced to undergo a metamorphosis when filtered through the techniques available to the resourceful artist. Bearden knew that

(15) regardless of individual painters' personal histories, tastes, or points of view, they must pay their craft the respect of approaching it through an acute awareness of the resources and limitations of the form to which they have dedicated their creative energies.

(20) But how did Bearden, so passionately dedicated to solving the more advanced problems of his painting technique, also succeed so well at portraying the realities of African-American life? During the Great Depression of the 1930s, Bearden painted scenes of

(25) the hardships of the period; the work was powerful, the scenes grim and brooding. Through his depiction of the unemployed in New York's Harlem he was able to move beyond the usual "protest painting" of the period to reveal instances of individual human suffering. His

(30) human figures, placed in abstract yet mysteriously familiar urban settings, managed to express the complex social reality lying beyond the borders of the canvas without compromising their integrity as elements in an artistic composition. Another important

(35) element of Bearden's compositions was his use of muted colors, such as dark blues and purples, to suggest moods of melancholy or despair. While functioning as part of the overall design, these colors also served as symbols of the psychological effects of

(40) debilitating social processes.

During the same period, he also painted happier scenes—depictions of religious ceremony, musical performance, and family life—and instilled them with the same vividness that he applied to his scenes of

(45) suffering. Bearden sought in his work to reveal in all its fullness a world long hidden by the clichés of sociology and rendered cloudy by the simplifications of journalism and documentary photography. Where any number of painters have tried to project the "prose" of

(50) Harlem, Bearden concentrated on releasing its poetry— its family rituals and its ceremonies of affirmation and celebration. His work insists that we truly see the African-American experience in depth, using the fresh light of his creative vision. Through an act of artistic

(55) will, he created strange visual harmonies out of the mosaic of the African-American experience, and in doing so reflected the multiple rhythms, textures, and mysteries of life.

In the Narrative passage on the previous page, we should immediately note the author's viewpoint. The author takes a stand regarding Bearden from the outset, and displays tone clearly through many word choices. For example, a "double triumph" is not empirical fact, but rather an indication that the author is a very big fan of Bearden's. In the remainder of this short paragraph, the author's positive tone is reflected with an impressive number of complimentary terms; added to "triumph" are such words as "commitment," "perfecting," "innovative," and "pioneered." And beyond his original artistic techniques, the author tells us, Bearden used his art to explore the African American experience. Note that the author attributes none of the opinions to critics or to anyone in particular, which means that the passage at this point represents the author's viewpoint.

Having relayed a very clear and positive tone in the first paragraph, the author uses the remainder of the passage to support this perspective. In the second paragraph, praises continue; from Bearden's unique combination of painting and collage, the author asserts, the artist's resourcefulness and understanding of his medium allowed him to bring commonplace subjects to a different level.

By the third paragraph, we already have a good idea of where this passage is going, and active readers can likely predict the tone of the remainder of the passage. This positive portrayal continues with a rhetorical question presented by the author: How was Bearden able to master his technique while providing such a realistic portrayal of African American life? In the 1930s, Bearden's work relayed the Depression era hardship, reflecting the individual suffering of Harlem's unemployed with muted colors such as dark blues and purples. The author explains that these types of colors played an aesthetic role while also allowing the artist to symbolize the debilitating effects of a "complex social reality."

In the final paragraph, the author maintains the positive (and at this point, predictable) tone by offering another compliment: Bearden portrays happy scenes as vividly as his more melancholy works. The point was to create depictions that rose above the standard, simple perceptions of sociology, journalism and documentary photos, to relay Harlem's "poetry": family ritual, celebration, and ceremony. Bearden, the author tells us, creates a new artistic perspective while providing greater depth in his portrayals of the African American experience.

Let us take a moment to analyze this passage using VIEWSTAMP.

VIEWSTAMP Analysis:

The **Viewpoint** presented in this passage is that of the author, who is a fan of Bearden's work.

The **Structure** of the passage is as follows:

> Paragraph One: Characterize Bearden's work as both technical innovation and artistic exploration of the African American experience.
>
> Paragraph Two: Describe Bearden's style, and how the artist transformed the commonplace with a resourceful understanding of his medium.
>
> Paragraph Three: Present rhetorical Question of how the artist was able to be so successful in achieving technical expertise and creating realistic portrayals. Point out that color choices play a role in both design and portrayal of emotion.
>
> Paragraph Four: Discuss Bearden's equally vivid happy scenes, and the fact that the artist's portrayals reflected many facets of African American life without oversimplification sometimes seen in other media.

The author's **Tone** is quite clearly positive with regard to Bearden throughout the passage: the author respects Bearden for his technical innovation, and especially for the ability of the artist to use his medium to create real, multi-faceted portrayals of the African American experience.

In this passage, Bearden's work is discussed from one perspective—that of the author, and there is really only one **Argument** made: that Bearden's work represents both technical innovation and the artistic ability to create vivid portrayals of African American life.

The **Main Point** of the passage is that Bearden's work represents a "double triumph": Bearden employs his technical artistic innovations to allow for the creation of more realistic and vivid portrayals of various facets of African American life.

When you encounter a narrative passage in which the author's perspective is presented so clearly, it is important that you recognize the general tone (which in this case is obviously positive) and understand the reasons for the author's appreciation, as an Author's Perspective question is likely to follow:

> The passage suggests that the author's attitude toward Bearden's innovative painting techniques is one of:

To prephrase this answer we need to consider not only the positive tone that recurs throughout the passage, but also the specific reasons for the author's appreciation. In this case, the author is very impressed with the artist's innovative technique, applied to the creation of realistic portrayals of the African American experience. The author's tone is both respectful and appreciative of Bearden and his work.

Now let us take a look at the question with the answers included. See if you can quickly locate the right choice:

14. The passage suggests that the author's attitude toward Bearden's innovative painting techniques is one of

   (A) admiration for how they aided Bearden in communicating his rich vision of African-American life
   (B) appreciation for how they transform complex social realities into simple and direct social critiques
   (C) respect for how they are rooted in the rhythms and textures of African-American experience
   (D) concern that they draw attention away from Bearden's social and political message
   (E) strong conviction that they should be more widely utilized by African-American artists

The correct answer choice is (A): This answer choice basically restates our prephrase: the author likes Bearden's innovative artistic technique, but this admiration is based in large part on the way this technique allowed Bearden to create such vivid depictions of the African-American experience.

Narrative with Positional Analysis

A variant of the narrative form occurs in passages in which the author explains the history of views on a subject, or outlines two or more alternative views on a subject. These positional analysis passages normally end with the author taking one of several possible positions; in some cases, the author will agree with one of the perspectives discussed in the passage, while in others the author will provide an entirely different perspective. The following provides an example wherein the author discusses the historical perspective on two different political systems, and then provides a different perspective: a reassessment of the two systems in the modern era.

Narratives with Positional Analysis contain multiple explanations, solutions, or theories, and the author then assesses those ideas, normally choosing one or combining two or more.

June 2003—Passage #1

Social scientists have traditionally defined multipolar international systems as consisting of three or more nations, each of roughly equal military and economic strength. Theoretically, the members of such
(5) systems create shifting, temporary alliances in response to changing circumstances in the international environment. Such systems are, thus, fluid and flexible. Frequent, small confrontations are one attribute of multipolar systems and are usually the result of less
(10) powerful members grouping together to counter threats from larger, more aggressive members seeking hegemony. Yet the constant and inevitable counterbalancing typical of such systems usually results in stability. The best-known example of a
(15) multipolar system is the Concert of Europe, which coincided with general peace on that continent lasting roughly 100 years beginning around 1815.

Bipolar systems, on the other hand, involve two major members of roughly equal military and
(20) economic strength vying for power and advantage. Other members of lesser strength tend to coalesce around one or the other pole. Such systems tend to be rigid and fixed, in part due to the existence of only one axis of power. Zero-sum political and military
(25) maneuverings, in which a gain for one side results in an equivalent loss for the other, are a salient feature of bipolar systems. Overall superiority is sought by both major members, which can lead to frequent confrontations, debilitating armed conflict, and,
(30) eventually, to the capitulation of one or the other side. Athens and Sparta of ancient Greece had a bipolar relationship, as did the United States and the USSR during the Cold War.

However, the shift in the geopolitical landscape
(35) following the end of the Cold War calls for a reassessment of the assumptions underlying these two theoretical concepts. The emerging but still vague multipolar system in Europe today brings with it the unsettling prospect of new conflicts and shifting
(40) alliances that may lead to a diminution, rather than an enhancement, of security. The frequent, small confrontations that are thought to have kept the Concert of Europe in a state of equilibrium would today, as nations arm themselves with modern
(45) weapons, create instability that could destroy the system. And the larger number of members and shifting alliance patterns peculiar to multipolar systems would create a bewildering tangle of conflicts.

This reassessment may also lead us to look at the
(50) Cold War in a new light. In 1914 smaller members of the multipolar system in Europe brought the larger members into a war that engulfed the continent. The aftermath—a crippled system in which certain members were dismantled, punished, or voluntarily
(55) withdrew—created the conditions that led to World War II. In contrast, the principal attributes of bipolar systems-two major members with only one possible axis of conflict locked in a rigid yet usually stable struggle for power-may have created the necessary
(60) parameters for general peace in the second half of the twentieth century.

This passage exemplifies the Narrative with Positional Analysis. The author begins by presenting the viewpoint of traditional Social Scientists, how they look at various types of international systems, and the power dynamics within each, and then provides the author's own, separate analysis. The passage opens with a discussion of the multipolar international system, which contains three or more equally strong nations. According to this traditional perspective ("Theoretically," line 4) shifting alliances lead to routine confrontations, counterbalancing power which in turn leads to stability for the system. The author ends this paragraph by providing an example of an international system: the Concert of Europe, in which the involved nations enjoyed peace for about 100 years.

The author continues this narrative passage with a discussion of a second type of system; bipolar systems, we are told, are comprised of only two nations of roughly equal strength (note: since there is no new source attributed in this paragraph, we can assume that the information continues to come from the viewpoint of the traditional Social Scientist). While weaker nations tend to support one side or another, the primary, single axis of power helps to create a more rigid system. With finite power available, the theory goes, both nations seek to dominate through confrontation and armed battle, until one succeeds. Again, as is common in the narrative style, the author provides us with some examples of the bipolar system: Ancient Greece which involved Athens and Sparta, and the Cold War between the United States and the USSR.

While the presence of multiple viewpoints might seem dangerous, you already have the tools to track these views. Of course, as you might expect in the presence of multiple views, the primary focus in positional analysis passages is the compare-and-contrast between the views.

While the author uses the first two paragraphs to provide viewpoints from the traditional Social Scientists' viewpoint (the historical perspective), in the third paragraph there is an important shift to the author's viewpoint and positional analysis: In the post-Cold War world, the old perspectives may require reassessment. Regular confrontation may have brought stability back in the days of the Concert of Europe, but conflict with modern weaponry in today's multipolar Europe could have the opposite effect. The author also points out another important part of the modern picture: the large number of members within the shifting system could create very complex multi-faceted conflict.

At this point in the story, the author has provided some traditional theory regarding the two different types of international systems, and then shifted in the third paragraph to the author's own viewpoint with regard to the potential instability of modern multipolar systems.

This basic theme (that the historical perspective may be wrong) is continued in the fourth paragraph, still from the author's viewpoint, suggesting that both World War I and World War II were facilitated by the multipolar systems involved, while the Cold War, with its bipolar system, may have allowed for a half century of general peace.

Having provided historical background in the beginning of this narrative, the author takes a distinct position, questioning the applicability of the old perspectives to modern day multipolar systems, and suggesting that bipolar systems may be better able to facilitate stability and ongoing peace.

VIEWSTAMP Analysis:

There are two basic **Viewpoints** presented in this passage: the traditional viewpoints, presented in the first two paragraphs, and that of the author, who presents a different assessment which begins in the third paragraph.

The **Structure** of the passage is as follows:

> Paragraph One: Introduce traditional viewpoint concerning multipolar systems, and provide example.
>
> Paragraph Two: Describe traditional viewpoint regarding bipolar systems, and provide examples of such systems.
>
> Paragraph Three: Shift from traditional viewpoint to author's viewpoint, suggest that multipolar systems may bring instability in the modern era.
>
> Paragraph Four: Continue the author's viewpoint; suggest that multipolar systems may have helped lead to both World Wars, while the bipolar Cold War may have caused roughly fifty years of peace enjoyed at the end of the twentieth century.

The **Arguments** presented in this passage are those of the traditionalists and that of the author. Traditional theory, as presented in the first and second paragraphs, asserts that mulitpolar systems can bring stability, while bipolar systems can lead to debilitating conflict. The author's argument is that modern times may call for a reassessment of these presumptions—in today's world, multipolar systems may bring instability, and perhaps the peace that existed in the latter 20th century is attributable to a bipolar system.

The author's **Main Point** is that traditional perspectives regarding bipolar and multipolar systems may need to be reassessed given the different conditions in modern times.

In a Narrative with Positional Analysis, the author always takes one position or another. Understanding this position is vital, as you will almost certainly see a question about the Author's Perspective in such a passage:

> With respect to the Cold War, the author's attitude can most accurately be described as

Again, the author's perspective is that modern multipolar systems may create instability, while the predictable struggles within a bipolar system bring the potential for more lasting peace. The Cold War is the author's primary example of this sort of peaceful bipolar dynamic. Let's look at the options:

4. With respect to the Cold War, the author's attitude can most accurately be described as

  (A) fearful that European geopolitics may bring about a similar bipolar system
  (B) surprised that it did not end with a major war
  (C) convinced that it provides an important example of bipolarity maintaining peace
  (D) regretful that the major European countries were so ambivalent about it
  (E) confident it will mark only a brief hiatus between long periods of European multipolarity

Answer choice (C) is the correct answer, and is nicely aligned with our prephrase; when we recognize how and why examples are used, it makes the correct answer much easier to locate.

The makers of the LSAT commonly include narratives like the one above, in which the author takes a position that is somehow contrary to the traditional approach. It is important that you note the various viewpoints represented, the sometimes subtle shifts between different perspectives, and reasons (if provided) for the author's opinions.

Narrative with Timeline

Another narrative variant that occurs is the specific history or chronology of an event. In these passages, the author outlines a series of events against the backdrop of time, or the order of events as they occurred. These passages are somewhat rare, only because the presence of a timeline gives students a natural structure that they can use to easily understand the passage.

Narrative with Causality

As discussed in Chapter Three, cause and effect reasoning sometimes appears in LSAT passages. In fact, some entire passages are devoted to explaining the causes behind a particular event or occurrence. The following passage is an example:

The proponents of the Modern Movement in architecture considered that, compared with the historical styles that it replaced, Modernist architecture more accurately reflected the functional
(5) spirit of twentieth-century technology and was better suited to the newest building methods. It is ironic, then, that the Movement fostered an ideology of design that proved to be at odds with the way buildings were really built.

(10) The tenacious adherence of Modernist architects and critics to this ideology was in part responsible for the Movement's decline. Originating in the 1920s as a marginal, almost bohemian art movement, the Modern Movement was never very popular with the public,
(15) but this very lack of popular support produced in Modernist architects a high-minded sense of mission—not content merely to interpret the needs of the client, these architects now sought to persuade, to educate, and, if necessary, to dictate. By 1945 the
(20) tenets of the Movement had come to dominate mainstream architecture, and by the early 1950s, to dominate architectural criticism—architects whose work seemed not to advance the evolution of the Modern Movement tended to be dismissed by
(25) proponents of Modernism. On the other hand, when architects were identified as innovators—as was the case with Otto Wagner, or the young Frank Lloyd Wright—attention was drawn to only those features of their work that were "Modern"; other aspects were
(30) conveniently ignored.

The decline of the Modern Movement later in the twentieth century occurred partly as a result of Modernist architects' ignorance of building methods, and partly because Modernist architects were
(35) reluctant to admit that their concerns were chiefly aesthetic. Moreover, the building industry was evolving in a direction Modernists had not anticipated: it was more specialized and the process of construction was much more fragmented than in
(40) the past. Up until the twentieth century, construction had been carried out by a relatively small number of tradespeople, but as the building industry evolved, buildings came to be built by many specialized subcontractors working independently. The architect's
(45) design not only had to accommodate a sequence of independent operations, but now had to reflect the allowable degree of inaccuracy of the different trades. However, one of the chief construction ideals of the Modern Movement was to "honestly" expose
(50) structural materials such as steel and concrete. To do this and still produce a visually acceptable interior called for an unrealistically high level of craftmanship. Exposure of a building's internal structural elements, if it could be achieved at all,
(55) could only be accomplished at considerable cost— hence the well-founded reputation of Modern architecture as prohibitively expensive.

As Postmodern architects recognized, the need to expose structural elements imposed unnecessary
(60) limitations on building design. The unwillingness of architects of the Modern Movement to abandon their ideals contributed to the decline of interest in the Modern Movement.

We see in this passage another narrative: this is the story of the decline of the Modern Movement in architecture, as told through the author's viewpoint. A central focus is the causal relationship, and the author attributes the decline of the movement in part to the Modernists' impractical devotion to aesthetics. The author opens the passage with a quick introduction to the Modern movement, and then quickly points out the impracticality of the movement's ideology. There is very clear tone in this introduction: from the author's viewpoint, this movement is very impractical.

Note that the author uses each paragraph to support the causal relationship between the Modern Movement's ideals and its downfall, and that the tone with regard to the Modern Movement remains negative without exception. The author begins the second paragraph with another assertion of the same causal relationship (between the Movement's impracticality and its decline), and goes on to provide a timeline from the 1920s, and the Modern Movement's fringe beginnings, to the early 1950s, when the movement was dominating both mainstream architecture and architectural criticism.

The third paragraph continues this presentation of the author's viewpoint, with a continued negative tone and more support for the causal argument, by way of several factors that led the ideals of Modernism to result in the decline of the movement. The movement's proponents, the author tells us, did not fully understand building methods, were impractically focused on aesthetics, and were not prepared for the fragmentation of the building industry.

The author uses the last paragraph to introduce another perspective, that of the Postmodernists, in order to further strengthen the author's assertion that the Modern Movement was impractical. The final sentence of the passage is merely a restatement of the author's main point, which is the author's causal assertion: the decline of the Modern Movement was due in part to the Modernist ideals and the unwillingness to change them.

VIEWSTAMP Analysis:
The author presents several **Viewpoints** in this passage. The passage begins with a presentation of a Modernist perspective on Modernism, followed by a quick shift to the author's viewpoint, which is the primary overriding perspective throughout the passage. In the second paragraph, the author provides some more, limited insight into the Modernist perspective (in a very biased tone), characterizing the Modernists as self important, dismissive of all non-Modernist styles, and believing it their mission to spread and sometimes dictate some architectural style. The passage continues to present the viewpoint of the author until the final paragraph, where the Postmodern architects are credited with recognizing the impracticality of Modernist architecture. Note that this perspective is provided to support the author's perspective on the Movement.

The **Structure** of the passage is as follows:

> Paragraph One: Introduce Modernist ideal; quickly shift to author's perspective, assert impracticality of the Movement.

> Paragraph Two: Reassert that Modernist ideals led to the Movement's decline; provide basic timeline of the rise of the Movement; assert bias in the pro-Modernist media.

> Paragraph Three: Expand on how Modernist ideals led to the decline of the Movement; discuss fragmentation of construction, and that chiefly aesthetic emphasis on structural exposure was prohibitively expensive.

> Paragraph Four: Present Postmodernist perspective, restate main point that impractical movement's ideals helped lead to its decline.

The **Arguments** in the passage are those of the Modernists (presented by the author in a very biased, limited way), and those made from the author's viewpoint. The Modernists would argue that their ideal of structural exposure was a more honest portrayal, and would apparently not agree that their concerns were chiefly aesthetic. The author argues that adherence to Modernist ideals was impractical, and these ideals helped to bring the decline of the Movement.

The **Main Point** of the passage is that adherence to Modernist ideals was impractical, chiefly aesthetic, prohibitively expensive, and helped to bring about the decline of the Movement.

In Causal passages, your focus must be on identifying the nature and scope of the cause; at least one of the questions will test your recognition of the causal relationship. For example, this passage is accompanied by a Global Purpose question:

> The author of the passage is primarily concerned with

We should prephrase an answer, and with regard to this passage our prephrase must contain some mention of the central causal relationship discussed by the author. The primary concern is with the causal relationship discussed throughout the passage: the cause of the Modern Movement's decline.

Take a look at the answer choices provided:

27. The author of the passage is primarily concerned with

   (A) analyzing the failure of a movement
   (B) predicting the future course of a movement
   (C) correcting a misunderstanding about a movement
   (D) anticipating possible criticism of a movement
   (E) contrasting incompatible viewpoints about a
         movement

Answer choice (A): This is the correct answer choice, consistent with our prephrase, and discussed throughout the passage. The author's main focus is on what led to the decline of the Modern Movement in architecture.

As we can see from reading causal passages such as the one discussed above, developing an understanding of the cause-and-effect relationship asserted by the author can sometimes be the key to the entire passage.

Narrative featuring Principle and Example

Many passages present an initial theory or principle, and use the remainder of the passage to discuss examples of the theory or provide evidence in support of the theory. In these passages you must recognize that the examples are not the main point of the passage, but rather just support for the principle under discussion. You can be assured that the Main Point or Global Purpose question in the passage will closely test whether you understood that explaining the principle was the reason the passage was written. Consider the following example:

The following passage was written in the mid-1990s.

The demand for electricity in certain countries has been projected recently to grow by 50 percent by the year 2010. Unfortunately, the increased use of fossil fuels to generate this electricity may ultimately damage
(5) human and environmental health. For example, emissions of air pollutants in these countries are expected to double over the next 25 years, even if energy is used efficiently, so that local urban air quality will likely deteriorate. Renewable sources of
(10) electricity, such as solar radiation, wind, and waterpower, are possible solutions to the problems caused by increasing demand for electricity. Unlike fossil fuels, renewable energy sources are available in virtually all geographic regions, and they allow
(15) electricity production without dangerous environmental pollutants. Additionally, these sources can usually be located closer to consumers than can plants that use fossil fuels, thus reducing transmission and distribution costs. Technologies for the successful long-term
(20) exploitation of these resources, however, are not always implemented successfully.

In rural Brazil, for example, millions of citizens do not have electricity, and the lack of necessary infrastructure has limited efforts to provide it. In 1992,
(25) an energy agency from the United States developed a joint project with two Brazilian states to install 800 household solar electrical systems and train local personnel to service them. Under the project's terms, local utilities install, maintain, and own the systems,
(30) and collect fees from users. Backers hoped the project would attract enough private investment for substantial expansion throughout Brazil. But the project directors rejected the relatively high bids of local Brazilian companies to produce the solar collectors and thus
(35) missed an opportunity to stimulate local production. Consequently, a short-term savings in start-up costs precluded the long-term benefits deriving from the development of local production capacity and technological skill, which eventually would have led to
(40) independence from costly foreign expertise. As a result, participating utilities can generate only enough income to cover operating and maintenance costs, which makes further investment and expansion unlikely. Thus, the movement toward a sustainable,
(45) rural electricity system in Brazil remains stalled.

But some efforts have avoided these pitfalls. In the mid-1980s, a Danish energy agency helped agencies in India build three modern wind turbine plants and gradually develop local technical capacity. Local
(50) participants were trained in planning, operation, maintenance, and construction of turbines. Indian firms subsequently began manufacturing turbines and, as more locally manufactured equipment became available, Indian utilities were able to increase their use
(55) of wind energy profitably. The success of these small projects spurred enthusiasm; Indian utilities were soon ordering more equipment and private investment in wind energy surged. Because the Danish agency, unlike its U.S. counterpart, recognized the importance
(60) of local involvement at all levels, the project has a good chance of remaining competitive and profitable for the long run.

You probably recognize this passage as a narrative, since the author recounts the stories of alternative energy production in two developing nations, all from the author's viewpoint. The author begins by introducing the problems with developing nations' increasing use of electricity (pollution, air quality), as well as possible solutions; renewable resources such as solar, wind, and water power are available in all regions without the pollution, and with lower distribution costs. Attempts to set up long term exploitation of these resources, though, are not always successful.

The passage continues from the author's viewpoint in the second paragraph, in which the author presents the example of an unsuccessful effort to develop alternative power in Brazil: American project directors there avoided local Brazilian production to reduce start-up costs. By doing so, however, the directors also failed to derive the benefits of local technological skill and production. Since costly foreign expertise is still required, local utilities are making only enough to cover costs. So the goal of a sustainable electricity system in rural Brazil, we are told, "remains stalled." Notice how the author recounts the facts without value judgment or opinion.

In the last paragraph of this narrative passage (which continues to present the author's viewpoint) we are provided with an example of more successful implementation, and the principle that the author believes drove that success: A Danish company worked with Indian agencies to develop three wind plants in India. Locals were trained on all levels, developing local capacity and encouraging private investment. The author believes that with this approach, problems like those experienced in Brazil might be avoided. The central principle, as discussed above, is provided by the author in the final sentence: local involvement is vital when facilitating renewable energy in the developing world. Thus, through the first two paragraphs the author simply describes the situation regarding alternative energy production in two developing nations, then takes a viewpoint and explains it in the final paragraph.

Since this is a narrative in which the author both presents and exemplifies a principle, we should not be surprised to discover that this passage is accompanied by both a Main Point and a Global Purpose question (be sure to prephrase the answers to both):

Which one of the following most accurately expresses the main point of the passage?

Again, the main point in this narrative is the principle which drove the success of the Danish/Indian project: To improve chances of success with alternative energy in developing countries, involve the locals to spur interest and lead to self sustenance. Consider, then, the entire question, including answer choices:

14. Which one of the following most accurately expresses the main point of the passage?

   (A) While some later efforts to implement renewable energy systems have been plagued and eventually halted by economic conflicts, early renewable energy projects relying more heavily on local involvement enjoyed a larger degree of success.

   (B) Investors in renewable energy projects should consider not only financial factors but also the potential gains in human and environmental health from using this technology—gains that are not always readily measurable.

   (C) Renewable energy sources represent a promising means for addressing many countries' energy demands and environmental concerns, but the necessary technologies can be implemented most effectively in countries that have continuing access to foreign investment or expertise.

   (D) Though renewable energy sources represent a promising means for meeting the rising energy demands of certain countries, the exploitation of these resources is unlikely to succeed unless long-term, local participation at all levels is seen as integral to renewable energy projects.

   (E) Certain types of renewable energy sources, such as wind-generated electricity systems, are more likely to be successful than other types, but continued investment and experimentation are necessary to establish which renewable energy projects will succeed.

Answer choice (D) restates our prephrase, with emphasis on the focal point of local participation in the development of renewable energy resources.

Let's consider the Global Purpose question in this passage:

> In the passage, the author is primarily concerned with

With purpose questions we should always try to prephrase the answer. In this case, the author is primarily interested in discussing alternative energy, and providing examples, both positive and negative, to illustrate an important component to success (that component is, of course, local participation). Consider the entire question:

18. In the passage, the author is primarily concerned with

    (A) summarizing the reasons why renewable energy resources should be used and explaining why certain promising technologies cannot be implemented profitably
    (B) arguing for the advantages of renewable energy resources and illustrating with examples what factors will favor their successful implementation
    (C) illustrating the advantages of adopting renewable energy resources by summarizing how they have been implemented in the past
    (D) comparing and contrasting two types of renewable energy technology and giving examples of the benefits and drawbacks of each
    (E) discussing two types of renewable energy resources and analyzing why one is more easily implemented than the other

The correct answer choice is consistent with our prephrase. The author praises renewable energy and presents examples to teach the lesson that successful implementation of these types of systems requires local participation. Thus, the correct answer choice is (B).

Principle-based narratives such as this one represent a particular type of persuasive strategy employed by the author. In the example above, the author wants us to learn a lesson about successful development of alternative energy, and chooses to teach this lesson by way of examples of both successful and unsuccessful efforts at implementation.

CHAPTER NINE: COMMON PASSAGE THEMES

Chapter Preview

In the previous chapter we discussed some common passage structures; here we will consider several themes commonly found in LSAT passages. Recognition of these themes can convey a significant testing advantage.

Recurrent Themes

Our discussion of recurrent themes is partially built around passage topics. As discussed earlier in Chapter Two, three passage types in particular—humanities passages featuring diversity, science passages, and law-related passages—appear on virtually every LSAT, so a familiarity with these types is beneficial. And, within these types, there are certain themes that are used again and again, which we will examine momentarily.

While we will examine the three most common topics of the LSAT Reading Comprehension section, we will not examine every topic that frequently appears. Humanities passages, for example, appear quite frequently, but other than our discussion of diversity and law we will not examine humanities passages as a separate entity. Why not? Because humanities passages *as a whole* have no definable structure or theme. That is, there is no constant element that can be drawn from these passages and used to your advantage. In earlier chapters we have already discussed the tools of analysis that allow you to attack any humanities passage, and there is no further information you need to be successful on these passages. This stands in sharp contrast to passages that feature diversity. In those passages, not only do you need the tools you already have, you need to further understand the aims of the test makers and themes they commonly feature.

Diversity Passages

As discussed in Chapter Two, almost every LSAT contains a humanities passage that features diversity elements. Diversity passages, as these are called, comprise one of the most important features of the LSAT, and understanding how and why they appear will give you a significant advantage during the test. Before proceeding, however, we offer a disclaimer: please understand that the following discussion is based on an analysis of existing LSAT passages, and the views discussed herein are those of the test makers or based on history. We back our conclusions using facts, and we are not making a value judgment about the existence of these passages. The truth is that these passages exist, and understanding their existence helps you perform better on the LSAT.

Diversity passages raise a sensitive topic. Prior to engaging in this discussion, we wish to reaffirm that we are not making a judgment about these passages, just reporting the facts. To be a good test taker, you must have knowledge of the actions of the test makers.

How Does Test Bias Play a Role in Test Content?

The history of standardized testing is filled with accounts of biased questions and attitudes. Testing bias occurs when the questions innately favor one group over another. In the early days of testing in the U.S., standardized tests were created by groups of predominantly Caucasian middle- to upper-class males, and questions from that era tend to represent their attitudes and values. Consider the following famous verbal analogy from the early days of the SAT:

RUNNER : MARATHON

   (A) envoy : embassy
   (B) martyr : massacre
   (C) oarsman : regatta
   (D) referee : tournament
   (E) horse : stable

To learn more about the history of standardized testing in the U.S., we recommend Nicholas Lemann's fascinating book, "The Big Test."

The correct answer to this question is (C). The problem, as was later revealed by statistical analysis, was that different groups performed quite differently on this question (as opposed to the same, which is the goal of an unbiased test). Rowing, a sport popular with the wealthy, was a sport unknown to large segments of the testing population. Students from urban areas or students who grew up on the Western plains, for example, were unlikely to be familiar with the sport or its terminology.

Closer to home, the LSAT also saw test content changes based on bias concerns. One obvious example was the removal of Family Tree games from the Logic Games section. Family Tree games revolved around the relationships stemming from nuclear family structures, and in today's society the nuclear family is not as prevalent as it once was.

The LSAT is made in the U.S., and used by U.S., Canadian, and some Australian law schools for admission purposes. Thus, although many non-North American students take the LSAT, the results of the test are used primarily for admission to North American law schools.

Over time, as such biases were revealed and understood to be harmful to testing populations that were not from certain backgrounds, the test content began to change because the test makers recognized that such questions were not a fair test of knowledge or abilities. As test makers came to recognize that the values of the test writer affected the scoring outcomes of various groups, they began to adjust the presentation and even the allowable content of the questions. In the quest to write questions that avoided even the perception of bias based on racial, cultural, and gender differences, certain topics became off-limits. For example, there are no questions about Christmas on a standardized test because not everyone celebrates Christmas (or Chanukah, or Kwanzaa, etc.). And, just as the makers of the exam do not want to create cultural confusion during the exam, they also want to avoid emotional upset. Thus, the test makers avoid emotional or controversial topics such as abortion or torture. There are other proscriptions that the test makers follow, but the point is that the test makers are aware of the history of bias in most exams, and the language you see on the exam is carefully chosen in an effort to remove bias.

So, in creating a widely-administered exam, the test makers seek to present an even, unbiased environment. However, the history of bias within the test remains, and in order to overcome accusations of possible bias against a wide array of groups, the test makers looked to expand the range of cultural, ethnic, and gender based topics within the exam. This is, of course, completely reasonable. The U.S. and Canada are societies that are comprised of a large number of different cultures, and individuals from many different social and ethnic backgrounds. Presenting a test that addresses and includes many different groups is not only natural, it is desirable.

Take a moment to place yourself in the shoes of a test maker. On the one hand, you desire to create a fair and unbiased test that disadvantages no person or group. On the other hand, the history of standardized testing is fraught with accusations of bias. When choosing how to represent certain groups, then, would you not take care to present traditionally underrepresented groups in a generally favorable light? By doing so, you run no risk of biasing the test but you do inoculate the test against claims of bias. Without making a judgment about the value of taking this approach, an examination of the last 25+ years of LSAT history shows undeniably that this is precisely the route taken by the test makers. The LSAT Reading Comprehension section tends to include at least one passage about a group (or member of a group) that has been traditionally viewed as underrepresented. As these passages contribute to the diversity of the test, we term them Diversity passages. As mentioned before, the mere presence of these passages is not surprising. What is most interesting about these passages, as we will see in a moment, is the striking consistency (and thus predictability) in the attitude that the test makers take towards these groups.

Before analyzing specific passages, let us take a moment to define underrepresented and overrepresented groups. For LSAT purposes, traditionally underrepresented groups typically focus on race and gender. Thus, there are a number of passages about African Americans, Women, Hispanic Americans, Asian Americans, and indigenous groups such as Native Americans and Native Canadians. Religious minorities and sexual orientation minorities, on the other hand, tend to be avoided because religion and sex are sensitive topics, and tests like the LSAT tend to avoid such topics except in the most general terms. The sole overrepresented group addressed on the LSAT is that of Caucasian males, typically those versed in Western thought.

Let us now examine the three most common presentations of Diversity passages on the LSAT: affirming underrepresented groups, undermining overrepresented groups, and mixed group passages.

The presence of diversity within standardized tests is not an accident. As noted in an ETS publication about testing guidelines, there are strict rules about test content:

"The ideal racial and ethnic balance in a test would reflect the diversity of the test-taking population. It is not feasible, however, to show members of every group in the test-taking population in every test. As a reasonable compromise, skills tests made for use primarily in the United States, strive to have about 20 percent of the items that mention people represent African American people, Asian American people, Latino American people, and/or Native American people."

1. Affirming Underrepresented Groups

Given the history of bias in standardized testing, it is no surprise that Law Services is very careful in how they present traditionally underrepresented groups. What is surprising is the consistency in the tone used by the test writers. In the dozens of passages addressing traditionally underrepresented groups that have appeared on the LSAT in the past 15+ years, every single passage has addressed these groups in a positive manner. That is, in each instance, the attitude of the author toward the person or group under discussion has been positive or encouraging. This type of consistency goes beyond mere chance, and reveals one of the core attitudes of the test makers. Knowing how the test makers will approach a traditionally underrepresented group then allows you to predict the general direction of certain answer choices. Consider the following question, with the preface that the passage was about Miles Davis, the prominent African American jazz musician. Take a moment to consider the answer choices, and then choose the one you feel would be most likely to be correct:

4.   Which one of the following best describes the
     author's attitude toward Miles Davis's music?

    (A)   uneasy ambivalence
    (B)   cautious neutrality
    (C)   grudging respect
    (D)   moderate commendation
    (E)   appreciative advocacy

Without reading the passage, but with knowing the consistent attitude held by the test makers, most students can predict the correct answer, which is (E). This result is contrary to the general aims of testing, because most students should *not* be able to choose the correct answer without having read the passage. The fact that they can shows the power of understanding the views of the test makers.

Of course, your job as a test taker is not to overly worry about the methods or aims of the test makers; your job is to simply understand that the test makers have certain patterns, and then to capitalize on those patterns whenever possible. Let us now examine how this pattern affects an entire passage. Please take approximately 2 to 3 minutes to read the following passage. As you read, keep the discussion above in mind.

The career of trumpeter Miles Davis was one of the most astonishingly productive that jazz music has ever seen. Yet his genius has never received its due. The impatience and artistic restlessness that

(5) characterized his work spawned one stylistic turn after another and made Davis anathema to many critics, who deplored his abandonment first of bebop and then of "cool" acoustic jazz for ever more innovative sounds.

(10) Having begun his career studying bebop, Davis pulled the first of many stylistic surprises when, in 1948, he became a member of an impromptu musical think tank that gathered in a New York City apartment. The work of this group not only

(15) slowed down tempos and featured ensemble playing as much as or even more than solos—in direct reaction to bebop—it also became the seedbed for the "West Coast cool" jazz style.

In what would become a characteristic zigzag,

(20) Davis didn't follow up on these innovations himself. Instead, in the late 1950s he formed a new band that broke free from jazz's restrictive pattern of chord changes. Soloists could determine the shapes of their melodies without referring back to

(25) the same unvarying repetition of chords. In this period, Davis attempted to join jazz phrasings, harmonies, and tonal qualities with a unified and integrated sound similar to that of a classical orchestral piece: in his recordings the rhythms, no

(30) matter how jazzlike, are always understated, and the instrumental voicings seem muted.

Davis's recordings from the late 1960s signal that, once again, his direction was changing. On *Filles de Kilimanjaro*, Davis's request that

(35) keyboardist Herbie Hancock play electric rather than acoustic piano caused consternation among jazz purists of the time. Other albums featured rock-style beats, heavily electronic instrumentation, a loose improvisational attack and a growing use of

(40) studio editing to create jagged soundscapes. By 1969 Davis's typical studio procedure was to have musicians improvise from a base script of material and then to build finished pieces out of tape, like a movie director. Rock groups had pioneered the

(45) process; to jazz lovers, raised on the ideal of live improvisation, that approach was a violation of the premise that recordings should simply document the musicians' thought processes in real time. Davis again became the target of fierce polemics by purist

(50) jazz critics, who have continued to belittle his contributions to jazz.

What probably underlies the intensity of the reactions against Davis is fear of the broadening of possibilities that he exemplified. Ironically, he was

(55) simply doing what jazz explorers have always done: reaching for something new that was his own. But because his career endured, because he didn't die young or record only sporadically, and because he refused to dwell in whatever niche he had

(60) previously carved out, critics find it difficult to definitively rank Davis in the aesthetic hierarchy to which they cling.

For the purposes of this discussion, we will dispense with the normal VIEWSTAMP analysis of the passage and simply note that the viewpoint expressed is that of the author, an obvious admirer of Davis'.

Paragraph One:

This passage begins with its main point, and clearly relays the author's attitude toward the subject: Miles Davis, despite his musical genius, has been critically disregarded or misunderstood. In the final sentence the author restates this idea, asserting that Davis has been overlooked because of work too innovative for critics to appreciate.

Paragraph Two:

Here we are provided with the first date along a timeline of Davis' artistic surprises: he began in bebop, but in 1948 moved on to a new style called "West Coast cool" (ironically started in New York City). with facets (slow tempos, ensemble play) that countered bebop's approach.

Paragraph Three:

In this paragraph the author provides another date for the timeline (the late 1950's) , and another shift in Davis' musical approach. His new band "broke free from jazz's restrictive pattern," allowing band members to shape their own melodies, then weaving these pieces into a unified sound understated rhythms and muted instrumentation.

Paragraph Four:

The author's attitude has been established, and the structure of this passage becomes increasingly clear at the start of the fourth paragraph: a discussion of further stylistic shifts, and yet another date. During the late 60's, Davis made several major changes, provided nearly in list form: electric piano, rock style beats, electronic instrumentation and studio editing. The author then provides an extensive description of Davis' studio process (provide basic structure, then edit together the improvised parts), and then revisits the theme of changes misunderstood by "purist" critics who belittled Davis' contribution.

Paragraph Five:

The author uses the final paragraph to reassert the attitude that Davis was a great innovator, and that this was the basis of the critics' lack of understanding: his career lasted long enough for a lot of innovations, and the many shifts in direction led to the critics' inability to understand the jazz great or give him the credit he deserved.

Although the exact course of a passage cannot be determined before reading the text, the topic sometimes allows you to predict the *general* course that a passage will take. This conveys an immense advantage upon you as a test taker because if you have some forewarning of the direction the author is about to take, then you can read faster and you can process information more quickly.

2. Undermining Overrepresented Groups

Let us take a moment to examine the other side of the coin. If the test makers consistently take a positive attitude towards traditionally underrepresented groups, then what attitude would you expect the test makers to take towards traditionally overrepresented groups? As you might expect, the attitude is often critical—if not wholly, then at least partially. This does make some sense, of course. If a test has been historically biased in favor of a certain group, one method to reverse that bias is to present a greater number of passages critical of that group. On the LSAT, this criticism most frequently appears in passages devoted to assessing the work of scholars, who, under the description of the overrepresented group we used earlier, are typically Caucasian males versed in Western thinking.

While this assertion may seem surprising, an analysis of every released LSAT from the modern era (1991 to the present) shows that usually when the test makers critique an individual or viewpoint, that person or perspective belongs to an historically well-represented group, that of Caucasian male authors. Please read the following passage with the discussion above in mind:

Fairy tales address themselves to two communities, each with its own interests and each in periodic conflict with the other: parents and children. Nearly every study of fairy tales has taken the perspective of the

(5) parent, constructing the meaning of the tales by using the reading strategies of an adult bent on identifying universally valid tenets of moral instruction for children.

For example, the plot of "Hansel and Gretel" is set

(10) in motion by hard-hearted parents who abandon their children in the woods, but for psychologist Bruno Bettelheim the tale is really about children who learn to give up their unhealthy dependency on their parents. According to Bettelheim, this story—in which the

(15) children ultimately overpower a witch who has taken them prisoner for the crime of attempting to eat the witch's gingerbread house—forces its young audience to recognize the dangers of unrestrained greed. As dependent children, Bettelheim argues, Hansel and

(20) Gretel had been a burden to their parents, but on their return home with the witch's jewels, they become the family's support. Thus, says Bettelheim, does the story train its young listeners to become "mature children."

There are two ways of interpreting a story: one is a

(25) "superficial" reading that focuses on the tale's manifest content, and the other is a "deeper" reading that looks for latent meanings. Many adults who read fairy tales are drawn to this second kind of interpretation in order to avoid facing the unpleasant truths that can emerge

(30) from the tales when adults—even parents—are portrayed as capable of acting out of selfish motives themselves. What makes fairy tales attractive to Bettelheim and other psychologists is that they can be used as scenarios that position the child as a

(35) transgressor whose deserved punishment provides a lesson for unruly children. Stories that run counter to such orthodoxies about child-rearing are, to a large extent, suppressed by Bettelheim or "rewritten" through reinterpretation. Once we examine his

(40) interpretations closely, we see that his readings produce meanings that are very different from those constructed by readers with different cultural assumptions and expectations, who, unlike Bettelheim, do not find inflexible tenets of moral instruction in the

(45) tales.

Bettelheim interprets all fairy tales as driven by children's fantasies of desire and revenge, and in doing so suppresses the true nature of parental behavior ranging from abuse to indulgence. Fortunately, these

(50) characterizations of selfish children and innocent adults have been discredited to some extent by recent psychoanalytic literature. The need to deny adult evil has been a pervasive feature of our society, leading us to position children not only as the sole agents of evil

(55) but also as the objects of unending moral instruction, hence the idea that a literature targeted for them must stand in the service of pragmatic instrumentality rather than foster an unproductive form of playful pleasure.

Again, for the purposes of discussion, we will dispense with the VIEWSTAMP analysis and focus primarily on the diversity elements within the passage.

Paragraph One:
This paragraph offers no indication that this passage will eventually contain diversity elements. Instead, the passage initially appears to be a discussion about the meaning of fairy tales.

Paragraph Two: The second paragraph begins with an example about Hansel and Gretel, but the author quickly pivots the discussion and introduces the views of psychologist Bruno Bettelheim (line 11). The remainder of the paragraph discusses Bettelheim's views.

Paragraph Three:
The author begins this paragraph with discussion of two approaches to the interpretation of a story: a superficial consideration of the basic content, and a deeper examination of the work for hidden "latent meanings." The author uses the second half of this paragraph to criticize Bettleheim, characterizing the psychologist as an inflexible writer who chose to suppress or reinterpret those stories which failed to provide the standard lessons warning children against transgression.

You also should not overlook the importance of understanding the subtext of lines 39-45. Note the nature of the attack in this section: Bettelheim has certain cultural views that he cannot put aside, and his intellectual views are biased by those notions. This type of ethnocentrism has been frequently attacked by the makers of the LSAT. Ironic, since it was this type of ethnocentrism that led to the early bias in standardized tests discussed at the start of this section!

Paragraph Four:
The start of the last paragraph continues the attack, noting somewhat dismissively that Bettelheim's suppressive views have been discredited to some extent in recent psychoanalytic literature.

The final lines serve as an attempt to draw the passage back to the ideas of the first paragraph, and are, quite likely, also an attempt by the test makers to draw some attention away from Bettelheim.

Of course, understanding the underlying intent of the test makers does not answer all of the questions for you. Some of the questions will address details of the passage, or specific viewpoint elements. However, some of the questions will be made easier with knowledge of the test makers' viewpoint. Consider, for example, the following question:

Which one of the following most accurately states the main idea of the passage?

While the context of the discussion is fairy tales, the main idea is that Bettelheim's view is incorrect. Consider then, the answer choices:

9. Which one of the following most accurately states the main idea of the passage?

    (A) While originally written for children, fairy tales also contain a deeper significance for adults that psychologists such as Bettelheim have shown to be their true meaning.
    (B) The "superficial" reading of a fairy tale, which deals only with the tale's content, is actually more enlightening for children than the "deeper" reading preferred by psychologists such as Bettelheim.
    (C) Because the content of fairy tales has historically run counter to prevailing orthodoxies about child-rearing, psychologists such as Bettelheim sometimes reinterpret them to suit their own pedagogical needs.
    (D) The pervasive need to deny adult evil has led psychologists such as Bettelheim to erroneously view fairy tales solely as instruments of moral instruction for children.
    (E) Although dismissed as unproductive by psychologists such as Bettelheim, fairy tales offer children imaginative experiences that help them grow into morally responsible adults.

As we know, the correct answer must attack Bettelheim. Answer choices (A), (B), (C), and (E) fail to attack Bettelheim, either at all or sufficiently. Only answer choice (D) directly attacks Bettelheim, by stating that "Bettelheim... erroneously view(s) fairy tales." Thus, answer choice (D) is correct. Statistically, this is a question that only about 60% of students answer correctly, yet, when placed against the background of our discussion of undermining overrepresented groups, answer choice (D) should jump off the page at you. This is how to improve your performance on the LSAT— when you can take advantage of the situation either through method or understanding, do so with authority.

3. Mixed Group Passages

Thus far, we have examined passages based primarily on single groups, either traditionally underrepresented or traditionally overrepresented groups. What happens, though, when a passage contains both groups? How do the test makers handle a situation, for example, when one of the members from the overrepresented group addresses one of the traditionally underrepresented groups, or vice versa? Let us take a moment to briefly discuss each scenario:

1. Member of an underrepresented group addresses a member of an overrepresented group.

   These scenarios occur relatively rarely, and thus they are not the focus of this section. When they do occur, it is normally because the member of the overrepresented group was critical of the member of the underrepresented group. Thus, the member of the underrepresented group is typically presented as being somewhat dismissive of the member of the overrepresented group (which is quite reasonable—who wouldn't be dismissive toward someone who criticized them?).

2. Member of an overrepresented group addresses a member of an underrepresented group.

   Although we find passages where members of an overrepresented group criticize a member of an underrepresented group, the response in those passages is predictable: that group or individual is then attacked. More interesting—and the focus of this section—are passages where members of an overrepresented group praise or commend members of an underrepresented group. For example, how would you expect the test takers to treat a Western Caucasian male scholar who wrote a study about the positive developments within a native culture? Such a scenario presents a bit of a dilemma for the test makers. Because the scholar is writing in a positive manner about a traditionally underrepresented group, the test makers endorse that position. But, perhaps because of the source of the commentary, the test makers usually also insert at least some mild criticism of the scholar. Thus, passages of this type, which we term "Assessing the Scholars," contain a fascinating display of the competing values of the test makers. Take a moment to consider the following passage, which falls into this category:

Most studies of recent Southeast Asian immigrants to the United States have focused on their adjustment to life in their adopted country and on the effects of leaving their homelands. James
(5) Tollefson's *Alien Winds* examines the resettlement process from a different perspective by investigating the educational programs offered in immigrant processing centers. Based on interviews, transcripts from classes, essays by immigrants, personal visits
(10) to a teacher-training unit, and official government documents, Tollefson relies on an impressive amount and variety of documentation in making his arguments about processing centers' educational programs.
(15) Tollefson's main contention is that the emphasis placed on immediate employment and on teaching the values, attitudes, and behaviors that the training personnel think will help the immigrants adjust more easily to life in the United States is often
(20) counterproductive and demoralizing. Because of concerns that the immigrants be self-supporting as soon as possible, they are trained almost exclusively for low-level jobs that do not require English proficiency. In this respect, Tollefson claims, the
(25) processing centers suit the needs of employers more than they suit the long-term needs of the immigrant community. Tollefson also detects a fundamental flaw in the attempts by program educators to instill in the immigrants the traditionally Western
(30) principles of self-sufficiency and individual success. These efforts often have the effect of undermining the immigrants' sense of community and, in doing so, sometimes isolate them from the moral support and even from business opportunities afforded by
(35) the immigrant community. The programs also encourage the immigrants to shed their cultural traditions and ethnic identity and adopt the lifestyles, beliefs, and characteristics of their adopted country if they wish to enter fully into the
(40) national life.
Tollefson notes that the ideological nature of these educational programs has roots in the turn-of-the-century educational programs designed to assimilate European immigrants into United
(45) States society. Tollefson provides a concise history of the assimilationist movement in immigrant education, in which European immigrants were encouraged to leave behind the ways of the Old World and to adopt instead the principles and
(50) practices of the New World.
Tollefson ably shows that the issues demanding real attention in the educational programs for Southeast Asian immigrants are not merely employment rates and government funding, but also

(55) the assumptions underpinning the educational values in the programs. He recommends many improvements for the programs, including giving the immigrants a stronger voice in determining their needs and how to meet them, redesigning the
(60) curricula, and emphasizing long-term language education and job training over immediate employment and the avoiding of public assistance. Unfortunately, though, Tollefson does not offer enough concrete solutions as to how these reforms
(65) could be carried out, despite his own descriptions of the complicated bureaucratic nature of the programs.

From a quick reading of the first sentence, this passage would appear to be a standard Affirming Underrepresented Groups passage. If so, we would expect a discussion that affirms some aspect of the Southeast Asian immigrant experience. However, as the first paragraph continues, the text makes clear that the discussion will focus on James Tollefson's *Alien Winds*, a book about the immigrant educational programs offered in immigrant processing centers. If Tollefson's book were about a different topic, we would then expect this passage to fall into the Undermining Overrepresented Groups category, and that Tollefson's views would be undermined within the passage. But, because Tollefson's book discusses an underrepresented group in a positive manner, the passage takes an entirely different approach to him.

Specifically, Tollefson has blamed the educational programs offered at the processing centers for causing certain difficulties encountered by immigrants, instead of blaming the immigrants themselves. This viewpoint is considered a positive assessment of the situation, as opposed to the normal critical position taken by many authors who are unable to look beyond the assumptions of their own culture and upbringing. Hence, the test makers will generally praise Tollefson, but because he is a member of an overrepresented group, they are also likely to criticize him in some small way as well.

Let us take a moment to review the passage, again focusing on the diversity elements and bypassing our VIEWSTAMP analysis:

> In the introductory paragraph of the passage, the author indicates that James Tollefson's work is distinct from most studies of southeast Asian immigrants (line 4-6). Unlike the majority of such inquiries, which tend to focus on immigrants' adaptation to change, Tollefson's work, *Alien Winds*, is a study of immigrant processing center educational programs, and is based on many sources, which the author calls "impressive" in amount and variety (line 11). This description is the first tangible sign that Tollefson is going to receive more lenient treatment than you would otherwise expect.

> The second paragraph begins with a review of Tollefson's main contention that the emphasis on immediate employment and on teaching employable qualities in the educational programs leads to problems for immigrants. The paragraph continues on to discuss the various supporting facts and theories advanced by Tollefson. The paragraph itself is quite dense and contains a number of disparate facts. Other than noting that Tollefson "detects a fundamental flaw" in the programs, the focus of the discussion in this paragraph is not on the diversity elements, but rather creating a section of text that can be used to generate questions for the problem set.

In the third paragraph, the author discusses the foundations of the educational programs that are the focus of the first two paragraphs of the passage. Aside from describing Tollefson's history as "concise," this paragraph does not touch on the author's attitude towards the groups under discussion.

Up to this point, the author has favorably reviewed Tollefson's approach in his book. Among other things, his work has been called "impressive" and "concise," and at the start of this paragraph the author mentions that Tollefson "ably shows" the real issues (line 51). Given that Tollefson is addressing an underrepresented group in a positive manner, this is not surprising. But, because Tollefson is also a member of an overrepresented group, the test makers typically feel some need to criticize. Consequently, in the final paragraph, starting at line 63, the author provides a light critique of *Alien Winds* as a closing note: the work presents good ideas but lacks sufficient suggestions for the implementation of the suggested reforms.

So, even though Tollefson is a member of an overrepresented group, there is a considerable reduction in the force of the criticism directed his way. This is likely because the general theme of diversity is dominant, and thus the test makers prefer to direct positive attention towards the underrepresented group.

Because such attitudes are central to the passage, there will often be a question about the author's opinion of the critiqued work. This passage is no exception:

> Which one of the following best describes the opinion
> of the author of the passage with respect to Tollefson's work?

The answer to this question is one that we should prephrase. Again, the general tone of the passage is positive with regard to examined work, but of course it is vital that we recognize both sides of the author's mixed review of *Alien Winds*: the author is impressed with Tollefson's subject matter, sources, and basic assertions regarding immigrant education and necessary changes, but does not feel that Tollefson provides specific direction for the application of these changes.

Consider then, the entire question:

24. Which one of the following best describes the opinion of the
author of the passage with respect to Tollefson's work?

    (A)   thorough but misguided
    (B)   innovative but incomplete
    (C)   novel but contradictory
    (D)   illuminating but unappreciated
    (E)   well documented but unoriginal

In this question, the first word in each answer choice could apply to the
author's view of Tollefson's work. Thus, the last word must provide the
principal basis for selecting the correct answer choice. Answer choice (B),
"incomplete" is directly supported by lines 63-67 and is thus correct. Note that
the last word in answer choice (D) is the most benign of the five choices.
As an aside, this particular format, where each answer choice contains one
or two descriptive words, generally requires less time to complete than other
questions. With that in mind, if you find yourself running out of time on a
Reading Comprehension passage, it is recommended that you skip ahead to
questions such as this one. You may be able to complete an extra question or
two in the remaining time by answering easier question types.

The ultimate lesson here is that in passages that mix underrepresented and
overrepresented groups, you must carefully examine the statements of each
group. The test makers will direct the passage in various directions depending
on the nature of what is being said, but, as we have seen throughout our
discussion, those directions are generally predictable.

Common Diversity Passage Themes

Thus far in this section we have examined how the test makers treat certain groups, and we have discovered that the test makers have consistent and predictable attitudes towards those groups. Further, there are also some recurrent themes *within* these types of passages that the test makers use to communicate the attitudes they hold. Let us examine two major Diversity themes, each of which addresses underrepresented groups:

1. The Blending of the Old and New

At one point, the first passage from five LSATs in a row was a Diversity passage featuring a blending of the old and new. These were the five passages that appeared from September 2006 to December 2007.

Of course, there are many more examples; these five were unique because they occurred consecutively.

These passages feature individuals or groups that blend old approaches and new approaches to create something unique and powerful. This "blended" approach bridges the gap between old and new by keeping some elements of the original approach but also by adopting elements of the new approach. The result is a synthesis of the two, and unique in and of itself. In all cases, the person or group who does the blending is praised as innovative or flexible.

Why is this theme used frequently in Diversity passages? Because the ability to adapt and to synthesize information is an extremely advanced and beneficial skill, and to attribute such a skill to any group is a positive statement (which is why in almost all instances, the ability to blend elements is praised). In a later passage we will see this theme at work, and if you wish to see other examples of this theme in actual LSAT Reading Comprehension passages, here are a few selected passages:

> September 2007, Passage #1—Ousmane Sembène
> June 2007, Passage #1—Rita Dove
> December 2006, Passage #1—Ezekiel Mphahlele
> September 2006, Passage #1—Mexican American Literature
> June 2002, Passage #3—The Invisible Man

2. Defiance of Classification

A number of LSAT passages discuss persons or groups that either cannot be classified by conventional means, confound their critics, or are underappreciated in their time. The message of these passages is that the person or subject under discussion is too unique or powerful to be classified, or is so progressive that their contemporaries could not understand the full merit of their work.

The Miles Davis passage discussed earlier perfectly exemplifies the concept of "Defiance of Classification," and these same basic ideas show up with surprising regularity.

Final Note

The message of this section is that the makers of the test have certain viewpoints that they hold, and that the history of standardized testing—along with elements of fairness and equal representation—has played a role in formulating those viewpoints. When the makers of a test hold certain viewpoints, those views are ingrained into the construction of the test, and certain patterns emerge. This general predictability is the theme of this section; the test makers have proven over the years to have an agenda, and your knowledge of this agenda—regardless of your view of it—is critical. While the test makers are not constrained to always follow the route they have taken in the past, the overwhelming evidence suggests that more often than not they will continue to do so. Thus, it is in your best interest to be informed about their actions.

The next section presents two Diversity practice passages, and thereafter we move on to discuss Law-Related and Science passages.

Asian American poetry from Hawaii, the Pacific island state of the United States, is generally characterizable in one of two ways: either as portraying a model multicultural paradise, or as
(5) exemplifying familiar Asian American literary themes such as generational conflict. In this light, the recent work of Wing Tek Lum in *Expounding the Doubtful Points* is striking for its demand to be understood on its own terms. Lum offers no romanticized notions of
(10) multicultural life in Hawaii, and while he does explore themes of family, identity, history, and literary tradition, he does not do so at the expense of attempting to discover and retain a local sensibility. For Lum such a sensibility is informed by the fact
(15) that Hawaii's population, unlike that of the continental U.S., has historically consisted predominantly of people of Asian and Pacific island descent, making the experience of its Asian Americans somewhat different than that of mainland
(20) Asian Americans.

In one poem, Lum meditates on the ways in which a traditional Chinese lunar celebration he is attending at a local beach both connects him to and separates him from the past. In the company of new
(25) Chinese immigrants, the speaker realizes that while ties to the homeland are comforting and necessary, it is equally important to have "a sense of new family" in this new land of Hawaii, and hence a new identity-one that is sensitive to its new environment.
(30) The role of immigrants in this poem is significant in that, through their presence, Lum is able to refer both to the traditional culture of his ancestral homeland as well as to the flux within Hawaiian society that has been integral to its heterogeneity. Even in a laudatory
(35) poem to famous Chinese poet Li Po (701-762 A.D.), which partly serves to place Lum's work within a distinguished literary tradition, Lum refuses to offer a stereotypical nostalgia for the past, instead pointing out the often elitist tendencies inherent in the work of
(40) some traditionally acclaimed Chinese poets.

Lum closes his volume with a poem that further points to the complex relationships between heritage and local culture in determining one's identity. Pulling together images and figures as vastly
(45) disparate as a famous Chinese American literary character and an old woman selling bread, Lum avoids an excessively romantic vision of U.S. culture, while simultaneously acknowledging the dream of this culture held by many newly arrived immigrants.
(50) The central image of a communal pot where each person chooses what she or he wishes to eat but shares with others the "sweet soup / spooned out at the end of the meal" is a hopeful one; however, it also appears to caution that the strong cultural
(55) emphasis in the U.S. on individual drive and success that makes retaining a sense of homeland tradition difficult should be identified and responded to in ways that allow for a healthy new sense of identity to be formed.

1. Which one of the following most accurately expresses the main point of the passage?

(A) The poetry of Lum departs from other Asian American poetry from Hawaii in that it acknowledges its author's heritage but also expresses the poet's search for a new local identity.

(B) Lum's poetry is in part an expression of the conflict between a desire to participate in a community with shared traditions and values and a desire for individual success.

(C) Lum writes poetry that not only rejects features of the older literary tradition in which he participates but also rejects the popular literary traditions of Hawaiian writers.

(D) The poetry of Lum illustrates the extent to which Asian American writers living in Hawaii have a different cultural perspective than those living in the continental U.S.

(E) Lum's poetry is an unsuccessful attempt to manage the psychological burdens of reconciling a sense of tradition with a healthy sense of individual identity.

2. Given the information in the passage, which one of the following is Lum most likely to believe?

(A) Images in a poem should be explained in that poem so that their meaning will be widely understood.

(B) The experience of living away from one's homeland is necessary for developing a healthy perspective on one's cultural traditions.

(C) It is important to reconcile the values of individual achievement and enterprise with the desire to retain one's cultural traditions.

(D) One's identity is continually in transition and poetry is a way of developing a static identity.

(E) One cannot both seek a new identity and remain connected to one's cultural traditions.

3. The author of the passage uses the phrase "the flux within Hawaiian society" (line 33) primarily in order to

    (A) describe the social tension created by the mix of attitudes exhibited by citizens of Hawaii
    (B) deny that Hawaiian society is culturally distinct from that of the continental U.S.
    (C) identify the process by which immigrants learn to adapt to their new communities
    (D) refer to the constant change to which the culture in Hawaii is subject due to its diverse population
    (E) emphasize the changing attitudes of many immigrants to Hawaii toward their traditional cultural norms

4. According to the passage, some Asian American literature from Hawaii has been characterized as which one of the following?

    (A) inimical to the process of developing a local sensibility
    (B) centered on the individual's drive to succeed
    (C) concerned with conflicts between different age groups
    (D) focused primarily on retaining ties to one's homeland
    (E) tied to a search for a new sense of family in a new land

5. The author of the passage describes *Expounding the Doubtful Points* as "striking" (lines 7-8) primarily in order to

    (A) underscore the forceful and contentious tone of the work
    (B) indicate that the work has not been properly analyzed by literary critics
    (C) stress the radical difference between this work and Lum's earlier work
    (D) emphasize the differences between this work and that of other Asian American poets from Hawaii
    (E) highlight the innovative nature of Lum's experiments with poetic form

6. With which one of the following statements regarding Lum's poetry would the author of the passage be most likely to agree?

    (A) It cannot be used to support any specific political ideology.
    (B) It is an elegant demonstration of the poet's appreciation of the stylistic contributions of his literary forebears.
    (C) It is most fruitfully understood as a meditation on the choice between new and old that confronts any human being in any culture.
    (D) It conveys thoughtful assessments of both his ancestral homeland tradition and the culture in which he is attempting to build a new identity.
    (E) It conveys Lum's antipathy toward tradition by juxtaposing traditional and nontraditional images.

In the field of historiography—the writing of history based on a critical examination of authentic primary information sources—one area that has recently attracted attention focuses on the responses
(5) of explorers and settlers to new landscapes in order to provide insights into the transformations the landscape itself has undergone as a result of settlement. In this endeavor historiographers examining the history of the Pacific Coast of the
(10) United States have traditionally depended on the records left by European American explorers of the nineteenth century who, as commissioned agents of the U.S. government, were instructed to report thoroughly their findings in writing.

(15)   But in furthering this investigation some historiographers have recently recognized the need to expand their definition of what a source is. They maintain that the sources traditionally accepted as documenting the history of the Pacific Coast have too
(20) often omitted the response of Asian settlers to this territory. In part this is due to the dearth of written records left by Asian settlers; in contrast to the commissioned agents, most of the people who first came to western North America from Asia during this
(25) same period did not focus on developing a self-conscious written record of their involvement with the landscape. But because a full study of a culture's historical relationship to its land cannot confine itself to a narrow record of experience, these
(30) historiographers have begun to recognize the value of other kinds of evidence, such as the actions of Asian settlers.

As a case in point, the role of Chinese settlers in expanding agriculture throughout the Pacific Coast
(35) territory is integral to the history of the region. Without access to the better land, Chinese settlers looked for agricultural potential in this generally arid region where other settlers did not. For example, where settlers of European descent looked at willows
(40) and saw only useless, untillable swamp, Chinese settlers saw fresh water, fertile soil, and the potential for bringing water to more arid areas via irrigation. Where other settlers who looked at certain weeds, such as wild mustard, generally saw a nuisance,
(45) Chinese settlers saw abundant raw material for valuable spices from a plant naturally suited to the local soil and climate.

Given their role in the labor force shaping this territory in the nineteenth century, the Chinese settlers
(50) offered more than just a new view of the land. Their vision was reinforced by specialized skills involving swamp reclamation and irrigation systems, which helped lay the foundation for the now well-known and prosperous agribusiness of the region. That
(55) 80 percent of the area's cropland is now irrigated and that the region is currently the top producer of many specialty crops cannot be fully understood by historiographers without attention to the input of Chinese settlers as reconstructed from their
(60) interactions with that landscape.

8. Which one of the following most accurately states the main point of the passage?

(A) The history of settlement along the Pacific Coast of the U.S., as understood by most historiographers, is confirmed by evidence reconstructed from the actions of Asian settlers.

(B) Asian settlers on the Pacific Coast of the U.S. left a record of their experiences that traditional historiographers believed to be irrelevant.

(C) To understand Asian settlers' impact on the history of the Pacific Coast of the U.S., historiographers have had to recognize the value of nontraditional kinds of historiographic evidence.

(D) Spurred by new findings regarding Asian settlement on the Pacific Coast of the U.S. historiographers have begun to debate the methodological foundations of historiography.

(E) By examining only written information, historiography as it is traditionally practiced has produced inaccurate historical accounts.

9. Which one of the following most accurately describes the author's primary purpose in discussing Chinese settlers in the third paragraph?

(A) to suggest that Chinese settlers followed typical settlement patterns in this region during the nineteenth century

(B) to argue that little written evidence of Chinese settlers' practices survives

(C) to provide examples illustrating the unique view Asian settlers had of the land

(D) to demonstrate that the history of settlement in the region has become a point of contention among historiographers

(E) to claim that the historical record provided by the actions of Asian settlers is inconsistent with history as derived from traditional sources

10. The passage states that the primary traditional historiographic sources of information about the history of the Pacific Coast of the U.S. have which one of the following characteristics?

(A) They were written both before and after Asian settlers arrived in the area.

(B) They include accounts by Native Americans in the area.

(C) They are primarily concerned with potential agricultural uses of the land.

(D) They focus primarily on the presence of water sources in the region.

(E) They are accounts left by European American explorers.

11. The author would most likely disagree with which one of the following statements?

(A)   Examining the actions not only of Asian settlers but of other cultural groups of the Pacific Coast of the U.S. is necessary to a full understanding of the impact of settlement on the landscape there.

(B)   The significance of certain actions to the writing of history may be recognized by one group of historiographers but not another.

(C)   Recognizing the actions of Asian settlers adds to but does not complete the writing of the history of the Pacific Coast of the U.S.

(D)   By recognizing as evidence the actions of people, historiographers expand the definition of what a source is.

(E)   The expanded definition of a source will probably not be relevant to studies of regions that have no significant immigration of non-Europeans.

12. According to the passage, each of the following was an aspect of Chinese settlers' initial interactions with the landscape of the Pacific Coast of the U.S. EXCEPT:

(A)   new ideas for utilizing local plants
(B)   a new view of the land
(C)   specialized agricultural skills
(D)   knowledge of agribusiness practices
(E)   knowledge of irrigation systems

13. Which one of the following can most reasonably be inferred from the passage?

(A)   Most Chinese settlers came to the Pacific Coast of the U.S. because the climate was similar to that with which they were familiar.

(B)   Chinese agricultural methods in the nineteenth century included knowledge of swamp reclamation.

(C)   Settlers of European descent used wild mustard seed as a spice.

(D)   Because of the abundance of written sources available, it is not worthwhile to examine the actions of European settlers.

(E)   What written records were left by Asian settlers were neglected and consequently lost to scholarly research.

14. Which one of the following, if true, would most help to strengthen the author's main claim in the last sentence of the passage?

(A)   Market research of agribusinesses owned by descendants of Chinese settlers shows that the market for the region's specialty crops has grown substantially faster than the market for any other crops in the last decade.

(B)   Nineteenth-century surveying records indicate that the lands now cultivated by specialty crop businesses owned by descendants of Chinese settlers were formerly swamp lands.

(C)   Research by university agricultural science departments proves that the formerly arid lands now cultivated by large agribusinesses contain extremely fertile soil when they are sufficiently irrigated.

(D)   A technological history tracing the development of irrigation systems in the region reveals that their efficiency has increased steadily since the nineteenth century.

(E)   Weather records compiled over the previous century demonstrate that the weather patterns in the region are well-suited to growing certain specialty crops as long as they are irrigated.

Paragraph One:

This passage focuses on Wing Tek Lum, a member of a traditionally underrepresented group. Aside from falling into the Affirming Underrepresented Groups category, this passage also exemplifies the Defiance of Classification that is an underlying theme in many Diversity passages. It is also common for an LSAT author to begin a passage by introducing traditional viewpoints, in order to then present a contrasting perspective. In this passage, the author starts with an introduction to the traditional viewpoints of Asian American poets from Hawaii: generally their work reflects either a multicultural utopia, or traditional themes found in Asian American literature (the example provided is that of generational conflict). The author presents these traditional perspectives in order to immediately distinguish the work of Wing Tek Lum from most examples of Hawaiian Asian American writings. Lum's work, *Expounding the Doubtful Points*, is very distinct (*striking*ly so, according to the author of the passage) in that the work does not portray Hawaii as a multicultural paradise, and even familiar themes are explored with the understanding that the experiences of Hawaiian Asian Americans is different from that of Asian Americans on the mainland.

This introductory paragraph provides vital information; the author introduces traditional viewpoints of Asian American poetry from Hawaii, and distinguishes the work of Wing Tek Lum. The passage to this point reflects the author's viewpoint, which takes on an extremely positive tone with regard to Lum and the work under review.

Paragraph Two:

In the second paragraph we see another theme common among Diversity passages: The Blending of Old and New. The author begins the paragraph discussing a poem about a Chinese lunar celebration. Lum appreciates the homeland connection provided by the traditional celebration, as well as the identity that comes with "a sense of new family." The recent Chinese immigrants in attendance provide Lum with a reference to the dynamic and multifaceted Hawaiian society, which the poet blends with reference to the beach celebration which reflects his ancestral tradition.

This paragraph ends with the author providing another example of Lum's Defiance of Classification: in a poem which praises Li Po, a Chinese poet from the eighth century, Lum chooses to underscore the elitism of some traditional Chinese poetry, rather than taking the more standard nostalgic perspective that might be expected in such a poem.

This second paragraph continues the positive tone from the introduction—the author's viewpoint: Lum is not like the rest; the poet blends the old with the new and provides a perspective which is distinct from the traditional.

Paragraph Three:

It is now clear that the entire passage presents the viewpoint of the author, who is very impressed with Lum. In this third paragraph, the author continues the positive tone with a discussion of the final poem from *Expounding the Doubtful Points*. By striking up the image of a famous Chinese American character alongside that of an old woman selling bread, Lum pays homage to the new immigrants' dreams without portraying an overly romantic notion of U.S. culture. As a closing note, the author of the passage references a Lum quote which is optimistic but cautionary: the American focus on drive and success might make it difficult for an immigrant to hold onto the homeland culture, but with the proper response, a "healthy new sense of identity" can emerge (this closing note provides another great example of the emphasis on Blending the Old and New).

VIEWSTAMP Analysis:

The entire passage is written from the **Viewpoint** of the author, who is very impressed with Lum's distinct approach to Asian American poetry.

The **Structure** of the passage is as follows:

> Paragraph One: Introduce the general topic of Asian American poetry from Hawaii, Lum's *Expounding the Doubtful Points*, and the work's "demand to be understood on its own terms."

> Paragraph Two: Discuss one of Lum's poems in which the poet Blends the Old and New, and another which distinguishes Lum's poetry from the traditional Chinese poetry.

> Paragraph Three: Discuss another poem which Blends Old and New, and show Lum's attitude to be optimistic but cautionary.

The author's **Tone** is clearly positive with regard to Lum, and respectful of the poet's focus on both tradition and "a sense of new family."

The **Argument** in the passage is the author's assertion that Lum's work defies the traditional characterizations, blending the old and the new to present a distinct perspective.

The author's **Main Point** is that Lum's poetry represents a departure from the norm, reflecting both a respect for tradition and an understanding of the importance of developing a new immigrant identity.

Question #1: GR, Main Point. The correct answer choice is (A)

Answer choice (A): This is the correct answer choice, as it restates the author's Main Point, discussed above; Lum is distinctive in that he focuses on both tradition and the importance of a new identity.

Answer choice (B): Although the poem discussed in the last paragraph does reference the conflict between homeland tradition and the American emphasis on success, this does not represent the main point of the passage.

Answer choice (C): Lum does highlight the elitist tendencies of some traditional Chinese poetry in lines 39-40, although this does not necessarily amount to rejection. And while the author does believe that Lum's work is distinct from other Asian American poetry from Hawaii, this is certainly not the same as rejecting popular literary traditions of Hawaii.

Answer choice (D): At the end of the first paragraph the author points out Lum's understanding that the Hawaiian Asian Americans' perspective differs from that of mainland Asian Americans (not referring solely to *writers*, however). In any case, this is certainly not the main point of the passage, so this answer choice is incorrect.

Answer choice (E): If we have an understanding of the tone of this passage, we can recognize that this answer choice is incorrect when we get to the phrase "unsuccessful attempt." The author of the passage is clearly a fan of Lum's, and believes that Lum is successful in his efforts to blend tradition with a new sense of identity.

Question #2: GR, Must, SP. The correct answer choice is (C)

With regard to Subject Perspective questions, it is always important to understand what the author has relayed about the subject in question. In this case, we know that the author is impressed with Lum's perspective, since the poet considers the importance of both the old and the new in the development of an identity.

Answer choice (A): The author of this passage never discusses Lum's focus on widespread understanding; there is a reference to the disparate imagery in Lum's poetry, but this is very different from a focus on making the work widely understandable.

Answer choice (B): Lum believes that it is possible to develop a healthy perspective on one's culture while living away from the homeland, but nothing in the passage suggests that leaving one's homeland is necessary for this sort of development.

Answer choice (C): This is the correct answer choice. This answer passes the Fact Test; we can confirm this choice with the information from the cautionary note in the last sentence of the passage. Lum believes that it is important to respond to the American drive for success in a way that allows for retention of one's homeland culture; this is an important reconciliation between traditional culture and one particular emphasis of the new culture.

Answer choice (D): The passage does not refer to poetry as a way to fight change; on the contrary, the author praises Lum's recognition of the "flux within Hawaiian society that has been integral to its heterogeneity." (lines 33-34)

Answer choice (E): This is an Opposite answer choice: it is completely contrary to the passage, in which the author praises Lum for his ability to remain connected to his homeland culture while understanding the importance of developing a new sense of identity.

Question #3: CR, Must. The correct answer choice is (D)

In responding to Specific Reference questions such as this one, it is advisable to examine the referenced quote in context. In this case, the author praises Lum for being "able to refer both to the traditional culture…as well as to the flux within Hawaiian society that has been integral to its heterogeneity." So, Lum references tradition, and the quote referenced in the question regards the dynamic nature that has been integral to the society's multi-faceted culture.

Answer choice (A): The author sees the flux as positive, and integral to the heterogeneity of the society; there is no discussion of social tension.

Answer choice (B): Since the author (and Lum) clearly believe that there are cultural distinctions between Hawaiian society and that of the mainland, this answer choice is incorrect.

Answer choice (C): The referenced quote is intended to describe an attribute of the Hawaiian society, not to identify specific adaptation processes.

Answer choice (D): This is the correct answer choice. As prephrased above, the quote refers to the changes that come with Hawaii's cultural diversity.

Answer choice (E): In context, "flux" references the changing nature of the society, not the changing attitudes of immigrants toward their cultural norms.

Question #4: GR, Must. The correct answer choice is (C)

There are references to other Asian American literature (not by Lum) in the first and second paragraphs of the passage. In the first paragraph, the author tells us that generally Asian American poetry characterized Hawaii as a multicultural paradise, or explores familiar themes such as generational conflict. At the end of the second paragraph, the author refers to Lum's assertion of elitism in some traditional Chinese poetry.

Answer choice (A): "Inimical" basically means adverse, or harmful, and the author does not characterize Asian American poetry as adverse to the process of developing a local sensibility. Note: if unsure of the meaning of a word such as "inimical," it is advisable to skip the answer while assessing the other choices.

Answer choice (B): The passage does not characterize Asian American literature as focused on the individual's drive to succeed—it is United States culture that maintains this focus, according to the final paragraph of the passage.

Answer choice (C): This is the correct answer choice. This conflict is described as an attribute of some Asian American poetry in the first paragraph; the author provides generational conflict as an example of a familiar theme in Asian American literature.

Answer choice (D): In the second paragraph of the passage the author discusses the comfort and necessity of retaining ties to one's homeland, but this is not presented as a *primary* focus of some Asian American literature.

Answer choice (E): Again, the search for a new sense of family in a new land is discussed with regard to Lum, but is not presented as a primary focus of some Asian American literature, so this answer choice is incorrect.

Question #5: SR, Must. The correct answer choice is (D)

Again, with specific reference questions we should always be sure to have the proper context associated with a referenced word or phrase. In this case, the author describes *Expounding the Doubtful Points* as "striking for its demand to be understood on its own terms." *Striking* is a rather strong term, intended to strongly distinguish Lum's work from much other Asian American poetry.

Answer choice (A): Lum's work is described by the author as neither forceful nor contentious, so this answer choice is incorrect.

Answer choice (B): Since there is no reference to the other critics' analysis of Lum's work, this answer choice cannot be correct.

Answer choice (C): The quote in this question does reference a radical difference—the difference between Lum's poetry and the work of *other* poets, not between Lum's recent and past work.

Answer choice (D): This is the correct answer choice. Unlike other examples of Asian American poetry from Hawaii, the author provides, Lum's work is strikingly distinct.

Answer choice (E): The term *striking* is used to describe the distinction between Lum's poetry and the work of others, with regard to Lum's characterizations of the culture in Hawaii, not with regard to his experimental poetic form.

Question #6: GR, Must, AP. The correct answer choice is (D)

Since this is an Author's Perspective question we should be sure to identify the tone reflected in the passage. In this case, the author's tone is very positive with respect to Lum's poetry; in particular the author is impressed with the poet's focus on the importance to immigrants of retaining a sense of homeland culture, coupled with the value of developing a new sense of identity and culture.

Answer choice (A): The passage contains no reference to the poetry's prospective use in support of political ideology, so this answer choice is incorrect.

Answer choice (B): At the end of the second paragraph, the author does refer to one of Lum's poems as "laudatory," but there is no specific reference to the poet's appreciation for the stylistic contributions of his literary forbears.

Answer choice (C): The author does not perceive Lum's poetry as choosing sides; rather, the author is impressed with the way the poet blends themes which reference the Old and the New.

Answer choice (D): This is the correct answer choice, and reflects the same theme as our prephrase: the author is impressed with Lum's references to the importance of both the homeland culture and a new sense of identity.

Answer choice (E): The use of the term *antipathy* (meaning distaste or aversion; roughly the opposite of sympathy) should tell us that this answer choice doesn't reflect the tone of the passage. Lum is not characterized by the passage as having an *aversion* to tradition; rather, Lum sees the importance of both tradition and a new sense of identity.

This passage, in which the author discusses how Chinese settlers influenced the Pacific Coast landscape, and the value of studying this influence, reflects two common themes discussed earlier in this chapter. First, this is a Diversity passage in which a traditionally underrepresented group is praised for its positive impact; second, the value of studying this influence represents the application of a new perspective to an old line of inquiry.

Paragraph One:

The author starts the passage by providing the definition of Historiography—the writing of history based on certain authentic sources. The author points to an area that has recently attracted attention. The focus on how explorers and settlers responded to their newfound landscapes can provide insight into the land's transformations during that era. Previously, settlers' accounts have been used as the primary source of information about the settling of the United States Pacific Coast; European American explorers have been the traditional sources of such accounts, as they were commissioned by the U.S. government to keep detailed written records of their findings.

Paragraph Two:

Now that we have some background, the author turns to historiographers' recent recognition of the need to expand their definition of a source. Historical accounts have often omitted the perspectives of Chinese settlers, in part because these people were less focused on documentation of such matters and therefore left less written records. The point here is to emphasize the importance of the Chinese in the development of the landscape. This provides the author with the opportunity to praise a traditionally underrepresented group, and to point out that ignoring the influence of the Chinese would leave a cultural study incomplete. This is why historiographers have come to rely on other sources of historical data. Note that reliance on new sources of data reflects the application of a new approach or perspective to old inquiries regarding the development of the U.S. Pacific Coast landscape.

Paragraph Three:

The third paragraph offers examples of the actions of the early Chinese settlers, showing how such evidence is relevant to the creation of a more complete cultural history of the area: with less access to more fertile soil, the Chinese found potential where the Europeans had not, using irrigation and taking advantage of some of the area's natural harvests, such as wild mustard, which had previously been seen only as a nuisance.

Paragraph Four:

In the last paragraph, the author again emphasizes the importance of the Chinese settlers in shaping this territory, given their vision and expertise in irrigation and swamp reclamation. In the final sentence, the author argues that historiographers should pay attention to the Chinese influence on this region's settlement, considering its modern day irrigated farmlands and various specialty crops.

<u>VIEWSTAMP Analysis:</u>

This passage presents the Viewpoint of the author, who believes that historiography can benefit from studying the effects of the early settlers on the U.S. Pacific Coast landscape.

The **Structure** of the passage is as follows:

<u>Paragraph One</u>: Introduce historiography, and its traditional sources of evidence.

<u>Paragraph Two</u>: Discuss the recent recognition of the need to expand on sources used, to include consideration of the actions of Chinese settlers.

<u>Paragraph Three</u>: List specific influences of the Chinese settlers.

<u>Paragraph Four</u>: Restate the importance of considering the effects of these settlers on the landscape that developed.

The **Tone** of the passage is positive with respect to the settlers, and supportive of the appropriate addition of relevant sources to the field of historiography

The primary **Argument** of the passage is that of the author, whose primary assertion is that the early Chinese settlers had a significant effect on the Pacific Coast landscape, and that this effect should be considered to develop a broader view of historiography.

The author's **Main Point** is to introduce the concept of historiography, and to point out the importance of non-traditional information sources, especially with respect to the actions of the Chinese settlers, in understanding the development of the Pacific Northwest landscape.

Question #8: GR, Main Point. The correct answer choice is (C)

Since this is a Main Point question, we should attempt to form a prephrase before beginning to assess the answer choices. The main point of this passage, roughly, is to introduce historiography and discuss the need to include early Chinese settlers' actions as a source of historical information.

Answer choice (A): Part of the point of this passage is that historiographers need to expand their definition of a source if they are to have a complete understanding of the development of the landscape. If historiographers need to pay attention to non-written evidence made by Chinese settlers, it must be that this new evidence would offer some insight, so it seems highly unlikely that such new sources might simply confirm what historians already knew.

Answer choice (B): The passage suggested that the attention to the influence of Chinese settlers is recent, but that doesn't mean that historiographers have traditionally assumed that such evidence is irrelevant. They might simply have failed to see the existence of such evidence.

Answer choice (C): This is the correct answer choice, as it sums up the author's main point in

---

writing this passage. The author states in lines 15-17 that historiographers have recognized a need to expand their definition of a source, and in lines 54-60 the author states that historiographers cannot understand the development of the U.S. Pacific Coast without considering the actions of Chinese settlers.

Answer choice (D): Since the passage never suggests that Pacific Coast historiographers are divided over whether to pay attention to new types of evidence, this answer choice is unfounded. Furthermore, since historiographers recognize the need for new types of evidence, there appears to be some consensus. Finally, adding a new type of evidence is not the same as challenging a methodological foundation.

Answer choice (E): The author's point is not that older accounts have been inaccurate, but rather that they have been incomplete. Further, since the author explicitly confines the discussion to the historiography of the U.S. Pacific Coast, we cannot justifiably select a response that refers to the whole of historiography.

Question #9: SR, P. The correct answer choice is (C)

Since this question specifically refers to the third paragraph, it is once again advantageous to have an understanding of the structure of the passage. The third paragraph provides examples of the integral role of the Chinese settlers on the landscape, which is what we should prephrase before moving on to the answer choices.

Answer choice (A): The examples in the third paragraph illustrate that Chinese settlers were atypical, and the author doesn't examine their settlement patterns.

Answer choice (B): It seems true that there is little written evidence of the practices of the Chinese settlers. But this is not because such records didn't survive, but because the Chinese settlers simply didn't leave "a self-conscious written record" (lines 21-27).
Further, since the question is about the function of the third paragraph, we can confidently eliminate this incorrect answer choice.

Answer choice (C): This is the correct answer choice. The author argues that considering the Chinese perspective on the landscape is critical to understanding the transformation of the U.S. Pacific Coast. The third paragraph develops that argument by showing how the Chinese perspective was distinctive from the European perspective.

Answer choice (D): This answer choice is incorrect, since no debate among the historiographers is even alluded to in the passage. On the contrary, there appears to be a consensus among historiographers that new sources must be considered to have a more complete perspective on the development of the region.

Answer choice (E): The author's claim is not that the new source of evidence is inconsistent with traditional accounts, but rather that information about the actions of the Chinese settlers would complement the sources already considered. The new sources, when considered along with the traditional, would offer a more complete historiography.

Question #10: CR, Must. The correct answer choice is (E)

Since this question concerns the traditional sources of information for historiographers, the relevant reference point, considering the organization of the passage, would be the first paragraph.

Answer choice (A): Since the passage offers no information as to the timing of the Chinese settlement relative to the writing of the traditional sources of historiography, this answer choice is incorrect.

Answer choice (B): No mention is made in the passage concerning Native American accounts, so we cannot confidently confirm or deny this assertion.

Answer choice (C): While it does seem likely that traditional sources are concerned with potential agricultural uses of the land, the author never specifies this, and certainly does not assert that this was a primary concern.

Answer choice (D): Once again, the author does not indicate precisely an American-European explorer's focus. The passage explicitly states that the Chinese were concerned with water sources, which should not be confused with American-European concern. Furthermore, once again there is no evidence as to the primary concern of any of the parties in the passage.

Answer choice (E): This is the correct answer choice, as it references the author's explicit statements in lines 8-14. Since historiographers have traditionally depended on the written records of European-American explorers, it makes sense that, traditionally, the primary sources have been the accounts of those explorers.

Question #11: GR, Must, AP. The correct answer choice is (E)

Since this question asks for the response that the author would most likely disagree with, we should look for the answer choice that cannot be true based on the information provided in the stimulus.

Answer choice (A): Since the author acknowledges that a specific new source is likely to be valuable to the formation of a complete cultural perspective, this answer choice provides an assertion with which the author would likely agree.

Answer choice (B): Since there has been a change in what historiographers of the U.S. Pacific Coast view as a source, some time might lapse before every historiographer knows of these new sources to be considered, so the author might agree with this assertion. In any case, there is no reason to assume that the author would disagree, so this answer choice is incorrect.

Answer choice (C): The author asserts that the historiography was incomplete without consideration of the acts of early Chinese settlers, so the same might be said for other sources not previously considered. Since the author would be likely to agree with this statement, this answer choice is incorrect.

Answer choice (D): Since this answer basically paraphrases the claims found in lines 15-17, this assertion is not one with which the author would disagree, so this answer is wrong.

Answer choice (E): This is the correct answer choice. The author's arguments relay the idea that, wherever written evidence neglects an important, contributing population, historiographers should investigate this new source of information. This assertion is based not on the fact that the settlers were non-European, but rather that they made important contributions. Thus the author would disagree with this answer choice, which asserts non-European participation is required to expand the definition of a source.

Question #12: GR, Must, X. The correct answer choice is (D)

This is another example of a question which becomes much easier when one considers passage organization. Since this question concerns early Chinese settler's interactions with the landscape, it seems that the relevant reference point would be the third paragraph, which deals almost exclusively with Chinese influences on the initial development of the region.

Answer choice (A): The new utilizations of local plants are discussed in lines 43-47, which describe the Chinese use of the wild mustard plant. Because this is an Except question, this answer choice, which accurately reflects information in the passage, should be eliminated.

Answer choice (B): The author specifically discusses the Chinese view of the land in lines 36-42, so this response provides an aspect discussed in the passage, and is therefore incorrect.

Answer choice (C): The discussion of Chinese ability to find unexpected agricultural potential in new areas and new plants, and use irrigation, as described in the third paragraph, is evidence that the Chinese had specialized agricultural skills. Since this is discussed in the passage, this answer choice is incorrect.

Answer choice (D): This is the correct answer choice, because the author makes no mention of initial Chinese knowledge of agribusiness practices. The Chinese settlers helped lay the foundations for what is now the well-known, prosperous agribusiness of the region (lines 50-54). Since the question asked about the settlers' initial interactions, and the passage discusses the agribusiness of a later era, this choice is the only answer that is unsupported, and it is therefore the correct response to this EXCEPT question.

Answer choice (E): Since the passage explicitly states in lines 48-54 that the Chinese settlers had knowledge of irrigation systems, this choice is supported, and incorrect.

Question #13: GR, Must. The correct answer choice is (B)

This question asks for the response that can be most reasonably inferred from the passage, so we must find the answer choice that is consistent with the author's reasoning. Often the most efficient approach to this sort of question is to review the choices and quickly eliminate any that are inconsistent with the passage, and then examine the remaining responses more closely.

Answer choice (A): While the early Chinese settlers did have important, transferable skills, there is no reason to presume that these were the result of having come from similar climates, and the passage offers no insight into whether the climate was the reason for their migration.

Answer choice (B): This is the correct answer choice, based on the fact that Chinese settlers brought these swamp reclamation skills to the Pacific Coast (lines 50-54). As for the fact that these methods were used in the 19th century, this is confirmed by the fact that the historiographers of the U.S. Pacific Coast region have, as explicitly stated, traditionally used nineteenth-century European-American accounts (lines 8-14), and the Chinese settlers discussed fall in the same period (lines 21-27).

Answer choice (C): According to the passage, it was the Chinese settlers who used the wild mustard seeds, while the European settlers generally viewed the plants as weeds (lines 43-47).

Answer choice (D): It is valuable to study the actions of the Chinese settlers because there was little recorded by them. The actions of the European settlers have presumably already been considered by the historiographers, and this is because of the abundance of written sources available.

Answer choice (E): Since the author explicitly states in lines 21-22 that written records never existed in many cases, this choice, which suggests that such written records did exist at one time, is unsupported.

Question #14: SR, Strengthen. The correct answer choice is (B)

This question asks which answer choice most effectively strengthens the author's claim in the last sentence, which basically states the main point of the passage: a complete historiography requires consideration of the actions of the early Chinese settlers. The correct answer choice will bolster this argument.

Answer choice (A): Since this response implies nothing directly about Chinese involvement in transforming the landscape, this answer is incorrect. Things change with time, and knowing what occurred during the past decade does not prove what occurred over a century ago. Further, the speed of the growth of the specialty crops relative to that of other crops has no clear relevance.

Answer choice (B): This is the correct answer choice, as this response would lend credibility to the claim that it was Chinese ancestors who converted the swamplands to grow the specialty crops currently cultivated by their Chinese-American descendants.

Answer choice (C): While this answer choice does provide evidence that irrigation is beneficial to agribusiness, it does nothing to provide support for the assertion that this benefit is attributable to early Chinese influence. Since this answer does not strengthen the claim from the last sentence in the passage, this choice is incorrect.

Answer choice (D): A steady increase in the efficiency of irrigation systems does not offer insight into their original source in the region. While this answer choice does appear to support the claim that irrigations improvements began in the nineteenth century, it does little to strengthen the claim that the early Chinese influence must be considered to form a more complete historiography.

Answer choice (E): Since we already know, given the passage, that agribusiness in the U.S. Pacific Coast region is thriving, it does not strengthen the author's argument to add reasons to believe that vegetation can grow well in that area. Although this response might make it more likely that irrigation is a good idea, it has nothing to do with whether such irrigation is attributable to early Chinese influence.

Law Related Passages

As we discussed in Chapter 2 on page 9, the LSAT Reading Comprehension section usually features one passage based on a law related issue. Therefore, a brief examination of law related passages is helpful to understanding the type of topics you will typically encounter.

Many students assume that because the LSAT is the test to gain admission to law school, the makers of the test must defend the legal system at every turn in the passages they present. This assumption is incorrect. Instead, the test makers treat the Law as a positive, benevolent, dynamic, and at times flawed system.

Seeing the legal system as having flaws is not unreasonable. A system as complex as law is bound to have areas where confusion, uncertainty, or change arises. This uncertainty within law can come from the rules, the witnesses, the attorneys, or even the judges. The test makers are happy to engage in frank discussions of the issues related to improving any aspect of the judicial system, and passages have addressed the following issues:

> Inferential errors made by juries
>
> How the Web affects copyright holders
>
> The blandness of legal writing
>
> Possible bias introduced by computer displays in court
>
> Indeterminacy in legal outcomes

If you encounter any unknown legal terminology while reading a Law related passage, do not be concerned. Any legal terms will be explained in the text.

The above is just a small sampling of issues that the LSAT has addressed regarding the legal system.

On the other hand, the test makers show no hesitation in discussing the law as a positive force, and as a remedy to right social injustice. For example, passages have addressed some of the following topics where the law is used as a remedy or an aid:

> The benefits of bankruptcy law revisions
>
> Native American rights to property
>
> Regulation of international waters

There are also a number of passages that deal with legal theory, and "big picture" issues related to the legal system. Various passages have addressed how to interpret law, how to model legal reasoning on computers, and the basis for punishment within the legal system. These passages tend to be more theoretical in nature and focus less on real world examples.

The makers of the test also do not limit themselves to addressing just the U.S. system of law. A number of previous passages have addressed the legal systems of Canada and England, and even South Africa.

In short, the law is treated as the complicated, powerful system it is, and the test makers examine both the faults and benefits of the system, as well as the theoretical underpinnings. Given that the name of the company that produces the LSAT is Law Services, and thus one would expect that they have a great deal of familiarity with law related elements, this is no surprise.

Two Special Topics

There are two topics that appear within Law related passages that bear further examination because in each case the viewpoint taken by the makers of the test is consistent, and thus predictable. You can then use this information to move more quickly within the passages.

1. Regulation

The legal system is used to correct possible damage and to regulate actions and industries. On the LSAT, passages occasionally appear that address the legal regulation of marketplaces and borders. In almost all cases the viewpoint presented by the authors is the same: regulation is either needed or should be expanded if already in place. Given that Law Services is an organization that ultimately assists in producing lawyers, and it is the law which regulates our society, the consistency of this viewpoint should come as no surprise.

2. Diversity

We have already discussed passages that contain Diversity elements and discussed the consistency of the viewpoint presented in those passages. When passages concerning law related issues include diversity elements, that consistency continues. In almost all cases, the test makers advocate legal remedies and relief for underrepresented groups.

A Law Related Passage Analyzed

Now that we have discussed some of the different ways law related passages are presented, let us take a moment to examine a law related passage, and then discuss some of the notable elements. Please take several minutes to read the following passage:

(5)

(10)

(15)

Individual family members have been assisted in resolving disputes arising from divorce or separation, property division, or financial arrangements, through court-connected family mediation programs, which differ significantly from court adjudication. When courts use their authority to resolve disputes by adjudicating matters in litigation, judges' decisions are binding, subject only to appeal. Formal rules govern the procedure followed, and the hearings are generally open to the public. In contrast, family mediation is usually conducted in private, the process is less formal, and mediators do not make binding decisions. Mediators help disputing parties arrive at a solution themselves through communication and cooperation by facilitating the process of negotiation that leads to agreement by the parties.

(20)

(25)

(30)

(35)

(40)

Supporters of court adjudication in resolving family disputes claim that it has numerous advantages over family mediation, and there is some validity to this claim. Judges' decisions, they argue, explicate and interpret the broader social values involved in family disputes, and family mediation can neglect those values. Advocates of court adjudication also argue that since the dynamics of power in disputes are not always well understood, mediation, which is based on the notion of relatively equal parties, would be inappropriate in many situations. The court system, on the other hand, attempts to protect those at a disadvantage because of imbalances in bargaining power. Family mediation does not guarantee the full protection of an individual's rights, whereas a goal of the court system is to ensure that lawyers can secure all that the law promises to their clients. Family mediation also does not provide a formal record of the facts and principles that influence the settlement of a dispute, so if a party to a mediated agreement subsequently seeks modification of the judgment, the task of reconstructing the mediation process is especially difficult. Finally, mediated settlements divert cases from judicial consideration, thus eliminating the opportunity for such cases to refine the law through the ongoing development of legal precedent.

(45)

(50)

(55)

But in the final analysis, family mediation is better suited to the unique needs of family law than is the traditional court system. Proponents of family mediation point out that it constitutes a more efficient and less damaging process than litigation. By working together in the mediation process, family members can enhance their personal autonomy and reduce government intervention, develop skills to resolve future disputes, and create a spirit of cooperation that can lead to greater compliance with their agreement. The family mediation process can assist in resolving emotional as well as legal issues and thus may reduce

(60)

stress in the long term. Studies of family mediation programs in several countries report that the majority of participants reach a full or partial agreement and express positive feelings about the process, perceiving it to be more rational and humane than the court system.

The passage concerns the value of family mediation programs versus the formalized process of court adjudication. Not unsurprisingly for a Law related passage, the author provides a frank discussion of the issue at hand, showing both positives and negatives of each option before concluding that the non-court solution is better for the needs of this particular situation.

Paragraph One:

The passage opens by explaining that family members can be assisted in dispute resolution in a variety of instances with family mediation programs, which are court-connected but significantly different than court adjudication. Whereas court decisions use formal rules in public hearings to produce binding results, family mediation is less formal, private, and not binding, and aimed at finding a mutually agreeable resolution.

Paragraph Two:

The second paragraph is dedicated to a discussion of the value of court adjudication of family disputes. The paragraph opens with the viewpoint of the supporters of court adjudication, and the author separately weighs in with the view that the supporters have some valid claims. Specifically, the supporters of the court make four claims:

1. Judges' decisions explain and interpret the broader social values present in family disputes, something that family mediation can neglect.

2. The court system protects the disadvantaged and ensures full protection of an individual's rights, whereas mediation does not guarantee full protection of rights and can be inappropriate in many instances because it is based on the notion of relatively equal parties.

3. Family mediation does not provide a formal record of the facts in a case, and thus modifying an agreement can be difficult.

4. Mediated settlements are not part of the formal system, and thus they eliminate opportunities for such cases to contribute to the development of the law and legal precedent.

You should diagram these four points using the circled numbered list notation (1, 2, 3, 4) off to the side of each item.

Paragraph Three:

In the last paragraph, the author states the main point of the passage, namely that family mediation is a better choice for resolving family disputes than the traditional court system. The author then provides the viewpoint of the proponents of family mediation, who state that mediation is more efficient and less damaging than litigation. As an aside, note how the passage uses the terms "court adjudication," "judge's decisions," "court system," and "litigation" to all refer to the generally same idea. The use of interchangeable names is not an accident; one of the goals of the test makers is to test your ability to track related ideas within sections of text, and using this technique gives them that opportunity. Returning to the passage, the paragraph closes with a recitation of the benefits of the family mediation process.

VIEWSTAMP Analysis:

The passage contains a viewpoint neutral section and then three distinct **Viewpoints:**

> The first paragraph is viewpoint neutral.
>
> The view of the supporters of court adjudication (line 17).
>
> The view of the author, who believes that family mediation programs are better than court adjudication in cases of family disputes (line 44), even though the court adjudication process has merit (line 19).
>
> The view of the proponents of family mediation (line 46).

The **Structure** of the passage is as follows:

> Paragraph One: Compare and contrast family mediation with court adjudication.
>
> Paragraph Two: Discuss four points raised by the supporters of court adjudication.
>
> Paragraph Three: State the Main Point and then outline the view of the proponents of family mediation, views that the author agrees with.

The author's **Tone** is positive towards family mediation, but also acknowledges the benefits of court adjudication. This is more a case of mediation being better suited for this particular task than court adjudication being entirely unsuitable.

The **Arguments** in the passage are mainly a set of benefits proposed by each side, with the author making the judgment that the family mediation benefits outweigh the court adjudication benefits.

The author's **Main Point** is family mediation is a better solution for resolving family disputes than is court adjudication.

The clear structure of this passage, along with the well-defined viewpoints, places you in an excellent position to answer the questions.

Two of the questions relate to the Global direction of the passage; one is a Main Point question and the other is a Global Purpose question. These two questions are easily answered by understanding the author's view that family mediation is a better solution for resolving family disputes than is court adjudication. Three other questions also relate directly to viewpoints: one involves the author, one involves the supporters of court adjudication, and one involves the proponents of family mediation. With the clear structure of the passage, these questions are also easy to answer. Here is one of the questions:

17. According to the passage, proponents of court adjudication of family disputes would be most likely to agree with which one of the following?

   (A)   Court adjudication of family disputes usually produces a decision that satisfies all parties to the dispute equally.
   (B)   Family mediation fails to address the underlying emotional issues in family disputes.
   (C)   Settlements of disputes reached through family mediation are not likely to guide the resolution of similar future disputes among other parties.
   (D)   Court adjudication presumes that the parties to a dispute have relatively equal bargaining power.
   (E)   Court adjudication hearings for family disputes should always be open to the public.

In this Subject Perspective question stem, note how the test makers decide to suddenly use the term "proponents of court adjudication" instead of "supporters of court adjudication," which they had used previously. This switch is made because "proponents" was previously used in relation to family mediation, and the test makers are hoping that the careless or hurried test taker will misunderstand which group the question refers to. A student could see "proponent" and easily make the mistake of thinking the question referred to the proponents of family mediation when in fact the question refers to the supporters of court adjudication (especially when "family disputes" appears shortly thereafter). This type of test making trick is not uncommon, and this is one reason why you must always read very carefully.

Because the question is about the supporters of court adjudication, you should know that the correct answer will likely be generated by the information in the second paragraph. There were four reasons given in that paragraph, so you should seek an answer that matches one or more of those four. The correct answer choice is (C), which is based on the final reason given in the second paragraph (lines 39-43). Note how some of the wrong answer choices mix up the viewpoints in an attempt to lure you in: answer choice (B) is an answer better attributed to the proponents of family mediation, and answer choice (D) ascribes the wrong view to court adjudication. Answer choice (E) is incorrect because the passage states that hearings are *generally* open to the public, not always open to the public (lines 9-10), and, more importantly, because no comment is made about how the supporters of court adjudication view the subject.

Law related passages, like all Reading Comprehension passages, are tailor-made for the VIEWSTAMP approach we advocate in this book. You will likely see a law related passage on the LSAT you take, but there is no specific viewpoint that the passage will take unless it addresses Regulation or Diversity. Simply focus on the VIEWSTAMP elements and you will be able to safely navigate any Law passage.

Two Law Related Practice Passages

The next four pages contain two actual LSAT Law related passage sets. After the two passages, a complete analysis of each passage and all of the corresponding questions is presented.

To most effectively benefit from this section, time yourself on the first passage. Attempt to finish the passage in 8 minutes and 45 seconds, but if you cannot, continue working until you complete all of the questions and then note your time. Then, read the entire explanation section for the first passage. Afterwards, move to the second passage and repeat the process.

In many Western societies, modern bankruptcy laws have undergone a shift away from a focus on punishment and toward a focus on bankruptcy as a remedy for individuals and corporations in financial
(5) trouble—and, perhaps unexpectedly, for their creditors. This shift has coincided with an ever-increasing reliance on declarations of bankruptcy by individuals and corporations with excessive debt, a trend that has drawn widespread criticism. However,
(10) any measure seeking to make bankruptcy protection less available would run the risk of preventing continued economic activity of financially troubled individuals and institutions. It is for this reason that the temptation to return to a focus on punishment of
(15) individuals or corporations that become insolvent must be resisted. Modern bankruptcy laws, in serving the needs of an interdependent society, serve the varied interests of the greatest number of citizens.

The harsh punishment for insolvency in centuries
(20) past included imprisonment of individuals and dissolution of enterprises, and reflected societies' beliefs that the accumulation of excessive debt resulted either from debtors' unwillingness to meet obligations or from their negligence. Insolvent debtors
(25) were thought to be breaking sacrosanct social contracts; placing debtors in prison was considered necessary in order to remove from society those who would violate such contracts and thereby defraud creditors. But creditors derive little benefit from
(30) imprisoned debtors unable to repay even a portion of their debt. And if the entity to be punished is a large enterprise, for example, an auto manufacturer, its dissolution would cause significant unemployment and the disruption of much-needed services.

(35) Modern bankruptcy law has attempted to address the shortcomings of the punitive approach. Two beliefs underlie this shift: that the public good ought to be paramount in considering the financial insolvency of individuals and corporations; and that
(40) the public good is better served by allowing debt-heavy corporations to continue to operate, and indebted individuals to continue to earn wages, than by disabling insolvent economic entities. The mechanism for executing these goals is usually a
(45) court-directed reorganization of debtors' obligations to creditors. Such reorganizations typically comprise debt relief and plans for court-directed transfers of certain assets from debtor to creditor. Certain strictures connected to bankruptcy—such as the fact
(50) that bankruptcies become matters of public record and are reported to credit bureaus for a number of years—may still serve a punitive function, but not by denying absolution of debts or financial reorganization. Through these mechanisms, today's
(55) bankruptcy laws are designed primarily to assure continued engagement in productive economic activity, with the ultimate goal of restoring businesses and individuals to a degree of economic health and providing creditors with the best hope of collecting.

6. Which one of the following most accurately expresses the main point of the passage?

(A) The modern trend in bankruptcy law away from punishment and toward the maintenance of economic activity serves the best interests of society and should not be abandoned.

(B) Bankruptcy laws have evolved in order to meet the needs of creditors, who depend on the continued productive activity of private citizens and profit-making enterprises.

(C) Modern bankruptcy laws are justified on humanitarian grounds, even though the earlier punitive approach was more economically efficient.

(D) Punishment for debt no longer holds deterrent value for debtors and is therefore a concept that has been largely abandoned as ineffective.

(E) Greater economic interdependence has triggered the formation of bankruptcy laws that reflect a convergence of the interests of debtors and creditors.

7. In stating that bankruptcy laws have evolved "perhaps unexpectedly" (line 5) as a remedy for creditors, the author implies that creditors

(A) are often surprised to receive compensation in bankruptcy courts

(B) have unintentionally become the chief beneficiaries of bankruptcy laws

(C) were a consideration, though not a primary one, in the formulation of bankruptcy laws

(D) are better served than is immediately apparent by laws designed in the first instance to provide a remedy for debtors

(E) were themselves active in the formulation of modern bankruptcy laws

8. The author's attitude toward the evolution of bankruptcy law can most accurately be described as

(A) approval of changes that have been made to inefficient laws

(B) confidence that further changes to today's laws will be unnecessary

(C) neutrality toward laws that, while helpful to many, remain open to abuse

(D) skepticism regarding the possibility of solutions to the problem of insolvency

(E) concern that inefficient laws may have been replaced by legislation too lenient to debtors

9. The primary purpose of the passage is to

   (A) offer a critique of both past and present approaches to insolvency
   (B) compare the practices of bankruptcy courts of the past with those of bankruptcy courts of the present
   (C) criticize those who would change the bankruptcy laws of today
   (D) reexamine today's bankruptcy laws in an effort to point to further improvements
   (E) explain and defend contemporary bankruptcy laws

10. Which one of the following claims would a defender of the punitive theory of bankruptcy legislation be most likely to have made?

   (A) Debt that has become so great that repayment is impossible is ultimately a moral failing and thus a matter for which the law should provide punitive sanctions.
   (B) Because insolvency ultimately harms the entire economy, the law should provide a punitive deterrent to insolvency.
   (C) The insolvency of companies or individuals is tolerable if the debt is the result of risk-taking, profit-seeking ventures that might create considerable economic growth in the long run.
   (D) The dissolution of a large enterprise is costly to the economy as a whole and should not be allowed, even when that enterprise's insolvency is the result of its own fiscal irresponsibility.
   (E) The employees of a large bankrupt enterprise should be considered just as negligent as the owner of a bankrupt sole proprietorship.

11. Which one of the following sentences could most logically be appended to the end of the last paragraph of the passage?

   (A) Only when today's bankruptcy laws are ultimately seen as inadequate on a large scale will bankruptcy legislation return to its original intent.
   (B) Punishment is no longer the primary goal of bankruptcy law, even if some of its side effects still function punitively.
   (C) Since leniency serves the public interest in bankruptcy law, it is likely to do so in criminal law as well.
   (D) Future bankruptcy legislation could include punitive measures, but only if such measures ultimately benefit creditors.
   (E) Today's bankruptcy laws place the burden of insolvency squarely on the shoulders of creditors, in marked contrast to the antiquated laws that weighed heavily on debtors.

12. The information in the passage most strongly suggests which one of the following about changes in bankruptcy laws?

   (A) Bankruptcy laws always result from gradual changes in philosophy followed by sudden shifts in policy.
   (B) Changes in bankruptcy law were initiated by the courts and only grudgingly adopted by legislators.
   (C) The adjustment of bankruptcy laws away from a punitive focus was at first bitterly opposed by creditors.
   (D) Bankruptcy laws underwent change because the traditional approach proved inadequate and contrary to the needs of society.
   (E) The shift away from a punitive approach to insolvency was part of a more general trend in society toward rehabilitation and away from retribution.

13. Which one of the following, if true, would most weaken the author's argument against harsh punishment for debtors?

   (A) Extensive study of the economic and legal history of many countries has shown that most individuals who served prison time for bankruptcy subsequently exhibited greater economic responsibility.
   (B) The bankruptcy of a certain large company has had a significant negative impact on the local economy even though virtually all of the affected employees were able to obtain similar jobs within the community.
   (C) Once imprisonment was no longer a consequence of insolvency, bankruptcy filings increased dramatically, then leveled off before increasing again during the 1930s.
   (D) The court-ordered liquidation of a large and insolvent company's assets threw hundreds of people out of work, but the local economy nevertheless demonstrated robust growth in the immediate aftermath.
   (E) Countries that continue to imprison debtors enjoy greater economic health than do comparable countries that have ceased to do so.

Computers have long been utilized in the sphere of law in the form of word processors, spreadsheets, legal research systems, and practice management systems. Most exciting, however, has been the
(5) prospect of using artificial intelligence techniques to create so-called legal reasoning systems—computer programs that can help to resolve legal disputes by reasoning from and applying the law. But the practical benefits of such automated reasoning
(10) systems have fallen short of optimistic early predictions and have not resulted in computer systems that can independently provide expert advice about substantive law. This is not surprising in light of the difficulty in resolving problems involving the
(15) meaning and applicability of rules set out in a legal text.

Early attempts at automated legal reasoning focused on the doctrinal nature of law. They viewed law as a set of rules, and the resulting computer
(20) systems were engineered to make legal decisions by determining the consequences that followed when its stored set of legal rules was applied to a collection of evidentiary data. Such systems underestimated the problems of interpretation that can arise at every
(25) stage of a legal argument. Examples abound of situations that are open to differing interpretations: whether a mobile home in a trailer park is a house or a motor vehicle, whether a couple can be regarded as married in the absence of a formal legal ceremony,
(30) and so on. Indeed, many notions invoked in the text of a statute may be deliberately left undefined so as to allow the law to be adapted to unforeseen circumstances. But in order to be able to apply legal rules to novel situations, systems have to be equipped
(35) with a kind of comprehensive knowledge of the world that is far beyond their capabilities at present or in the foreseeable future.

Proponents of legal reasoning systems now argue that accommodating reference to, and reasoning from,
(40) cases improves the chances of producing a successful system. By focusing on the practice of reasoning from precedents, researchers have designed systems called case-based reasoners, which store individual example cases in their knowledge bases. In contrast
(45) to a system that models legal knowledge based on a set of rules, a case-based reasoner, when given a concrete problem, manipulates the cases in its knowledge base to reach a conclusion based on a similar case. Unfortunately, in the case-based systems
(50) currently in development, the criteria for similarity among cases are system dependent and fixed by the designer, so that similarity is found only by testing for the presence or absence of predefined factors. This simply postpones the apparently intractable
(55) problem of developing a system that can discover for itself the factors that make cases similar in relevant ways.

21. Which one of the following most accurately expresses the main point of the passage?

(A) Attempts to model legal reasoning through computer programs have not been successful because of problems of interpreting legal discourse and identifying appropriate precedents.

(B) Despite signs of early promise, it is now apparent that computer programs have little value for legal professionals in their work.

(C) Case-based computer systems are vastly superior to those computer systems based upon the doctrinal nature of the law.

(D) Computers applying artificial intelligence techniques show promise for revolutionizing the process of legal interpretation in the relatively near future.

(E) Using computers can expedite legal research, facilitate the matching of a particular case to a specific legal principle, and even provide insights into possible flaws involving legal reasoning.

22. The logical relationship of lines 8-13 of the passage to lines 23-25 and 49-53 of the passage is most accurately described as

(A) a general assertion supported by two specific observations

(B) a general assertion followed by two arguments, one of which supports and one of which refutes the general assertion

(C) a general assertion that entails two more specific assertions

(D) a theoretical assumption refuted by two specific observations

(E) a specific observation that suggests two incompatible generalizations

23. In the passage as a whole, the author is primarily concerned with

(A) arguing that computers can fundamentally change how the processes of legal interpretation and reasoning are conducted in the future

(B) indicating that the law has subtle nuances that are not readily dealt with by computerized legal reasoning programs

(C) demonstrating that computers are approaching the point where they can apply legal precedents to current cases

(D) suggesting that, because the law is made by humans, computer programmers must also apply their human intuition when designing legal reasoning systems

(E) defending the use of computers as essential and indispensable components of the modern legal profession

24. The passage suggests that the author would be most likely to agree with which one of the following statements about computerized automated legal reasoning systems?

    (A) These systems have met the original expectations of computer specialists but have fallen short of the needs of legal practitioners.
    (B) Progress in research on these systems has been hindered, more because not enough legal documents are accessible by computer than because theoretical problems remain unsolved.
    (C) These systems will most likely be used as legal research tools rather than as aids in legal analysis.
    (D) Rule systems will likely replace case-based systems over time.
    (E) Developing adequate legal reasoning systems would require research breakthroughs by computer specialists.

25. It can be most reasonably inferred from the passage's discussion of requirements for developing effective automated legal reasoning systems that the author would agree with which one of the following statements?

    (A) Focusing on the doctrinal nature of law is the fundamental error made by developers of automated legal systems.
    (B) Contemporary computers do not have the required memory capability to store enough data to be effective legal reasoning systems.
    (C) Questions of interpretation in rule-based legal reasoning systems must be settled by programming more legal rules into the systems.
    (D) Legal statutes and reasoning may involve innovative applications that cannot be modeled by a fixed set of rules, cases, or criteria.
    (E) As professionals continue to use computers in the sphere of law they will develop the competence to use legal reasoning systems effectively.

26. Based on the passage, which one of the following can be most reasonably inferred concerning case-based reasoners?

    (A) The major problem in the development of these systems is how to store enough cases in their knowledge bases.
    (B) These systems are more useful than rule systems because case-based reasoners are based on a simpler view of legal reasoning.
    (C) Adding specific criteria for similarity among cases to existing systems would not overcome an important shortcoming of these systems.
    (D) These systems can independently provide expert advice about legal rights and duties in a wide range of cases.
    (E) These systems are being designed to attain a much more ambitious goal than had been set for rule systems.

27. Which one of the following is mentioned in the passage as an important characteristic of many statutes that frustrates the application of computerized legal reasoning systems?

    (A) complexity of syntax
    (B) unavailability of relevant precedents
    (C) intentional vagueness and adaptability
    (D) overly narrow intent
    (E) incompatibility with previous statutes

28. The examples of situations that are open to differing interpretations (lines 25-30) function in the passage to

    (A) substantiate the usefulness of computers in the sphere of law
    (B) illustrate a vulnerability of rule systems in computerized legal reasoning
    (C) isolate issues that computer systems are in principle incapable of handling
    (D) explain how legal rules have been adapted to novel situations
    (E) question the value of reasoning from precedents in interpreting legal rules

Practice Passage I—September 2006 Passage #2 Answer Key

Paragraph One:

The author begins this passage discussing the shift in Western bankruptcy laws away from an emphasis on punishment and toward a focus on bankruptcy as a remedy. This approach has drawn criticism as declarations of bankruptcy have increased.

Following a viewpoint-neutral introduction, the author's viewpoint is presented: we should resist the temptation to make bankruptcy protection less available, because this protection helps to ensure continued economic activity. Modern bankruptcy laws, the author argues, recognize interdependence and serve the interests of the greatest number of citizens.

Paragraph Two:

In the second paragraph the author presents the historical (from past centuries) viewpoint on bankruptcy, when harsh punishments were imposed based on the belief that excessive debt came from negligence or unwillingness to pay. Those who broke sacred social payment contracts were removed from society through imprisonment.

Having presented the old way of dealing with debtors, the author points out two disadvantages of the historical approach: a focus on separation and punishment does not repay creditors, and under the old approach large entities' bankruptcies can lead to further detriment for society.

Paragraph Three:

At this point in the passage, the author has discussed the old approach to bankruptcy, and why we should avoid a similar approach. In this paragraph, the author examines modern bankruptcy law, which is based on a primary concern for public good in consideration of bankruptcy issues. The public good is better served by continued economic activity than by the presence of disabled, insolvent entities. Modern bankruptcy involves reorganization, court transfers of assets, and some debt relief, and these reorganizations are made public and have credit bureau ramifications, so there is some punitive aspect. But providing these individuals and corporations with bankruptcy protection helps to ensure continued productivity and provides creditors with the best chance of collecting their debts.

VIEWSTAMP Analysis:

The **Viewpoints** presented in this passage are those of the historical view (from "centuries past"), and those of the the more modern perspective, which are shared by the author. The historical view on bankruptcy in Western societies maintained a focus on punishment, while the more modern perspective (and the one to which the author subscribes) approaches the issue with a view toward continued productivity.

The **Structure** of the passage is as follows:

> Paragraph One: Introduce shift in bankruptcy in Western societies, from focus on punishment to focus on continued productivity. Shift from viewpoint-neutral discussion to the author's viewpoint, author asserts that bankruptcy protection should continue to be available in the interest of the common good.

Paragraph Two: Present historical perspective on insolvent debtors; point out that the old debtors' prison approach provides little benefit for the creditor, and slowing or stopping individual or corporate productivity can yield negative results.

Paragraph Three: Discuss modern bankruptcy law, and the beliefs that have driven changes from the old ways (public good, continued productivity should be the main considerations). Present specific mechanisms, and restate the goal of modern bankruptcy law, to help those in debt while also trying to provide creditors with the best chance to collect.

The **Tone** of the passage is quite positive with respect to modern bankruptcy law, and negative with regard to the historical view on bankruptcy. The author clearly believes that modern laws provide a more practical approach to helping all parties involved.

The author's main **Argument** is that modern bankruptcy law is preferable to laws from past centuries, and that we should not be tempted to go back to the traditional perspective.

The **Main Point** of the passage is that the changes to bankruptcy laws that have taken place are for the best, so we should avoid the old approach and focus more on productivity and the greater good than on punishment.

Question #6: GR, Main Point. The correct answer choice is (A)

Before looking at the choices, you should be sure to prephrase the answer to any Main Point question. In this case, the Main Point is that bankruptcy laws in Western societies have changed to better serve the interests of the greater good.

Answer choice (A): This is the correct answer choice, as it provides a basic restatement of our prephrase above. The author believes that bankruptcy laws have changed, and we should not go back to a system that focuses on punishment rather than on the greater good of society.

Answer choice (B): Although the author points out that modern bankruptcy laws do help creditors, the author does not claim that creditors' needs caused the evolution of these laws, so this answer choice is incorrect.

Answer choice (C): Modern bankruptcy laws are based in part on humanitarian concerns, but the author does not assert that the earlier approach was more efficient. In fact, the passage specifically points out that the imprisonment of debtors could not benefit creditors (line 29).

Answer choice (D): According to the passage, the old approach was focused on punishment and was an inefficient means of dealing with insolvency. The author does not discuss the issue of deterrence, and does not assert that a lack of deterrence caused the discussed changes in the laws.

Answer choice (E): Economic interdependence allows for the interests of debtors and creditors to be aligned, but the author does not claim that increased interdependence has triggered current laws, so this answer choice is incorrect.

Question #7: SR, Must. The correct answer choice is (D)

The "unexpected remedy" implies that the creditors may not have expected to gain from laws meant to help debtors.

Answer choice (A): The author does not imply that creditors are surprised to get any compensation in bankruptcy court, so this answer should be eliminated.

Answer choice (B): There is no implication that the creditors would be the chief beneficiaries, only that they might benefit.

Answer choice (C): This is a potentially tricky wrong answer choice. The referenced implication is that the creditors might unexpectedly benefit from laws that serve an interdependent society, but the author does not discuss whether the creditors were considered when the bankruptcy laws were formulated.

Answer choice (D): This is the correct answer choice. The implication, as prephrased, is that creditors may, surprisingly, benefit from laws intended to help debtors.

Answer choice (E): There is no implication that the creditors were involved in formulating modern bankruptcy laws. Further, the author implies that the creditors were surprised to benefit from the laws, so it seems unlikely that they were involved in their formulation.

Question #8: GR, AP. The correct answer choice is (A)

The author's attitude is that the old laws were counterproductive and detrimental, and the modern approach to bankruptcy makes more sense for all parties involved.

Answer choice (A): This is the correct answer choice, and reflects our prephrase above. The author approves of the modern approach as more reasonable and effective than the historical approach.

Answer choice (B): This answer goes too far. The author agrees with the changes that have taken place, but does not go so far as to claim that no further changes to the laws will ever be necessary.

Answer choice (C): The author's attitude is not neutral; it is supportive of the changes that have taken place, so this answer choice is incorrect.

Answer choice (D): The author is not skeptical, but supportive of the idea that bankruptcy under the modern approach can serve the interests of both debtors and creditors.

Answer choice (E): The author supports modern legislation, and never suggests that newer laws are too lenient, so this answer choice should be eliminated.

Question #9: GR, P. The correct answer choice is (E)

The author's main purpose is to discuss the old and new approaches to bankruptcy, and explain why the modern approach is preferable.

Answer choice (A): The passage does discuss both past and present approaches, but the purpose is more than to provide a critique of each. The author clearly wants to support the modern approach and warn against going back to the historical approach.

Answer choice (B): The author does compare the old approach to the new approach, but this is not the primary purpose, which is to lend support to the modern perspective on bankruptcy.

Answer choice (C): The author does not seek to criticize currently proposed changes, but to warn against the historical, punishment-based perspective.

Answer choice (D): The author supports the modern perspective on bankruptcy, and does not discuss further improvements.

Answer choice (E): This is the correct answer choice. The author discusses the basis of the modern approach, and provides several points in support of this perspective.

Question #10: GR, SP. The correct answer choice is (A)

To prephrase the answer to this question, we should consider what drove the historical perspective. This comes from the discussion in the second paragraph, in which the author explains that insolvent debtors were seen as negligent or unwilling to pay, and it was necessary to punish and remove these contract breakers from society.

Answer choice (A): This is the correct answer choice. The historical perspective saw the insolvent as deserving of punishment. Punishment was a primary focus of the old perspective, so a propoent of this perspective would likely call for punitive sanctions.

Answer choice (B): This is a popular wrong answer, as it seems a reasonble defense of a punitive approach. The passage does not present *deterrence* as a driving justification for the historical approach, however, so this answer choice is incorrect.

Answer choice (C): A proponent of the historical perspective would likely have little tolerance for insolvency, regardless of the long term prospects.

Answer choice (D): This answer choice represents the modern perspective, and that of the author, rather than the viewpoint associated with the historical approach to bankruptcy.

Answer choice (E): There is no reference or implication regarding this specific assigment of negligence, so we cannot be sure of the historical perspective on this issue.

Question #11: SR, E. The correct answer choice is (B)

If we are to prephrase an answer to this passage expansion question, it is valuable to consider how the passage ended. In this case the closing point was that modern bankruptcy laws may be punitive on some level, but they are intended to promote economic activity and help all parties involved. The right answer choice will likely either continue this general theme, or reference the passage in general.

Answer choice (A): This response would make no sense at the end of this passage. The author is a fan of today's bankruptcy laws, and would not have such a positive tone with regard to original intent.

Answer choice (B): This is the correct answer choice, as this response logically restates the point with which the author ends the passage.

Answer choice (C): There is no reference to criminal law in the passage, so this answer choice would not logically follow.

Answer choice (D): The author mentions the punitive facet of current bankruptcy law, but never references prospective punitive measures in the future, so this answer choice should be eliminated.

Answer choice (E): The author believes that modern law favors all parties concerned/involved, in stark contrast to this answer choice.

Question #12: GR, Must. The correct answer choice is (D)

As with all Must questions, the correct answer choice must pass the Fact Test.

Answer choice (A): We can rule out this answer choice based on the word "always," since the author makes no such absolute claims. Further, in the one example discussed, it seems that a change in policy was followed by a gradual change in philosophy among creditors.

Answer choice (B): There is no reference or implication that the courts led the way, so this answer choice is incorrect.

Answer choice (C): The author implied that benefit to creditors may have been unexpected, but this is not the same as claiming a bitter opposition on the part of the creditors.

Answer choice (D): This is the correct answer choice. The author discusses several points of inadequacy of the historical approach, and asserts that the new laws are an improvement, so we can assume that the changes were a result of these inadequacies.

Answer choice (E): Since there are no discussions or implications of such broad societal trends, this cannot be the right answer choice.

Question #13: CR, Weaken. The correct answer choice is (E)

The author's argument *against* harsh punishment for debtors is that this treatment is economically counterproductive. The correct answer choice will somehow weaken or cast doubt on this point.

Answer choice (A): This answer choice does not weaken the basic argument that bankrupt individuals cannot be productive while in prison.

Answer choice (B): This choice supports the author's argument against harsh punishment.

Answer choice (C): This answer choice would not weaken the general claims about non-productivity, only that there may have been many who needed bankruptcy but had been afraid to make a claim.

Answer choice (D): A single example of immediate growth does not disprove the author's more general claims about bankruptcy, so this answer choice is incorrect.

Answer choice (E): This is the correct answer choice, as it strengthens the assertion that harsh debtor punishment is good for an economy.

Paragraph One:

The author begins this passage by stating that computers have been commonly used for basic functions in law, with interesting prospects in the area of "legal reasoning systems." These are defined as "computer programs that can help to resolve legal disputes by reasoning from and applying the law." Early efforts to use artificial intelligence in this way have been unable to produce expert legal advice. According to the author this is to be expected, considering the complexity of any system of legal rules. The final sentence in the paragraph provides the first bit of tone in the passage, reflecting the author's skepticism regarding the prospects for computer legal reasoning.

Paragraph Two:

Here the author discusses early efforts to create legal reasoning systems, which began with programs based on sets of rules, or doctrine. These were found ineffective because of the legal interpretations required at every level. Since many laws are written vaguely and require some degree of interpretation, access to the vast information required for this interpretation is beyond computer capability now or in the near future. Note that while the first paragraph closed with the author's skeptical viewpoint, this paragraph is generally informational, and viewpoint-neutral.

Paragraph Three:

In the final paragraph the author presents current thoughts on the creation of legal reasoning systems. Here, the author introduces the perspective of proponents, who say that basing decisions on past similar cases might improve prospects for a working system. The problem is that the case-based reasoning program would have to recognize similar cases and issues, and criteria for this similarity would have to be predetermined within the program. Here we see another manifestation of the author's skeptical tone: this new approach, the author points out, is sure to have serious challenges as well, because at some point it will be necessary to enable the program to determine relevant precedent.

VIEWSTAMP Analysis:

The **Viewpoints** presented in this passage are those of the proponents of legal systems, who believe in the prospects of case-based legal systems, and of the author, who is skeptical about the possibility of finding a solution to this very complex problem.

The **Structure** of the passage is as follows:

> Paragraph One: Introduce the concept of legal reasoning systems, and discuss how early attempts have been unable to automate legal reasoning.

> Paragraph Two: Discuss early attempts to base legal reasoning systems on sets of legal rules; this doctrinal approach required interpretations at each level. Point out that computers are currently not capable of storing the comprehensive knowledge required to create a rule-based automated system.

> Paragraph Three: Introduce another approach suggested by legal reasoning systems proponents—case-based reasoners attempt to reach conclusions based on similar case precedents. Assert that there still exists the underlying problem of creating a program that can assess legally relevant similarities.

Practice Passage II—December 2006 Passage #4 Answer Key

The author's **Tone** is skeptical regarding the possibility of creating a fully functional legal reasoning system that is capable of determining relevant precedent or dispensing expert legal advice.

The **Arguments** in the passage are those of the legal reasoning proponents, who assert that the chances of developing such a system are improved with the use of precedent-based reasoning, and of the author, who is skeptical about the prospects.

The **Main Point** of this passage is to discuss attempts at reasoning systems, and the challenges of developing programs with comprehensive legal knowledge or understanding of relevant precedents.

Question #21: GR, Main Point. The correct answer choice is (A)

The question stem asks for the main point of the passage, which is to introduce the concept of legal reasoning systems and the challenges associated with the development of artificial intelligence-based legal reasoning systems.

Answer choice (A): This is the correct answer choice, discussing the same points emphasized in our prephrased answer above.

Answer choice (B): This answer choice is incorrect, because computer programs are presently used in law, as discussed in the first sentence of the passage.

Answer choice (C): While earlier, doctrinal approaches apparently were not successful, and case-based programs represent the latest effort to develop legal reasoning systems, it is still unclear whether they will be able to provide a better solution, so this answer choice is incorrect.

Answer choice (D): While there is promise, the author highlights the challenges involved going forward, and never makes the assertion that revolutionary results will be achieved in the near future.

Answer choice (E): While this may be true, the main point of the passage involves the challenges associated with developing legal reasoning systems, so this answer choice is incorrect.

Question #22: SR, O. The correct answer choice is (A)

With specific reference, passage organization questions such as this one, we need to understand the organization and specific context of the passage. In lines 8-13, the author is summarizing the main point: the benefits of legal reasoning systems have fallen short of predictions. In lines 23-25, the discussion focuses on how rule-based systems have proven inadequate because of the problems of interpretation. In lines 49-53, the discussion surrounds how case-based systems are limited. The first statement is a general statement: the benefits of legal reasoning systems have fallen short of expectations. The second statement is one example of how the first portion of the passage is true. The third statement is another example to support the first referenced assertion.

Answer choice (A): This is the correct answer choice. The first statement is the general assertion that legal reasoning systems have fallen short of predictions, and the other referenced statements are specific observations that lend support to the general assertion.

Answer choice (B): Since both later points support the first, this answer choice is incorrect.

Answer choice (C): The first reference is a general assertion, but the later two referenced excerpts are facts in support and not the author's *assertions*.

Answer choice (D): Since the two observations support the first assertion, this answer choice should be eliminated.

Answer choice (E): The first referenced quote is a general assertion, rather than a specific observation.

Question #23: GR, P. The correct answer choice is (B)

The question stem asks for the author's primary concern. Again, the author is primarily interested in discussing the concept of legal reasoning systems and the associated challenges.

Answer choice (A): Although the author does allude to the potential benefits of legal reasoning systems, this is not the primary concern.

Answer choice (B): This is the correct answer choice, as the author is interested in discussing the challenges of such systems—the subtleties of law that make interpretation and determinations of relevance difficult.

Answer choice (C): There is no such demonstration—the author focuses on the challenges that are sure to come with systems based on precedent, so this answer choice should be eliminated.

Answer choice (D): The passage provides no such suggestion, and while this may be true, it is not supported by the passage and certainly not the primary focus.

Answer choice (E): While the author could be a proponent of the use of computers in the law office, the primary concern is to note that legal reasoning systems are sure to bring challenges during development.

Question #24: GR, AP. The correct answer choice is (E)

This question regarding the author's perspective cannot be perfectly prephrased, but it is advisable to know the author's basic attitude, which is that computer reasoning systems are a good idea but have yet to be successfully implemented.

Answer choice (A): The passage specifically states in line 10 that these systems have fallen short of original predictions, so this choice is incorrect.

Answer choice (B): The hindrance to progress has come from difficulties in subtle interpretations, not lack of accessibility to legal documents.

Answer choice (C): The author highlights the challenges that will go along with developing a system for legal analysis, but is not so skeptical as to presume that such efforts will be futile.

Answer choice (D): Rule systems represented the early attempts at legal reasoning systems, while case-based systems are the latest approach.

Answer choice (E): This is the correct answer choice. In rule systems, the author notes that these systems would have to be equipped with knowledge "that is far beyond their capabilities at present or in the foreseeable future" (lines 34-37). For case-based systems, lines 50-57 state that the criteria for these systems are system dependent and fixed by their designers, and that there is a problem of developing a system that can determine relevant precedents.

Question #25: GR, AP. The correct answer choice is (D)

Since this is another author's perspective question, it is again helpful to note that there are various reasons presented which drive the author's uncertainty about whether computer-based reasoning can be implemented successfully.

Answer choice (A): With regard to the doctrinal model, the author discusses the challenges associated but does not suggest that the choice of this focus was a fundamental error. Rather, the challenges go along with the task itself, for which a solution has not yet been found.

Answer choice (B): The chief problem with legal reasoning systems is not memory but the limitations of the programming, so this answer choice is incorrect.

Answer choice (C): In the examples provided in the second paragraph of the passage, it is not rules programming that is the problem. Rather, it is an inability to equip the systems with the comprehensive knowledge required for expert interpretation that has resulted in difficulties.

Answer choice (D): This is the correct answer choice. The rule-based system appears to require more comprehensive legal knowledge than computers are currently capable of, and at the end of the passage (line 54) the author notes the "intractable problem of developing a system that can discover for itself the factors that make cases similar in relevant ways."

Answer choice (E): The incompetence of the legal practitioners is not the source of the problems with legal reasoning systems; the challenge lies in the creation of the programming.

Question #26: CR, Must. The correct answer choice is (C)

The question stem asks what can be inferred concerning case-based reasoning systems. Active readers with a good grasp of this passage's organization recognize that this discussion comes from the last paragraph of the passage.

Answer choice (A): In lines 49-57, the author notes that the major problem is the human limitations created by the programmers, not the lack of storage capacity. In fact, inadequate storage is not mentioned at all.

Answer choice (B): The author will likely agree that case-based systems currently appear to have more potential than rule-based systems, but this is not because they are based on a simpler view of legal reasoning.

Answer choice (C): This is the correct answer choice, rephrasing the author's assertion at the end of the passage that there remains the "intractable problem of developing a system that can discover for itself the factors that make cases similar in relevant ways." (54-57).

Answer choice (D): The author is focused on the challenges associated with developing a program that can independently provide such advice, but such programs have not yet been successfully developed, so this answer choice should be eliminated.

Answer choice (E): There is nothing in the passage to suggest that there is a more ambitious goal for case systems versus rule systems. Rather, the two models simply represent two different approaches to the same problem.

Question #27: GR, Must. The correct answer choice is (C)

An important characteristic of many statutes that frustrates the application of computerized legal reasoning systems is the vagueness that is often written into statutes to allow for (and require) flexible interpretation.

Answer choice (A): The complexity of the syntax is never mentioned, so this is incorrect.

Answer choice (B): It is not the unavailability of relevant precedents that is the problem, but rather the flexible determination of the relevance of various precedents, so this answer choice should be eliminated.

Answer choice (C): This is the correct answer choice, reflecting our prephrased answer above. This is noted in lines 31-33: "a statute may be deliberately left undefined so as to allow the law to be adapted to unforeseen circumstances."

Answer choice (D): The problem is not an overly narrow intent. It is the opposite—the built-in flexibility—that is mentioned as a challenging attribute.

Answer choice (E): There is no reference to statutes' incompatibility, so this answer choice cannot be correct.

Question #28: SR, P. The correct answer choice is (B)

This question stem asks what function is served by the examples of situations that are open to differing interpretations (lines 25-30). These are offered to show that rule-based systems underestimated the complexity of interpretation that can arise at each stage of a legal argument.

Answer choice (A): Given the fact that the author focuses on the inability thus far to create legal reasoning systems, this answer choice is incorrect.

Answer choice (B): This is the correct answer choice, consistent with our prephrase above.

Answer choice (C): Since the issues exemplify the challenges of rule based systems, this answer choice is incorrect.

Answer choice (D): The referenced examples show the difficulties of adapting to novel situations, so this answer choice should be eliminated.

Answer choice (E): The discussion of precedents is pertinent to case-based systems rather than rule-based systems, which is the context for the referenced examples, so this answer choice is incorrect.

Science Passages

The spectrum of topics covered in the Reading Comprehension section is quite broad, but one topic that consistently appears is Science. On average, each Reading Comprehension section contains one passage based on Science.

Types of Science Passages

Up until the October 1991 LSAT, all LSAT Reading Comprehension Science passages addressed the topic in a social science environment. For example, a passage would discuss the effects of technology on society, and examine the social implications of the new technology. Passages of this type, which we term Soft Science passages, still appear on the LSAT today. These passages are relatively easy because they focus more on social impact, or alternatively, they address scientific ideas that the average person is somewhat familiar with, such as oil drilling or renewable energy resources.

Starting in October 1991 with the infamous Waterbugs passage, the makers of the LSAT began to introduce passages based on scientific topics that the average student had never previously encountered, or knew little about. These passages, which we term Hard Science passages, still exist on today's LSAT, and appear more frequently than Soft Science passages. The introduction of Hard Science often increases the difficulty of the section and includes a broader variety of subject matter on the test. In a moment we will discuss how to attack Science passages, but in the meantime, consider some of the Science passages that have appeared on the LSAT:

Hard Science passages appear more frequently than Soft Science passages.

> Embryos and the genetic mechanisms of early polarity
>
> Brain neurotransmitter theory
>
> Gravity, dark matter and neutrinos
>
> Max Planck and radiation wave theory

To most students, those topics appear at least a bit intimidating. However, you should not be overly concerned about any individual Science passage, as discussed next.

Why You Should Not Fear Science Passages

The makers of the LSAT state that LSAT question topics "reflect a broad range of academic disciplines and are intended to give no advantage to candidates from a particular background," but many LSAT students come from a humanities background and these test takers often worry about passages containing scientific topics. If the topic of science concerns you, please keep in mind these two points:

1. As discussed in Chapter Two, the topic of a passage does not affect the underlying logical relationship of the parts of the passage. Thus, regardless of the topic, you can still use the VIEWSTAMP approach and succeed.

2. One of the fears of test takers is encountering concepts that they do not know or that sound intimidating. Naturally, someone who encounters terms like "riddled basins of attraction" or "rubisco" are unlikely to have seen them before and would seemingly have a valid reason for worrying that they will be at a disadvantage in working with the passage containing those terms. However, you should not worry because the LSAT will *not* assume that you know anything about advanced technical or scientific ideas. Any term or idea beyond the domain of general public knowledge will be explained for you. Consider the following items:

    These points are also true for Logical Reasoning questions.

    A. Example: "But for decades cosmologists (scientists who study the universe) have attempted to account for..."

    In this example, the term "cosmologists" is immediately followed by a parenthetical definition that explains that cosmologists are scientists who study the universe. So, even if you do not know what a cosmologist is, the test makers provide you with the definition.

    B. Example: "among the more attractive candidates are neutrinos, elementary particles created as a by-product of nuclear fusion, radioactive decay, or catastrophic collisions between particles."

    In this example, the definition of "neutrinos" is set off by a comma, and the remainder of the sentence provides the explanation of the term.

    C. Example: "This is because the boundary between one basin of attraction and another is riddled with fractal properties; in other words, the boundary is permeated by an extraordinarily high number of physical irregularities such as notches or zigzags."

    In this example the definition of "fractal properties" is slightly separated from the term, but the definition is still relatively close. Note that there is no rule that says that the definition has to immediately follow the term in question. The definition will sometimes be a number of lines away. If this occurs, simply note the term and continue reading until you encounter the explanation.

D. Example: "Until recently, biologists were unable to explain the fact that pathogens—disease-causing parasites—have evolved to incapacitate, and often overwhelm, their hosts."

This example uses dashes to provide the definition of the term "pathogen." Once you know that a pathogen is simply a disease-causing parasite, the passage doesn't seem quite as complex.

E. Example: "When genes are inserted into an individual's cells and tissues to treat a disease, this treatment is known as gene therapy."

While in the first four examples the definition followed the term, in this example the definition actually precedes the term. While this arrangement occurs less frequently than the definition following the term, you should still be aware that the test makers have the option of placing the definition either before or after the term, and either in immediate proximity or separated by a number of lines.

The important point to draw from this discussion is that nothing you will encounter in a Science passage (or any other passage) will remain unexplained, and that you already have the methods in hand to attack Science passages effectively.

Remember, although on occasion you will see a passage that references an ominous looking word or idea (whether Science or Law or any other subject matter), you will not need to know or be assumed to know anything more about those elements than what you are told by the test makers. When you read a science-based passage, focus on understanding the relationship of the ideas and do not be intimidated by the terminology used by the author.

Handling Scientific Elements

While we are fully confident that any student can handle the science elements that appear in a passage, there is value in revisiting how to diagram certain elements that tend to appear in Science passages.

1. Handling Scientific Terminology

   When you encounter scientific terms or phrases, underline the phrase and make note of the definition by marking the section with the "DEF" notation. If necessary, you can reduce the scientific term to an acronym.

2. Handling Dense Sections of Scientific Explanation

   If you encounter an extended section of dense scientific terminology, bracket off the section and do not worry too much about understanding every single idea within the section. You can return to the bracketed area when you are asked to do so by a question, and focus on understanding the ideas at that point.

If necessary, return to Chapter Four for a refresher in diagramming.

A Science Passage Analyzed

On the following page an actual LSAT Science passage is presented, along with a complete analysis of the passage and all of the corresponding questions.

To most effectively benefit from this section, time yourself on the passage. Attempt to finish the passage in 8 minutes and 45 seconds, but if you cannot, continue working until you complete all of the questions and note your time. While reading, remember to apply the VIEWSTAMP approach advocated throughout the book. Then, read the entire explanation section and consider what elements you missed, and what you need to do to improve.

Sometimes there is no more effective means of controlling an agricultural pest than giving free rein to its natural predators. A case in point is the cyclamen mite, a pest whose population can be
(5) effectively controlled by a predatory mite of the genus *Typhlodromus*. Cyclamen mites infest strawberry plants; they typically establish themselves in a strawberry field shortly after planting, but their populations do not reach significantly damaging
(10) levels until the plants' second year. *Typhlodromus* mites usually invade the strawberry fields during the second year, rapidly subdue the cyclamen mite populations, and keep them from reaching significantly damaging levels.
(15) *Typhlodromus* owes its effectiveness as a predator to several factors in addition to its voracious appetite. Its population can increase as rapidly as that of its prey. Both species reproduce by parthenogenesis-a mode of reproduction in which unfertilized eggs
(20) develop into fertile females. Cyclamen mites lay three eggs per day over the four or five days of their reproductive life span; *Typhlodromus* lay two or three eggs per day for eight to ten days. Seasonal synchrony of *Typhlodromus* reproduction with the
(25) growth of prey populations and ability to survive at low prey densities also contribute to the predatory efficiency of *Typhlodromus*. During winter, when cyclamen mite populations dwindle to a few individuals hidden in the crevices and folds of leaves
(30) in the crowns of the strawberry plants, the predatory mites subsist on the honeydew produced by aphids and white flies. They do not reproduce except when they are feeding on the cyclamen mites. These features, which make *Typhlodromus* well-suited for
(35) exploiting the seasonal rises and falls of its prey, are common among predators that control prey populations.
    Greenhouse experiments have verified the importance of *Typhlodromus* predation for keeping
(40) cyclamen mites in check. One group of strawberry plants was stocked with both predator and prey mites; a second group was kept predator-free by regular application of parathion, an insecticide that kills the predatory species but does not affect the cyclamen
(45) mite. Throughout the study, populations of cyclamen mites remained low in plots shared with *Typhlodromus,* but their infestation attained significantly damaging proportions on predator-free plants.
(50)   Applying parathion in this instance is a clear case in which using a pesticide would do far more harm than good to an agricultural enterprise. The results were similar in field plantings of strawberries, where cyclamen mites also reached damaging levels when
(55) predators were eliminated by parathion, but they did not attain such levels in untreated plots. When cyclamen mite populations began to increase in an untreated planting, the predator populations quickly responded to reduce the outbreak. On average,
(60) cyclamen mites were about 25 times more abundant in the absence of predators than in their presence.

20. Which one of the following most accurately expresses the main point of the passage?

(A)   Control of agricultural pests is most effectively and safely accomplished without the use of pesticides, because these pesticides can kill predators that also control the pests.

(B)   Experimental verification is essential in demonstrating the effectiveness of natural controls of agricultural pests.

(C)   The relationship between *Typhlodromus* and cyclamen mites demonstrates how natural predation can keep a population of agricultural pests in check.

(D)   Predation by *Typhlodromus* is essential for the control of cyclamen mite populations in strawberry fields.

(E)   Similarity in mode and timing of reproduction is what enables *Typhlodromus* effectively to control populations of cyclamen mites in fields of strawberry plants.

21. Based on the passage, the author would probably hold that which one of the following principles is fundamental to long-term predatory control of agricultural pests?

(A)   The reproduction of the predator population should be synchronized with that of the prey population, so that the number of predators surges just prior to a surge in prey numbers.

(B)   The effectiveness of the predatory relationship should be experimentally demonstrable in greenhouse as well as field applications.

(C)   The prey population should be able to survive in times of low crop productivity, so that the predator population will not decrease to very low levels.

(D)   The predator population's level of consumption of the prey species should be responsive to variations in the size of the prey population.

(E)   The predator population should be vulnerable only to pesticides to which the prey population is also vulnerable.

22. Which one of the following is mentioned in the passage as a factor contributing to the effectiveness of *Typhlodromus* as a predator?

(A)   its ability to withstand most insecticides except parathion

(B)   its lack of natural predators in strawberry fields

(C)   its ability to live in different climates in different geographic regions

(D)   its constant food supply in cyclamen mite populations

(E)   its ability to survive when few prey are available

23. Suppose that pesticide X drastically slows the reproductive rate of cyclamen mites and has no other direct effect on cyclamen mites or *Typhlodromus*. Based on the information in the passage, which one of the following would most likely have occurred if, in the experiments mentioned in the passage, pesticide X had been used instead of parathion, with all other conditions affecting the experiments remaining the same?

(A) In both treated and untreated plots inhabited by both *Typhlodromus* and cyclamen mites, the latter would have been effectively controlled.

(B) Cyclamen mite populations in all treated plots from which *Typhlodromus* was absent would have been substantially lower than in untreated plots inhabited by both kinds of mites.

(C) In the treated plots, slowed reproduction in cyclamen mites would have led to a loss of reproductive synchrony between *Typhlodromus* and cyclamen mites.

(D) In the treated plots, *Typhlodromus* populations would have decreased temporarily and would have eventually increased.

(E) In the treated plots, cyclamen mite populations would have reached significantly damaging levels more slowly, but would have remained at those levels longer, than in untreated plots.

24. It can be inferred from the passage that the author would be most likely to agree with which one of the following statements about the use of predators to control pest populations?

(A) If the use of predators to control cyclamen mite populations fails, then parathion should be used to control these populations.

(B) Until the effects of the predators on beneficial insects that live in strawberry fields are assessed, such predators should be used with caution to control cyclamen mite populations.

(C) Insecticides should be used to control certain pest populations in fields of crops only if the use of natural predators has proven inadequate.

(D) If an insecticide can effectively control pest populations as well as predator populations, then it should be used instead of predators to control pest populations.

(E) Predators generally control pest populations more effectively than pesticides because they do not harm the crops that their prey feed on.

25. The author mentions the egg-laying ability of each kind of mite (lines 20-23) primarily in order to support which one of the following claims?

(A) Mites that reproduce by parthenogenesis do so at approximately equal rates.

(B) Predatory mites typically have a longer reproductive life span than do cyclamen mites.

(C) *Typhlodromus* can lay their eggs in synchrony with cyclamen mites.

(D) *Typhlodromus* can reproduce at least as quickly as cyclamen mites.

(E) The egg-laying rate of *Typhlodromus* is slower in the presence of cyclamen mites than it is in their absence.

26. Which one of the following would, if true, most strengthen the author's position regarding the practical applicability of the information about predatory mites presented in the passage?

(A) The individual *Typhlodromus* mites that have the longest reproductive life spans typically also lay the greatest number of eggs per day.

(B) The insecticides that are typically used for mite control on strawberry plants kill both predatory and nonpredatory species of mites.

(C) In areas in which strawberry plants become infested by cyclamen mites, winters tend to be short and relatively mild.

(D) *Typhlodromus* are sometimes preyed upon by another species of mites that is highly susceptible to parathion.

(E) *Typhlodromus* easily tolerate the same range of climatic conditions that strawberry plants do.

27. Information in the passage most strongly supports which one of the following statements?

(A) Strawberry crops can support populations of both cyclamen mites and *Typhlodromus* mites without significant damage to those crops.

(B) For control of cyclamen mites by another mite species to be effective, it is crucial that the two species have the same mode of reproduction.

(C) Factors that make *Typhlodromus* effective against cyclamen mites also make it effective against certain other pests of strawberry plants.

(D) When *Typhlodromus* is relied on to control cyclamen mites in strawberry crops, pesticides may be necessary to prevent significant damage during the first year.

(E) Strawberry growers have unintentionally caused cyclamen mites to become a serious crop pest by the indiscriminate use of parathion.

A Science Passage Analyzed

This passage contains a classic structure, and one that has been used in Science passages before: the opening lines state a principle or belief, and then the remaining lines provide examples that illustrate the theory or belief. The passage, which appears to be solely about cyclamen mites, is actually about demonstrating the statement in the first sentence (using natural predation to control agricultural pests).

Paragraph One:

The passage opens with the assertion that will be shown throughout the passage: sometimes the most effective agent for controlling an agricultural pest is its natural predators (lines 1-3). The example that is used to discuss this statement is that of the cyclamen mites, who infest strawberry plants. Cyclamen mites can be controlled by another mite, that of the genus *Typhlodromus*. The remainder of the paragraph establishes a timeline: cyclamen mites infest strawberry fields shortly after planting but their levels do not become damaging until the second year (lines 6-10). In the second year, mites from the genus *Typhlodromus* appear and subdue the cyclamen mite population before damage occurs (lines 10-14).

Regarding the scientific terminology in this paragraph, you are not expected to know anything about mites, and certainly nothing about their specific names or genus. You simply need to know that there are two types of mites—cyclamen mites and mites from the genus *Typhlodromus*—and that *Typhlodromus* mites are predators of the cyclamen mites, which feed on strawberries.

Paragraph Two:

The second paragraph is devoted to a discussion of why *Typhlodromus* mites are effective predators, and three main reasons are presented. The first is their voracious appetite (line 16), the second is that their population can increase as rapidly as that of the cyclamen mites (line 17-18), and the third is that they have a population that seasonally matches the population of their prey (lines 23-27). The author closes the paragraph by noting that such features are common among predators that control prey populations (in other words, these features of *Typhlodromus* mites are not unique). You should diagram these three points using the numbered list notation (circled 1, 2, 3) off to the side of each item.

There are two scientific terms used in the paragraph. The first, "parthenogenesis," is immediately defined after the dash in line 18. The second term, "seasonal synchrony," is finally defined in line 35, more than 10 lines later. However, this term is relatively easy to figure out from context, and so most readers are able to move forward from line 23 without confusion.

Paragraphs Three and Four:

These paragraphs offer proof for the opening statement in the form of experimental results. As recounted in the third paragraph, using greenhouse experiments, researchers demonstrated the importance of the predator *Typhlodromus* mites. In the fourth paragraph, the results were similar when live field plantings were done.

The third paragraph also offers up another ominous looking term—"parathion"—but then immediately defines it as an insecticide that kills the *Typhlodromus* predator mites but not the cyclamen mites.

VIEWSTAMP Analysis:

The passage contains just a single **Viewpoint:**

> The view of the author, who believes that at times the best means of controlling an agricultural pest is giving free rein to its natural predators.

The **Structure** of the passage is as follows:

> Paragraph One: Assert a principle, begin explanation of an example.
>
> Paragraph Two: Discuss three advantages of the predator *Typhlodromus* mite.
>
> Paragraph Three: Provide proof in the form of experimental results.
>
> Paragraph Four: Provide further proof from field tests, which confirmed the greenhouse experiment results.

The author's **Tone** is confident in the stated principle, and positive that the example of the mites and corresponding experiment results provide proof of the principle.

The **Arguments** in the passage are mainly an explanation of how the example of the mites illustrates the assertion that opens the passage.

The author's **Main Point** is that at times the best means of controlling an agricultural pest is giving free rein to its natural predators, as exemplified by the relationship of the two mite types.

Overall, this passage looks forbidding at first glance. The passage appears to be filled with scientific terms and references, and many students may simply bail out after glancing at the text. While there are some sections that are a bit dense and will require re-examination during the questions (such as lines 23-37 and lines 52-59), the overall structure of the passage and the general message is clear.

Question #20: GR, Main Point. The correct answer choice is (C)

This question should be easy, as long as you realize that the first sentence of the passage sets up a framework for the remaining discussion. If you did not realize this point, you may fall for an answer choice such as (D).

Answer choice (A): This answer choice is incorrect because of the phrase "most effectively." The author simply noted that predator control was "sometimes" the most effective method, not that pesticides were never the most effective method. Pesticides just were not the most effective method in this situation.

Answer choice (B): The phrase, "Experimental verification is essential" is problematic. The author neither states this point nor would it be the main point even if stated in the passage.

Answer choice (C): This is the correct answer choice, as indicated in the passage analysis.

Answer choice (D): This answer choice focuses on the cyclamen mite example but never references the first sentence of the passage, and so it is incorrect. Remember, examples are never the main point of the passage; the principle that the examples explain is usually the main point.

Aside from the fact that this point—even if it were true—is not the main point, the author never states this point in the passage. The author instead states that the *Typhlodromus* mite is effective in controlling cyclamen mites (lines 3-6), and important to keeping the cyclamen mites in check (lines 38-40), but not *essential*.

Answer choice (E): This answer addresses a minor point within the passage, not the broad overall theme of the passage.

Question #21: GR, Must, Author's Perspective, PR. The correct answer choice is (D)

This question asks you to identify the author's perspective regarding a principle of long-term predatory control of pests. Aside from knowing that the author believes that it can be an effective method, we also know that the author believes the *Typhlodromus* mite has several features that make it an effective predator (as related in the second paragraph).

Answer choice (A): This answer choice is incorrect because of the phrase "just prior." In lines 17-18, the author states that "Its population can increase *as rapidly as* that of its prey" (italics added for emphasis). The *Typhlodromus* mite is effective because it matches or responds to the cyclamen mite, not because it anticipates the cyclamen mite.

Answer choice (B): This answer choice does not address the principle of predatory *control*, just a principle of theory viability.

Answer choice (C): The author does not offer any opinions on whether the *prey* population should be able to survive.

Answer choice (D): This is the correct answer choice. Lines 23-33 support this statement as a principle the author believes in.

Answer choice (E): The reference to the use of pesticides and their effect on the predator population was part of the discussion of experimental results. The author was not implying that the predators should be vulnerable only to pesticides that also affect the prey.

Question #22: GR, Must. The correct answer choice is (E)

This question asks you to identify the advantages of the *Typhlodromus* mite, and you should immediately refer to the second paragraph for more information.

Answer choice (A): This is not mentioned as a factor contributing to the effectiveness of the *Typhlodromus* mite.

Answer choice (B): This is not mentioned in the passage.

Answer choice (C): Although the *Typhlodromus* mite can live during different seasons (lines 23-28), no mention is made of the *Typhlodromus* mite living in different geographic regions.

Answer choice (D): This is not given as a factor in why the *Typhlodromus* mite is an *effective* predator.

Answer choice (E): This is the correct answer choice. As mentioned in lines 27-32, this is an advantage of the *Typhlodromus* mite.

Question #23: CR, Must. The correct answer choice is (A)

The question stem supposes a situation wherein the *Typhlodromus* mite is unaffected by a particular pesticide, but the cyclamen mite has its reproductive rate slowed. Although pesticides are discussed in the third paragraph, the issue of reproductive rates is one that appears in the second paragraph. Hence, you should refer to the second paragraph for more information. From that paragraph, we know that the *Typhlodromus* mite can already keep up with the cyclamen mite, so if the cyclamen mite reproductive rate slowed, the effect would be that there would be less food for the *Typhlodromus* mite. The question stem also references the experiments discussed in the passage, so that reference takes you to the third and fourth paragraphs. Because those paragraphs reference greenhouse and field tests, the conclusion is that there is likely to be no change in how cyclamen mites are affected by the *Typhlodromus* mite, and the only impact would be on the food supply of the *Typhlodromus* mite.

Answer choice (A): This is the correct answer choice. In both experiments, the cyclamen mite would still be controlled.

Answer choice (B): You cannot make a comparison between these two populations; given that cyclamen mites were 25 times more prevalent in the absence of predators (lines 59-61), they may have had a higher population even with the pesticide than when the *Typhlodromus* mite was present without pesticides.

Answer choice (C): Given the meaning of seasonal synchrony, it is unlikely that it would be lost just because the cyclamen mite population was lower than normal. The likely scenario is that the *Typhlodromus* mite would simply respond with lower numbers.

Answer choice (D): Although the first half of this answer sounds valid, the second half is unknown. Therefore, this answer choice is incorrect.

Answer choice (E): There is no way to draw this conclusion based on the information in the question stem or passage.

Question #24: GR, Must, Author's Perspective. The correct answer choice is (C)

We know from our initial analysis that the author believes at times the best means of controlling an agricultural pest is giving free rein to its natural predators.

Answer choice (A): Parathion was just the pesticide used in the experiments discussed in the passage, and it was a pesticide used to control *Typhlodromus* mites, not cyclamen mites.

Answer choice (B): No, the author would disagree with this statement. He or she has already stated that at times the best means of controlling an agricultural pest is giving free rein to its natural predators.

Answer choice (C): This is the correct answer choice. This conditional answer choice indicates that insecticides should be used only if natural predators could not do the job. The contrapositive, which states that if natural predators can do the job then insecticides should not be used, is a statement that the author would agree with based on the statements in the passage. Thus, this answer choice is correct.

Answer choice (D): No, this answer choice is incorrect, in part because the passage is not about controlling *predator* populations. Plus, the author is pro-predator control, not anti-predator control.

Answer choice (E): The passage is about the effectiveness of control (lines 1-3), and harm to the crops does not play a role.

Question #25: SR, Purpose. The correct answer choice is (D)

The question stem refers you to lines 20-23, so return to line 15 to gain context for what is presented in lines 20-23. The overall message of this paragraph is the effectiveness of the *Typhlodromus* mites, and the point made specifically in lines 17-18 is in reference to the ability of the *Typhlodromus* mites to increase population as rapidly as cyclamen mites. Hence, answer choice (D) is correct.

Answer choice (A): The information in lines 20-23 seems to suggest that this answer choice is incorrect.

Answer choice (B): While this statement appears to be true for *Typhlodromus* mites in relation to cyclamen mites, the passage does not address all predatory mites (as does this answer). In addition, even if this statement were true, making that point still would not be the purpose of the author in lines 20-23.

Answer choice (C): The synchrony discussed in the passage is based on seasonal populations, not reproductive rates.

Answer choice (D): This is the correct answer choice.

Answer choice (E): There is no mention made of differences in *Typhlodromus* mite reproductive rates in the presence or absence of cyclamen mites.

Question #26: GR, Strengthen. The correct answer choice is (E)

In this question, you are asked to select an answer choice that supports the author's overall contention about the applicability of predatory mites. To prephrase this question is somewhat difficult because there is no way to know what aspect of the author's position the test makers will choose to support.

Answer choice (A): The passage is about the mites as a whole, not individual mites. This information does not support the author.

Answer choice (B): This answer indicates that the pesticides typically used for mite control kill all mites. This information has no material effect on the applicability of predatory mites.

Answer choice (C): The severity of winter was not a germane issue to the argument made by the author. The author simply stated that *Typhlodromus* mites could survive the winter (lines 27-32).

Answer choice (D): This answer indicates that in a field sprayed with parathion, the predators of the *Typhlodromus* mites would also be affected. However, because parathion affects the *Typhlodromus* mites as well, this information is not helpful.

Answer choice (E): This is the correct answer choice. This answer shows that the *Typhlodromus* mites can survive in the habitats of the cyclamen mites, and thus would be able to prey upon them.

Question #27: GR, Must. The correct answer choice is (A)

In a Global Must Be true question, do not worry about prephrasing an answer because there are too many options. Simply move from the question stem directly to the answer choices.

Answer choice (A): This is the correct answer choice. This answer choice is supported by lines 10-14.

Answer choice (B): Although the passage states that *Typhlodromus* mites and cyclamen mites have the same mode of reproduction (line 18), the passage does not suggest that this is a necessary element for effective predatory control.

Answer choice (C): The example in the passage just discusses how *Typhlodromus* mites can control cyclamen mites; the effectiveness of *Typhlodromus* mites against other strawberry plant pests is not addressed.

Answer choice (D): This answer choice is incorrect. As stated in lines 6-10, during the first year of a cyclamen mite infestation, the population does not reach a significantly damaging level. Hence, it is unlikely that pesticides would be needed.

Answer choice (E): Although certain experiments seem to suggest that the indiscriminate application of parathion could create the situation described in this answer choice, nowhere does the passage suggest that this is an actual problem.

Two Science Practice Passages

The next several pages contain two actual LSAT Science passage sets. After the two passages, a complete analysis of each passage and all of the corresponding questions is presented.

To most effectively benefit from this section, time yourself on the first passage. Attempt to finish the passage in 8 minutes and 45 seconds, but if you cannot, continue working until you complete all of the questions and then note your time. Then, read the entire explanation section for the first passage. Afterwards, move to the second passage and repeat the process.

The pronghorn, an antelope-like mammal that lives on the western plains of North America, is the continent's fastest land animal, capable of running 90 kilometers per hour and of doing so for several
(5) kilometers. Because no North American predator is nearly fast enough to chase it down, biologists have had difficulty explaining why the pronghorn developed its running prowess. One biologist, however, has recently claimed that pronghorns run as
(10) fast as they do because of adaptation to predators known from fossil records to have been extinct for 10,000 years, such as American cheetahs and long-legged hyenas, either of which, it is believed, were fast enough to run down the pronghorn.

(15) Like all explanations that posit what is called a relict behavior—a behavior that persists though its only evolutionary impetus comes from long-extinct environmental conditions—this one is likely to meet with skepticism. Most biologists distrust explanations positing relict
(20) behaviors, in part because testing these hypotheses is so difficult due to the extinction of a principal component. They typically consider such historical explanations only when a lack of alternatives forces them to do so. But present-day observations sometimes yield
(25) evidence that supports relict behavior hypotheses.

In the case of the pronghorn, researchers have identified much supporting evidence, as several aspects of pronghorn behavior appear to have been shaped by enemies that no longer exist. For example,
(30) pronghorns—like many other grazing animals—roam in herds, which allows more eyes to watch for predators and diminishes the chances of any particular animal being attacked but can also result in overcrowding and increased competition for food. But, since
(35) pronghorns have nothing to fear from present-day carnivores and thus have nothing to gain from herding, their herding behavior appears to be another adaptation to extinct threats. Similarly, if speed and endurance were once essential to survival, researchers would
(40) expect pronghorns to choose mates based on these athletic abilities, which they do—with female pronghorns, for example, choosing the victor after male pronghorns challenge each other in sprints and chases.

Relict behaviors appear to occur in other animals
(45) as well, increasing the general plausibility of such a theory. For example, one study reports relict behavior in stickleback fish belonging to populations that have long been free of a dangerous predator, the sculpin. In the study, when presented with sculpin, these
(50) stickleback fish immediately engaged in stereotypical antisculpin behavior, avoiding its mouth and swimming behind to bite it. Another study found that ground squirrels from populations that have been free from snakes for 70,000 to 300,000 years still clearly recognize
(55) rattlesnakes, displaying stereotypical antirattlesnake behavior in the presence of the snake. Such fear, however, apparently does not persist interminably. Arctic ground squirrels, free of snakes for about 3 million years, appear to be unable to recognize the

(60) threat of a rattlesnake, exhibiting only disorganized caution even after being bitten repeatedly.

16. Which one of the following most accurately states the main point of the passage?

(A) Evidence from present-day animal behaviors, together with the fossil record, supports the hypothesis that the pronghorn's ability to far outrun any predator currently on the North American continent is an adaptation to predators long extinct.

(B) Although some biologists believe that certain animal characteristics, such as the speed of the pronghorn, are explained by environmental conditions that have not existed for many years, recent data concerning arctic ground squirrels make this hypothesis doubtful.

(C) Research into animal behavior, particularly into that of the pronghorn, provides strong evidence that most present-day characteristics of animals are explained by environmental conditions that have not existed for many years.

(D) Even in those cases in which an animal species displays characteristics clearly explained by long-vanished environmental conditions, evidence concerning arctic ground squirrels suggests that those characteristics will eventually disappear.

(E) Although biologists are suspicious of hypotheses that are difficult to test, there is now widespread agreement among biologists that many types of animal characteristics are best explained as adaptations to long-extinct predators.

17. Based on the passage, the term "principal component" (line 21) most clearly refers to which one of the following?

(A) behavior that persists even though the conditions that provided its evolutionary impetus are extinct

(B) the original organism whose descendants' behavior is being investigated as relict behavior

(C) the pronghorn's ability to run 90 kilometers per hour over long distances

(D) the environmental conditions in response to which relict behaviors are thought to have developed

(E) an original behavior of an animal of which certain present-day behaviors are thought to be modifications

18. The last paragraph most strongly supports which one of the following statements?

   (A)   An absence of predators in an animal's environment can constitute just as much of a threat to the well-being of that animal as the presence of predators.
   (B)   Relict behaviors are found in most wild animals living today.
   (C)   If a behavior is an adaptation to environmental conditions, it may eventually disappear in the absence of those or similar conditions.
   (D)   Behavior patterns that originated as a way of protecting an organism against predators will persist interminably if they are periodically reinforced.
   (E)   Behavior patterns invariably take longer to develop than they do to disappear.

19. Which one of the following describes a benefit mentioned in the passage that grazing animals derive from roaming in herds?

   (A)   The greater density of animals tends to intimidate potential predators.
   (B)   The larger number of adults in a herd makes protection of the younger animals from predators much easier.
   (C)   With many animals searching it is easier for the herd to find food and water.
   (D)   The likelihood that any given individual will be attacked by a predator decreases.
   (E)   The most defenseless animals can achieve greater safety by remaining in the center of the herd.

20. The passage mentions each of the following as support for the explanation of the pronghorn's speed proposed by the biologist referred to in line 8 EXCEPT:

   (A)   fossils of extinct animals believed to have been able to run down a pronghorn
   (B)   the absence of carnivores in the pronghorn's present-day environment
   (C)   the present-day preference of pronghorns for athletic mates
   (D)   the apparent need for a similar explanation to account for the herding behavior pronghorns now display
   (E)   the occurrence of relict behavior in other species

21. The third paragraph of the passage provides the most support for which one of the following inferences?

   (A)   Predators do not attack grazing animals that are assembled into herds.
   (B)   Pronghorns tend to graze in herds only when they sense a threat from predators close by.
   (C)   If animals do not graze for their food, they do not roam in herds.
   (D)   Female pronghorns mate only with the fastest male pronghorn in the herd.
   (E)   If pronghorns did not herd, they would not face significantly greater danger from present-day carnivores.

The survival of nerve cells, as well as their performance of some specialized functions, is regulated by chemicals known as neurotrophic factors, which are produced in the bodies of animals,
(5) including humans. Rita Levi-Montalcini's discovery in the 1950s of the first of these agents, a hormonelike substance now known as NGF, was a crucial development in the history of biochemistry, which led to Levi-Montalcini sharing the Nobel Prize
(10) for medicine in 1986.

In the mid-1940s, Levi-Montalcini had begun by hypothesizing that many of the immature nerve cells produced in the development of an organism are normally programmed to die. In order to confirm this
(15) theory, she conducted research that in 1949 found that, when embryos are in the process of forming their nervous systems, they produce many more nerve cells than are finally required, the number that survives eventually adjusting itself to the volume of
(20) tissue to be supplied with nerves. A further phase of the experimentation, which led to Levi-Montalcini's identification of the substance that controls this process, began with her observation that the development of nerves in chick embryos could be
(25) stimulated by implanting a certain variety of mouse tumor in the embryos. She theorized that a chemical produced by the tumors was responsible for the observed nerve growth. To investigate this hypothesis, she used the then new technique of tissue culture, by
(30) which specific types of body cells can be made to grow outside the organism from which they are derived. Within twenty-four hours, her tissue cultures of chick embryo extracts developed dense halos of nerve tissue near the places in the culture where she
(35) had added the mouse tumor. Further research identified a specific substance contributed by the mouse tumors that was responsible for the effects Levi-Montalcini had observed: a protein that she named "nerve growth factor" (NGF).
(40) NGF was the first of many cell-growth factors to be found in the bodies of animals. Through Levi-Montalcini's work and other subsequent research, it has been determined that this substance is present in many tissues and biological fluids, and that it is
(45) especially concentrated in some organs. In developing organisms, nerve cells apparently receive this growth factor locally from the cells of muscles or other organs to which they will form connections for transmission of nerve impulses, and sometimes from
(50) supporting cells intermingled with the nerve tissue. NGF seems to play two roles, serving initially to direct the developing nerve processes toward the correct, specific "target" cells with which they must connect, and later being necessary for the continued
(55) survival of those nerve cells. During some periods of their development, the types of nerve cells that are affected by NGF—primarily cells outside the brain and spinal cord—die if the factor is not present or if they encounter anti-NGF antibodies.

15. Which one of the following most accurately expresses the main point of the passage?

(A) Levi-Montalcini's discovery of neurotrophic factors as a result of research carried out in the 1940s was a major contribution to our understanding of the role of naturally occurring chemicals, especially NGF, in the development of chick embryos.

(B) Levi-Montalcini's discovery of NGF, a neurotrophic factor that stimulates the development of some types of nerve tissue and whose presence or absence in surrounding cells helps determine whether particular nerve cells will survive, was a pivotal development in biochemistry.

(C) NGF, which is necessary for the survival and proper functioning of nerve cells, was discovered by Levi-Montalcini in a series of experiments using the technique of tissue culture, which she devised in the 1940s.

(D) Partly as a result of Levi-Montalcini's research, it has been found that NGF and other neurotrophic factors are produced only by tissues to which nerves are already connected and that the presence of these factors is necessary for the health and proper functioning of nervous systems.

(E) NGF, a chemical that was discovered by Levi-Montalcini, directs the growth of nerve cells toward the cells with which they must connect and ensures the survival of those nerve cells throughout the life of the organism except when the organism produces anti-NGF antibodies.

16. Based on the passage, the author would be most likely to believe that Levi-Montalcini's discovery of NGF is noteworthy primarily because it

(A) paved the way for more specific knowledge of the processes governing the development of the nervous system

(B) demonstrated that a then new laboratory technique could yield important and unanticipated experimental results

(C) confirmed the hypothesis that many of a developing organism's immature nerve cells are normally programmed to die

(D) indicated that this substance stimulates observable biochemical reactions in the tissues of different species

(E) identified a specific substance, produced by mouse tumors, that can be used to stimulate nerve cell growth

17. The primary function of the third paragraph of the passage in relation to the second paragraph is to

   (A) indicate that conclusions referred to in the second paragraph, though essentially correct, require further verification
   (B) indicate that conclusions referred to in the second paragraph have been undermined by subsequently obtained evidence
   (C) indicate ways in which conclusions referred to in the second paragraph have been further corroborated and refined
   (D) describe subsequent discoveries of substances analogous to the substance discussed in the second paragraph
   (E) indicate that experimental procedures discussed in the second paragraph have been supplanted by more precise techniques described in the third paragraph

18. Information in the passage most strongly supports which one of the following?

   (A) Nerve cells in excess of those that are needed by the organism in which they develop eventually produce anti-NGF antibodies to suppress the effects of NGF.
   (B) Nerve cells that grow in the absence of NGF are less numerous than, but qualitatively identical to, those that grow in the presence of NGF.
   (C) Few of the nerve cells that connect with target cells toward which NGF directs them are needed by the organism in which they develop.
   (D) Some of the nerve cells that grow in the presence of NGF are eventually converted to other types of living tissue by neurotrophic factors.
   (E) Some of the nerve cells that grow in an embryo do not connect with any particular target cells.

19. The passage describes a specific experiment that tested which one of the following hypotheses?

   (A) A certain kind of mouse tumor produces a chemical that stimulates the growth of nerve cells.
   (B) Developing embryos initially grow many more nerve cells than they will eventually require.
   (C) In addition to NGF, there are several other important neurotrophic factors regulating cell survival and function.
   (D) Certain organs contain NGF in concentrations much higher than in the surrounding tissue.
   (E) Certain nerve cells are supplied with NGF by the muscle cells to which they are connected.

20. Which one of the following is most strongly supported by the information in the passage?

   (A) Some of the effects that the author describes as occurring in Levi-Montalcini's culture of chick embryo extract were due to neurotrophic factors other than NGF.
   (B) Although NGF was the first neurotrophic factor to be identified, some other such factors are now more thoroughly understood.
   (C) In her research in the 1940s and 1950s, Levi-Montalcini identified other neurotrophic factors in addition to NGF.
   (D) Some neurotrophic factors other than NGF perform functions that are not specifically identified in the passage.
   (E) The effects of NGF that Levi-Montalcini noted in her chick embryo experiment are also caused by other neurotrophic factors not discussed in the passage.

Paragraph One:

In this scientific passage, the author begins with a brief discussion of the 90 mph North American pronghorn and the interesting question of why it is able to run so much faster than any of its predators. The introduction is viewpoint neutral, and in line 8 the author introduces the viewpoint of "one biologist," who claims that the speed was developed to escape from some predators before extinction over 10,000 years ago. The author provides two examples of such predators: the American cheetah and the long-legged hyena.

Paragraph Two:

In this paragraph the author expands upon the explanation begun in the introduction and continues the passage in a neutral, academic tone, basically reporting the facts. "Relict behavior" is currently exhibited behavior that was developed in response to conditions that no longer exist. This theory generally draws skepticism since it cannot be tested, and is usually a last resort for scientists, but seems to be supported in some cases by present-day evidence.

Paragraph Three:

Here the author introduces current evidence to support the idea of relict behavior: pronghorns herd even though they have no predators to fear and herding can result in overcrowding, and pronghorns choose mates based on physical prowess.

Paragraph Four:

The author ends the passage with further examples that strengthen the claim of the existence of relict behavior, and discusses the lengths of time that relict behaviors seem to persist (and eventually disappear).

VIEWSTAMP Analysis:

This passage is fairly **Viewpoint** neutral, discussing the possible existence of relict behavior and presenting evidence in its favor.

The **Structure** of the passage is as follows:

Paragraph One: Introduce the pronghorn, the possibility of behavior based on outdated necessity, and two examples of extinct predators of the pronghorn.

Paragraph Two: Introduce the concept of relict behavior, and that the theory elicits skepticism but is supported by modern day evidence.

Paragraph Three: Introduce specific examples of modern evidence supporting the existence of relict behavior.

Paragraph Four: Provide further examples of possible relict behavior, and one example of lost relict behavior.

This is a basic science passage with little real argumentation. The only real **Argument** is that of the author, who believes that relict behavior likely exists.

The **Main Point** of the passage is that the pronghorn's relative speed may be a relict behavior based on the need to escape predators that no longer exist.

Question #16: GR, Main Point. The correct answer choice is (A)

The main point of the passage, as prephrased above, is to introduce the pronghorn, and to introduce and provide evidence to support the notion of relict behavior.

Answer choice (A): This is the correct answer choice, as it reflects the same basic information discussed above.

Answer choice (B): The example of the squirrel serves to show that at some point relict behavior dissipates, but it does not weaken the argument for the existence of relict behavior.

Answer choice (C): The author does not suggest that most behavior is relict, only that relict behavior does appear to exist.

Answer choice (D): The ground squirrel is one case and does not provide enough evidence to draw such a broad conclusion regarding all relict behavior.

Answer choice (E): The author discusses the logical skepticism of a theory that is difficult to test, but does not assert that there is widespread agreement about the existence of relict behavior.

Question #17: SR, Must. The correct answer choice is (D)

For this Specific Reference question, we should be sure that we know the context of the reference: There is skepticism about the theory of relict behavior, partly because it is so difficult to test due to the absence of a principal component. In the case of the pronghorn, this refers to the long extinct predators that may have led to the pronghorn's speed and other relict behavior.

Answer choice (A): Since the behavior that persists is not absent, we can rule out this choice.

Answer choice (B): The principal component does not refer to the ancestor of the pronghorn, so this answer choice is incorrect.

Answer choice (C): This ability is not absent, so this answer choice must be wrong.

Answer choice (D): This is the correct answer choice, aligned with our prephrase. In the case of the pronghorn, the referenced environmental condition would be the extinct predators.

Answer choice (E): The passage does not talk about original behavior that is different from modern day behavior, so this answer choice should be eliminated.

Question #18: SR, Must. The correct answer choice is (C)

Since this passage references the last paragraph, we should consider what information was provided there. There are other examples that appear evidentiary of relict behavior, and there is one example when relict behavior has apparently ended.

Answer choice (A): There is no reference to any detriment associated with the absence of predators, so this answer choice can be safely eliminated.

Answer choice (B): The word that makes this answer choice a definite loser is "most"—the author would not claim that most animals display relict behavior.

Answer choice (C): This is the correct answer choice, as it refers to the end of the paragraph, and the example of the squirrel whose relict behavior apparently no longer exists.

Answer choice (D): There is no such claim in the passage, so this answer choice is incorrect.

Answer choice (E): The author of this passage never makes any such comparison, so this answer choice is incorrect.

Question #19: CR, Must. The correct answer choice is (D)

The answer to this Concept Reference question should be prephrased: the benefits of the herd, discussed in the third paragraph, are the greater number of eyes watching out, and the lower likelihood that any one animal will be attacked.

Answer choice (A): The author does not discuss density in the passage, so although this may sound like reasonable speculation, it must be eliminated because it cannot be confirmed by the information provided.

Answer choice (B): This is another choice that seems like it could be true, but since it is not discussed in the passage, this answer choice must be incorrect.

Answer choice (C): This answer choice seems reasonable enough, but since it is not discussed in the passage, it cannot be correct.

Answer choice (D): This is the correct answer choice, as it presents one of the two benefits listed in our prephrase.

Answer choice (E): This answer choice seems like it could be true, but it is not offered specifically as a benefit, so it must not be correct.

Question #20: SR, Must X. The correct answer choice is (B)

Since this is an Except question, the four incorrect answer choices will support the biologist's explanation, and the correct answer will not.

Answer choice (A): This evidence is mentioned, so this choice is one of the four wrong answers that is mentioned in the passage.

Answer choice (B): This is the correct answer choice. There is no discussion of the absence of "carnivores," only the absence of predators.

Answer choice (C): This is discussed in the third paragraph, so this answer choice should be eliminated.

Answer choice (D): This is alluded to in the third paragraph, so we can safely eliminate this choice from contention as well.

Answer choice (E): This evidence is presented in the final paragraph, so this answer choice must be incorrect.

Question #21: SR, Must. The correct answer choice is (E)

In the third paragraph of the passage the author discusses the various behaviors of the pronghorn that may be explained as relict behavior.

Answer choice (A): This choice is far more absolute than provided for by the author, who only says that herding is beneficial, not that herding grazers never get attacked.

Answer choice (B): The point is that they do not need to graze in herds, but they still do, so it must have something to do with past stimuli.

Answer choice (C): There is nothing mentioned in the passage that allows this conditional relationship to be drawn, so this answer choice should be eliminated.

Answer choice (D): While the third paragraph does refer to a preference for athletic prowess, there is no assertion that only the fastest is chosen to mate.

Answer choice (E): This is the correct answer choice. Again, since the point is that they herd without the necessity for herding protection, this answer choice must be true.

In this passage, the author discusses some of the specific research that led to Rita Levi-Montalcini's Nobel Prize winning discovery of NGF, or "Nerve Growth Factor," and the broad ramifications of this and subsequent discoveries regarding neurotrophic factors.

Paragraph One:
The author begins this passage with an introduction to the concept of neurotrophic factors: Chemicals which regulate the survival of nerve cells in animals. The first of these agents, known as NGF, was discovered in the 1950s by Rita Levi-Montalcini, who in 1986 shared the Nobel Prize for this discovery. As is common in science passages such as this one, the tone of the author is somewhat academic and the passage to this point is fairly viewpoint neutral.

Paragraph Two:
In the second paragraph, the author continues this viewpoint-neutral, factual account, taking us back in time, to the mid-1940s, at which point Levi-Montalcini had hypothesized that many immature nerve cells are normally programmed to die. She did research to confirm this study, and in 1949 found that embryos produce many more nerve cells than are needed, adjusting downward to suit the tissue's necessity. A later phase of the research dealt with chick embryos, whose nerve development could be stimulated with tumor implantation. Levi-Montalcini hypothesized this to be caused by a chemical produced by tumors. The technique of tissue culture, which grows cells outside an organism, was used to investigate and then prove her hypothesis. Further research identified the tumor substance responsible for the observed effects, and Levi-Montalcini called it NGF, which stands for "nerve growth factor."

Paragraph Three:
The third paragraph continues in the same neutral, scientific tone, discussing that NGF was the first of many cell-growth factors found in animals. Levi-Montalcini's work, supplemented by later research, led to the determination that NGF is present in many tissues and fluids, and in heavy concentrations in some organs. This growth factor appears to be supplied by muscle cells, by organs over which nerve impulses will be transmitted, or sometimes by cells that are interspersed with the nerve tissues. The cells affected by NGF, generally those outside the brain and spinal cord, die if NGF is absent, or if anti-NGF antibodies are present.

VIEWSTAMP Analysis:
This passage, like many (but not all) science passages, is fairly **Viewpoint-neutral**. The author does believe that Levi-Montalcini played an important role, but this assertion appears to be well-founded and factual.

The **Structure** of the passage is as follows:

Paragraph One: Introduce NGF, its function, and its Nobel Prize winning discoverer.

Paragraph Two: Provide background on the hypothesis, research that led to discovery.

Paragraph Three: Provide further information about subsequent research which shed light on sources of NGF within an organism.

The author's **Tone** is academic and viewpoint neutral.

There are no real **Arguments** advanced in this passage, as is not uncommon in science passages.

The author's **Main Point** is that Levi-Montalcini's discovery of NGF was based on significant research and yielded important results in the history of biochemistry.

Question #15: GR, Main Point. The correct answer choice is (B)

Again, with Main Point questions we should always try to prephrase an answer before looking at the choices provided. In this case, the main point of this passage is to introduce the reader to the important scientific discovery of NGF, as well as the steps taken by the scientist in confirming early hypotheses, and further details about NGF uncovered through subsequent research.

Answer choice (A): The first half of this answer choice looks good, but the importance of the scientist's discovery was not to simply increase our understanding of chick embryos. Since the ramifications of Levi-Montalcini's discovery were further-reaching, this choice is wrong.

Answer choice (B): This is the correct answer choice. Most importantly, this response concludes that the discovery of NGF was pivotal to biochemistry, a fact reflected in the first paragraph.

Answer choice (C): This answer choice is relevant only to the second paragraph. Since the question asks for the main point of the passage, this answer should be eliminated. Furthermore, the passage states that Levi-Montalcini used the tissue-culture technique, not that she *devised* it.

Answer choice (D): This response confines its observations to the last paragraph, and does not reflect the main point of the passage. Furthermore, the passage actually stated that NGF is produced by tissues *to which the nerve cells will connect*, and this choice contrarily claims that NGF is produced only when nerve cells have already connected.

Answer choice (E): Once again, this response should be immediately eliminated simply because it is relevant only to the last paragraph. Furthermore, this choice is false given the passage, because it leaves out the possibility that nerve cells die if NGF is simply removed.

Question #16: GR, AP. The correct answer choice is (A)

This question asks why the discovery of NGF is important, from the perspective of the author. Since the author referenced the Nobel Prize and the importance this discovery to biochemistry in general, and because an entire paragraph is dedicated to the discoveries that Levi-Montalcini's findings made possible, we should look for an answer that underscores the significance of this contribution.

Answer choice (A): This is the correct answer choice. The last paragraph describes the more specific understanding that subsequent research led to, and the first paragraph describes the contribution to biochemistry as "crucial," and indicates that the contribution led to Levi-Montalcini's eventually winning the Nobel Prize.

Answer choice (B): Since Levi-Montalcini actually expected many of the results that she eventually observed, there is no support for the idea that the author believes anything about "unanticipated" results.

Answer choice (C): It seems that the discoveries in the last paragraph have been the most important from the author's perspective, rather than this particular confirmation. The author refers to the development as "crucial" to biochemistry, and it is advisable to look for a choice that explains the crucial nature of the development.

Answer choice (D): Levi-Montalcini's experiments did show observable reactions in the tissues of different species; however, the ultimate significance in these experiments lies in the fact that they led to the expansion of knowledge of how the nervous system develops and functions.

Answer choice (E): The experiments did identify a substance, produced by mouse tumors, that stimulates nerve growth. However, that was not the ultimate finding of this important scientific discovery, so this choice is wrong.

Question #17: SR, O. The correct answer choice is (C)

This question exemplifies the value of understanding passage organization. Again, the second paragraph describes the experiments, and the third paragraph describes subsequent developments, so the correct response should reflect such a relationship. In reviewing the answer choices, it is advisable to eliminate any response that is not aligned with this description, and verify or rule out the remaining choices based on the information in the passage.

Answer choice (A): The third paragraph offers no indication that Levi-Montalcini's conclusions required further confirmation. In fact, the third paragraph deals with some of the findings that are built on discoveries dealt with in the second paragraph.

Answer choice (B): In the third paragraph, the author discusses how science has built upon Levi-Montalcini's conclusions, which is rather contrary to the idea that science has undermined those conclusions.

Answer choice (C): This is the correct answer choice, as the third paragraph deals with further scientific developments based on discoveries discussed in the second paragraph.

Answer choice (D): In the third paragraph the author does not introduce any new, analogous substances, so this answer is incorrect.

Answer choice (E): Since the third paragraph discusses no experimental techniques, this response cannot be a description of its function.

Question #18: GR, Must. The correct answer choice is (E)

In approaching this Must Be True question, we should eliminate responses that are contrary to facts and inferences within the passage.

Answer choice (A): This answer choice states that nerve cells produce anti-NGF, and is therefore unsupported by the passage, which never indicates precisely where anti-NGF is produced.

Answer choice (B): This choice asserts that cells not affected by NGF are less numerous than those affected by NGF, and that the different cells have the same qualities. While the passage does support the idea that there are different types of cells, not all of which are affected by NGF, no further detail is offered as to similarities or quantitative comparisons.

Answer choice (C): The passage does suggest that a significant number of nerve cells probably die off in the process of an organism's development. However, since the passage never offers any information about the relative number of surviving cells, the conclusion that "few" cells are needed is unsupported.

Answer choice (D): Nothing in the passage indicates that some nerve cells have the capacity to change into other types of living tissue, so this answer choice is incorrect.

Answer choice (E): This is the correct answer choice, as it is supported by the discussion in the second paragraph. The passage states that an embryo initially produces more nerve cells than needed, and that the extra cells die off, which already supports the idea that the embryo produces nerve cells that do not end up connecting to anything. Furthermore, the second paragraph indicates that NGF governs the process by which some nerve cells develop and others die off (lines 14-26), and the third paragraph explains, in detail, that NGF is the causal factor that helps direct nerve cells toward target cells. It is reasonable to conclude that since some nerve cells will die off, they do not receive NGF, and do not connect with target cells.

Question #19: CR, Must. The correct answer choice is (A)

There is only one specifically described experiment, and that is the one that tests Levi-Montalcini's hypothesis that a chemical produced by mouse tumors stimulated nerve growth.

Answer choice (A): This is the correct answer choice. Lines 20-28 deal with Levi-Montalcini's hypothesis that a mouse tumor produces a chemical that stimulates nerve growth, and lines 28-39 provide a description of the experiment.

Answer choice (B): This choice contains true information; in lines 14-20, the passage informs us that Levi-Montalcini actually did test the hypothesis that many nerve cells are pre-programmed to die. However, the passage does not *describe* that experiment, offering no details about the *process* of the experiment.

Answer choice (C): The author indicates in the first paragraph that NGF is not the only neurotrophic factor, and mentions anti-NGF antibodies in the last paragraph; however, the author never provides the particulars of experiments that tested any such hypothesis or produced these results.

Answer choice (D): The information in this answer choice may be true, given the fact that NGF is "especially concentrated in some organs." However, the passage does not deal with organs' NGF concentration relative to that of surrounding tissue. Further, this is not the hypothesis that the passage described the *testing experiment* for, so this answer choice is incorrect.

Answer choice (E): While this is apparently the case, given the information in the third paragraph, the passage never deals with any specific experiment that confirmed this hypothesis.

Question #20: GR, Must. The correct answer choice is (D)

Once again, for Must Be True questions, we should seek to eliminate all answer choices that are unconfirmed by, or clearly contrary to the information within the passage.

Answer choice (A): Since the author never discusses neurotrophic factors other than NGF, this response is unsupported.

Answer choice (B): This answer choice is only partially accurate, and therefore incorrect. It is true that NGF was the first neurotrophic factor to be identified, and that other such substances have since been found. However, the passage never offers any information about the relative degree to which these various factors are currently understood, so this answer is incorrect.

Answer choice (C): The passage only deals with the scientist's discovery of NGF. While there is discussion of other such factors, there is no reference to her having discovered them. This answer choice is thus unsupported and incorrect.

Answer choice (D): This is the correct answer choice. In the first paragraph, the author describes NGF as the *first* such agent discovered, and that neurotrophic factors regulate nerve cell survival as well as "some specialized functions." Since these further functions are not specified within the passage, and the role of NGF as discussed seems to be relevant only to growth and survival, the assertion in this answer choice seems quite likely.

Answer choice (E): Since the experiments discussed in the passage only concern NGF with respect to nerve growth, there is no reason to assume that the observed effects were caused by other neurotrophic factors. Other factors certainly *might have* come into play, but we cannot assume that this was the case.

CHAPTER TEN: SECTION STRATEGY AND MANAGEMENT

Approaching the Section Strategically

For many students, the Reading Comprehension section is a troublesome section because of the volume of reading involved. How you approach the section depends in part on how good you are at Reading Comprehension. If Reading Comprehension is your strength, and if anything less than completion of the section means failure to you, then much of what is contained in this chapter will not apply to you. On the other hand, if you are one of the many students who has difficulty with the Reading Comprehension section, then the following advice is designed to assist you.

Section Structure

Many students believe that the passages in the Reading Comprehension section are presented in order of difficulty, and that each passage set is more difficult than the previous passage set. This is false. The difficulty of individual passages varies greatly, and the last passage in a section may be easier than, say, the second passage in the same section.

Questions are also not presented in order of difficulty, and you cannot tell beforehand which question in a passage set will be the most difficult. However, there are two statistics that are helpful when considering the task at hand:

1. Over 90% of the questions in Reading Comprehension are Must Be True questions. Because these questions are based directly on what you have read, you should never be intimidated by any individual question—the information needed to answer the question is on the page.

2. In over 80% of passages, the first question is a Main Point question. As we know from Chapter Two, you must always seek to identify the main point, and when you do so, most of the time you will be immediately repaid in the questions.

Time Management: The Nexus of Speed and Accuracy

Time management is critical to your success on this section. Each section of the LSAT is 35 minutes in length, and since there are always four passage sets per section, you have exactly 8 minutes and 45 seconds to complete each passage set and transfer your answers. However, this assumes you will complete all four passage sets. For a number of students that is not possible or advisable. Strong performance on the LSAT depends on two factors: speed and accuracy. If you rush to complete every question but miss most of them, you will not receive a high score. On the other hand, if, by slowing down, you increase your accuracy, you may be able to increase your score despite doing fewer questions. Consider the following comparison:

	Student #1	Student #2	Student #3
Questions completed in section	28	24	20
Accuracy Rate	50%	75%	100%
Total Correct Answers	14	18	20

Of course our preference is to have you complete each question and answer them all correctly. That should always be your goal. But as you practice with the techniques, you will naturally find a level of comfort. That may be doing all four passages, or it may involve doing fewer passages.

Obviously, actual performance in a section depends on a variety of factors, and each student must assess their own strengths and weaknesses. Regardless, the message is the same: you *might* benefit from slowing down and attempting fewer passages. The following table displays the amount of time that should be allotted to each passage, depending on how many are attempted:

# Passages Attempted	Time per Passage Attempted
2	17 minutes and 30 seconds
3	11 minutes and 40 seconds
4	8 minutes and 45 seconds

The amount of time listed includes time for transferring answers. You cannot transfer your answers after the 35 minutes have expired.

If you rush through the four passages and only get 14 correct, then perhaps a better choice would be to attack only three passages, spend more time on each passage, and try for a higher accuracy rate. Practice will dictate which strategy is superior, but please keep in mind that there is a point of diminishing returns. Spending 35 minutes on one passage and answering all seven questions correctly does not lead to a very high LSAT score! Instead, you must seek the level that provides you with the best combination of speed and accuracy. We strongly believe that you should attempt *at least* three passages unless there is a compelling reason to the contrary.

Doing Fewer Passages

Prior to the test, if practice has proven that you should attempt three passages or fewer, it would make sense to select the passages according to your test-taking strengths. This requires two steps:

1. Know your personal strengths and weaknesses in the Reading Comprehension section. Assess which kinds of passages you prefer, and be detailed in your assessment. For example, do you like passages about Law? Like Comparative Reading passage sets? Like Science passages but dislike passages about History?

2. Choose the best passages to work on when you begin the section. As the section begins, look for the passage types you prefer. Usually a quick reading of the first few lines of the passage reveals whether you will like the passage. Know that sometimes the test makers use "easy" topics to present difficult passages, so your selections will not be infallible.

Apply this strategy after you have proven that you cannot complete four passages with accuracy.

At the beginning of each Reading Comprehension section, quickly scan the first few lines of the first passage. If it looks like a passage you would like to do or one that seems easy to do, start with that passage. If, on the other hand, the first passage appears hard or is of a type you dislike, move to the second passage and scan the first few lines. Complete the same analysis to decide if you want to do the passage.

One factor to keep in mind when analyzing passages is the number of questions in a passage. Suppose two passages appear equally attractive to you. In this case you should do the passage with the greater number of questions, the theory being you get "more for your money" when there are more questions.

All else being equal, do the passage with more questions.

Your actions within each passage set are also important, and you can never let a single question consume too much time. You must keep focused, and if you do not see a clear path to solving the question, move on.

If you do decide to do only three passages but you find yourself with an extra minute or two at the end of the section, use one of the approaches discussed in the Limited Time Strategies section later in this section.

An excellent
countdown
practice timer
can be purchased
through our
website at
powerscore.com.

Time pressure is the top concern cited by test takers, and one of the most important tools for test success is a timer. Your timer should be a constant companion during your LSAT preparation. Although not all of your practice efforts should be timed, you should attempt to do as many questions as possible under timed conditions in order to acquaint yourself with the difficulties of the test. After all, if the LSAT was a take-home test, no one would be too worried about it.

When using a timer, keep in mind the current Law Services test center regulations concerning time: "Supervisors will keep the official time. You may take an analog (nondigital) wristwatch to the test center. No other timers— including electronic and countdown timers—are allowed." (from the LSAT & LSDAS Registration & Information Book).

Thus, your in-test timer must be a basic analog wristwatch. Although this rule is, at times, randomly enforced, you do not want to find yourself in a position of bringing only a digital timer and then having your timer taken away when you have come to depend on it. Second, the supervisors typically will call a warning with five minutes remaining. Since you have a watch this warning announcement should come as no surprise to you. As you progress through the section, check your watch every 4-5 minutes for tracking purposes. There is no need to check it every minute!

Even though you can only take a wristwatch to the test center, while practicing you should at first use a countdown timer so that you get a perfectly accurate picture of how fast you read and answer questions. The countdown timer is important because, unlike a wristwatch, the timer has a "stop" button that allows you to freeze your time when you finish a section. Thus, you will get the best picture of your capabilities, and that will assist you in creating the personal Pacing Guideline discussed in the next section.

Practice doing as many passages as possible with your timer so that you can develop a comfortable and familiar pace.

A timer is invaluable because it is an odometer for the section. With sufficient practice you will begin to establish a comfortable test-taking speed and the timer allows you to make sure you are maintaining this appropriate speed. If you go too quickly or too slowly you can then make adjustments during the test. Memorize the following time-markers:

# Passages Attempted	Timer Marking Points (counting up from 0 to 35:00 minutes)
2	Move to passage #2 at 17 minutes and 30 seconds
3	Move to passage #2 at 11 minutes and 40 seconds; Move to passage #3 at 23 minutes and 20 seconds;
4	Move to passage #2 at 8 minutes and 45 seconds; Move to passage #3 at 17 minutes and 30 seconds; Move to passage #4 at 26 minutes and 15 seconds

Memorize these marking points!

The above table assumes that each passage is done in exactly the allotted time. If you spend more time on one of the passages, you must make up that time in another passage to stay on pace. If you do one of the passages more quickly, that gives you the luxury of spending more time on a later passage.

Remember, the LSAT is what is known as a "speeded" test. The test makers presume that the average student cannot finish each section in the allotted time (i.e., that they are "speeded" up). So, most people do not finish all the questions in any of the sections. Increasing speed usually requires a lot of practice and analysis of your performance. The tools we use—passage analysis, knowledge of question-generating formations and questions types, etc.—are designed to help you increase your speed once you are familiar with them. Yes, they take some time to adjust to at first, but this is true of any organized system. Keep practicing and work on becoming comfortable with the timed aspect of the test, and your LSAT score will improve.

Pacing Guidelines

Every test taker must have a plan of action before they start a section. As you practice, you should strive to determine your personal Pacing Guideline. For example, how much time do you plan to spend on the first passage? The first two passages? How much time do you expect will have elapsed when you reach question #10? Question #20? Before you pick up a pencil and take the actual test, you should be able to answer these questions.

First off, we are not advocating that you create a strict timeline that controls where you are every moment in the section or that dictates when you quit working on a question. Instead, you must create a loose blueprint for completing the section—one that uses your particular strengths to create an achievable set of goals. To give you a better sense of how the idea works, here is an example of a Pacing Guideline for a high scorer:

> Complete each passage in eight minutes or less, unless a passage has eight questions.

> Last three minutes of the section: double-check my work; return to any question I noted as especially challenging.

Clearly, this Guideline is an aggressive one that assumes that the test taker is good enough to complete all the questions accurately and still have time remaining. Your personal Guideline does not have to be the same! Take a moment, however, to review the above Guideline:

- The test taker assumes that he or she can work fast, but makes an adjustment for the number of questions.

- Despite being good enough to expect to finish all the questions, the test taker doesn't just sit back and relax for the last few minutes. Instead, he or she uses that time to re-check troublesome problems.

- The Guideline is relatively loose and contains a minimum of components.

Here is how to create and use your own Pacing Guideline:

1. During your practice sessions, focus on determining how fast you can do a typical Reading Comprehension passage set while retaining a high degree of accuracy. To do this, you will need to time yourself religiously.

2. Make a benchmark for where you should be after either of the first two passage sets. If your Guideline is too complex to remember without writing down, it is too complex to use!

3. Try to take into account the difficulty level of a passage and a high or low number of questions.

4. Do not make your Pacing Guideline too detailed. The difficulty of the questions (and entire sections) varies, so you do not want to create a rigid Guideline that cannot account for these differences. For example, do not make a Guideline that specifies where you will be at 5, 8, 12, 15 minutes, etc. That is too specific and will be unusable if you run into a hard (or very easy) passage early in the section. Try to make your Guideline broad enough to characterize several different points in the section. If you have more than four or five sections in your Guideline, it is getting too detailed!

5. Make sure you are comfortable with your plan and that your goals are achievable. This is not a plan of what you hope will happen, but rather what your practice has proven you can do.

6. Use the Guideline to help monitor your performance during the test. If you end up working faster than expected and you are beating your goals, then you will know that things are going exceedingly well and that should bolster your confidence. On the other hand, if you find yourself falling behind the marking points, then you will know that you must bear down and work a bit more quickly.

Implementing the steps above should not be too difficult, but you would be surprised at how many people fail to prepare even the most basic plan of action for each section. In many ways, it is as if they have been asked to run a triathlon but they practice only infrequently and do not keep track of how fast they can go without burning out. Athletes at all levels measure their performance frequently, and the LSAT is just a triathlon for the mind. The important thing is that you find a Guideline that works for you and that you have confidence in. Then, follow it on test day and always remember that you might have to be flexible to account for the unexpected.

You should have a different Pacing Guideline for each section.

Within each Pacing Guideline there is room to make decisions during the test. With practice you will discover your strengths and weaknesses, and you can alter your approach during the test to maximize your abilities. Despite all efforts, however, you might find yourself running out of time as you approach the last passage. If this occurs, there are two broad-based, special strategies you can employ to handle this problem.

Please keep in mind that these two strategies only apply if you arrive at the last passage and do not have time to fully read the passage and answer at least three questions.

1. Go Global—Skim the Passage and Answer the Global Questions

   In general, we strongly advise against skimming. The passages are designed in a way that easily defeats skimming as an effective strategy, and students who skim the passages are simply unable to answer all of the questions correctly. However, when time is running low, skimming might be able to help you answer several questions very quickly. To employ this stratagem, skim the passage very quickly, attempting to glean the gist of the passage and the author's general position. Then, find all of the Global questions and attempt to answer each. Hopefully, you will encounter at least one Main Point and Global Purpose question, and you can use your very generalized knowledge of the passage to answer those quickly.

These two strategies are not mutually exclusive. If you use the first approach and still have time left, implement the second approach.

2. Go Local—Read the Questions First and do only the Specific Reference Questions.

   With this approach you employ another stratagem we normally are strongly against: you read the questions first and then attempt to find the answer to each in the passage. The key is to select carefully the questions to do. By choosing to do only the Specific Reference questions, you can use the line references to return to specific areas of the passage and gain the knowledge needed to answer the questions. Thus, with this stratagem you do not read or skim the passage at all; you just read small sections very closely.

The choice of strategy is yours, but it is dependent on the nature of the questions. If you know you are low on time, when you arrive at the passage you should glance at the questions and attempt to determine if there are more Specific Reference questions or more Global questions. Then use that information and your personal preferences to decide which strategy to use. You cannot predetermine which strategy to choose; you must make the decision when you reach and review the passage.

Even if you are able to read through the last passage and complete (or nearly complete) all of the questions, there are still mini-strategies you can employ within the last passage. The following two "endpassage" strategies can save valuable time at the *end of a section*:

1. When you find an attractive answer, choose it and move on

   As time winds down, you can make allowances in your approach to the questions. For example, if you are on question #26 (of 28 total) with only one minute remaining in the section and you find that answer choice (A) is extremely attractive, you can choose it and move on to the final question. Normally you would read all the answer choices, but when time is low, you can alter that approach if it is expedient to do so.

2. Jump to the shortest questions

   Another example of "endpassage" management would be if you only have one minute left, but two questions to complete. In this instance, you choose the shorter of the two problems. Then you can return to the other problem if time allows.

Remember, good test takers are flexible in their approach and they adapt to changing circumstances. And even when circumstances change, they maintain focus and a positive attitude.

Note how your strategy can change depending on how much time remains. This is not inconsistency; rather, it is just an acknowledgment of the realities of testing. If slightly altering an approach as time runs out helps gain you an extra point, then by all means you should do it.

Once you have answered a question, it is critical you correctly transfer that answer choice selection.

Transferring your answers from the test booklet to your answer sheet is one of the most important tasks that you perform during the LSAT. Our research indicates that approximately 10% of all test takers make some type of transcription error during a typical five-section test. Since one question can translate into a difference of several percentile points, we strongly advise you to follow one of the two approaches discussed below. The method you choose is entirely dependent upon your personal preferences.

1. Logical Grouping. This method involves transferring several answer choices at once, at logical break points throughout each section. For the Reading Comprehension and Logic Games sections, transfer answer choices after you complete the questions for each passage or passage set. For the Logical Reasoning section, transfer answer choices after you complete each two-page question group. This method generally allows for faster transferring of answers, but some students find they are more likely to make errors in their transcription.

2. Question By Question. As the name implies, this method involves filling in the answer ovals on your answer sheet after you complete each individual question. This method generally consumes more time than the Logical Grouping method, but it usually produces a higher transfer accuracy rate. If you use the Logical Grouping method and find yourself making errors, use this method instead.

Filling in the ovals

Be sure to blacken the entire oval for the answer choice you select. Do not use checks or Xs, and do not select two answers.

Although Law Services prints dire warnings against making stray marks on the answer sheet or incompletely filling in the ovals, these errors are not fatal to your LSAT score. If you believe that Law Services has incorrectly scored your test due to an answer sheet problem, you can have your answer sheet hand scored for an additional fee. Although rarely an issue, machine scoring errors can occur from stray marks, incompletely or improperly filled-in ovals, partially erased answers, or creases in your answer sheet. Remember, answers in your test booklet will not be scored, and two fully blackened answer choices to the same question will not be reviewed by hand scoring.

Three in a row?

The test takers have many tricks to keep you psychologically off-balance.

Unlike the SAT, the LSAT often has three identical answer choices to consecutive questions (such as three D's), and on several occasions, four identical answer choices in a row have appeared. On the June 1996 LSAT, six of seven answer choices in one section were (C), and on the June 2008 LSAT, four of five answer choices in one section were (B). The use of multiple answer choices in a row is one of the psychological weapons employed by the test makers to unnerve test takers. Any test taker seeing four (D)'s in a row on their answer sheet understandably thinks they have made some type of error, primarily because most tests avoid repetition in their answer choices. If you see three or four answer choices in a row, do not become alarmed, especially if you feel you have been performing well on the section. We are still waiting for the day that the LSAT has five identical correct answers in a row, but we will not be too surprised when it happens.

Guessing Strategy ████████████████████

Because the LSAT does not assess a scoring penalty for incorrect answer choices, you should always guess on every question that you cannot complete during the allotted time. However, because some answer choices are more likely to occur than others, you should not guess randomly. The following tables indicate the frequency of appearance of Reading Comprehension answer choices over the years.

Never leave an answer blank on the LSAT! There is no penalty for wrong answers and so it is in your best interest to guess on any problem you cannot complete.

All Reading Comprehension Answer Choices June 1991 - June 2010*

	A%	B%	C%	D%	E%
% appearance of each answer choice throughout the entire section	19.7	19.9	20.1	21.8	18.5

The table above documents the percentage each answer choice appeared as a percentage of all Reading Comprehension answer choices between June 1991 and June 2010 inclusive. If history holds, when guessing on the LSAT Reading Comprehension section, you would be best served by always guessing answer choice (D). Do *not* choose random answer choices, and do *not* put in a pattern such as A-B-C-D-E etcetera. Although guessing answer choice (D) does not guarantee you will get the questions correct, if history is an indicator then guessing answer choice (D) gives you a better chance than guessing randomly. Consider the following comparison of students guessing on five consecutive answer choices:

We discuss guessing strategy and many other LSAT concepts in the Free LSAT Help Section of the powerscore.com website.

Correct Answer Choice	Student #1 Answer Choices (Pattern)	Student #2 Answer Choices (Random)	Student #3 Answer Choices (All D's)
B	A	D	D
D	B	C	D
E	C	A	D
A	D	E	D
C	E	B	D
# Correct =	0	0	1

Guessing randomly reduces each question to an independent event with a 1 in 5 chance of success.

Although one question may not seem significant, it adds up over four sections, and depending on where you are in the scoring scale, it can increase your score several points. And every point counts! By guessing answer choice (D), you increase your chances of getting an answer correct.

The next table summarizes the percentage appearance of answer choices in just the last five answer choices of the Reading Comprehension section.

Last Five Answer Choices Per Reading Comprehension Section June 1991 - June 2010*

	A%	B%	C%	D%	E%
% appearance of each answer choice throughout last five answer choices of the Reading Comprehension section	17.8	21.5	18.8	22.8	19.1

*These statistics do not include the unreleased February 1998, February 2001, February 2002, February 2003, February 2004, February 2005, February 2006, February 2007, February 2008, February 2009, and February 2010 LSAT administrations.

Within the last five questions, the guessing strategy dictates that you should also guess answer choice (D). Notice the significant statistical deviation of answer choice (A). Answer choice (A) is not a good answer choice to guess in the last five answer choices!

Please keep in mind that the above advice holds only for pure guessing. If you are attempting to choose between two answer choices, do not choose on the basis of statistics alone!

On a related note, if you are a strong test taker who correctly answers most questions but occasionally does not finish a section, quickly review the answer choices you have previously selected and use the answer that appears least as your guessing answer choice. For example, if you have completed twenty questions in a section, and your answers contain a majority of (A)'s, (C)'s, (D)'s, and (E)'s, guess answer choice (B) for all of the remaining questions.

Chapter Eleven: The June 2008 LSAT Reading Comprehension Section

Taking the June 2008 LSAT Reading Comprehension Section ▮

This chapter contains the complete text of the June 2008 LSAT Reading Comprehension section, including an answer key and complete explanations for each question. For the closest possible re-creation of the conditions of the LSAT, take this exam as a 35-minute timed exercise.

When attacking the section, remember to use the techniques and approaches we have discussed within this book, and to remain focused and positive.

After completing the section, refer to the answer key to compute your section score, and then refer to the explanations to learn how to solve each question. Carefully reading the explanation for each question and each answer choice will improve your ability to apply the techniques and methods you have learned.

Good luck!

This passage was adapted from an article published in 1996.

The Internet is a system of computer networks that allows individuals and organizations to communicate freely with other Internet users throughout the world. As a result, an astonishing
(5) variety of information is able to flow unimpeded across national and other political borders, presenting serious difficulties for traditional approaches to legislation and law enforcement, to which such borders are crucial.

(10) Control over physical space and the objects located in it is a defining attribute of sovereignty. Lawmaking presupposes some mechanism for enforcement, i.e., the ability to control violations. But jurisdictions cannot control the information and
(15) transactions flowing across their borders via the Internet. For example, a government might seek to intercept transmissions that propagate the kinds of consumer fraud that it regulates within its jurisdiction. But the volume of electronic communications
(20) crossing its territorial boundaries is too great to allow for effective control over individual transmissions. In order to deny its citizens access to specific materials, a government would thus have to prevent them from using the Internet altogether. Such a draconian
(25) measure would almost certainly be extremely unpopular, since most affected citizens would probably feel that the benefits of using the Internet decidedly outweigh the risks.

One legal domain that is especially sensitive to
(30) geographical considerations is that governing trademarks. There is no global registration of trademarks; international protection requires registration in each country. Moreover, within a country, the same name can sometimes be used
(35) proprietarily by businesses of different kinds in the same locality, or by businesses of the same kind in different localities, on the grounds that use of the trademark by one such business does not affect the others. But with the advent of the Internet, a business
(40) name can be displayed in such a way as to be accessible from any computer connected to the Internet anywhere in the world. Should such a display advertising a restaurant in Norway be deemed to infringe a trademark in Brazil just because it can be
(45) accessed freely from Brazil? It is not clear that any particular country's trademark authorities possess, or should possess, jurisdiction over such displays. Otherwise, any use of a trademark on the Internet could be subject to the jurisdiction of every country
(50) simultaneously.

The Internet also gives rise to situations in which regulation is needed but cannot be provided within the existing framework. For example, electronic communications, which may pass through many
(55) different territorial jurisdictions, pose perplexing new questions about the nature and adequacy of privacy protections. Should French officials have lawful access to messages traveling via the Internet from Canada to Japan? This is just one among many

(60) questions that collectively challenge the notion that the Internet can be effectively controlled by the existing system of territorial jurisdictions.

1. Which one of the following most accurately expresses the main point of the passage?

   (A) The high-volume, global nature of activity on the Internet undermines the feasibility of controlling it through legal frameworks that presuppose geographic boundaries.

   (B) The system of Internet communications simultaneously promotes and weakens the power of national governments to control their citizens' speech and financial transactions.

   (C) People value the benefits of their participation on the Internet so highly that they would strongly oppose any government efforts to regulate their Internet activity.

   (D) Internet communications are responsible for a substantial increase in the volume and severity of global crime.

   (E) Current Internet usage and its future expansion pose a clear threat to the internal political stability of many nations.

2. The author mentions French officials in connection with messages traveling between Canada and Japan (lines 57-59) primarily to

(A) emphasize that the Internet allows data to be made available to users worldwide
(B) illustrate the range of languages that might be used on the Internet
(C) provide an example of a regulatory problem arising when an electronic communication intended for a particular destination passes through intermediate jurisdictions
(D) show why any use of a trademark on the Internet could be subject to the jurisdiction of every country simultaneously
(E) highlight the kind of international cooperation that made the Internet possible

3. According to the passage, which one of the following is an essential property of political sovereignty?

(A) control over business enterprises operating across territorial boundaries
(B) authority over communicative exchanges occurring within a specified jurisdiction
(C) power to regulate trademarks throughout a circumscribed geographic region
(D) control over the entities included within a designated physical space
(E) authority over all commercial transactions involving any of its citizens

4. Which one of the following words employed by the author in the second paragraph is most indicative of the author's attitude toward any hypothetical measure a government might enact to deny its citizens access to the Internet?

(A) benefits
(B) decidedly
(C) unpopular
(D) draconian
(E) risks

5. What is the main purpose of the fourth paragraph?

(A) to call into question the relevance of the argument provided in the second paragraph
(B) to provide a practical illustration that questions the general claim made in the first paragraph
(C) to summarize the arguments provided in the second and third paragraphs
(D) to continue the argument that begins in the third paragraph
(E) to provide an additional argument in support of the general claim made in the first paragraph

Passage A

Drilling fluids, including the various mixtures known as drilling muds, play essential roles in oil-well drilling. As they are circulated down through the drill pipe and back up the well itself, they lubricate the
(5) drill bit, bearings, and drill pipe; clean and cool the drill bit as it cuts into the rock; lift rock chips (cuttings) to the surface; provide information about what is happening downhole, allowing the drillers to monitor the behavior, flow rate, pressure, and
(10) composition of the drilling fluid; and maintain well pressure to control cave-ins.

Drilling muds are made of bentonite and other clays and polymers, mixed with a fluid to the desired viscosity. By far the largest ingredient of drilling
(15) muds, by weight, is barite, a very heavy mineral of density 4.3 to 4.6. It is also used as an inert filler in some foods and is more familiar in its medical use as the "barium meal" administered before X-raying the digestive tract.

(20) Over the years individual drilling companies and their expert drillers have devised proprietary formulations, or mud "recipes," to deal with specific types of drilling jobs. One problem in studying the effects of drilling waste discharges is that the drilling
(25) fluids are made from a range of over 1,000, sometimes toxic, ingredients—many of them known, confusingly, by different trade names, generic descriptions, chemical formulae, and regional or industry slang words, and many of them kept secret by companies or individual
(30) formulators.

Passage B

Drilling mud, cuttings, and associated chemicals are normally released only during the drilling phase of a well's existence. These discharges are the main environmental concern in offshore oil production, and
(35) their use is tightly regulated. The discharges are closely monitored by the offshore operator, and releases are controlled as a condition of the operating permit.

One type of mud—water-based mud (WBM—is a mixture of water, bentonite clay, and chemical
(40) additives, and is used to drill shallow parts of wells. It is not particularly toxic to marine organisms and disperses readily. Under current regulations, it can be dumped directly overboard. Companies typically recycle WBMs until their properties are no longer
(45) suitable and then, over a period of hours, dump the entire batch into the sea.

For drilling deeper wells, oil-based mud (OBM) is normally used. The typical difference from WBM is the high content of mineral oil (typically 30 percent).
(50) OBMs also contain greater concentrations of barite, a powdered heavy mineral, and a number of additives. OBMs have a greater potential for negative environmental impact, partly because they do not disperse as readily. Barite may impact some
(55) organisms, particularly scallops, and the mineral oil may have toxic effects. Currently only the residues of OBMs adhering to cuttings that remain after the cuttings are sieved from the drilling fluids may be discharged overboard, and then only mixtures up to a
(60) specified maximum oil content.

6. A primary purpose of each of the passages is to

(A) provide causal explanations for a type of environmental pollution
(B) describe the general composition and properties of drilling muds
(C) point out possible environmental impacts associated with oil drilling
(D) explain why oil-well drilling requires the use of drilling muds
(E) identify difficulties inherent in the regulation of oil-well drilling operations

7. Which one of the following is a characteristic of barite that is mentioned in both of the passages?

(A) It does not disperse readily in seawater.
(B) It is not found in drilling muds containing bentonite.
(C) Its use in drilling muds is tightly regulated.
(D) It is the most commonly used ingredient in drilling muds.
(E) It is a heavy mineral.

8. Each of the following is supported by one or both of the passages EXCEPT:

(A) Clay is an important constituent of many, if not all, drilling muds.
(B) At least one type of drilling mud is not significantly toxic to marine life.
(C) There has been some study of the environmental effects of drilling-mud discharges.
(D) Government regulations allow drilling muds to contain 30 percent mineral oil.
(E) During the drilling of an oil well, drilling mud is continuously discharged into the sea.

9. Which one of the following can be most reasonably inferred from the two passages taken together, but not from either one individually?

   (A) Barite is the largest ingredient of drilling muds, by weight, and also the most environmentally damaging.

   (B) Although barite can be harmful to marine organisms, it can be consumed safely by humans.

   (C) Offshore drilling is more damaging to the environment than is land-based drilling.

   (D) The use of drilling muds needs to be more tightly controlled by government.

   (E) If offshore drilling did not generate cuttings, it would be less harmful to the environment.

10. Each of the following is supported by one or both of the passages EXCEPT:

    (A) Drillers monitor the suitability of the mud they are using.

    (B) The government requires drilling companies to disclose all ingredients used in their drilling muds.

    (C) In certain quantities, barite is not toxic to humans.

    (D) Oil reserves can be found within or beneath layers of rock.

    (E) Drilling deep oil wells requires the use of different mud recipes than does drilling shallow oil wells.

11. Based on information in the passages, which one of the following, if true, provides the strongest support for a prediction that the proportion of oil-well drilling using OBMs will increase in the future?

    (A) The cost of certain ingredients in WBMs is expected to increase steadily over the next several decades.

    (B) The deeper an offshore oil well, the greater the concentration of barite that must be used in the drilling mud.

    (C) Oil reserves at shallow depths have mostly been tapped, leaving primarily much deeper reserves for future drilling.

    (D) It is unlikely that oil drillers will develop more efficient ways of removing OBM residues from cuttings that remain after being sieved from drilling fluids.

    (E) Barite is a common mineral, the availability of which is virtually limitless.

12. According to passage B, one reason OBMs are potentially more environmentally damaging than WBMs is that OBMs

    (A) are slower to disperse
    (B) contain greater concentrations of bentonite
    (C) contain a greater number of additives
    (D) are used for drilling deeper wells
    (E) cannot be recycled

Aida Overton Walker (1880-1914), one of the most widely acclaimed African American performers of the early twentieth century, was known largely for popularizing a dance form known as the cakewalk
(5) through her choreographing, performance, and teaching of the dance. The cakewalk was originally developed prior to the United States Civil War by African Americans, for whom dance was a means of maintaining cultural links within a slave society. It
(10) was based on traditional West African ceremonial dances, and like many other African American dances, it retained features characteristic of African dance forms, such as gliding steps and an emphasis on improvisation.

(15) To this African-derived foundation, the cakewalk added certain elements from European dances: where African dances feature flexible body postures, large groups and separate-sex dancing, the cakewalk developed into a high-kicking walk performed by a
(20) procession of couples. Ironically, while these modifications later enabled the cakewalk to appeal to European Americans and become one of the first cultural forms to cross the racial divide in North America, they were originally introduced with satiric
(25) intent. Slaves performed the grandiloquent walks in order to parody the processional dances performed at slave owners' balls and, in general, the self-important manners of slave owners. To add a further irony, by the end of the nineteenth century, the cakewalk was
(30) itself being parodied by European American stage performers, and these parodies in turn helped shape subsequent versions of the cakewalk.

While this complex evolution meant that the cakewalk was not a simple cultural phenomenon—
(35) one scholar has characterized this layering of parody upon parody with the phrase "mimetic vertigo—it is in fact what enabled the dance to attract its wide audience. In the cultural and socioeconomic flux of the turn-of-the-century United States, where
(40) industrialization, urbanization, mass immigration, and rapid social mobility all reshaped the cultural landscape, an art form had to be capable of being many things to many people in order to appeal to a large audience.

(45) Walker's remarkable success at popularizing the cakewalk across otherwise relatively rigid racial boundaries rested on her ability to address within her interpretation of it the varying and sometimes conflicting demands placed on the dance. Middle-
(50) class African Americans, for example, often denounced the cakewalk as disreputable, a complaint reinforced by the parodies circulating at the time. Walker won over this audience by refining the cakewalk and emphasizing its fundamental grace.
(55) Meanwhile, because middle- and upper-class European Americans often felt threatened by the tremendous cultural flux around them, they prized what they regarded as authentic art forms as bastions of stability; much of Walker's success with this

(60) audience derived from her distillation of what was widely acclaimed as the most authentic cakewalk. Finally, Walker was able to gain the admiration of many newly rich industrialists and financiers, who found in the grand flourishes of her version of the
(65) cakewalk a fitting vehicle for celebrating their newfound social rank.

13. Which one of the following most accurately expresses the main point of the passage?

(A) Walker, who was especially well known for her success in choreographing, performing, and teaching the cakewalk, was one of the most widely recognized African American performers of the early twentieth century.

(B) In spite of the disparate influences that shaped the cakewalk, Walker was able to give the dance broad appeal because she distilled what was regarded as the most authentic version in an era that valued authenticity highly.

(C) Walker popularized the cakewalk by capitalizing on the complex cultural mix that had developed from the dance's original blend of satire and cultural preservation, together with the effects of later parodies.

(D) Whereas other versions of the cakewalk circulating at the beginning of the twentieth century were primarily parodic in nature, the version popularized by Walker combined both satire and cultural preservation.

(E) Because Walker was able to recognize and preserve the characteristics of the cakewalk as African Americans originally performed it, it became the first popular art form to cross the racial divide in the United States.

14. The author describes the socioeconomic flux of the turn-of-the-century United States in the third paragraph primarily in order to

(A) argue that the cakewalk could have become popular only in such complex social circumstances

(B) detail the social context that prompted performers of the cakewalk to fuse African and European dance forms

(C) identify the target of the overlapping parodic layers that characterized the cakewalk

(D) indicate why a particular cultural environment was especially favorable for the success of the cakewalk

(E) explain why European American parodies of the cakewalk were able to reach wide audiences

15. Which one of the following is most analogous to the author's account in the second paragraph of how the cakewalk came to appeal to European Americans?

(A) Satirical versions of popular music songs are frequently more popular than the songs they parody.

(B) A style of popular music grows in popularity among young listeners because it parodies the musical styles admired by older listeners.

(C) A style of music becomes admired among popular music's audience in part because of elements that were introduced in order to parody popular music.

(D) A once popular style of music wins back its audience by incorporating elements of the style of music that is currently most popular.

(E) After popular music begins to appropriate elements of a traditional style of music, interest in that traditional music increases.

16. The passage asserts which one of the following about the cakewalk?

(A) It was largely unknown outside African American culture until Walker popularized it.

(B) It was mainly a folk dance, and Walker became one of only a handful of people to perform it professionally.

(C) Its performance as parody became uncommon as a result of Walker's popularization of its authentic form.

(D) Its West African origins became commonly known as a result of Walker's work.

(E) It was one of the first cultural forms to cross racial lines in the United States.

17. It can be inferred from the passage that the author would be most likely to agree with which one of the following statements?

(A) Because of the broad appeal of humor, satiric art forms are often among the first to cross racial or cultural divisions.

(B) The interactions between African American and European American cultural forms often result in what is appropriately characterized as "mimetic vertigo."

(C) Middle-class European Americans who valued the cakewalk's authenticity subsequently came to admire other African American dances for the same reason.

(D) Because of the influence of African dance forms, some popular dances that later emerged in the United States featured separate-sex dancing.

(E) Some of Walker's admirers were attracted to her version of the cakewalk as a means for bolstering their social identities.

18. The passage most strongly suggests that the author would be likely to agree with which one of the following statements about Walker's significance in the history of the cakewalk?

(A) Walker broadened the cakewalk's appeal by highlighting elements that were already present in the dance.

(B) Walker's version of the cakewalk appealed to larger audiences than previous versions did because she accentuated its satiric dimension.

(C) Walker popularized the cakewalk by choreographing various alternative interpretations of it, each tailored to the interests of a different cultural group.

(D) Walker added a "mimetic vertigo" to the cakewalk by inserting imitations of other performers' cakewalking into her dance routines.

(E) Walker revitalized the cakewalk by disentangling its complex admixture of African and European elements.

19. The passage provides sufficient information to answer which one of the following questions?

(A) What were some of the attributes of African dance forms that were preserved in the cakewalk?

(B) Who was the first performer to dance the cakewalk professionally?

(C) What is an aspect of the cakewalk that was preserved in other North American dance forms?

(D) What features were added to the original cakewalk by the stage parodies circulating at the end of the nineteenth century?

(E) For about how many years into the twentieth century did the cakewalk remain widely popular?

In principle, a cohesive group—one whose members generally agree with one another and support one another's judgments—can do a much better job at decision making than it could if it were
(5) noncohesive. When cohesiveness is low or lacking entirely, compliance out of fear of recrimination is likely to be strongest. To overcome this fear, participants in the group's deliberations need to be confident that they are members in good standing and that the others will continue to value their role in the
(10) group, whether or not they agree about a particular issue under discussion. As members of a group feel more accepted by the others, they acquire greater freedom to say what they really think, becoming less
(15) likely to use deceitful arguments or to play it safe by dancing around the issues with vapid or conventional comments. Typically, then, the more cohesive a group becomes, the less its members will deliberately censor what they say out of fear of being punished socially
(20) for antagonizing their fellow members.

But group cohesiveness can have pitfalls as well: while the members of a highly cohesive group can feel much freer to deviate from the majority, their desire for genuine concurrence on every important
(25) issue often inclines them not to use this freedom. In a highly cohesive group of decision makers, the danger is not that individuals will conceal objections they harbor regarding a proposal favored by the majority, but that they will think the proposal is a good one
(30) without attempting to carry out a critical scrutiny that could reveal grounds for strong objections. Members may then decide that any misgivings they feel are not worth pursuing—that the benefit of any doubt should be given to the group consensus. In this way, they
(35) may fall victim to a syndrome known as "groupthink," which one psychologist concerned with collective decision making has defined as "a deterioration of mental efficiency, reality testing, and moral judgment that results from in-group pressures."
(40) Based on analyses of major fiascoes of international diplomacy and military decision making, researchers have identified groupthink behavior as a recurring pattern that involves several factors: overestimation of the group's power and morality,
(45) manifested, for example, in an illusion of invulnerability, which creates excessive optimism; closed-mindedness to warnings of problems and to alternative viewpoints; and unwarranted pressures toward uniformity, including self-censorship with
(50) respect to doubts about the group's reasoning and a concomitant shared illusion of unanimity concerning group decisions. Cohesiveness of the decision-making group is an essential antecedent condition for this syndrome but not a sufficient one, so it is important
(55) to work toward identifying the additional factors that determine whether group cohesiveness will deteriorate into groupthink or allow for effective decision making.

20. Which one of the following most accurately expresses the main point of the passage?

(A) Despite its value in encouraging frank discussion, high cohesion can lead to a debilitating type of group decision making called groupthink.
(B) Group members can guard against groupthink if they have a good understanding of the critical role played by cohesion.
(C) Groupthink is a dysfunctional collective decision-making pattern that can occur in diplomacy and military affairs.
(D) Low cohesion in groups is sometimes desirable when higher cohesion involves a risk of groupthink behavior.
(E) Future efforts to guard against groupthink will depend on the results of ongoing research into the psychology of collective decision making.

21. A group of closely associated colleagues has made a disastrous diplomatic decision after a series of meetings marked by disagreement over conflicting alternatives. It can be inferred from the passage that the author would be most likely to say that this scenario

(A) provides evidence of chronic indecision, thus indicating a weak level of cohesion in general
(B) indicates that the group's cohesiveness was coupled with some other factor to produce a groupthink fiasco
(C) provides no evidence that groupthink played a role in the group's decision
(D) provides evidence that groupthink can develop even in some groups that do not demonstrate an "illusion of unanimity"
(E) indicates that the group probably could have made its decision-making procedure more efficient by studying the information more thoroughly

22. Which one of the following, if true, would most support the author's contentions concerning the conditions under which groupthink takes place?

(A) A study of several groups, each made up of members of various professions, found that most fell victim to groupthink.

(B) There is strong evidence that respectful dissent is more likely to occur in cohesive groups than in groups in which there is little internal support.

(C) Extensive analyses of decisions made by a large number of groups found no cases of groupthink in groups whose members generally distrust one another's judgments.

(D) There is substantial evidence that groupthink is especially likely to take place when members of a group develop factions whose intransigence prolongs the group's deliberations.

(E) Ample research demonstrates that voluntary deference to group opinion is not a necessary factor for the formation of groupthink behavior.

23. The passage mentions which one of the following as a component of groupthink?

(A) unjustified suspicions among group members regarding an adversary's intentions

(B) strong belief that the group's decisions are right

(C) group members working under unusually high stress, leading to illusions of invulnerability

(D) the deliberate use of vapid, clichéd arguments

(E) careful consideration of objections to majority positions

24. It can be inferred from the passage that both the author of the passage and the researchers mentioned in the passage would be most likely to agree with which one of the following statements about groupthink?

(A) Groupthink occurs in all strongly cohesive groups, but its contribution to collective decision making is not fully understood.

(B) The causal factors that transform group cohesion into groupthink are unique to each case.

(C) The continued study of cohesiveness of groups is probably fruitless for determining what factors elicit groupthink.

(D) Outside information cannot influence group decisions once they have become determined by groupthink.

(E) On balance, groupthink cannot be expected to have a beneficial effect in a group's decision making.

25. In the passage, the author says which one of the following about conformity in decision-making groups?

(A) Enforced conformity may be appropriate in some group decision situations.

(B) A high degree of conformity is often expected of military decision-making group members.

(C) Inappropriate group conformity can result from inadequate information.

(D) Voluntary conformity occurs much less frequently than enforced conformity.

(E) Members of noncohesive groups may experience psychological pressure to conform.

26. In line 5, the author mentions low group cohesiveness primarily in order to

(A) contribute to a claim that cohesiveness can be conducive to a freer exchange of views in groups

(B) establish a comparison between groupthink symptoms and the attributes of low-cohesion groups

(C) suggest that there may be ways to make both cohesive and noncohesive groups more open to dissent

(D) indicate that both cohesive and noncohesive groups may be susceptible to groupthink dynamics

(E) lay the groundwork for a subsequent proposal for overcoming the debilitating effects of low cohesion

27. Based on the passage, it can be inferred that the author would be most likely to agree with which one of the following?

(A) Highly cohesive groups are more likely to engage in confrontational negotiating styles with adversaries than are those with low cohesion.

(B) It is difficult for a group to examine all relevant options critically in reaching decisions unless it has a fairly high degree of cohesiveness.

(C) A group with varied viewpoints on a given issue is less likely to reach a sound decision regarding that issue than is a group whose members are unified in their outlook.

(D) Intense stress and high expectations are the key factors in the formation of groupthink.

(E) Noncohesive groups can, under certain circumstances, develop all of the symptoms of groupthink.

JUNE 2008
READING COMPREHENSION SECTION
ANSWER KEY

1.	A	8.	E	15.	C	22.	C
2.	C	9.	B	16.	E	23.	B
3.	D	10.	B	17.	E	24.	E
4.	D	11.	C	18.	A	25.	E
5.	E	12.	A	19.	A	26.	A
6.	B	13.	C	20.	A	27.	B
7.	E	14.	D	21.	C		

The June 2008 LSAT Reading Comprehension Section Analyzed ■

The following pages contain an analysis of each passage and complete explanations for each question. The analysis of each passage includes a diagram for the passage and the VIEWSTAMP breakdown. Please note that the diagram of each passage is only one possible way to diagram the passage; each student will diagram the passage slightly differently. Our representation is intended to show one such method, and to point out some of the more notable features within the text.

When reviewing the questions, we strongly recommend that you read the explanations for the questions you answered correctly and incorrectly. The goal is to improve both your speed and accuracy, and by reviewing even those questions you answered correctly, you may pick up tips that help you go faster next time.

This passage was adapted from an article published in 1996.

_VN (5)

The Internet is a system of computer networks that allows individuals and organizations to communicate freely with other Internet users throughout the world. As a result, an astonishing variety of information is able to flow unimpeded across national and other political borders, presenting <u>serious difficulties for traditional approaches to legislation and law enforcement</u>, to which such <u>borders are crucial</u>.

Def.

MP

(10)   Control over physical space and the objects located in it is a defining attribute of <u>sovereignty</u>. Lawmaking presupposes some mechanism for enforcement, i.e., the ability to control violations. But jurisdictions cannot control the information and

Def.

(15) transactions flowing across their borders via the Internet. For <u>example</u>, a government might seek to intercept transmissions that propagate the kinds of consumer fraud that it regulates within its jurisdiction. But the volume of electronic communications

EX

(20) crossing its territorial boundaries is too great to allow for effective control over individual transmissions. In order to deny its citizens access to specific materials, a government would thus have to prevent them from using the Internet altogether. Such a draconian

_VA (25) measure would almost certainly be extremely unpopular, since most affected citizens would probably feel that the benefits of using the Internet decidedly outweigh the risks.

One legal domain that is <u>especially sensitive</u> to

(30) geographical considerations is that governing <u>trademarks</u>. There is no global registration of trademarks; international protection requires registration in each country. <u>Moreover</u>, within a country, the same name can sometimes be used

(35) proprietarily by businesses of different kinds in the same locality, or by businesses of the same kind in different localities, on the grounds that use of the trademark by one such business does not affect the others. But with the advent of the Internet, a business

(40) name can be displayed in such a way as to be accessible from any computer connected to the Internet anywhere in the world. Should such a display advertising a restaurant in Norway be deemed to infringe a trademark in Brazil just because it can be

Q

(45) accessed freely from Brazil? <u>It is not clear that any particular country's trademark authorities possess, or should possess, jurisdiction over such displays</u>. Otherwise, any use of a trademark on the Internet could be subject to the jurisdiction of every country

(50) simultaneously.

<u>The Internet also gives rise to situations in which regulation is needed but cannot be provided</u> within the existing framework. For <u>example</u>, electronic communications, which may pass through many

EX

(55) different territorial jurisdictions, pose perplexing new questions about the nature and adequacy of privacy protections. Should French officials have lawful access to messages traveling via the Internet from Canada to Japan? This is just one among many

Q

(60) questions that collectively challenge the notion that the Internet can be effectively controlled by the existing system of territorial jurisdictions.

In this passage, the author discusses some of the problems associated with the Internet and its free flow of information across international and political borders.

Paragraph One:

The author uses the first paragraph of this passage to provide a brief introduction to the Internet and the problems associated with the free flow of information: the traditional approach to regulation relied on borders that have dissipated in the face of the flow of information over the Internet.

Paragraph Two:

In the second paragraph, the author expands further on the problems of open communication facilitated by the Internet. Power requires some degree of control, and the ability to respond to violations of sovereign laws. Because there are so many electronic transmissions, it would be impossible for a given jurisdiction to respond specifically to all those which may violate its laws. For a government to maintain complete control over such transmissions would require complete denial of Internet access; this move would likely be very unpopular with those who benefit from the Internet, and is described by the author as draconian, which means that from the author's viewpoint, this level of control would be far too harsh.

Paragraph Three:

At this point in the passage, we have been introduced to a basic problem associated with the Internet: the lack of sovereign control over the vast flow of information. The author continues this theme by introducing trademarks, an area of specific concern. A trademark must be registered in each individual country in order to achieve international protection. In some cases trademarked names may overlap among businesses, presuming no adverse effects. Today, however, a name can be displayed over the Internet worldwide, making the issue of trademark infringement much more complex. Here the author provides an example of a modern trademark dilemma by posing a rhetorical question: does a Norwegian advertisement infringe on a Brazilian name because the ad is accessible in Brazil? Two possible answers—either no authority has (or should have) jurisdiction, or Internet content is subject to everyone's jurisdiction—are provided by the author to conclude this paragraph.

Paragraph Four:

In the final paragraph the author presents another rhetorical question regarding third parties and the inadequacy of the traditional framework for regulation of the Internet. The author closes on a note that is overtly skeptical in tone, questioning whether traditional jurisdictional approaches will ever be applicable to the Internet.

<u>VIEWSTAMP Analysis</u>:

The only **Viewpoint** presented in this passage is that of the author, who presents problems of the Internet that traditional jurisdictional approaches seemingly cannot solve.

The **Structure** of the passage is as follows:

> <u>Paragraph One</u>: Introduce the Internet, problems of the information flowing across borders.
>
> <u>Paragraph Two</u>: Expand on reasons that traditional jurisdictional approach does not work on the Internet, and why limiting communications is an all-or-nothing proposition.
>
> <u>Paragraph Three</u>: Introduce the specific problem of trademarks, third parties, and whether anyone has or should have jurisdiction over Internet transmissions.
>
> <u>Paragraph Four</u>: Close with the clearest example of tone of the passage, obviously skeptical with regard to the prospects for the application of traditional regulation to the Internet.

The author's **Tone** in this passage is fairly academic, and skeptical with regard to prospective applicability of the traditional framework to regulation of the Internet.

The main **Argument** of the passage is the author's argument that Internet communications present significant problems concerning intellectual property and jurisdiction.

The **Main Point** of the passage is that the Internet has enabled communications that present new problems which traditional jurisdictional approaches may not be able to solve.

Question #1: GR, Main Point. The correct answer choice is (A)

The answer to this question is prephrased in the VIEWSTAMP Analysis above.

Answer choice (A): This is the correct answer choice, a sophisticated way of saying that the old jurisdictional approach does not work with regard to information which flows over the Internet.

Answer choice (B): There is no reference to the Internet's strengthening government control over speech, so this answer choice cannot be correct.

Answer choice (C): While this may be implied by the author's assertion beginning in line 24 ("Such a draconian measure would almost certainly be extremely unpopular"), this choice does not represent the main point of the passage.

Answer choice (D): While it could be true that more open lines of communication could facilitate crime, there is no such reference in the passage, so this is certainly not the main point.

Answer choice (E): The author does not claim that there is a clear threat to many nations' stability, so this answer choice is incorrect.

Question #2: SR, P. The correct answer choice is (C)

The reference in this question is to the complex issue of third party jurisdiction.

Answer choice (A): The reference is not to underscore the wide availability of information, so this answer choice is incorrect.

Answer choice (B): The referenced scenario is not intended to celebrate the diversity of language spoken on the Internet.

Answer choice (C): This is the correct answer choice, as it references the third-party (intermediate) jurisdiction from our prephrase.

Answer choice (D): This is a tricky answer choice, as it references another problem with the Internet, but this separate point is made in line 50.

Answer choice (E): The reference is not intended to highlight cooperation, so this answer choice is incorrect.

Question #3: GR, Must. The correct answer choice is (D)

The author specifies control over physical space as an essential property of political sovereignty at the beginning of the second paragraph (lines 10-11)

Answer choice (A): This is not mentioned as an essential property of sovereignty, so this answer choice should be eliminated.

Answer choice (B): This is not our prephrased essential property, so it cannot be correct.

Answer choice (C): The power to regulate trademarks is certainly not essential to political sovereignty.

Answer choice (D): This is the correct answer choice, as it perfectly restates our prephrase, and the reference point at the beginning of the second paragraph.

Answer choice (E): The author does not assert that political sovereignty requires absolute control over all commercial transactions.

Question #4: SR, AP. The correct answer choice is (D)

During the discussion of the possibility of restricting all access, on line 24, the author says "such a draconian measure would almost certainly be unpopular." The author's viewpoint is that this measure is unnecessarily harsh (this is the definition of draconian), and would not go over well with the people.

Answer choice (A): "Benefits" does not in any way reflect the author's attitude in this context.

Answer choice (B): "Decidedly" modifies "unpopular," but does not reflect the author's attitude regarding the prospect of complete denial of access to the Internet.

Answer choice (C): "Unpopular" reflects the author's attitude about the reaction of the people, but not the author's attitude about restriction of access.

Answer choice (D): This is the correct answer choice. "Draconian" means overly harsh, which reflects the author's view of across-the-board restriction of Internet access.

Answer choice (E): The word "risks" does not reflect the author's attitude, so this answer choice is incorrect.

Question #5: SR, P. The correct answer choice is (E)

The fourth paragraph provides another example of a scenario that the traditional jurisdictional approach is not equipped to handle.

Answer choice (A): The author does not contradict an earlier assertion, so this answer choice should be eliminated.

Answer choice (B): Again, the author does not question any claims made earlier in the passage.

Answer choice (C): The last paragraph is not a summary, but an additional example which continues the theme of earlier paragraphs.

Answer choice (D): This is almost right. The last paragraph does build on an earlier argument, but that argument is made throughout the passage, not begun in the third paragraph.

Answer choice (E): This is the correct answer choice. The reference in the fourth paragraph supports the general argument made in the first paragraph.

Passage A

V_N

Drilling fluids, including the various mixtures known as drilling muds, play essential roles in oil-well drilling. As they are circulated down through the drill pipe and back up the well itself, they lubricate the (1) drill bit, bearings, and drill pipe; clean and cool the (2) drill bit as it cuts into the rock; lift rock chips (3) (cuttings) to the surface; provide information about what is happening downhole, allowing the drillers to (4) monitor the behavior, flow rate, pressure, and composition of the drilling fluid; and maintain well (5) pressure to control cave-ins.

(5)

(10)

Drilling muds are made of bentonite and other clays and polymers, mixed with a fluid to the desired viscosity. By far the largest ingredient of drilling

(15) muds, by weight, is barite, a very heavy mineral of density 4.3 to 4.6. It is also used as an inert filler in some foods and is more familiar in its medical use as the "barium meal" administered before X-raying the digestive tract.

(20) Over the years individual drilling companies and their expert drillers have devised proprietary formulations, or mud "recipes," to deal with specific types of drilling jobs. One problem in studying the effects of drilling waste discharges is that the drilling

(25) fluids are made from a range of over 1,000, sometimes toxic, ingredients—many of them known, confusingly, by different trade names, generic descriptions, chemical formulae, and regional or industry slang words, and many of them kept secret by companies or individual

(30) formulators.

Passage B

Drilling mud, cuttings, and associated chemicals are normally released only during the drilling phase of a well's existence. These discharges are the main environmental concern in offshore oil production, and

(35) their use is tightly regulated. The discharges are closely monitored by the offshore operator, and releases are controlled as a condition of the operating permit.

One type of mud—water-based mud (WBM)—is a mixture of water, bentonite clay, and chemical

(40) additives, and is used to drill shallow parts of wells. It is not particularly toxic to marine organisms and disperses readily. Under current regulations, it can be dumped directly overboard. Companies typically recycle WBMs until their properties are no longer

(45) suitable and then, over a period of hours, dump the entire batch into the sea.

For drilling deeper wells, oil-based mud (OBM) is normally used. The typical difference from WBM is the high content of mineral oil (typically 30 percent).

(50) OBMs also contain greater concentrations of barite, a powdered heavy mineral, and a number of additives. OBMs have a greater potential for negative environmental impact, partly because they do not disperse as readily. Barite may impact some

(55) organisms, particularly scallops, and the mineral oil may have toxic effects. Currently only the residues of OBMs adhering to cuttings that remain after the cuttings are sieved from the drilling fluids may be discharged overboard, and then only mixtures up to a

(60) specified maximum oil content.

Recall that for Comparative Reading passages, our analysis is a bit different from the standard VIEWSTAMP approach. Instead, we will distill each passage separately, then consider the similarities and differences between the two passages and their authors.

Passage A

Paragraph One: This factual paragraph is a viewpoint-neutral account of drilling fluids ("muds") and the various roles they play in the drilling process. Examples are lubricating, cleaning and cooling the drill bit, bringing cuttings to the surface, providing information to drillers, and maintaining well pressure.

Paragraph Two: This paragraph continues the author's viewpoint-neutral presentation of facts, turning specifically to the ingredient bentonite, which is mixed with fluid to achieve desired viscosities. The main ingredient of drilling muds, we are told, is barite, which is also used in various other products, including inert food filler and as part of the procedure to x-ray the digestive tract.

Paragraph Three: In the final paragraph, the author indicates that drilling companies have devised their own mud recipes, and many use a different mix. Some of the ingredients are toxic, and there are multiple names for each chemical. This makes it difficult to study the effects of drilling waste discharge.

Passage B

Paragraph One: This paragraph opens with a discussion of drilling releases that are an environmental concern: mud, cuttings, and chemicals. We are also told that the drilling requires permits and is closely monitored in offshore drilling.

Paragraph Two: Here the author continues the fairly viewpoint-neutral presentation of facts, introducing one type of non-toxic mud called WBM, which companies are currently allowed to dump freely.

Paragraph Three: Here the author discusses OBM (oil-based mud), made with more mineral oil, more barite, and more potential environmental impact. Legal dumping of OBM is much more restricted.

Passage Similarities:

Both passages are primarily concerned with muds and chemicals involved in the drilling process. Both passages are presented in an academic tone, relaying the facts without forming any real argumentation.

Passage Differences:

Only the author of the first passage deals with many specific uses of drilling muds, while the author of the second passage focuses more specifically on environmental impacts. Only the second passage deals with WBMs and OBMs.

Question #6: PC, P. The correct answer choice is (B)

The passage similarities are outlined on the previous page.

Answer choice (A): Only the second passage is focused on specific environmental impacts, so this answer choice can be eliminated.

Answer choice (B): This is the correct answer choice. The author of passage A discusses the common composition of drilling muds in the second paragraph, and the author of passage B describes two types of drilling muds (WBM and OBM) in the second and third paragraphs of that passage.

Answer choice (C): Again, the second passage focuses primarily on environmental impact, but the first passage does not.

Answer choice (D): The first passage provides a discussion of the uses of drilling muds, but the second does not.

Answer choice (E): Some of these difficulties are discussed in the last paragraph of passage A, but this area is not covered in passage B.

Question #7: PC, Must. The correct answer choice is (E)

Passage B describes barite as a "heavy, powdered material," and adds that it may impact some organisms. Passage A describes barite as heavy, and the largest ingredient by weight, and the author provides its density and lists some of its uses. An attribute referenced in both passages is that barite is heavy, so this is a good prephrase for the answer to this passage commonality question.

Answer choice (A): This is the description of OBMs provided in the last paragraph of passage B, but it is not a description of barite.

Answer choice (B): This is not accurate based on either account, so this answer choice should be eliminated (incidentally, the author of passage B provides that OBMs have greater concentrations of barite, which implies that WMBs contain barite as well).

Answer choice (C): The author of passage B discusses the monitoring and regulation, but passage A does not discuss regulation per se.

Answer choice (D): Passage A describes barite as the largest ingredient by weight, but the author of passage B does not discuss this.

Answer choice (E): This is the correct answer choice and restates our prephrase.

Question #8: PA, Must X. The correct answer choice is (E)

This is a passage aggregate question, which means that we should consider all of the information provided in both passages in determining the correct answer choice. Since it is an except question, the right answer will be the one which is not discussed in either passage.

Answer choice (A): The first passage describes drilling muds as "made of bentonite and other clays," (line 12), which implies that clay is a standard ingredient.

Answer choice (B): Passage B describes WBMs as "not particularly toxic to marine life" (line 41).

Answer choice (C): The author of passage A describes problems "in studying the effects" of drilling discharge, which implies that some study has been done.

Answer choice (D): In passage B, OBMs are described as having typically 30 percent mineral oil.

Answer choice (E): This is the correct answer choice. Passage B specifies that discharge happens *only* during drilling, but this is not the same as claiming that discharge takes place *always* during drilling. Since there is no reference to, or implication of, continuous discharge during drilling, this answer choice is unsupported, making it the correct response to this passage aggregate except question.

Question #9: PA, Must, the correct answer choice is (B)

This passage aggregate question requires information from both passages to be answered.

Answer choice (A): We know from the first passage that barite is the largest ingredient by weight (line 14), but neither passage supports the assertion that barite is the most damaging to the environment.

Answer choice (B): This is the correct answer choice. Passage B states in line 54 that barite "may impact some organisms," and passage A tells us that barite is used as filler in food, and as a "meal" taken prior to x-ray of the digestive tract.

Answer choice (C): This comparison cannot be made based on the information provided in the passages, so this answer choice should be eliminated.

Answer choice (D): The author of the second passage asserts that there are already tight controls and monitoring systems in place, and the author of the first passage references the difficulty of studying discharge, but neither asserts that tighter controls are necessary.

Answer choice (E): Cuttings are not described in either passage as having environmental impact on their own, so this answer choice is incorrect.

Question #10: PA, Must X. The correct answer choice is (B)

Because all of the answer choices except one are supported by one or both passages, the correct answer will be the choice that is not supported by either passage.

Answer choice (A): Passage A tells us that drilling muds allow drillers to monitor fluid and maintain well pressure (line 8), so this supported answer choice should be eliminated.

Answer choice (B): This is the correct answer choice. Neither passage references such a requirement, and passage A even tells us that many formulations are kept secret.

Answer choice (C): As discussed above, barite is used as food filler and is ingested for x-ray of the digestive tract, implying non-toxicity, so this answer choice is supported by the passages and should be eliminated.

Answer choice (D): Since one of the uses of drilling fluids listed in passage A is "cleaning and cooling the drill bit as it cuts into the rock" (line 5), this answer choice is supported and should be eliminated from contention.

Answer choice (E): In the last paragraph of passage B, the author tells us, "For drilling deeper wells, oil-based mud is normally used." This implies that different formulations are required for drilling deeper wells.

Question #11: PA, Must. The correct answer choice is (C)

Interestingly, this is the fourth Passage Aggregate question in a row. The correct answer choice to this question will provide some reason for increased use of OBMs. From passage B, we know that OBMs are used for drilling deeper wells.

Answer choice (A): Since we cannot know how the cost of OBM's ingredients will change, this answer choice would not necessarily support a conclusion that OBM's proportional use will rise.

Answer choice (B): This answer choice would not make it any more or less likely that OBM's proportional use will increase.

Answer choice (C): This is the correct answer choice. If most future drilling is deep well drilling, this would increase the likelihood that the proportional use of OBMs would increase.

Answer choice (D): This answer choice would not increase the likelihood of using OBMs—if anything it would weight against the likelihood of increased use.

Answer choice (E): Neither author discusses the availability of barite, so this answer choice is incorrect.

Question #12: PE, Must. The correct answer choice is (A)

Passage B tells us that OBMs may be more damaging because they do not disperse as readily (lines 53-54). Barite is an ingredient that may have toxic effects, and OBMs have greater concentrations of barite (from line 50, and 54-56).

Answer choice (A): This is the correct answer choice, and restates the prephrased answer above.

Answer choice (B): There is no reference to greater concentrations of bentonite, and there is no way of knowing based on the passages whether such concentrations would be harmful.

Answer choice (C): Passage B describes OBMs as having "a number of additives," but this does not necessarily mean a greater number of additives, and further, we don't know if this would make OBMs more damaging.

Answer choice (D): OBMs are used for drilling deeper wells (line 47), but this does not necessarily make OBMs more damaging.

Answer choice (E): Passage B only mentions recycling in reference to WBMs, but this does not mean that OBMs cannot be recycled.

Aida Overton Walker (1880-1914), one of the most widely acclaimed African American performers of the early twentieth century, <u>was known largely for popularizing a dance form known as the cakewalk</u>

(5) through her choreographing, performance, and teaching of the dance. The cakewalk was <u>originally developed</u> prior to the United States Civil War by African Americans, for whom dance was a means of maintaining cultural links within a slave society. It

(10) <u>was based on</u> traditional West African ceremonial dances, and like many other African American dances, it <u>retained features</u> characteristic of African dance forms, such as gliding steps and an emphasis on improvisation.

(15) To this African-derived foundation, <u>the cakewalk added certain elements</u> from European dances: where African dances feature flexible body postures, large groups and separate-sex dancing, the cakewalk developed into a high-kicking walk performed by a

(20) procession of couples. Ironically, while these modifications later enabled the cakewalk to appeal to European Americans and become one of the first cultural forms to cross the racial divide in North America, they were originally introduced with <u>satiric</u>

(25) <u>intent</u>. Slaves performed the grandiloquent walks in order to parody the processional dances performed at slave owners' balls and, in general, the self-important manners of slave owners. To add a further irony, by the end of the nineteenth century, the cakewalk was

(30) itself being parodied by European American stage performers, and these parodies in turn helped shape subsequent versions of the cakewalk.

While this complex evolution meant that the cakewalk was not a simple cultural phenomenon—

(35) one scholar has characterized this layering of parody upon parody with the phrase "<u>mimetic vertigo</u>—it is in fact what enabled the dance to attract its wide audience. In the cultural and socioeconomic flux of the turn-of-the-century United States, where

(40) industrialization, urbanization, mass immigration, and rapid social mobility all reshaped the cultural landscape, an art form had to be capable of being many things to many people in order to appeal to a large audience.

(45) Walker's <u>remarkable</u> success at popularizing the cakewalk across otherwise relatively <u>rigid racial boundaries rested on her ability to address</u> within her interpretation of it <u>the varying and sometimes conflicting demands</u> placed on the dance. Middle-

(50) class African Americans, <u>for example</u>, often denounced the cakewalk as disreputable, a complaint reinforced by the parodies circulating at the time. Walker won over this audience by refining the cakewalk and emphasizing its fundamental grace.

(55) Meanwhile, because middle- and upper-class <u>European Americans</u> often felt threatened by the tremendous cultural flux around them, they prized what they regarded as authentic art forms as bastions of stability; much of Walker's success with this

(60) audience derived from her distillation of what was widely acclaimed as the most authentic cakewalk. <u>Finally</u>, Walker was able to gain the admiration of many newly rich industrialists and financiers, who found in the grand flourishes of her version of the

(65) cakewalk a fitting vehicle for celebrating their newfound social rank.

CC

Circle
of
Parody

Def.

V_AUTH

V_AA

EX

①

②

③

V_EA

Paragraph One:

This paragraph presents the discussion of a prominent African American woman. The focus on a member of a traditionally underrepresented group makes this a Diversity passage, which means that we should expect the tone to be generally positive. Aida Overton Walker is best known for popularizing the cakewalk, a dance which reflected African dance moves, developed before the Civil War by African Americans.

Paragraph Two:

In this paragraph the author expands on the cakewalk, which also incorporated European moves and high kicking processions. Originally intended by African Americans to parody self-important slave-owners, the dance was later re-parodied by Europeans, shaping later versions. Note the theme of bridging cultural gaps, which is a positive theme within the "blending" subset of Diversity themes.

Paragraph Three:

In this paragraph the author discusses why the dance enjoyed wide appeal; the layers of parody ("mimetic vertigo") appealed to many during an era when the culture was shifting rapidly.

Paragraph Four:

In this final paragraph, the author's tone becomes more overtly positive, discussing the reasons for Walkers "remarkable" success (note the author's choice of very strong language here). Walker, we are told, held different appeal for different people. She won over African Americans with refined, fundamental grace, she appealed to Europeans as an authentic bastion of artistic stability, and she gained admiration from the newly rich, who celebrated the grand flourishes of her style.

VIEWSTAMP Analysis:

The main **Viewpoint** presented here is that of the author, who is clearly a fan of Walker. The other viewpoints presented are those of the various members of Walker's fan base, all of whom had their own distinct reason for finding her and her dance appealing.

The **Structure** of the passage is as follows:

Paragraph One: Introduce Walker and the foundation of the cakewalk.

Paragraph Two: Expand on the cakewalk and the European influence, as well as the multi-layered parody involved in its performance.

Paragraph Three: Discuss further reasons for the popularity of the dance, and the term "mimetic vertigo."

Paragraph Four: Discuss the various reasons for the respective appreciation from many different groups, from African Americans to Europeans to newly wealthy industrialists.

The **Tone** of the passage is quite positive with regard to Walker, her dance, and its widespread appeal.

The author does not really present much of an **Argument** in this passage, except that there were many reasons for Walker's widespread appeal.

The **Main Point** of the passage is that Aida Walker made the cakewalk an international success, as the dance successfully blended art and parody, and thus appealed to many different groups for many different reasons.

Question #13: GR, Main Point. The correct answer choice is (C)

The answer to this question is prephrased above.

Answer choice (A): This wrong answer may be tempting, since it references the opening sentence of the passage, but this is not the main point as prephrased above.

Answer choice (B): This answer choice may not be inaccurate, but only references a small piece of information from the passage, so it cannot represent the main point.

Answer choice (C): This is the correct answer choice. The cakewalk had broad appeal for many reasons, including the complex cultural mix and the use of parody.

Answer choice (D): There were parodies of the dance, but this is certainly not the main point of the passage.

Answer choice (E): It was the mix of influences that allowed the dance to cross racial divides, so this answer choice is incorrect.

Question #14: SR, P. The correct answer choice is (D)

The reference to the socioeconomic flux serves to show why the cakewalk became so popular—popularity required being able to appeal to a broad audience, and the multiple layers of parody helped enable the cakewalk to do this.

Answer choice (A): The author does not assert that the flux was necessary, only that it helped explain the popularity of the cakewalk.

Answer choice (B): The flux is not described to show how the dance fused forms, so this answer choice should be eliminated.

Answer choice (C): The description is not provided to show the parodies' targets, but rather to explain why the cakewalk was successful.

Answer choice (D): This is the correct answer choice. The flux is described because of its role in the cakewalk's popularity.

Answer choice (E): The socioeconomic flux is not referenced to explain why European American parodies of the cakewalk were able to reach wide audiences, so this answer choice is incorrect.

Question #15: SR, Parallel. The correct answer choice is (C)

The account in the second paragraph details how a dance that was meant partly as a satire became popular with those it was meant to parody.

Answer choice (A): This is not quite the same as the dance's appeal to the targets of the parody. This answer choice instead compares the original with a parody, so this choice should be eliminated.

Answer choice (B): The use of one style to increase popularity in another is not analogous to the referenced portion of the passage, so this answer choice is incorrect.

Answer choice (C): This is the correct answer choice. In this choice, popular music fans appreciate music intended as a popular music parody, much like cakewalk fans appreciate a dance meant as a dance parody.

Answer choice (D): Since this choice lacks any element of parody, it should be eliminated.

Answer choice (E): The appropriation of one style of music by another is not analogous to the reference from the passage, so this answer choice is incorrect.

Question #16: GR, Must. The correct answer choice is (E)

Answer choice (A): The author does not assert that the dance was "largely unknown," but rather that Walker made it widely popular.

Answer choice (B): The author does not say that the cakewalk was mainly a folk dance, and provides no information regarding how many people performed the dance professionally.

Answer choice (C): The passage does not say that performances as parody dropped off, so this answer choice should be eliminated.

Answer choice (D): The origins were not thought to *result* from Walker's work, so this answer choice is clearly incorrect.

Answer choice (E): This is the correct answer choice, verified by the fact that the author makes this exact point starting in line 23.

Question #17: GR, AP. The correct answer choice is (E)

To answer this author's perspective question, it is helpful to be familiar with the tone of the passage, and the fact that the author is appreciative of Walker's influence and ability to achieve such broad-based popularity.

Answer choice (A): The author does not make any such broad claims regarding satire's ability to cross boundaries, so this answer choice is incorrect.

Answer choice (B): The passage provides only one instance of layered parody. This is not the same as asserting that such interactions "often result" in mimetic vertigo.

Answer choice (C): Since the passage provides no discussion of other African American dances that became popular with the Europeans, this answer choice can be eliminated.

Answer choice (D): Separate-sex dancing in the United States is not discussed in the passage.

Answer choice (E): This is the correct answer choice. The author tells us at the end of the last paragraph that the newly rich appreciated Walker's grand flourishes as a way to celebrate their newfound social rank.

Question #18: GR, AP. The correct answer choice is (A)

The author believes that Walker was integral in the popularization of the cakewalk, varying her interpretation based on the "sometimes conflicting demands placed on the dance" (lines 48-49), and that "much of Walker's success with this audience derived from her distillation of what was widely acclaimed as the most authentic cakewalk" (lines 59-61).

Answer choice (A): This is the correct answer choice. Walker's popular style was a distilled version, meaning that it was made up of elements that were already present in the dance.

Answer choice (B): The author does not credit Walker with accentuating the satire, but with reaching a broad audience with an interpretation that had broad-based appeal.

Answer choice (C): Walker's interpretation was appealing to many different groups, but this does not mean that she had a different interpretation for each cultural group.

Answer choice (D): There is no reference in the passage to Walker's adding another layer of parody, so this answer choice is incorrect.

Answer choice (E): Walker did not disentangle the various elements, she brought them together in a refined style that appealed to many different groups of people.

Question #19: GR. Must. The correct answer choice is (A)

Answer choice (A): This is the correct answer choice, as the author provides in the first paragraph that the cakewalk "retained features characteristic of African dance forms, such as gliding steps and an emphasis on improvisation" (lines 12-14).

Answer choice (B): The author does not mention the first dancer to perform the cakewalk professionally. Walker is credited with popularizing the dance.

Answer choice (C): The passage provides no discussion of other North American dance forms that preserved aspects of the cakewalk.

Answer choice (D): The author does not provide specific additional features added to the parodies, so this answer choice should be eliminated.

Answer choice (E): The cakewalk is described as having achieved widespread popularity, but the passage does not specify the number of years that the dance enjoyed popularity.

In principle, a cohesive group—one whose
members generally agree with one another and
support one another's judgments—can do a much
better job at decision making than it could if it were   Def.

(5)   noncohesive. When cohesiveness is low or lacking
entirely, compliance out of fear of recrimination is
likely to be strongest. To overcome this fear,
participants in the group's deliberations need to be
confident that they are members in good standing and

(10)   that the others will continue to value their role in the
group, whether or not they agree about a particular
issue under discussion. As members of a group feel
more accepted by the others, they acquire greater
freedom to say what they really think, becoming less

(15)   likely to use deceitful arguments or to play it safe by
dancing around the issues with vapid or conventional
comments. Typically, then, the more cohesive a group
becomes, the less its members will deliberately censor
what they say out of fear of being punished socially

(20)   for antagonizing their fellow members.
But group cohesiveness can have pitfalls as well:
while the members of a highly cohesive group can
feel much freer to deviate from the majority, their
desire for genuine concurrence on every important

(25)   issue often inclines them not to use this freedom. In a
highly cohesive group of decision makers, the danger
is not that individuals will conceal objections they
harbor regarding a proposal favored by the majority,
but that they will think the proposal is a good one

(30)   without attempting to carry out a critical scrutiny that
could reveal grounds for strong objections. Members
may then decide that any misgivings they feel are not
worth pursuing—that the benefit of any doubt should
be given to the group consensus. In this way, they

(35)   may fall victim to a syndrome known as
"groupthink," which one psychologist concerned with
collective decision making has defined as "a
deterioration of mental efficiency, reality testing, and   Def.
moral judgment that results from in-group pressures."

(40)   Based on analyses of major fiascoes of international
diplomacy and military decision making,
researchers have identified groupthink behavior as a
recurring pattern that involves several factors:
overestimation of the group's power and morality,

(45)   manifested, for example, in an illusion of   ①
invulnerability, which creates excessive optimism;
closed-mindedness to warnings of problems and to   ②
alternative viewpoints; and unwarranted pressures
toward uniformity, including self-censorship with   ③

(50)   respect to doubts about the group's reasoning and a
concomitant shared illusion of unanimity concerning
group decisions. Cohesiveness of the decision-making NEC
group is an essential antecedent condition for this   not
syndrome but not a sufficient one, so it is important   SUF

(55)   to work toward identifying the additional factors that
determine whether group cohesiveness will deteriorate
into groupthink or allow for effective decision
making.

Paragraph One:

In this introductory paragraph, the author discusses the concept of cohesiveness, which improves a group's decision-making ability. Low cohesiveness leads to compliance (and presumably lower quality decision-making), and comes from a lack of confidence from members who question their own standing. The greater the cohesiveness, the less self-censorship, the better the decision-making.

Paragraph Two:

In this paragraph, the author introduces one peril of cohesiveness: members may feel free to diverge, but choose to accept the group's decisions rather than put ideas through real scrutiny. Here the author introduces a new concept, "groupthink," and defines it as a lack of good judgment that comes from too much deference to the group's decisions.

Paragraph Three:

Here the author discusses examples of major diplomatic and military mistakes caused by groupthink, and provides a list of several factors that lead to this pattern: overestimation of the group's abilities, excessive optimism, failure to consider other viewpoints, and pressure toward uniformity. The author closes by stating that cohesiveness is necessary to good decision making, but it is important to avoid the factors that lead to groupthink.

VIEWSTAMP Analysis:

This passage is presented from the neutral viewpoint of the author, who relays facts about cohesiveness, decision making, and groupthink.

The Structure of the passage is as follows:

> Paragraph One: Introduce the concept of cohesiveness and why it is important for good group decision-making.

> Paragraph Two: Introduce and define the problem of groupthink as one possible by-product of cohesiveness.

> Paragraph Three: Discuss specific factors of groupthink, and highlight the importance of recognizing factors that take positive cohesion and lead to negative groupthink.

The **Tone** of the passage is academic, as the author relays basic information about the importance of cohesion in a group, and the dangers of groupthink.

The **Argument** advanced is that of the author in the last paragraph, which is that it is important to recognize factors that can cause cohesion to deteriorate into groupthink.

The **Main Point** of the passage is that cohesion is vital to good group decision making, but that it is important to avoid counter-productive groupthink in a cohesive group.

Question #20: GR, Main Point. The correct answer choice is (A)

The answer to this question in prephrased in the VIEWSTAMP analysis on the previous page.

Answer choice (A): This is the correct answer choice, restating the main point as prephrased in our analysis. Cohesion can be valuable but can also lead to detrimental groupthink.

Answer choice (B): The author does not suggest that a good understanding of the importance of cohesion will protect against groupthink.

Answer choice (C): This is an accurate description but does not reflect the main point of the passage, so this answer choice should be eliminated.

Answer choice (D): The author does not compare low-cohesion decision making to high-cohesion groupthink, so this answer choice might not even be accurate, let alone reflect the main point of the passage.

Answer choice (E): The author maintains that it is important to try to recognize the factors that can contribute to groupthink, but does not assert that this will depend exclusively on a particular area of research.

Question #21: GR, AP. The correct answer choice is (C)

It is difficult to know exactly what the author would say about this scenario, since the passage regards groupthink in cohesive groups. Meetings ruined by conflict and disagreement are not reflective of cohesion or groupthink.

Answer choice (A): The author does not discuss chronic indecision, so this answer choice should be eliminated.

Answer choice (B): The group appears to have lacked cohesiveness, which is counter to this response.

Answer choice (C): This is the correct answer choice, as the group displayed no symptoms of cohesiveness or groupthink.

Answer choice (D): The referenced scenario provides no indication of groupthink, so this answer choice is incorrect.

Answer choice (E): There is no indication that more thorough study would have led to more efficient decision making, and there is no reason to believe that the author would make such an assertion.

Question #22: GR, Strengthen. The correct answer choice is (C)

The correct answer choice will lend credibility to the argument that groupthink can develop when individuals avoid real scrutiny based on faith in the decision of the group.

Answer choice (A): This response would strengthen the argument that groupthink is common, but this would not strengthen the argument regarding specific conditions that give rise to groupthink.

Answer choice (B): Respectful dissent is the opposite of the agreement that comes from groupthink.

Answer choice (C): This is the correct answer choice, as it would strengthen the assertion that groupthink tends to take place where there is too much faith in the judgments of the group.

Answer choice (D): This answer choice provides a different incentive for forced unanimity, so it does not support the author's view of the conditions that lend themselves to groupthink.

Answer choice (E): This answer contradicts the author's viewpoint, so this answer choice should be eliminated.

Question #23: GR, Must. The correct answer choice is (B)

Answer choice (A): The author does not mention suspicion of others as a component of groupthink, so this answer choice is incorrect.

Answer choice (B): This is the correct answer choice. The danger of groupthink is that individuals may think that a group decision is good based on deference to the group and faith in the group perspective.

Answer choice (C): The individuals may think that the group is invulnerable, but that is based on overestimation of the group, not on unusually high stress conditions.

Answer choice (D): We might speculate that this could be a component of a groupthink mentality, but it is not provided by the passage and should thus be eliminated.

Answer choice (E): This answer choice is wrong on two counts; neither careful consideration nor minority objections are described as components of groupthink.

Question #24: GR, Must. The correct answer choice is (E)

Answer choice (A): Neither the author nor the referenced researchers would agree that groupthink occurs in *all* cohesive groups, so this answer choice can be safely eliminated.

Answer choice (B): This assertion is almost certainly inaccurate, since there are likely to be conditions that are common to formation of a groupthink mentality.

Answer choice (C): The author asserts that it is important to continue to seek the factors that can lead to groupthink, so this answer choice is incorrect.

Answer choice (D): The passage does not suggest that groupthink decisions are absolute and not susceptible to outside influence, so this answer choice should be eliminated.

Answer choice (E): This is the correct answer choice. It is safe to say that both the author and the researchers would agree that groupthink tends to be detrimental to good decision-making.

Question #25: GR, Must. The correct answer choice is (E)

Answer choice (A): Since the author does not comment on whether or not enforced conformity is ever acceptable, this answer choice should be eliminated.

Answer choice (B): Although we may assume this to be the case, the author does not comment on military expectation of conformity, so this answer choice is incorrect.

Answer choice (C): This is another answer choice that seems to be a reasonable assertion, but since it is not discussed in the passage it cannot be the right answer choice.

Answer choice (D): The passage does not provide a comparison between the relative frequency of voluntary versus involuntary conformity, so this answer choice must be incorrect.

Answer choice (E): This is the correct answer choice, as the passage specifically provides beginning in line 5: "When cohesiveness is low or lacking entirely, compliance out of fear of recrimination is likely to be strongest."

Question #26: SR, P. The correct answer choice is (A)

The author mentions low cohesiveness in order to lead into the fact that high cohesiveness allows for more free thought but might also lead to groupthink.

Answer choice (A): This is the correct answer choice. The reference to low cohesiveness leads to the discussion of high cohesiveness and greater freedom for individuals to say what they really think.

Answer choice (B): There is no such comparison between groupthink and low-cohesion groups, so this answer choice is incorrect.

Answer choice (C): The author does not discuss how to make non-cohesive groups more open to dissent, so this answer choice should be eliminated.

Answer choice (D): Groupthink relies on a high degree of cohesion, so non-cohesive groups are not susceptible to groupthink dynamics.

Answer choice (E): This passage does not focus much on low-cohesion groups, and the author alludes to no such proposal or groundwork.

Question #27: GR, AP. The correct answer choice is (B)

Answer choice (A): Since there is no discussion of confrontational negotiating styles, this answer choice can safely be eliminated.

Answer choice (B): This is the correct answer choice. The passage begins by outlining the fact that low cohesiveness can make members of a group hesitant to speak their minds, which would obviously be detrimental to the group decision-making dynamic.

Answer choice (C): The soundness of decisions made by groups with varied viewpoints is never compared to that of groups with a unified position, so this answer choice should be eliminated.

Answer choice (D): The passage presents several factors associated with groupthink, but the author never asserts that these are key factors in forming groupthink.

Answer choice (E): This may or may not be true, but, because this issue is never discussed or alluded to by the author, this answer choice must be incorrect.

CHAPTER TWELVE: TEST READINESS

The day before the test

Be sure you have received your LSAT admission ticket from Law Services. Double-check the information on the admission ticket for accuracy.

If you are not familiar with your test center, drive by the test center and examine the testing room and parking situation. This will alleviate any anxiety or confusion on the day of the test.

On the day before the LSAT, we recommend that you study very little, if at all. The best approach for most students is to simply relax as much as possible. Read a book, go see a movie, or play a round of golf. If you feel you must study, we recommend that you only briefly review each of the concepts covered in this book.

Eat only bland or neutral foods the night before the test and try to get the best sleep possible.

Do not study hard the day before the test. If you haven't learned the material by then, that final day won't make much difference.

The morning of the test

Attempt to follow your normal routine when you get up. For example, if you read the paper every morning, do so on the day of the test. If you do not regularly drink coffee, do not start on the morning of the LSAT. Constancy in your routine will allow you to focus on your primary objective: performing well on the test.

Dress in layers, so you will be warm if the test center is cold, but also able to shed clothes if the test center is hot.

Take along a clear plastic bag with all your pencils, sharpeners, highlighters, etc. Your bag, according to Law Services, can only be a maximum of one gallon and must be stored under your chair.

For the September/October, December, and February LSAT administrations, all students must arrive at the test center no later than 8:30 AM. For the June LSAT administration, all students must arrive at the test center no later than 12:30 PM.

We strongly believe that performing well requires you to believe that you can perform well. As you prepare to leave for the test, run though the test in your head, visualizing an exceptional performance. Imagine how you'll react to each logic game, reading passage, and logical reasoning question. Many athletes use this same technique to achieve optimal performance.

Even though test regulations require you to be at the center at a certain hour, the test will not begin immediately. Bring the morning newspaper or other reading material so that you have something to do while waiting.

Upon check-in, test supervisors will ask you to present your admission ticket, one form of acceptable personal identification, and a thumbprint. Supervisors are instructed to deny admission to anyone who does not present a government-issued photo ID with a signature.

The test supervisors will assign each examinee a seat. You are not permitted to choose your own seat.

Once you are seated, the test supervisors will read you the rules and regulations of the test, and have you write a certifying statement that attests that the person taking the test is the person whose name appears on the answer sheet and that you are taking the test for the sole purpose of admission to law school. Typically, the actual test will not begin until at least thirty to forty-five minutes after you are seated.

You are allowed only a limited number of items on your testing desk, so check with LSAC prior to your test for the exact list and for any new policies.

The test supervisors keep the official time, but they are not obligated to use a digital timer. They should announce a five-minutes-remaining warning for each test section.

You may work only on the assigned section. Testing supervisors may circulate throughout the testing room to ensure that all examinees are working in the appropriate section. Blackening of answer spaces on your answer sheet must be done before time is called for any given section. You will not be permitted time after the test to clean up your answer sheet or transfer answers from your test book to your answer sheet.

If you find it necessary to leave the room during the test, you must obtain permission from the supervisor. You will not be permitted to make up any missed time.

All test materials, including test books and answer sheets, are the property of Law Services and must be returned to Law Services by test supervisors after every administration. Legal action may be taken against an examinee who removes a test book and/or reproduces it.

If you engage in any misconduct or irregularity during the test, you may be dismissed from the test center and may be subject to other penalties for misconduct or irregularity. Actions that could warrant such consequences are creating a disturbance; giving or receiving help; working on or reading the test during a time not authorized by the supervisor; removing test materials or notes from the testing room; taking part in an act of impersonation or other forms of cheating; or using books, calculators, ear plugs, headsets, rulers,

---

Yes, you read that correctly. You will be thumbprinted at the test center. This is done for test security purposes.

LSAC updates the test center regulations often, so be sure to check with LSAC prior to your test for any new policies.

Be sure to ask the test supervisors how they will keep time. There have been many problems with sections being mis-timed.

papers of any kind, or other aids. The penalties for misconduct are high: you may be precluded from attending law school and becoming a lawyer.

If you encounter a problem with the test supervision or test center itself, report it to a test supervisor. Reportable problems include: power outages, mis-timing of test sections, and any unusual disturbances caused by an individual.

If you feel anxious or panicked for any reason before or during the test, close your eyes for a few seconds and relax. Think of other situations where you performed with confidence and skill.

After the test

Test results will be available online approximately three weeks after the test, and a hard copy of your score will arrive approximately four weeks after the test.

Thank you for choosing to purchase the *PowerScore LSAT Reading Comprehension Bible*. We hope you have found this book useful and enjoyable, but most importantly we hope this book helps raise your LSAT score.

In all of our publications we strive to present the material in the clearest and most informative manner. If you have any questions, comments, or suggestions, please do not hesitate to email us at lsatbibles@powerscore.com. We love to receive feedback and we do read every email that comes in!

Also, if you haven't done so already, we strongly suggest you visit the website for this book at:

www.powerscore.com/lsatbibles

This free online resource area contains supplements to the book material, provides updates as needed, and answers questions posed by students. There is also an official evaluation form that we encourage you to use.

If we can assist you in any way in your LSAT preparation or in the law school admissions process, please do not hesitate to contact us. We would be happy to help.

Thank you and best of luck on the LSAT!

A PPENDIX ONE

Consolidated Answer Key

The *PowerScore LSAT Reading Comprehension Bible* contains many passages that have appeared on previously released LSATs, and the answers to every LSAT question used in this book are found in the passage explanations. The consolidated answer key in this section contains two parts: the first part provides a quick chapter-by-chapter answer key for students who need to find the answers quickly, and the second part provides a comprehensive listing of the source of all the complete LSAT passages used in this book. The second part is especially helpful for students who are taking practice LSATs and want to know ahead of time which passages we have used in this book. They can then skip those passages ahead of taking the test, or avoid taking certain tests until later.

Chapter-by-Chapter Answer Key

The chapter-by-chapter answer key lists every passage in this book in the presented order and provides the correct answer for each question used from each passage. You can use this answer key as a quick reference when you are solving problems. Each problem is explained in more detail in the text of the chapter.

Chapter Six: Putting It All Together

Practice Passage I: June 2006 Passage #1, Questions 1-6
1. A   2. D   3. E   4. B   5. C   6. E

Practice Passage II: December 2005 Passage #1, Questions 1-5
1. A   2. D   3. E   4. B   5. C

Chapter Seven: Comparative Reading Passages

Passage Analysis: December 2007 Passage #3, Questions 15-19
15. A   16. C   17. D   18. C   19. D

Practice Passage I: October 2008 Passage #2, Questions 7-13
7. A   8. E   9. B   10. E   11. A   12. C   13. A

Practice Passage II: September 2007 Passage #2, Questions 7-12
7. D   8. B   9. A   10. C   11. B   12. D

Chapter Eight: Common Passage Structures

Narrative with Authorial Position Passage: October 2001 Passage #2, Question 14
14. A

Narrative with Positional Analysis Passage: June 2003 Passage #1, Question 4
4. C

Narrative with Causality Passage: October 2004 Passage #4, Question 27
27. A

Narrative featuring Principle and Example Passage: October 2003 Passage #3, Questions 14, 18
14. D   18. B

Chapter Nine: Common Passage Themes

Affirming Underrepresented Groups Passage: December 2002 Passage #2, Question 9
9. D

Mixed Group Passage: December 1996 Passage #4, Question 24
24. B

Diversity Practice Passage I: December 2007 Passage #1, Questions 1-6
1. A   2. C   3. D   4. C   5. D   6. D

Diversity Practice Passage II: October 2004 Passage #2, Questions 8-14
8. C   9. C   10. E   11. E   12. D   13. B   14. B

Passage Analysis: October 2005 Passage #3, Question 17
17. C

Law Related Practice Passage I: September 2006 Passage #2, Questions 6-13
6. A   7. D   8. A   9. E   10. A   11. B   12. D   13. E

Law Related Practice Passage II: December 2006 Passage #4, Questions 21-28
21. A   22. A   23. B   24. E   25. D   26. C   27. C   28. B

Sample Discussion Passage: December 2007 Passage #4, Questions 20-27
20. C   21. D   22. E   23. A   24. C   25. D   26. E   27. A

Science Practice Passage I: June 2005 Passage #3, Questions 16-21
16. A   17. D   18. C   19. D   20. B   21. E

Science Practice Passage II: October 2004 Passage #3, Questions 15-20
15. B   16. A   17. C   18. E   19. A   20. D

Chapter-by-Chapter Answer Key

Chapter Eleven: The June 2008 LSAT Reading Comprehension Section

Passage #1, Questions 1-5
1. A   2. C   3. D   4. D   5. E

Passage #2, Questions 6-12
6. B   7. E   8. E   9. B   10. B   11. C   12. A

Passage #3, Questions 13-19
13. C   14. D   15. C   16. E   17. E   18. A   19. A

Passage #4, Questions 20-27
20. A   21. C   22. C   23. B   24. E   25. E   26. A   27. B

This section contains a reverse lookup that cross references each passage according to the source LSAT. The tests are listed in order of the PrepTest number (if any). The date of administration is also listed to make the process easier. If a test is not listed, then no questions from that exam were used in this book.

Passages listed under each test begin by listing the *Reading Comprehension Bible* chapter the passage appears in, the page number, the passage date, and then the question numbers.

For information on obtaining the publications that contain the LSATs listed below, please visit the *PowerScore Free LSAT Help area* at www.powerscore.com/lsat/help/pub_ident.cfm

PrepTest 20—October 1996 LSAT

> Chapter 9, Page 219, October 1996, Passage #1, Question 4 (Affirming Underrepresented Groups)

PrepTest 21—December 1996 LSAT

> Chapter 9, Page 226, December 1996, Passage #4, Question 24 (Mixed Group Passages)

PrepTest 35—October 2001 LSAT

> Chapter 8, Page 199, October 2001, Passage #2, Question 14 (Narrative with Authorial Position)

PrepTest 39—December 2002 LSAT

> Chapter 9, Page 222, December 2002, Passage #2, Question 9 (Undermining Overrepresented Groups)

PrepTest 40—June 2003 LSAT

> Chapter 8, Page 203, June 2003, Passage #1, Question 4 (Narrative with Positional Analysis)

PrepTest 41—October 2003 LSAT

> Chapter 8, Page 210, October 2003, Passage #3, Questions 14, 18 (Narrative featuring Principle and Example)

PrepTest 44—October 2004 LSAT

> Chapter 2, Page 45, October 2004, Passage #1, Question 5 (Passage Structure)
> Chapter 9, Page 234, October 2004, Passage #2, Questions 8-14 (Diversity Practice Passage II)
> Chapter 9, Page 290, October 2004, Passage #3, Questions 15-20 (Science Practice Passage II)
> Chapter 8, Page 207, October 2004, Passage #4, Question 27 (Narrative with Causality)

Test-by-Test Passage Use Tracker

PrepTest 46—June 2005 LSAT

Chapter 2, Page 54, June 2005, Passage #1 (A Sample Passage Analyzed)
Chapter 9, Page 288, June 2005, Passage #3, Questions 16-21 (Science Practice Passage I)

PrepTest 47—October 2005 LSAT

Chapter 9, Page 251, October 2005, Passage #3, Question 17 (A Law Related Passage Analyzed)

PrepTest 48—December 2005 LSAT

Chapter 6, Page 150, December 2005, Passage #1, Questions 1-5 (Two Passages Analyzed)

PrepTest 49—June 2006 LSAT

Chapter 6, Page 148, June 2006, Passage #1, Questions 1-6 (Two Passages Analyzed)

PrepTest 50—September 2006 LSAT

Chapter 9, Page 258, September 2006, Passage #2, Questions 6-13 (Law Practice Passage I)

PrepTest 51—December 2006 LSAT

Chapter 9, Page 260, December 2006, Passage #4, Questions 21-28 (Law Practice Passage II)

PrepTest 52—September 2007 LSAT

Chapter 7, Page 182, September 2007, Passage #2, Questions 7-12 (Practice Passage II)

PrepTest 53—December 2007 LSAT

Chapter 9, Page 232, December 2007, Passage #1, Questions 1-6 (Diversity Practice Passage I)
Chapter 7, Page 172, December 2007, Passage #3, Questions 15-19 (Passage Analysis)
Chapter 9, Page 278, December 2007, Passage #4, Questions 20-27 (A Science Passage Analyzed)

PrepTest 54—June 2008 LSAT

Chapter 11, Page 314, June 2008, Passage #1, Questions 1-5
Chapter 11, Page 316, June 2008, Passage #2, Questions 6-12
Chapter 11, Page 318, June 2008, Passage #3, Questions 13-19
Chapter 11, Page 320, June 2008, Passage #4, Questions 20-27

PrepTest 55—October 2008 LSAT

Chapter 7, Page 180, October 2008, Passage #2, Questions 7-13 (Practice Passage I)

THE POWERSCORE LSAT READING COMPREHENSION BIBLE

MORE INFORMATION

Additional PowerScore Resources

We believe that the *PowerScore LSAT Reading Comprehension Bible* is the single best written resource for attacking the Reading Comprehension section of the LSAT.

Because new LSATs appear every several months, and access to accurate and up-to-date information is critical, we have devoted a section of our website to *Reading Comprehension Bible* students. This online resource area offers updates on recent LSAT Reading Comprehension sections, discussions of additional Reading Comprehension concepts, and general information. The *LSAT Reading Comprehension Bible* online area can be accessed at:

www.powerscore.com/lsatbibles

If you would like to comment on the *Reading Comprehension Bible*, or make suggestions for additional sections, please send us a message at lsatbibles@powerscore.com. We thank you for purchasing this book, and we look forward to hearing from you!

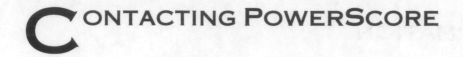

CONTACTING POWERSCORE

POWERSCORE INTERNATIONAL HEADQUARTERS:

PowerScore Test Preparation
57 Hasell Street
Charleston, SC 29401

Toll-free information number: (800) 545-1750
Website: www.powerscore.com
Email: lsat@powerscore.com

POWERSCORE LSAT PUBLICATIONS INFORMATION:

For information on the *LSAT Logic Games Bible, LSAT Logic Games Bible Workbook, LSAT Logical Reasoning Bible, LSAT Reading Comprehension Bible*, or *LSATs Deconstructed Series*.

Website: www.powerscore.com/pubs.htm

POWERSCORE FULL-LENGTH LSAT COURSE INFORMATION:

Complete preparation for the LSAT.
Classes available nationwide.

Web: www.powerscore.com/lsat
Request Information: www.powerscore.com/contact.htm

POWERSCORE VIRTUAL LSAT COURSE INFORMATION:

45 hours of online, interactive, real-time preparation for the LSAT.
Classes available worldwide.

Web: www.powerscore.com/lsat/virtual
Request Information: www.powerscore.com/contact.htm

POWERSCORE WEEKEND LSAT COURSE INFORMATION:

Fast and effective LSAT preparation: 16 hour courses, 99th percentile instructors, and real LSAT questions.

Web: www.powerscore.com/lsat/weekend
Request Information: www.powerscore.com/contact.htm

PowerScore LSAT Tutoring Information:

One-on-one meetings with a PowerScore LSAT expert.

Web: www.powerscore.com/lsat/content_tutoring.cfm
Request Information: www.powerscore.com/contact.htm

PowerScore Law School Admissions Counseling Information:

Personalized application and admissions assistance.

Web: www.powerscore.com/lsat/content_admissions.cfm
Request Information: www.powerscore.com/contact.htm

THE POWERSCORE LSAT READING COMPREHENSION BIBLE